Fundamentals of
Tax Policy

Fundamentals of Tax Policy

Richard Almy

Alan Dornfest, AAS

Daphne Kenyon, Ph.D.

KANSAS CITY, MISSOURI

Cover Credits: (clockwise from top left)
iStockphoto / Creativeye99
iStockphoto / zlisjak
Getty Images / uschools

Managing Editor: Christopher Bennett
Editor: Barbara Simmons
Designer: Mackenzie Miller

ISBN
Soft Cover: 978-0-88329-188-7
eBook: 978-0-88329-223-5

Copyright © 2008, 2020 by the International Association of Assessing Officers, 314 W. 10th Street, Kansas City, Missouri 64105-1616.

All rights reserved including rights of reproduction and use in any form or by any means, including the making of copies by any photo process or by any electronic or mechanical device (printed, written, or oral), or recording for sound or visual reproduction, or for use in any knowledge or retrieval system or device, unless permission in writing is obtained from the copyright proprietor.

Printed in the United States of America.

Foreword

On behalf of the International Association of Assessing Officers, I am honored to present *Fundamentals of Tax Policy*, the first book from IAAO whose sole focus is tax policy.

IAAO is an international leader in the mass appraisal and ad valorem taxation community. Its members have been valuing property of all types for almost 75 years by using proven valuation techniques that are taught and promulgated by IAAO. Our professional association has a rich history of developing educational materials, valuation techniques, and professional standards for the mass appraisal community. IAAO maintains three pillars of knowledge in ad valorem taxation—mass appraisal, tax policy, and tax administration.

Fundamentals of Tax Policy expands the IAAO collection of core knowledge. The text is intended to provide a basic understanding and overview of the many factors that shape tax policy. This text provides a foundation for further investigation and learning on tax policy issues.

IAAO is grateful to the authors, Richard Almy, Alan Dornfest, AAS, and Daphne Kenyon, Ph.D., for sharing their extensive knowledge and perspective in this area.

Guy Griscom

IAAO President, 2008

Fundamentals of Tax Policy
Table of Contents

Preface	xxiii
About the Authors	xxv
Acknowledgments	xxvii
Chapter 1: Introduction to Tax Policy	1
Scope	1
Public and Tax Policy Focus	2
Audience	2
Federalism Perspective	3
International Property Tax Policy	3
Major Concepts	4
What Is Property?	4
What Is a Tax?	5
How Are Taxes Classified?	6
What Is a Property Tax?	7
Property-Based Wealth as Underpinning for Tax	8
Influences on Tax Policy	9
The Legal Structure	9
Informal Processes	9
Policy Implementation	10
Historical Perspective on Property Tax Policy—The U.S. Model	11
Goals of Property Tax Policy	11
Early Federal Developments	11
State Property Tax Policy	11
Early Developments	11
Comments on Double Taxation	12
Ongoing and Recent History	12
Looking Ahead	17
References	18
Suggested Reading	18

Chapter 2: Principles, Politics, and Economics of Taxation 19
Underlying Systems 19
Democratic Form of Government 19
Basic Elements of a Mixed-Market Economy 20
Advantages of a Competitive Market System 21
Roles of Public and Private Sectors 21
Functional and Economic Roles of Government 23
Stabilization 23
Redistribution 23
Allocation 24
Government Provision Does Not Require Government Production 24
Government Failures 25
Size of Public Sector 26
Qualities of a Good Tax System 27
Fairness and Equity 28
Neutrality 29
Uniformity 30
Buoyancy 31
Practicality and Cost-Effectiveness 31
Public Acceptance 32
Openness and Transparency 33
References 33

Chapter 3: Fundamental Elements of the Property Tax 35
Property Taxation from a Systems Perspective 35
Important Legal Issues 36
The Legal Setting in the United States 37
Controversial Areas 40
Classification 40
Equality 43
Procedural Matters 45
Fiscal Arrangements 47
Powers of Taxation and Revenue Assignments 47
Rate-Setting Mechanisms 47
Fixed Rates 47
Budget-Based Rates 48

Table of Contents

- Single versus Compound Rates ... 48
- When Is a Rate Too High or Too Low? ... 48
- Compensating for Fiscal Capacity Differences ... 49
- Administrative Arrangements ... 50
  - Supervision and Equalization ... 50
  - Assessment and Valuation ... 51
  - Billing, Collection, and Enforcement ... 52
  - Appeals ... 52
  - Administrative Issues ... 53
    - Funding Property Tax Administration ... 53
    - Institutional Linkages ... 54
    - Role of the Private Sector in Property Tax Administration ... 55
    - Self-Assessment ... 56
    - Qualifications of Property Tax Officials ... 57
- Basic System Design Features ... 57
  - Who Is Responsible for Paying the Property Tax? ... 58
    - Subjects of Property Taxes ... 58
    - Establishing Liability for Taxation ... 58
  - What Property Is Taxable? ... 59
  - What Is the Basis of Assessment? ... 60
    - Non-value Bases ... 60
    - Value Bases ... 61
  - Revaluation and Reassessment ... 62
  - Strategies for Providing Tax Relief ... 63
    - Options ... 63
    - Spillover Effects and Administrative Considerations ... 66
- Important Administrative Provisions ... 67
  - Notice and Publicity ... 67
  - Appeal ... 68
  - Billing, Payment, and Enforcement Provisions ... 69
  - Other Features ... 69
- Conclusions ... 70
- References ... 70
- Suggested Reading ... 71

Chapter 4: The Role of Property Tax in Intergovernmental Finance 73
    Distribution of Powers 73
        The Case for Multiple Governments 73
            Economic 73
            Political 74
        Administrative Assignments—Types of Federalism 75
            Federal versus Unitary Governments 75
            Number of Governments in the United States 75
            Alternative Theories of Federalism 76
            Local Government—The U.S. Model 78
        Financing Distributive Powers 78
    Government Revenue and Resources 79
    Taxes Used by State and Local Governments 80
        Changes in Patterns of Local Government Revenues 82
        Significance of Various Local Government Funding Sources 82
        Regional Variations of Funding Sources 85
        Summary of Local Government Revenue Sources 85
    Property Taxes 87
    General Sales Taxes 88
        History 88
        The Sales Tax Base 88
        Sales Tax Rates 94
        Sales Tax Policy Issues 94
            Regressivity 94
            Border Effects and Out-of-State Sellers 96
            Revenue Elasticity 98
            Political Acceptability 99
    Individual Income Tax 99
        History 99
        The Individual Income Tax Base 99
        State Individual Income Tax Rates 100
        Individual Income Tax Administration 102
        Issues of Income Tax Policy 103
    Corporate Income Taxes 104
    Selective Sales Taxes 107
        Sumptuary Taxes 107

Table of Contents

- Taxes on Alcoholic Beverages 109
- Tobacco Taxes 108
- Gambling Taxes and Other Gaming Revenues 108
- Benefit-Based Excise Taxes 110
  - Motor Fuel Taxes 110
  - Other Benefit Taxes 112
  - Privilege Taxes 113
  - User Fees and Charges 113
- Intergovernmental Revenue 114
  - Intergovernmental Grants 112
    - Categorical Grants 114
    - Block Grants 114
    - General Revenue Sharing 114
    - Matching versus Lump-Sum Grants 114
    - Open-Ended versus Close-Ended Grants 115
    - School Aid Grants 115
    - Foundation Grants 115
    - Guaranteed Tax Base Grants 115
    - Flat Grants 116
  - PILOT (Payment in Lieu of Taxes) 116
    - Federal PILOT/PILT Policy 116
    - State Policies 116
  - Indirect Aid through the Tax Code 117
- Other Intergovernmental Fiscal Issues 117
  - Mandates 117
  - Rules of the Game 118
- Problems and Challenges 119
  - Tax Competition and Jurisdictional Issues 119
  - Growing Importance of the Service Sector of the Economy 120
  - Growing Importance of Remote Sales and Multistate Businesses 120
  - Equalization Issues 121
    - School Funding and Equalization 121
    - Uniformity versus Wealth 121
    - Revenue Sharing and Equalization 124
- Summary 125
- References 125

Chapter 5: Tax Analysis 127

Approaching the Analysis 127
Defining the Problem 127
Identifying the Level of Precision 127
Collecting Data 128
Using Positive versus Normative Approaches 128

Types of Analyses 129
Descriptive Studies 129
Forecasts 130
Principles and Techniques of Revenue Forecasting 130
Forecasting Issues 130
Qualitative Techniques 131
Quantitative Techniques 132
Analytical Studies 133
Sources of State and Local Taxes and Other Revenues 133
Analysis of Revenue Trends 136

Measurement of Tax Burden 138
Comparison of Fiscal Structures 139
Comparison of Overall Revenue Burdens 146
Relative Reliance on Different Sources of Revenue 142
Comparison of Overall Tax Burdens 146
Differences in Fiscal Capacity, Need, and Effort 151
Other Fiscal Measures and Information Sources 155
Observations on Tax Burden and Incidence 156
Analysis of Effects of Taxes 157
Effects of Taxes in Relation to Tax Base 157
Initial versus Ultimate Incidence of Taxes 159
Incidence of Property Tax 159
Technical Issues Related to Tax Incidence 161
Tax Elasticity 161

Conclusions 163
References 164

Chapter 6: Analysis of Selected Property Tax Features 165

Budget- versus Rate-Driven Systems 166
    Alternatives to Strict Budget- or Rate-Driven Systems 169
    Truth-in-Taxation Systems 169
Valuation System Basis 170
    Alternatives to Current Market Value 170
    Controls on the Distribution of the Property Tax Burden
    through Valuation System Alternatives 172
        Value Constraints 172
        Comments on Value Constraints 173
        Acquisition Value 175
        Acquisition Value in California—A Case Study 176
Site Value Taxation 180
Classification Systems 181
Targeted Controls on Property Taxes—Individuals 182
    Exemptions 182
        Partial Exemptions 183
        Full Exemptions 184
        De Facto Exemptions 185
        Controls on Exemptions 185
    Property Tax Deferrals, Circuit Breakers, and Tax Credits 185
    Abatements and Tax Increment Financing (TIF) 187
Summary 189
References 190

Chapter 7: Components of Model Property Tax Administrative Systems 193

Administrative Arrangements, Practices, and Issues 194
    Who Should Do What? 194
    Administrative Policy Setting 199
Effective Management 200
    Planning and Budgeting 200
        Planning 200
        Estimating Resource Requirements and Budgeting 201
    Work Management 202
        Organization 203
        Managing People 203
    Quality Assurance 204

        Professional Ethics 204
        Standards of Performance 204
        Documented Rules and Procedures 205
        Data Edits 205
        Security Procedures 205
    Ratio Studies 206
        Data Assembly 207
        Stratification 207
        Data Analysis 207
        Evaluation of Results 210
        Reporting 210
    Computer Support 210
        CAMA System Features 210
        Use of GIS in Valuation 212
Supervision and Equalization 213
    Standards and Specifications 214
        Appraisal Accuracy (Ratio Study) Standards 214
        Re-inspection and Reappraisal Standards 215
        Appraiser Qualifications 215
        Forms, Codes, and Data Formats 215
    Technical Assistance 216
        Legal Opinions and Interpretations 216
        Manuals, Bulletins, and Newsletters 216
        Education and Training 216
        Computer Services 216
        Valuation Assistance 216
        Cadastral Mapping 216
        Public Relations 216
        Financial Aid 217
    Performance Monitoring 217
    Equalization and Other Corrective Actions 219
        Direct Equalization 219
        Reassessment Orders 221
        Indirect Equalization 222

Table of Contents

- Initial Assessment Processes 223
  - Immovable Property Valuation 223
    - Preliminary Analyses 226
    - Valuation Modeling 227
    - Spatial Analyses Using a GIS 228
    - Value Review and Reconciliation 229
    - Keeping Values Current 230
  - Cadastral Data Management 230
    - Types of Cadastres 230
    - Cadastral Mapping 231
    - Cadastral Numbers 232
    - Immovable Property Attribute Data Collection 232
    - Market Data Collection 235
  - Movable Property Assessment and Valuation 237
    - Locating Movable Property for Tax Purposes 238
    - Discovering and Inventorying Taxable Movable Property 238
    - Valuation and Assessment 240
    - Quality Assurance 241
  - Assessment 242
    - Classification of Property for Purposes of Taxation 242
    - Identification of Taxpayers 242
    - Administration of Exemptions and Tax Relief Programs 243
    - Roll Preparation 244
    - Notices 244
- Tax Billing and Collection 244
  - Billing 245
    - Coverage Options 246
    - Delivery Options 246
  - Collection 246
  - Sanctions and Enforced Collection of Arrears 247
- Taxpayer and Stakeholder Relations 248
- Review and Appeal 249
- References 253

Chapter 8: Systems of Government and Taxation: A Global Perspective 255
    Types of Government 255
    Types of Taxes 256
    Utilization of Taxes 257
        Utilization of Taxes on Property 262
    Profiles of Property Taxes on Immovable Property 264
    Examples of Diversity 265
        Local Autonomy and Administration: Hungary, the Netherlands,
        and South Africa 266
            Hungary 267
            Netherlands 268
            South Africa 269
        Diversity in Policy, Administration and Practice: United Kingdom 270
            Council Tax 270
            Nondomestic Rates (the Uniform Business Rate) 272
            Administration 272
            The Northern Ireland Residential Revaluation 272
        Other Recent Reforms 273
            Russia 273
            The Baltic Countries 276
            China 279
        Technological Diversity 281
            Systems That Use Self-assessment 281
            Highly Computerized Systems: The Scandinavian Countries 283
    Issues 286
        Fiscal Decentralization 287
        Tax Harmonization and Competition 287
        Strengthening Private Property and Cost-Effective, Transparent
        Property Taxation 288
    References 289

Table of Contents

Chapter 9 : Prospects and Challenges 293
    Tax Policy and the Assessing Officer 293
    Information Clearinghouse Roles 295
        Provider of Property Tax Data 295
        Interpreter of Property Tax Data 298
        Policy Advocate 298
        Problems versus Solutions 299
    The Property Tax as an Institution 299
    Sustainability Issues 302
    Potential Solutions to Aspects of Property Tax Considered Unfair 303
        Countering a Populist Argument 304
        Stabilizing the PropertyTax 306
    The Future of the Property Tax 307
    References 309

Appendix A. Regressivity versus Progressivity of the Property Tax 311

Appendix B. Economic Effects of Property Taxation 317

Appendix C. Legal (Statutory) Incidence versus Economic Incidence 319

Appendix D. Partial versus General Equilibrium Analysis (Sector Analysis) ... 323

Appendix E. Criteria for Evaluating Effects of Taxes 327

Glossary 331

Index 355

List of Figures

1-1	Significance of Property Taxes in Local Government Finance in the United States, 1962–2005	13
1-2	State and Local Property Tax Revenue Compared with Other Tax Revenue for FY 2005	14
1-3	State and Local Per-Capita Property Taxes in Comparison to Other Major Taxes for FY 2005	14
2-1	Supply of Oranges Decreases	20
3-1	Typical Property Tax System External Linkages	54
4-1	Major Sources of School Funding, 1977 versus 1997	83
4-2	Major Sources of County Funding, 1977 versus 1997	84
4-3	Major Sources of Municipality Funding, 1977 versus 1997	84
4-4	Major Sources of Special District Funding, 1977 versus 1997	84
4-5	Tax Tunes: "The Day the Sales Tax Died" by Billy Hamilton, Deputy Comptroller, State of Texas	97
4-6	Percentage Distribution of Total Public Elementary-Secondary School System Revenue in 2004–2005	122
6-1	Disparity Ratios for Properties in Los Angeles County: 1975 Base Year	177
6-2	Montana Web Page Describing a $400 Property Tax Refund	187
7-1	Responsibility for Original Assessment in the United States	198
7-2	Generalized Valuation Process	225
7-3	Schematic Diagram of Mass Valuation System	227
7-4	Ways to Achieve Uniqueness in Parcel Identifiers	232
8-1	Total Taxes as a Percentage of GDP for General Government in Selected Countries	258
8-2	Taxes as a Percentage of Revenue for General Government in Selected Countries	259
8-3	Utilization of Main Types of Taxes by Percentage of Total Taxes for General Government in Selected Countries	261
8-4	Box Plots of the Utilization of Taxes by Type of State	262
8-5	Recurrent Taxes on Property as a Percentage of Total Taxes in Selected Countries	263
9-1	Conceptual Approach to Reviewing Property Tax Policies and Practices	294
C-1	Incidence of a Unit Sales Tax	319
C-2	Incidence of Social Security Tax with Respect to Wages	320
D-1	Example of Laffer Curve	325
E-1	Loss of Consumer Surplus	328

List of Tables

1-1	Synopsis of Contents by Chapter	17
2-1	A Menu of Potential Government Responses to Market Failures	25
2-2	State, Local, and Federal Government Spending as a Percentage of GDP in the United States	26
2-3	Government Spending as a Percentage of GDP in Selected Countries in 2006	27
3-1	Federal Constitutional and Statutory Provisions Affecting Taxation and Limiting the States' Powers of Taxation	38
3-2	Effect of Homeowner Exemption	42
4-1	Local Governments in the United States in 2002	76
4-2	Optimal Tax Assignment	79
4-3	State and Local Tax Collection by Source as a Percentage of Total Tax Collections in 2005	81
4-4	Local Government General Revenue by Source for FY 2005	86
4-5	State Sales Tax Rates as of January 1, 2007	89
4-6	Number of Services Taxed by Category in Each State in 2007	91
4-7	State and Local Sales Tax Rates in the Largest City in Each State	95
4-8	State Individual Income Tax Rates for Tax Year 2007 as of January 1, 2007	101
4-9	State Corporate Income Tax Rates and Apportionment Factors in 2007	105
4-10	State Excise Tax Rates on Cigarettes as of January 1, 2007	109
4-11	Motor Fuel Excise Tax Rates as of January 1, 2007	111
4-12	Formulas for State Aid to Education in 2003	116
4-13	Percentage Distribution of Elementary-Secondary Public School System Revenue by Source and State in 2004–2005	123
5-1	State and Local Government Finances by Level of Government, 2004–2005	134
5-2	State and Local Government Revenue for Selected Years	136
5-3	Total State and Local Government Revenue, Population, and Personal Income by State, FY 2004–2005	140
5-4	Distribution of Total State and Local Government Revenue by State, 2004–2005	145
5-5	Distribution of State and Local Own-Source General Revenue by State, 2004–2005, as Percentage of General Revenue from Own Sources	145
5-6	Property Tax Burden by State Based on Total Personal Income for FY 2005	147
5-7	Overall Tax Burden by State Based on Total Personal Income for FY 2005	149
5-8	Per-Capita Overall Tax Burden by State for FY 2005	151
5-9	Indexes of Fiscal Capacity, Need, and Effort by State, 1995–1996	153
5-10	Examples of Tax Expenditures	159

5-11	Examples of Income Elasticity	162
5-12	Examples of Rate Elasticity	162
6-1	Budget- versus Rate-Driven Property Tax Systems	167
6-2	Contrasting Rate- and Budget-Driven Tax Systems	168
6-3	Advantages and Disadvantages of Current Market Value	171
6-4	The Effect of Assessed Value Change Constraints on Property Tax Distribution	173
6-5	Constrained Values That Result in Tax Increases for Certain Properties with Lower Assessed Value Increases	174
6-6	Characteristics and Advantages of Property Tax System Controls	179
6-7	Limitations and Disadvantages of Property Tax System Controls	179
6-8	Effect of Classification on Individual Property Taxes	181
6-9	Purpose and Examples of Property Tax Exemptions (Full or Partial)	183
6-10	Common Full Property Tax Exemptions in the United States and Canada in 1999	184
6-11	Features of Property Tax Deferrals, Circuit Breakers, and Credits	186
6-12	Advantages and Disadvantages of Tax Abatements and TIFs	188
6-13	Tax Shifting as a Result of a TIF	189
7-1	Arguments for Centralized and Decentralized Assessment Administration	195
7-2	Overview of Required Job Skills for Tax Administration Staff	202
7-3	Sample Sales Data	208
7-4	Calculation of the Coefficient of Dispersion	209
7-5	Examples of Supervisory Activities in Tax Administration	214
7-6	Illustration of Direct Equalization on a Single Property	220
7-7	The Effect of Equalization on the Distribution of Property Taxes	220
7-8	Effect of Equalization on Effective Tax Rates	221
7-9	Illustration of Indirect Equalization	222
7-10	Content of an Assessment Notice	244
7-11	Billing Information	245
8-1	Median, Minimum, and Maximum Utilization of Main Categories of Taxes in Percentages of Total Taxes for General Government in Selected Countries	260
8-2	Median, Minimum, and Maximum Utilization of Categories of Recurrent Taxes on Property in Percentages of Total Taxes in Selected Countries	263
8-3	Information Sources for Countries Profiled	265
8-4	Property Taxation in Hungary, the Netherlands, and South Africa	267
8-5	Property Taxation in the United Kingdom	271
8-6	Council Tax Value Bands in England	271
8-7	Recurrent Property Taxes in the Russian Federation	283
8-8	Property Taxation in the Baltic Countries	277

List of Tables

8-9	Recurrent Property Taxes in China	280
8-10	Examples of Technological Diversity	284
9-1	Examples of Useful Information Sharing by Assessing Officers	295
9-2	Proportion of Property Tax Paid by Various Property Classes in Idaho in 2006	297
9-3	Who Spends the Property Tax in Idaho	297
9-4	Key Arguments Favoring the Property Tax	302
9-5	Property Tax Issues and Solutions	304
A-1	Models for Analyzing a Hypothetical Change in Property Taxation	315

Preface

Tax policy discussions and education have been a fundamental part of IAAO for many years. In 2004, the mission of IAAO in terms of promoting innovation and excellence in tax policy was addressed by Course 402, "Property Tax Policy," Workshop 403, "Property Tax Policy Alternatives and Modules," the *Standard on Tax Policy*, and various miscellaneous mentions in other association materials. However, a comprehensive text discussing tax policy in the context of mass appraisal and related disciplines did not exist. In July of that year, a project for developing the first-ever IAAO book on tax policy, *Fundamentals of Tax Policy*, was proposed. In conjunction with the other educational materials, the text would delineate a fundamental component of the core knowledge of IAAO.

The 2004 Executive Board approved the project plan and assigned the task of developing the book to the Communications Committee in collaboration with the Education Subcommittee. The committees were fortunate in finding the right people to make the publication happen. The product you hold in your hands would not have been possible without the expertise and dedication of its three authors: Richard Almy, Alan Dornfest, AAS, and Daphne Kenyon, Ph.D. The association thanks them for their invaluable efforts throughout the development process. Now, four years later, IAAO has realized its goal with the debut of this publication.

Fundamentals of Tax Policy explores the concepts and philosophy of taxation, the underlying systems for taxation, and the effects of taxation, thus offering insight into current tax policy debates. The goal is to present a broad overview of general tax policy with an emphasis on property tax policy. This book is directed at local, state, and provincial assessing officers and tax officials, members of the academic community, legislators, tax researchers, and governmental administrators. It is intended to provide a broad perspective on fundamental tax policy principles. Table 1-1, on pages 16 and 17, summarizes the content of each chapter and the appendixes.

The writing of a book is a lengthy, arduous, yet wondrous journey. That is why I find it truly gratifying to see this effort sustained through four different terms of administration at IAAO. It is a testimony to the commitment of IAAO to provide high-quality educational materials to its members and other appraisal professionals around the world.

Marion R. Johnson, CAE
IAAO President, 2006–2007

About the Authors

Richard Almy has worked in the tax policy arena with a general, multijurisdictional focus. As a member of the IAAO staff, he helped draft IAAO policy statements and shape the policy arguments in briefs of amicus curiae that IAAO filed with the U.S. Supreme Court. He was instrumental in research projects that identified policies supporting or detracting from market-value assessment, that evaluated efforts to tax farm and open-space land preferentially, and that evaluated measures to limit increases in assessments, property tax obligations, property tax levies, and local government spending. He helped IAAO identify questionable exemptions. In his consulting work he has systematically evaluated state and national property tax systems.

Alan Dornfest, AAS, is an internationally recognized expert in the area of property tax policy. He has been supervisor of property tax policy for the Idaho State Tax Commission since 1977. His responsibilities involve extensive research into the effects of property tax policy decisions, as well as practical experience in implementing policy and assisting assessing officers through development of administrative rules and training materials. Dornfest also imparts information and guidance on tax policy directly to a broad array of state and local government officials, including city and taxing district officials, state legislators, county commissioners, and members of the academic community. In addition to analysis of property taxes and the incidence of such taxes, Dornfest has considerable experience developing comparative tax burden studies for non-property taxes and coordinates the Idaho tax information submitted to the District of Columbia annually for further incorporation into its tax comparison study.

Daphne A. Kenyon, Ph.D. is an economist who works half time as visiting fellow at the Lincoln Institute of Land Policy and half time doing consulting through D. A. Kenyon & Associates, her public finance consulting firm in Windham, New Hampshire. Currently she also serves on the New Hampshire State Board of Education and on the Education Commission of the States. Previously, Kenyon served as president of The Josiah Bartlett Center for Public Policy; professor and chair in the Economics Department at Simmons College; senior economist with the Office of Tax Analysis at the U.S. Department of the Treasury, the Urban Institute, and the U.S. Advisory Commission on Intergovernmental Relations; and assistant professor at Dartmouth College. Her research and consulting have focused on state and local public finance, education policy, health care policy, and taxation. Since 1999, she has worked on school finance and property tax reform issues as a consultant, think-tank president, and visiting fellow for the Lincoln Institute of Land Policy. Kenyon earned her B.A. in economics from Michigan State University and her M.A. and Ph.D. in economics from the University of Michigan.

Acknowledgments

IAAO thanks the reviewers of this book: Robert Brown; Larry Clark, CAE; Jeanette Duncan, CAE; William J. McCluskey; Jeffery Spelman, CAE; and Timothy Wooten. Their expertise, perspectives, and comments added significant value to the content.

IAAO also thanks members of the Communications Committee, the Education Subcommittee, and the chairs of the Professional Development Committee for their support and encouragement. Their participation from 2003 through 2008 in the planning and logistics made this publication a reality.

Communication Committee members during this period were Marvin Anderson (2003 chair; 2006–2007 chair); Debra Asbury, AAS; William Birkle, AAS; C. Kevin Bokoske; Marion Johnson, CAE (2004 chair); John Lindsay (2008 chair); Elysa Lovelady; Gary McCabe, CAE; Dave McMullen; L. Wade Patterson; Jeffery Spelman, CAE (2005 chair); Guy W. Stark; John Taylor; Debbie Wheeler.

Chairs of the Professional Development Committee during this period were Rick Stuart, CAE, (2003 chair); Jim Todora (2004–2005 chair); and Fred Chmura, AAS (2006–2007 and 2008 chair).

Education Subcommittee members during this period were Patrick Alesandrini, CAE; Stephen Behrenbrinker, CAE; Larry Clark, CAE (2003 chair, 2005 chair); Barry Couch, CAE; Stuart K. Dalgleish, CAE; Jeanette Duncan, AAS; Anthony Hagenstein, CAE (2004 chair); Patricia Hedwall, CAE; Lillian Johnson; Josephine Lim; Michael Lomax; Kellianne Nagy, CAE; Jack Pasternacki; Richard Petree; Robert Reardon; William "Pete" Rodda; David B. Sanford, CAE; Steven R. Thomas, CAE, PPS; Jim Todora, CAE (2008 chair); Christine Van Staden; Paul Welcome, CAE (2006–2007 chair).

Much of the material in this book was drawn from the materials for Course 402 "Property Tax Policy" and from Chapters 1 and 2 of *Assessment Administration*. The contributions of those earlier authors are gratefully acknowledged.

Chapter 1
Introduction to Tax Policy

> *Without [good] tax policy, all the rest is moot.*
> —Anonymous respondent to 1995 survey of IAAO members
> on the need for a standard on property tax policy

Scope

In today's increasingly mobile global economy, states, regions, and even nations are in open competition for economic growth and sustenance. In this environment tax policy has become increasingly important in sustaining, encouraging, or discouraging certain outcomes. Few, if any, politicians from either major political party in the United States publicly espouse any position other than that taxes must be kept low. However, while taxes and the perception of high taxes reduce public support, the availability of public services increases support. Typically, public policy surveys find that large numbers of people who want lower taxes also want more support for services, particularly popular and widely used services, such as schools and roads. The disconnect between these two positions fuels continual attempts to tinker with the underlying systems that enable and govern both the taxes and the services. Examples of questions that must be answered to gain understanding of these policy directions are as follows:

- What determines whether taxes are high or low?
- When is it more appropriate or less appropriate for government to provide services?
- What are the pros and cons of various ways for funding government services?
- What makes taxes good or bad, supportable or unsupportable?
- Which type of tax is best?
- What are the strengths and weaknesses of each major tax?
- Who should have the authority to levy taxes?
- What should be the basis for taxes?
- What controls on taxes should be available?
- What are the underlying economic effects of taxation?
- How does taxation provide more than simply a revenue stream?

Specific to property tax policy, this book addresses the following questions:
- How is today's property tax evolving with respect to exemptions and the tax base?
- How is assessment administration changing?
- What legal issues affect property tax systems?
- How are property taxes controlled?
- Can a fair and equitable tax system be designed?
- What is the effect of equalization?
- What are the trade-offs if other taxes are substituted for property taxes?

This book explores the concept behind and the philosophy of taxation, the underlying systems for taxation, and the effects of taxation, thus covering many current tax policy debates.

Although many of the examples are based on U.S. experience, Chapter 8 in its entirety and various sections of other chapters provide a global perspective. Nevertheless, the material for the book as a whole is largely derived from U.S. sources, and the policy discussions are most germane to the United States, Canada, and other nations following the federal model of governmental separation of powers.

Public and Tax Policy Focus

Policies are purposeful courses of action that govern the operation of various systems. When these courses of action are governmentally established, they are considered to be public policy. When such policies provide direction with respect to methods and systems for funding government programs, they constitute tax policy.

The goal of this book is to provide a broad overview of general tax policy with an emphasis on property tax policy. By so doing, the authors hope to furnish a greater understanding of the interwoven nature of tax systems and aspects of such systems that are preferred or are less favorable.

Audience

Local, state, and provincial assessing officers and tax officials, members of the academic community, legislators, tax researchers, and governmental administrators must work within the systems of taxation and may recommend and advocate changes to them. This book is directed at providing this group with a broad perspective on fundamental tax policy principles. Assessing officers and other property tax administrators are expected to constitute much of this target audience. In countries such as the United States and Canada, most assessing officers operate at a local level (i.e., municipal or county) and provide access both to taxpayers and to the broader target audience identified above. While assessing officers can be presumed to have a great deal of knowledge about implementation and administration of property tax systems, their visibility and accessibility places them in a unique position to shed light on the policies underlying the current property tax system and to explain and distinguish the role of the property tax in the context of overall tax policy. This role is increasingly critical at a time when, despite continued conceptual support from the academic community, the property tax remains entrenched in the dubious position of least liked among all state and local taxes (at least in the United States). It is the intent of this book to assist assessing officers in fulfilling this role.

Federalism Perspective

Federalism is a form of government in which power is constitutionally divided between a central or national government and states or regional authorities. It is the operative system in the United States, Canada, and some other countries and is defined in greater detail in Chapter 4, "Role of Property Tax in Intergovernmental Finance." Although this book discusses tax policy under alternative government structures, the major focus is on federal models, because the property tax may be the only efficient and effective way to adequately fund the large number of local governments that federalism tends to promote. Note that the U.S. model divides authority only between the Federal Government and the states. The Constitution is silent on the issue of local governments and the authority or power they should have. For this reason and despite the delegation of responsibilities due to federalism, the authority and ability of local governments to levy taxes derive strictly from the states, although local governments are subject to federal restrictions.

International Property Tax Policy

Internationally, property tax policy revolves around several issues. First, there is the question of the underlying structure of government. In a federal system, much authority for setting property tax rates and even determining what component of property is subject to the tax often is vested with local, or at least subnational, governmental entities. There can be a sense or degree of independence, despite an overarching federal presence. An alternate model is the unitary system, in which local and regional governfments derive their powers, including taxation, from the national government. In these cases, property tax laws are determined by national legislatures. Local governments have varying degrees of authority regarding tax bases and exemptions and may have some discretion in setting tax rates. However, all authority derives from the national government, rather than being conceived as the shared authority system of federal models. International property tax systems are discussed to a greater extent in Chapter 8, "Systems of Government and Taxation: A Global Perspective."

Second, there is the issue of emerging democracies. This issue is most apparent in post-Soviet Eastern Europe, where countries that formerly had little or no private ownership of property, and therefore no base for property tax, have moved rapidly into more or less decentralized systems. These systems now permit private ownership and need funding sources that are based more on tangible assets than on income and other less discoverable tax bases. In many of these countries, property tax has emerged as a viable and equitable revenue source.

Major Concepts

What Is Property?

Ideas about property have been evolving since primitive times. Essentially, property is a cultural concept having to do with legal relationships among people about the things that can be possessed. Without laws to define property and governments to protect property rights, property does not exist. The concept of privately owned real property was—and remains—alien in some primitive societies, particularly nomadic ones; land was communally or tribally held. In early settlements, an individual's or family's dominion over a plot of land was based on a chief's allocation decision, and tenure was based more on custom than on defined rights.

Private ownership of real estate—and land in particular—was morally anathema to many socialist thinkers. With the formation of socialist governments in the twentieth century, much previously privately owned property was nationalized. Following the collapse of the Soviet Union in 1991, because private property is central to western market economies, many formerly Communist countries began restitution and privatization programs, which are returning nationalized property to former owners, current occupants, or purchasers.

Roman law recognized the two broad, overlapping ways of physically classifying property: (1) tangible versus intangible and (2) immovable (real) versus movable (personal). Real property comprises the rights, interests, and benefits connected with real estate. Real estate consists of land, improvements *to* land, such as clearing and grading; improvements *on* or attached to land, such as buildings; and appurtenances, such as easements to cross or give access to land. Except for appurtenances, real estate is tangible. Personal property or chattel is defined by exception: any property that is not real is personal. Personal property is characterized by its mobility, hence the term *movables*, and real property is known as *immovables*. The distinction between movable and immovable property is not always clear, causing administrative and valuation problems when there are differences in the way the two classes of property are taxed. Internationally, other terminology differences may be another source of confusion. The term *property* may not include land, and the term *land* may include buildings and other improvements to land.

What Is a Tax?

Taxes are the main source of government revenue.

> *The legal definition of tax depends on the context and the legal system. Typical elements that define a tax are that it is compulsory..., required by law..., made to the government for revenue purposes..., and not made in return for a service or other benefit thus distinguishing it from fees... .*
>
> —(Thuronyi 2005, 375)

In practice, it can be difficult to determine whether a revenue-raising instrument is a tax. In order to present comparable statistics, the International Monetary Fund (IMF) and the Organization for Economic Cooperation and Development (OECD) have developed largely complementary systems for classifying government revenues and expenditures (International Monetary Fund 2001, 48). According to the IMF, the main categories of *taxes* are (1) taxes on income, profits, and capital gains; (2) taxes on property; (3) taxes on goods and services; (4) taxes on international trade and transactions; and (5) other taxes.

Taxes are one way—but not the only way—for governments to derive necessary revenue. Governments often receive revenue from sales of goods and services, interest on funds held, rent from property owned, gifts, donations, and user fees and charges. Governments also share revenue, and such intergovernmental revenue sources can be significant. Although taxes are easily distinguishable from most of these other sources of revenue, user fees and charges often substitute for taxes and appear more like taxes than the other revenue sources. The main difference is that taxes are broad and do not necessarily provide the payer with a particular direct benefit. For example, paying motor fuel or property taxes for maintenance of highways can lead to generally improved highways, but a pothole in front of a particular taxpayer's house may not be repaired in a timely fashion. Contrast this general benefit from a tax with a specific benefit from a user fee, such as a toll for the maintenance of the next five miles of a particular highway. The expectation from paying the toll is that the revenue will be used for maintaining that specific stretch of roadway and that the toll payer is the user and will directly benefit from paying the fee.

Commonly, some government services, such as sewer, water, and trash disposal services, are funded through a combination of fees and property taxes. In some cases, the taxes are for capital expenses (i.e., building a new wastewater treatment plant) and fees are for ongoing operational expenses; however, this model is not universally true.

Because the differences between taxes and fees have blurred, there is a growing expectation that paying of a tax entitles the taxpayer to a specific type or amount of service. This is particularly problematic with the property tax, which often is subjected to the argument that if a taxpayer does not directly use a particular service (e.g., has no children in the school system), there should be no requirement to pay the tax that supports that service. The maker of such an argument fails to recognize the distinction that taxes are costs of government services not directly related to any particular taxpayer's use of those services. This point of view of course relates to the perceived appropriateness of the services provided by government, an issue that is explored more fully in Chapter 2, "Principles, Policies, and Economics of Taxation."

How Are Taxes Classified?

A tax can be recurrent, that is, assessed repeatedly, usually annually, or nonrecurrent, that is, assessed in connection with an event or transaction, such as the sale of real estate. Categories of property taxes include the following:

- Recurrent taxes on moveable (personal) and immovable property (land and buildings)—the main focus of this book
- Recurrent taxes on net wealth
- Estate, inheritance, and gift taxes
- Nonrecurrent taxes on capital and financial transactions (e.g., a real estate transfer tax).

Taxes that may be based on property values or that resemble property taxes but are classified differently include capital gains taxes and taxes on the imputed rental income of owner-occupied homes (these are classified as income taxes). In some former Communist countries, fees for the use of land resemble land taxes but could be classified differently.

A country, such as the United States, may use a different classification system and nomenclature. For example, the U.S. Census Bureau uses the following categories: (1) property taxes; (2) sales and gross receipts taxes; (3) selective sales and gross receipts taxes; (4) license taxes; (5) income taxes; and (6) other taxes (U.S. Census Bureau 2006, 4–9).

The main lesson from this discussion is that in comparing tax systems, care needs to be taken in interpreting statistics. It is no simple matter to classify taxes consistently. A further complication is that when statistics are presented by *level* of government, different taxes can be reflected in the total. The detail necessary to analyze, say, recurrent property taxes may not exist.

Taxes can be classified in other ways. One classification scheme distinguishes between direct and indirect taxes. Direct taxes are imposed on people, for example, income taxes. Indirect taxes are imposed on commodities or assets, for example, a sales tax on clothing and a property tax on land. From an economic perspective, this distinction is not helpful, as people ultimately pay all taxes (see Chapter 2).

An additional distinction can be made between specific and *ad valorem* taxes. A specific tax (sometimes called a unit tax or an excise tax) is a tax that is a fixed amount on a unit—a package of cigarettes, a bottle of wine, or a gallon of gasoline. A specific tax does not depend on the value of the unit. An ad valorem tax, on the other hand, depends on the value of the product. The tax rate is usually stated as a percentage of the value—a 5 percent sales tax, a 10 percent income tax, or a 1-mill property tax. Characteristics and administrative aspects of specific taxes are explored more thoroughly in Chapter 4, "Role of Property Tax in Intergovernmental Finance."

What Is a Property Tax?

Property tax is a form of recurrent taxation based on ownership or possession of property. For property tax to exist, there must be an underlying legal and cultural framework that defines property rights and enables possession of property. Property taxes take several forms and can be levied against various components or uses of property. In the United States, Canada, and some other nations, property taxes are *ad valorem*; that is, they are calculated in proportion to the value of the property (not necessarily market value or current market value). Around the world, property taxes may be based on value and sometimes on area without regard to value and can be levied against an occupant or user of property rather than the owner as the taxpayer.

The tax base or definition of taxable property against which the tax is to be applied must be established for the tax to be administered. In the nineteenth century, the general property tax was levied against both tangible and intangible property (often including bank deposits and other cash). As taxpayers came to acquire more and more intangible assets and as such assets increasingly were difficult to discover, the general property tax became administratively cumbersome and therefore increasingly inequitable. By the early twentieth century, it had evolved into a tax mostly on tangible property, although certain intangible components have been retained (i.e., labor necessary to build a house). As the twentieth century ended, more intangibles that had remained taxable were removed from the tax base in many states (e.g., goodwill, contracts, patents, and the like).

In addition to narrowing the base to tangible property, there has been a movement away from taxation of personal property (e.g., household goods, vehicles, inventory, machinery and equipment) in both the United States and Canada.

Finally, every property tax system makes allowances for exemptions. These are granted for a myriad of reasons, including business incentives, administrative complexity, and charitable and religious causes. Property taxation principles and exemption policy are discussed in greater detail in Chapter 6, "Analysis of Selected Property Tax Prescriptions."

Property-Based Wealth as Underpinning for Tax

The IAAO *Standard on Property Tax Policy* (IAAO 2004, 2.2:6) states

> *The property tax provides for balance and equity in the total tax system by taxing the one element of ability to pay overlooked by other state and local taxes. The property tax allocates the cost of government according to ability to pay as measured by property wealth.*

This seemingly self-evident statement leads to much debate, since, in modern society, there has been a blurring of the historical linkage between property ownership and the ability to convert that ownership into income and therefore have an ability to pay taxes.

In the United States, for example, home ownership is highly prized, with about 70 percent of all households living in owner-occupied homes. Depending on economic conditions and life situations, some homeowners (and other property owners) find themselves with a valuable asset but limited liquid resources with which to pay tax. The same argument often is made for owners of agricultural land who sometimes are perceived to have insufficient income from the land to pay the taxes. The IAAO *Standard on Property Tax Policy* (IAAO 2004, 2.2.3:7) addresses this issue further:

> *Historically, ownership of property has been highly correlated with, and at times was the only measure of, wealth. In modern society, however, income is considered the closest measure of ability to pay, and the link between property and wealth has become less obvious. However, one has only to note the availability of loans that use property or equity in property as collateral to recognize that the link to wealth and ultimately to income still exists. Businesses may be unprofitable and not currently generating income. Undeveloped land may be idle and have no income stream. Few would deny that either of these assets has value. However, property is owned in anticipation of future benefits, and courts have generally ruled in favor of zero or minimal value only when no future use can reasonably be anticipated. It is not unrealistic, therefore, to suggest that property still is a form of wealth and that only the property tax enables this wealth component to be used to pay for costs of government...without a property tax, some sectors of society with wealth would be exempt from participation in the costs of government. A balanced tax structure demands a property tax component.*

Although this position has a legal basis and represents sound economic theory, it ignores the public policy and political issues. Policy makers do not ignore these public pressures and have responded to ability-to-pay concerns by crafting property tax exemptions and other forms of tax relief, such as lower levels of assessment for residential and agricultural property, tax credits for lower income home owners, and other safety nets that are constantly being revised and refined. These mechanisms are discussed in greater detail in Chapter 6.

Influences on Tax Policy

The Legal Structure

In the broadest sense, the precepts of tax policy are provided in national or, in federal nations, state constitutions. In general, while constitutions lay out the framework for taxation, authorize it, and perhaps establish some fundamental principles (such as uniformity in property tax or the power of legislative bodies to grant exemptions), constitutional guidance tends to be broad and general. Legislatures provide statutes to create specific provisions for systems of taxation. Statutes can be more detailed or less detailed depending on the degree of discretion to be granted to the administrative agencies that implement statutory provisions. Typically, when statutes are very detailed, administrators have more guidance but less discretion. While these provisions establish the legislative branch as firmly in control of the specifics of policy, they can have unintended consequences. Assume, for example, a legislature intends to exempt intangible property from property tax; it may define the term generally or provide a list of the types of intangibles to be exempted (goodwill, contracts, cash, stock). In the latter (list) approach, a similar intangible (patents, for example) can be missed, despite a probable intent to exempt it. A statute that includes a list of specifics can preclude administrative flexibility and require frequent amendments to eliminate unintended inequities. The alternative approach is to define the policy (i.e., the exemption) more loosely and provide guidance to agencies with authority to administer the law and to establish rules or regulations to interpret and administer the policy.

Regardless of the specificity of any statute, there often is a need for interpretive rules to help front-line administrators implement the policy. Inevitably, disputes arise for resolution by the judicial system. Such resolution provides case law (especially when resolved by supreme courts), which forms precedent for future decisions.

Informal Processes

Statutes and administrative rules always entail formal development, passage, or promulgation processes. Legislative intent can be discernable through less formal processes such as speeches, minutes of committee hearings, and statements of intent provided by legislative committees or other bodies.

Policy Implementation

Policy implementation addresses the question of whether and to what extent statutorily set policies become operative. Regarding tax policy, taxpayers may be required to comply with some provision for which government may or may not have enforcement authority or ability. The use tax provides a clear example of the dilemma posed by a policy without clear administrative avenues. When individuals living in states that impose sales tax make online (electronic) purchases of goods that normally would be subject to the sales tax, these individuals are required to pay use tax, provided that the seller does not have a physical presence (nexus) in the purchaser's state. However, because under current U.S. law, the responsibility for collecting this tax is on the buyer, rather than the seller (as is the case with the general sales tax), the use tax is virtually unenforceable. Governments do not have the tools to effectively implement the policy behind this type of use tax. In the property tax arena, the same fundamental issues apply to the personal property tax, particularly when it is imposed through self-reporting mechanisms and when even property with *de minimus* value is required to be reported and taxed.

Aside from taxpayer compliance issues, governments can be remiss, can misunderstand, or can have insufficient resources with which to fully implement policy. While statutorily set policy is considered nominal, the degree of actual implementation is known as street-level or de facto policy.

Beginning in the last quarter of the twentieth century, there has been a marked shift from questioning the property tax as a valid source of state revenue to questioning the use of this tax to provide funding for local governments. This public pressure had its inception with the tax revolt in California that culminated in Proposition 13 and subsequent property tax limitation measures are discussed further throughout this book.

Historical Perspective on Property Tax Policy—The U.S. Model

Goals of Property Tax Policy

Tax policy goals range from providing stable revenue sources for government to redistributing wealth. Before these issues can be addressed, it is worthwhile to review the devolution of the property tax system in the United States from its beginnings as an exercise in federal tax power to its repudiation by the Federal Government in favor of other funding mechanisms. Perhaps analogously, state governments also embraced and later moved away from the property tax as a major funding source. In the United States today, property tax remains a mainstay for local governments. Interestingly, beginning in the 1990s several states reinstituted state-level property taxes, typically to provide more uniform school funding; this issue is discussed more fully in Chapter 4.

Early Federal Developments

The Constitution of the United States established the federal power to tax, a provision that previously had been denied to the federal government under the Articles of Confederation. In 1798 the federal government imposed a property tax, passed by Congress under the direct tax authority in the Constitution. The amount of tax to be raised was apportioned among the states based on population. The property tax was an *ad valorem* tax, based on the value of houses, and it was used in a progressive rate structure under which higher valued houses paid higher rates. Both federal and state officials were involved in assessment, collection, and administration. Although this first U.S. property tax was repealed and later reinstituted, the states generally began levying property taxes in response to debt repayment difficulties following an economic downturn in 1837 (Fisher 1996).

State Property Tax Policy

Early Developments

As property taxes became widespread in the form of state taxes in the United States, concerns over equity grew. Although some states began the practice earlier, following the Civil War most states adopted constitutional provisions requiring property taxes to be uniform and proportional. These concepts generally are understood as implying that one uniform rate should be applied in proportion to the value of taxable property, regardless of class or type.

In addition to concerns about uniformity, state tax policy needed to address questions on the breadth or applicability of the property tax. Historically, property ownership had been equated with wealth and ability to pay. Over time, wealth increasingly included intangible property, such as stock, bonds, mortgages, and cash. The general property tax envisioned by the principle of uniformity and codified in most states by the late nineteenth century included intangible property in the tax base. However, upon analysis of the effects of taxing such intangibles, economists such as Professor Seligman of Columbia University pointed out that there was a serious potential for double taxation. For example, if tangible property with a mortgage is taxed at its full value and the mortgage is then taxed, the same value is being taxed twice (albeit once to the owner of the tangible property and once to the holder of the mortgage). In his 1905 essay Seligman condemned this feature of the general property tax as:

> ...against the cardinal rules of uniformity, of equality and of universality of taxation...the general property tax is so flagrantly inequitable that its retention can be explained only through ignorance or inertia.

Concerns of this type gradually eroded support for the general property tax and pushed state governments to eliminate inclusion of many intangible property types in the early twentieth century.

Comments on Double Taxation

The term *double taxation* has become an overused pejorative argument. The general property tax, through its taxation of intangibles such as mortgages, resulted in two parties paying the same tax on the same underlying wealth—hence double taxation. This should not be confused with multiple but different taxes being applied to the same goods or services, as when sales tax and property tax both apply to an item.

Ongoing and Recent History
Level of Government Using Property Tax

The twentieth century saw continued and accelerating major developments in property tax policy. Among the most significant was the decline in the importance of the property tax as a source of revenue for states. After providing 43 percent of all state government revenue in 1902, property taxes were responsible for less than 1 percent of state government general revenue one hundred years later in 2002 (with the trend continuing at 0.9 percent in 2005). Two factors enabling this decline were the inception of the first modern state income tax (in Wisconsin) in 1911 and the widespread adoption of state income and sales taxes to lessen reliance on the property tax during the Great Depression in 1929 and much of the following decade. These substitute sources of tax revenue sometimes were available for use by local governments as well. However, even when states have permitted use of non-property taxes by local governments, administrative difficulties, economic competition between localities,

Chapter 1 Introduction to Tax Policy

and other considerations, which are discussed in greater detail in Chapter 4, have limited implementation by local governments. With the growth of local governments (i.e., municipalities, school districts, counties, special-purpose districts), property taxes have proven irreplaceable as a revenue mainstay.

Nevertheless, even for local governments, property tax has diminished in significance. In 1962, 48 percent of local government general revenue and 88 percent of local government tax revenue was derived from property tax. By 2005, these percentages had fallen to 28 percent and 72 percent, respectively. However, as shown in Figure 1-1, most of these declines were prior to 1982 and in direct response to the tax revolts of that period, such as Proposition 13 in California, which cut property taxes by more than $6 billion over a short time period (Fisher 1996).

FIGURE 1-1. Significance of Property Taxes in Local Government Finance in the United States, 1962-2005

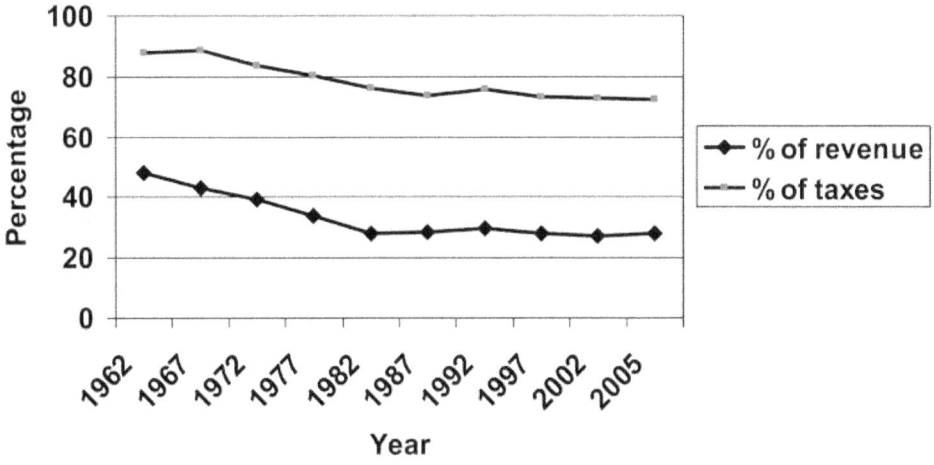

SOURCE: WWW.census.gov

Despite the reduction in the proportions of revenue and tax related to the property tax, note that no state in the United States (and no Canadian province) has eliminated the property tax. Rather, in the United States the tax has evolved from a state tax to a local tax. Furthermore, despite its predominance as a local tax, the magnitude of the property tax in the United States remains at a level at which it constitutes the predominant tax for state and local governments combined. This is demonstrated in Figure 1-2, which compares the three major tax types and overall tax revenue for all state and local governments for fiscal year 2005.

FIGURE 1-2. State and Local Property Tax Revenue Compared with Other Tax Revenue for FY 2005

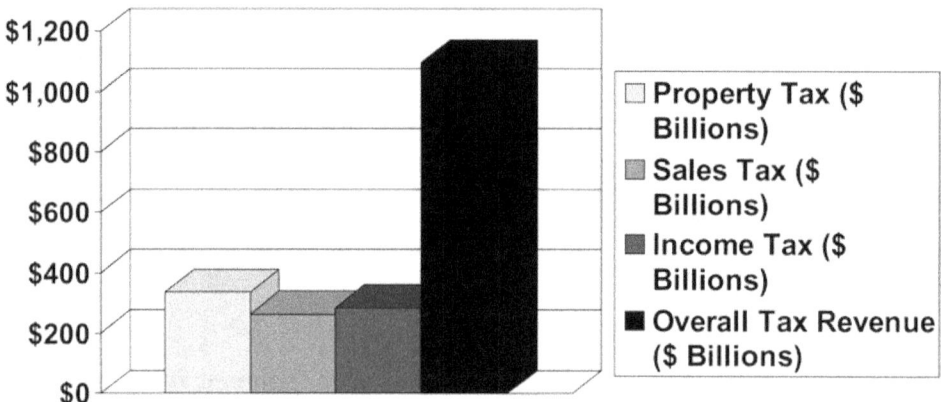

Source: www.census.gov

Figure 1-3 shows the same effect when the major taxes are compared on a per-capita basis. Both figures use a combination of individual and corporate income taxes for the income tax amounts.

FIGURE 1-3. State and Local Per-Capita Property Taxes in Comparison to Other Major Taxes for FY 2005

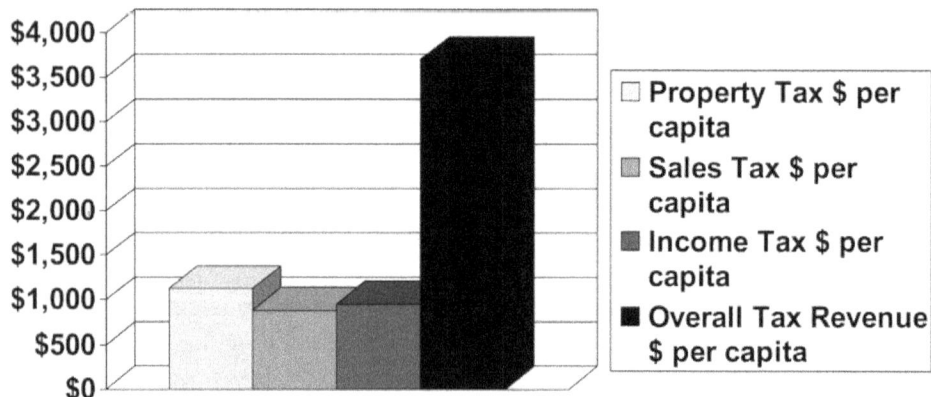

Source: www.census.gov

Tax Base

The definition of what is included in the tax base as taxable property has continued to narrow throughout the twentieth century and into the twenty-first century. By the end of the nineteenth century, some states had already responded to concerns about the general property tax by eliminating mortgages and certain other intangibles from the tax base. Although certain intangible elements, such as view, add to (or detract from) market value and thereby remain taxable or at least included in the value to be taxed, the general property tax of the nineteenth century no longer exists in the United States. It has been replaced with a tax on tangible property that has been gradually eroding into a tax on tangible real property. While specific exemptions and related policy decisions are discussed in greater detail in Chapter 6, the general direction away from a broad based tax and toward an increasingly narrow based one represents major continuing redirection of U.S. property tax policy and has implications for the future of the property tax in this country.

Assessment Administration

Assessment administration has followed a somewhat similar pattern, with most states adopting limited direct responsibility for the determination of the value of taxable property. Direct responsibility tends to be vested in local government assessors operating at a municipal or county level. The major impetus in the twentieth century has been toward increasing assessor professionalism through training, education, technology, and the creation and availability of professional standards of practice through organizations such as The Appraisal Foundation and IAAO. Assessment administration is discussed in greater detail in Chapter 3, "Fundamental Elements of the Property Tax."

Tax Limits

Although high taxes create economic distortions and generally are frowned upon, many of the most constraining property tax limits have originated in grassroots movements. Simple limits on specific tax rates have been utilized for a long time. As explained in greater detail in Chapter 6, these limits tend to provide stable and predictable property taxes when the tax base does not change through exemption or rapid increases or decreases in the value of taxable property. During times of rapid inflation, such as the 1970s, rate limits tend to be ineffective. As a result of this and other factors (see Chapter 6), revenue and value increase caps have become commonplace and usually constrain tax increases to a much greater extent than was the case with simple rate limits.

School Finance Issues

In addition to general ability-to-pay issues, the ability to provide a base level of services can also be adversely affected by using property wealth as an underpinning for the revenue needed for these services. This is especially true for school finance, which generally is accomplished through a combination of state and local funding mechanisms and taxes. In the United States, the property tax remains the predominant source of funding for schools, but there are large disparities among school districts in terms of property wealth. Nominally, this would lead to large disparities in per-pupil funding. However, states have been compelled by the courts to imbed a degree of uniform funding. Their efforts have led to equalization systems that attempt to level the playing field by lowering state aid to property-rich school districts while raising the amount of state funds distributed to property-poor school districts. Although this type of equalization can work, it complicates the tax and spending systems and can lead to less transparency and greater public disaffection. Equalization is discussed in greater detail in Chapter 4 and Chapter 7, "Components of Model Property Tax Administrative Systems."

Looking Ahead

This introductory section is intended to provide some background on the major topics discussed in greater detail in subsequent chapters. Table 1-1 presents a brief synopsis of the remaining chapters.

TABLE 1-1. Synopsis of Contents by Chapter

Chapter Number and Title	Description
2. Principles, Politics, and Economics of Taxation	Describes the purpose and function of government given a capitalistic economic system, a democratic form of government, and encouragement of private ownership; also covers government's economic roles.
3. Fundamental Elements of the Property Tax	Provides history and fundamental principles of property tax; includes discussion of the tax base, tax collection issues, controls on tax amounts, and issues related to specialized property types; also presents key principles of a model property tax system, advantages and disadvantages of the property tax, and ability-to-pay issues.
4. Role of Property Tax in Intergovernmental Finance	Describes the distribution of powers in federal governments and related financing issues, available taxes, and issues related to the administration and usefulness of these taxes; presents the major precepts of taxation and reviews underlying political issues; also discusses the applicability of each tax to different levels of government; concludes with discussion of equalization and school finance.
5. Tax Analysis	Discusses the meaning and measurement of tax burden and incidence and presents ways by which fiscal structures of states can be compared.
6. Analysis of Selected Property Tax Features	Reviews general property tax principles and model tax system precepts; also discusses use of market value as an underpinning for property tax; reviews the case for and against continued use of market value; also discusses various other valuation base systems and other methods for redistributing the property tax burden; concludes with a discussion of exemptions and tax relief mechanisms, including those designed to further economic development.
7. Components of Model Property Tax Administrative Systems	Discusses varying administrative roles and models related to property tax administration; frequency of appraisal, equalization systems, and administrative issues.
8. Systems of Government and Taxation: A Global Perspective	Discusses international uses of property taxes, with a preliminary discussion of various governmental structures; presents major tax types in use internationally and an overview of property tax systems in place around the world; covers the property tax base, major features of the tax, and use of the tax; compares property tax with other forms of taxation from this global perspective.
9. Prospects and Challenges	Discusses the role of the assessing officer as information provider and clearinghouse, and the interrelationship between the assessing officer and the policy maker; concludes with a review of the issues that currently affect the sustainability of the property tax in the United States.
Appendix A. Regressivity versus Progressivity of the Property Tax	Presents a discussion of the traditional view, new view, and benefit view of property taxation.
Appendix B. Economic Effects of Property Taxation	Examines the economic effects of property taxation, with respect to economic development, and discusses alternative property tax system approaches along these lines.

References

Fisher, G.W. 1996. *The worst tax? A history of the property tax in America.* Lawrence, KS: The University Press of Kansas.

International Monetary Fund. 2001. *Government finance statistics manual 2001.* http://www.imf.org/external/pubs/ft/gfs/manual/index.htm (accessed August 22, 2007).

International Association of Assessing Officers (IAAO). 2004. *Standard on property tax policy.* Chicago, IL: IAAO.

Seligman, E.R.A. *Essays in taxation.* New York: Macmillan Company, 1905, originally published in 1895. Quoted in Fisher, G.W. 1996. *The worst tax? A story of the property tax in America.* Lawrence, KS: University Press of Kansas.

Thuronyi, V. 2005. Tax. In *The encyclopedia of taxation & tax policy,* 2nd ed., J.J. Cordes, R.D. Ebel, and J.G. Gravelle, eds. Washington, DC: The Urban Institute Press.

U.S. Census Bureau. 2006. *2006 government finance and employment classification manual.* http://www.census.gov/govs/www/class06.html (accessed August 22, 2007).

Suggested Reading

Stocker, F.B., ed. 1991. *Proposition 13: A ten-year retrospective.* Cambridge, MA: Lincoln Institute of Land Policy.

Chapter 2
Principles, Politics, and Economics of Taxation

Underlying Systems

Democratic Form of Government

Democracy is a system of government that gives ultimate political power to the people. According to the *American Heritage Dictionary* (2000), democracy is "government by the people, exercised either directly or through elected representatives." There are a number of common elements of modern democracies:

- Free and fair elections, which make those in power accountable to the people
- Majority rule
- Guarantees of basic human rights for all
- Constitutional limits on government power
- Equal access to political resources and influence for all citizens. (In elections each person is entitled to one vote.)
- Underlying values of tolerance, cooperation, and compromise. (Fellow citizens allow each other the freedom to pursue different religions or lifestyles.)

There is a distinction between direct democracy and representative democracy. *Representative* democracy exists when citizens elect representatives to make decisions, enact laws, and administer laws on their behalf. In the United States, the national government operates as a representative democracy, as the president, vice president, and Congress are elected to represent U.S. citizens. *Direct* democracy exists when citizens employ no intermediaries or representatives to make their decisions. New England towns that use the town meeting form of government are one example of a direct democracy; citizens' referenda, common in the western United States, are another example.

Political systems and economic systems are related. Most modern democracies have market economic systems, and some experts maintain that a market system is a precondition for a democracy. Concentration of economic power, however, can undermine the effective working of a democracy.

Basic Elements of a Mixed-Market Economy

The U.S. economy is most often known as a mixed-market economy; that is, markets are used to make most economic decisions, but government has a role in setting the framework within which markets operate. The opposite of a *market economy* is a *command economy*, such as the former Soviet Union, in which most economic decisions are directed by government. For example, in a pure market economy, individuals and business firms operating within a market, with freely fluctuating prices, determine which persons will become accountants and which will become painters. In a pure command economy, government directs certain individuals to train and work as accountants and others as painters.

Figure 2-1 is a basic diagram of market supply and demand, often used to analyze price changes in a market economy. In a product market, such as the market for oranges, the demand curve (D) represents the amounts that consumers are willing to pay for various quantities of oranges. The supply curves (S', S) represent the amounts that producers (farmers in this case) are willing to supply at various prices (P_1, P_0). Figure 2-1 shows the effect on the price of oranges of a freeze that destroys part of the orange crop; the supply of oranges decreases, increasing the price (see the shift from price-quantity pair $P_0 Q_0$ to $P_1 Q_1$).

Less frequently, the U.S. economic system is referred to as a *capitalist* system. This terminology emphasizes another aspect of the economic system, the private ownership of land and capital (machinery and equipment). The opposite of capitalism is *socialism*, in which land and capital are owned by the government rather than by private individuals.

FIGURE 2-1. Supply of Oranges Decreases

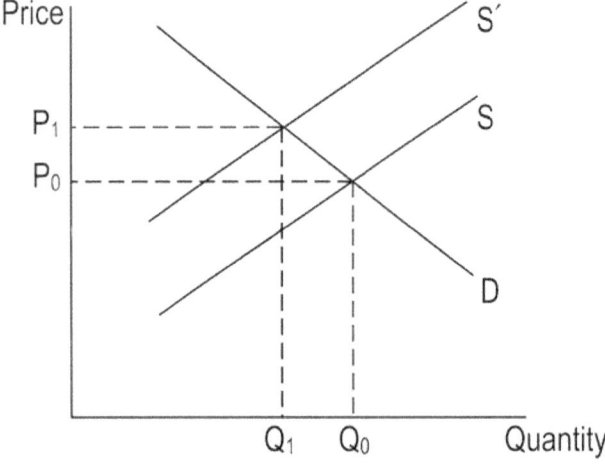

Advantages of a Competitive Market System

A market economy employs less coercion to coordinate economic activity than a command economy. In addition, competitive markets, in which no single buyer or seller dominates the market, provide the advantages of efficiency and economic growth. There are two types of efficiency: productive and allocative. *Productive* efficiency refers to the production of a good or service at the lowest average cost. For example, if certain conditions are satisfied, a competitive market economy tends to produce cars at the least possible cost. *Allocative* efficiency refers to the production of goods and services in an amount that satisfies consumer demand. For example, if U.S. consumers prefer cars to boats, a competitive market system will produce more cars than boats.

Competitive markets also promote economic growth. The pressure of competition provides an incentive for business firms to respond to consumer demands but keep costs low. Competitive markets also provide an array of choices to consumers, workers, and investors.

Competitive markets require certain elements, such as many buyers and sellers and the availability of low-cost information about price and quality of goods and services. These elements do not always exist, however, and this provides a justification for government.

Roles of Public and Private Sectors

As noted above, government plays an important role in the U.S. economy. The important question arises, When should the private sector produce a good or service and when should the government produce a good or service?

Private provision is best when nonrival benefits exist and nonpayers can be excluded from enjoyment of the good or service. A simple example is an ice cream cone. Nonrival benefits exist because only one person can eat the cone. Furthermore, if a person does not pay for the cone, it is simple to prevent him or her from obtaining it. Economists refer to this type of good as a *private* good.

The opposite type of good is a *public* good, for which nonrival benefits exist and it is difficult or too expensive to exclude nonpayers. An example of a local public good is mosquito abatement. When a town sprays for mosquitoes, it protects everyone from annoying bug bites and exposure to diseases such as West Nile virus. The fact that Mrs. Jones is protected does not detract from the protection afforded her next-door neighbor Mr. Smith. Thus mosquito abatement is a nonrival good within the neighborhood that has been sprayed. Furthermore, it is too expensive or difficult to exclude nonpayers from benefiting from mosquito abatement. If Mr. Smith decides to protest his property tax bill and refuses to pay his taxes, it is impractical to prevent his benefiting from the mosquito abatement program in his neighborhood.

Goods and services with nonrival benefits and the inability to exclude nonpayers are typically not provided by private firms or, if provided, are provided in an inefficiently small amount (an example of *allocative* inefficiency). Therefore, provision of public goods is one reason that government has an important role in a mixed-market economy.

The existence of public goods is one example of a market failure, but there are others. Another example is the existence of spillovers or externalities, which can be either negative or positive. Spillovers exist when some person or firm not party to an economic transaction receives either benefits or costs.

First, consider a negative externality. If Mr. Johnson drives a car with a defective exhaust system, he imposes a cost on other drivers following him who must breathe this exhaust. These other drivers are not part of the market transaction in which Mr. Johnson buys and maintains his car, and because they are not part of the market transaction, he has no incentive to take their wishes into account. In an unregulated market economy, there is a tendency for production and consumption decisions to generate too many negative spillovers. Government can alleviate this problem by placing a tax on pollution or setting emission standards for automobiles.

Second is the instance of a positive externality, in which the free market tends to produce too little of the good or service in question. An example of a positive externality is vaccinations. Not only does a vaccination protect the individual, it also protects others who come in contact with that individual. However, these contacts are not party to the economic transaction between patient and provider. Without government intervention, the free market would result in too few individuals receiving vaccinations. In this case, government intervenes by requiring vaccinations or providing them for free.

The benefits of a market economy derive mainly from its competitive aspect. In some sectors of the economy, there naturally arises a highly competitive market. In other sectors, monopolies (single sellers) or oligopolies (few sellers) arise. Markets dominated by monopolies or oligopolies are said to be imperfectly competitive markets. In these markets, business firms are not as responsive to consumer demand; there is less pressure to produce at the lowest average cost; and prices tend to be higher. In some cases, the government response can be to provide the good or service in question, such as in the case of cable television, or to regulate a private monopoly, such as in the case of public utilities. In other cases, the government can formulate antitrust policies to increase the competition in a market.

Another problem with market economies is that there is no assurance that they will generate a fair distribution of income. It is entirely possible that a few individuals will become very wealthy, while others many not earn enough to live. Business cycles are also an issue; market economies are subject to recessions, depressions, and excessive inflation.

Each of these market failures provides a possible justification for government action. Such government action is typically divided into the categories of stabilization, redistribution, and allocation.

Functional and Economic Roles of Government

Stabilization

The stabilization function refers to the influence of government on the overall level of economic activity, such as smoothing economic cycles and attempting to put the economy on a more stable path of growth. Stabilization tools are unemployment compensation, deficit spending by government, tax policy, and interest rate manipulation by the U.S. Federal Reserve System.

Although all government actions affect economic activity to some degree, public finance scholars believe national governments are in the best position to use fiscal policy to improve the general health of the economy. One reason is that the effects of any stabilization policies used by state or local governments will spill over their borders. For example, if Massachusetts were to spend more on public works projects in order to stimulate the economy, some of the second-round effects on employment or consumer spending are likely to affect neighboring states. A construction worker in Massachusetts might be a resident of Rhode Island, or a construction worker in Massachusetts might spend part of his paycheck in New Hampshire. Another reason the national government is best suited for the stabilization function is that it has policy tools that state and local governments do not have, such as the ability to use deficit spending and to conduct monetary policy (i.e., influence the money supply or vary the level of interest rates).

Redistribution

The redistribution function involves government actions to change the purely market-based allocation of wealth, income, and goods into one that society deems more equitable. Examples are cash transfers from high-income individuals to low-income individuals, rent subsidies, farm price supports, public transportation, and so on. As with stabilization, national governments are in a superior position to use taxation to redistribute income and wealth among individuals. State and local governments have more difficulty performing this function because people and businesses are mobile. High-income individuals and businesses that are taxed to fund redistributive programs can leave, while generous redistributive programs can attract low-income individuals. Nevertheless, state and local governments can and frequently do provide welfare and employment programs.

Allocation

Even in a market economy in which the private sector provides goods and services, government involvement in resource allocation is necessary because markets do not produce the socially optimal mix of goods and services. Government activities in the allocation category are government-guaranteed student loans, regulation of a natural monopoly like cable television, the creation of a government-run information clearinghouse like the U.S. Food and Drug Administration, government production of a public good like mosquito abatement, government-set automobile emission standards, and government provision of free and compulsory primary and secondary public education.

A government, on behalf of its residents, must articulate the demand for public goods and services, because in private markets residents cannot accurately express their willingness to pay. The political system, rather than individual consumers, makes consumption decisions. In theory, consumers make their preferences known to their elected representatives, and consumers' actions at the polls induce politicians to adopt service provisions that correspond to their constituents' preferences.

Table 2-1 shows the main types of market failures and the government function and possible government policies linked to each one.

Government Provision Does Not Require Government Production

Just because government has the responsibility to provide a particular service does not necessarily mean that it has to deliver that service. Consider the case of K-12 education. In the United States, local governments typically operate public schools in order to carry out their obligation to provide elementary and secondary education. However, there are alternatives to government operation of schools. For example, in some parts of the United States, vouchers allow parents to choose to send their children to public or private schools. Across the United States a significant fraction of parents home-school their children. A third alternative is for local government to contract with a private education company to operate schools.

TABLE 2-1. A Menu of Potential Government Responses to Market Failures

Failure of Market Economy	Government Intervention	Current Examples of Government Policy
Inefficiency Monopoly Spillovers/externalities Public goods	**Allocation Function** Encourage competition Intervene in markets Provide public goods	Antitrust laws, deregulation Antipollution laws, antismoking ordinances Build lighthouses, provide mosquito abatement
Inequality Unacceptable inequalities of income and wealth	**Distribution Function** Redistribute income	Progressive taxation of income and wealth, income support or transfer programs (e.g., food stamps)
Macroeconomic Problems Business cycles (high inflation or unemployment) Slow economic growth	**Stabilization Function** Stabilize through macroeconomic policies Stimulate growth	Monetary policies (e.g., changes in money supply and interest rates); fiscal policies (e.g., changes in tax and spending programs) Raise national savings rate by reducing budget deficit or increasing budget surplus

Source: Samuelson and Nordhaus, 2001, o, 40.

Government Failures

An important caution is that just because a market failure exists does not automatically mean that government should intervene. Table 2-1 is carefully labeled to indicate market failures and *potential* government responses—just as markets can fail, so can governments.

Government failure in an attempt to correct market failures is usually related to (1) lack of information, (2) the influence of special interest groups, (3) bureaucratic costs, and/or (4) the disincentives generated by taxation. Information on the social and private benefits and costs of a particular activity is necessary to avoid crafting government policies that fail. For example, appropriate government environmental policies depend upon good information about the additional benefits and costs generated by policies requiring lower levels of various chemicals in drinking water.

In addition, even if a government possesses the information necessary to appropriately intervene in the market economy, politics and the undue influence of special interest groups can steer this intervention on the wrong course. Also, because the organization and management of government entities are often large and bureaucratic, the actual cost of intervention can be quite high even if information and politics do not cause problems. Finally, raising taxes, which is typically necessary to fund government programs, imposes collection and disincentive effects that must be considered when determining the degree of government intervention in the market economy.

Size of Public Sector

The best way to measure the size of government relative to the size of the private economy is to examine total government expenditures as a percentage of gross domestic product (GDP), the market value of all goods and services produced in the economy. This measure is not perfect (it does not measure the role of government regulations, for example), but it is the best measure available. Table 2-2 shows that in 1929 state, local, and federal expenditures accounted for less than 10 percent of the economy. By 1950, government as a fraction of the private economy had more than doubled, and in 2005, government spending accounted for nearly one-third of the total economy.

TABLE 2-2. State, Local, and Federal Government Spending as a Percentage of GDP in the United States

Year	U.S. Government Spending as Percentage of GDP
1929	9.9%
1940	18.8
1950	20.7
1960	22.7
1970	27.6
1980	29.0
1990	30.6
2000	29.4
2006	36.3

Source: Chairman of the Council of Economic Advisors. Economic report of the President. various years, http://www.gpoaccess.gov/eop/index.html (accessed December 31, 2007).

One perspective on the size of the public sector in the United States is provided by libertarian think tanks such as the Cato Institute or by the anti-tax movement that has grown in importance since the late 1970s. According to this perspective, government has an automatic tendency to grow; furthermore, government growth threatens individual liberties and government programs are often inefficient.

At the same time, government in the United States is smaller relative to the private economy than in many other countries. Table 2-3 shows that government accounts for almost 40 percent of the total economy in Canada and more than 50 percent of the total economy in France and Sweden.

TABLE 2-3. Government Spending as a Percentage of GDP in Selected Countries in 2006

Country	Government Spending as Percentage of GDP
Australia	34.4%
Canada	39.3
France	53.4
Germany	45.7
Japan	38.1
Sweden	55.5
United Kingdom	45.0
United States	36.6

Source: OECD. 2007. "OECD in Figures 2007," http://fiordiliji.sourceoecd.org/vl=3776716/cl=37/nw=1/rpsv/figures_2007/en/page26.htm (accessed March 3, 2008).

Qualities of a Good Tax System

> *To tax and to please, no more than to love and be wise, is not given to men.*
> —Edmund Burke ([1774] 1899)

Shortly after Burke's observation, Adam Smith propounded four canons of taxation in his landmark treatise, *Wealth of Nations* ([1776] 1904):

- "The subjects of every state ought to contribute towards the support of the government, as nearly as possible, in proportion to their respective abilities; that is, in proportion to the revenue that they respectively enjoy under the protection of the state" (B.V. Ch.2 "Of the Sources of the General or Public Revenue of the Society." V.2.25).

- "The tax which each individual is bound to pay ought to be certain, and not arbitrary. The time of payment, the manner of payment, the quantity to be paid, ought all to be clear and plain to the contributor, and to every other person" (V.2.26).

- "Every tax ought to be levied at the time, or in the manner, in which it is most likely to be convenient for the contributor to pay it" (V.2.27).

- "Every tax ought to be contrived as both to take out and keep out of the pockets of the people as little as possible, over and above what it brings into the public treasury of the state" (V.2.28).

In Smith's time, the first canon implied proportional taxation. The idea of progressive taxation (taxing high-income people at higher rates than low-income people, or more valuable property at higher rates than less valuable property) came later. The second canon implies that a tax obligation must be legally sanctioned;

it also implies evenhanded administration. Finally, it implies that the system is transparent in the sense that it can be understood. The third canon makes the obvious, but sometimes ignored, point that tax compliance is greater if paying taxes is made as easy and painless as possible. There are two aspects to the fourth canon: the costs of the tax administration in assessing and collecting a tax and the costs of taxpayers in complying with reporting demands.

Later scholars (such as the Musgraves [1989]) added other principles and perspectives, which are rooted in economic theory and common sense. Some criteria are complementary; others are mutually exclusive. The scholarly principles reflect ideas about good government—a theoretical perspective. There also is a practical politics perspective. As Burke's aphorism suggests, policy conflicts are inevitable. However, a tax is sustainable as a source of revenue only so long as it is politically acceptable. In the words of the art historian, Bernard Berenson (1952), "Governments last as long as the under-taxed can defend themselves against the overtaxed."

To be politically acceptable, the tax must meet certain broadly agreed-upon criteria that tend to define a good tax system. Notions of *fairness*, *equity*, and *uniformity* predominate.

Fairness and Equity

Fairness and equity have to do with a sense that there is no favoritism or bias in the design or administration of a tax. The two basic principles of an equitable tax system are the *benefit principle* and the *ability-to-pay principle*. The benefit principle suggests that a tax is considered equitable when it pays for services that consumers desire. The gas tax is based on the benefit principle since gas taxes are usually earmarked for road maintenance and only road users pay the gas tax.

Taxation based on the ability-to-pay principle rests on two beliefs: *horizontal equity* and *vertical equity*. Horizontal equity calls for equal treatment of taxpayers who are the same in all relevant economic aspects. This means that two economically identical taxpayers pay the same tax. However, there are two problems with this criterion. First, there may be differences in policy makers' judgments as to what constitutes all *relevant* economic aspects. For example, in the United States, if two households are identical in wage income, but one has a blind member while the other has a deaf member, the household with the blind member pays less in taxes—a value judgment passed by Congress. Second, there may be some looseness in the meaning of *being treated equally*. For example, suppose there are two identical families in terms of income received, yet one chooses to buy a house using a mortgage while the other chooses to rent an apartment of identical size. In the United States, the family that buys the house may pay less in taxes because of the mortgage interest deduction. Again, this is a policy decision.

The second ability-to-pay belief is that taxpayers with a greater ability should pay more. Vertical equity essentially means that taxpayers who are in unequal economic positions should be treated differently. In practice, this means that people with low incomes should pay less in taxes than those with high incomes. Again, there are difficulties in implementation. For example, how much more in taxes should those with high incomes pay? Taxes whose rates increase as income, value, or other measures increase are said to be *progressive*. Taxes whose rates decrease as income, value, or other measures increase are said to be *regressive*. Finally, taxes whose rates remain constant as income, value, or other measures change are said to be *proportional*. (Regressive taxes are different from regressive assessments; see the Glossary.)

Neutrality

Neutrality means that a tax does not distort economic decisions. A uniform, broadly based tax is likely to be neutral. Neutrality fosters economic *efficiency*. An efficient tax encourages an optimal mix of the factors of production (labor, capital, management, and land), which according to economic theory increases general welfare. In theory, when a perfectly competitive market is at equilibrium for all goods, services, and factors, it is impossible to make any individual better off (in his or her own judgment) without making someone else worse off. Then any change caused by a tax would lead to a movement away from this equilibrium. When imposition of a tax distorts otherwise efficient economic decisions, the tax is said to create a deadweight loss or an excess burden. The excess burden is not the same as the tax burden.

A simple example of the excess burden of a tax follows. Suppose that a state places a very high tax on rice cereal. Consumers would try to avoid this tax, if possible, and if the tax were high enough, all those who preferred rice cereal might switch to corn or wheat cereal. If all consumers switched to another type of cereal, the rice cereal tax would not raise any revenue. But the tax would create an excess burden on consumers by inducing former rice-cereal consumers to switch to their second-choice cereal. If the loss in satisfaction imposed on rice-cereal consumers from this onerous tax could be measured, that would be an estimate of the excess burden of the tax.

High taxes on one factor of production tend to shift investment toward others with lower taxes. In a situation of perfect competition, producers and consumers follow the signals sent by the price system to allocate resources optimally, increasing the general welfare. To the extent that a tax changes prices, it might change the allocation of resources. If these resources were once allocated efficiently, that would no longer be the case. What causes these resource reallocations are the behavioral changes that consumers and producers undertake in response to the tax. However, the initial effect of a tax must be distinguished from its ultimate repercussion (see Chapter 5, "Tax Analysis"). For example, a tax levied on the owners of apartment buildings might be passed along to tenants in the form of higher rents.

Uniformity

Uniformity means a tax is proportional to some other measure. In assessment administration, the idea is that taxes should be proportional, not variant, across the property value spectrum; that is, assessment ratios or effective tax rates should not vary significantly with property value (unless the tax is deliberately designed to be progressive or regressive).

Departures from a policy of uniformity are common. They may be deliberate or unintended. Examples of deliberate departures are progressive income taxes and classified (differential) property tax systems. Other examples of deliberate departures from uniformity are incentive and disincentive measures designed to further social and economic policies. The list of possible objectives is endless. In property taxation, common objectives are making housing more affordable (particularly for families with limited income); encouraging good works by nonprofit organizations; encouraging economic development; preserving farmland, forests, open space, wetlands, and historic buildings; protecting the environment; and expressing gratitude for military service in times of war.

Adhering to a policy of uniformity in property taxation has several requirements. By definition, an *ad valorem* tax is proportional to value. Arguably, a uniform relationship between property value and property taxes can be maintained only if current market value is the basis of assessments. Property tax laws address uniformity in two ways: (1) tax rates and (2) assessment ratios. In the case of assessment ratios, it may be necessary to distinguish between legal ratios (the percentage of appraised values that assessed values represent) and actual ratios (the percentage of market values that assessed values represent). Both ratios must be uniform to achieve uniform effective tax rates. Second, the responsibility for any departures from uniformity needs to be clear. That is, taxpayers need to be able to distinguish between, on the one hand, differentials in tax burdens caused by differential tax rates, assessment ratios, exemptions, limits on changes in assessments, and the like and, on the other hand, differentials caused by non-uniform valuations. This also is a transparency requirement. In addition, uniformity requires that all taxable property in a tax district has been discovered and is accurately described. Tax obligations need to be enforced vigorously.

A policy of uniformity can have *buoyancy* and acceptability benefits. When effective tax rates are uniform, governments can more easily identify a publicly acceptable rate of tax. Of course, in keeping with the ability-to-pay concept, high-income taxpayers may acquiesce to a higher rate of taxation than low-income taxpayers. Consequently, there may be fiscal benefits to setting a rate of tax that is higher than low-income taxpayers can afford and providing them relief in other ways. When effective tax rates are not uniform, which occurs when valuations are out of date, governments take their rate-setting cues from relatively overvalued taxpayers. As a result, they decide upon a general rate of tax lower than the rate the undervalued would accept. Consequently, revenues are less than those when valuations are uniform.

Buoyancy

Buoyancy refers to the ability of tax yields to rise (and fall) with the economy and with revenue needs. Buoyancy is a characteristic of value-based property tax systems, but assessed valuations must be updated as the underlying market values change. *Stability* refers to the ability of the tax system to generate a stable level of revenue over time in the face of economic fluctuations. This characteristic refers to the entire system—and it implies that multiple taxes are superior to a system with but one tax. The label *balanced revenue system* sometimes is used in this context. Sometimes stability is referred to as the resiliency of a tax system, meaning how the system responds to changing economic conditions (see the discussion of tax *elasticity* in Chapter 5).

Under a multiple tax system, for example, if there were to be a recession, sales and income tax revenues would likely fall, but property tax revenues would likely remain stable. User fees would likely fall somewhere in between. A multiple tax system would lead to a situation in which any tax rate on a particular base is likely to be lower than that under a single tax system. A tax on the capital value, or current market value, of immovable property can be an important part of a balanced revenue system. Such a tax has a stable and reliable base, which is attractive during economic swings. If revaluations are frequent, the base also can be buoyant during periods of economic growth or inflation. On the other hand, in states with assessment caps, levy limits, or other property tax limitations, the property tax will be much less buoyant than in states without such limits.

In a similar vein, taxes on immovable property are considered to be good local taxes because the immovability of the tax base makes clear which government is entitled to the tax revenue. Local government services often are provided to properties or their owners and occupants (the benefit principle). Many public services provided through property taxes are thought to protect property investments and, indeed, may increase property value. At the same time, the tax captures for local government some of the increases in the value of property partially created by public expenditures. Having a dedicated source of revenue promotes local autonomy. The visibility of property taxes focuses attention on the overall quality of governance and promotes accountability. The property tax is the only tax that affords taxpayers the opportunity to review and challenge not only their assessments but also the assessments on similar or surrounding properties.

Practicality and Cost-Effectiveness

In keeping with Smith's fourth canon, taxes need to be administratively practical and cost-effective. Administrative practicality has several facets. Simplicity is one: the base should be easily measurable, evasion difficult, and taxpayers compliant. For example, one reason some e-commerce transactions are not taxed is the difficulty of determining who should pay the tax; that is, who should pay the tax on an item bought by an individual who lives in a state with no sales tax, purchased from a merchant in a state with a high sales tax, and delivered to a third party in a state with a low sales tax? These problems can be minimized by common tax codes and tax cooperation, but they also have costs. As noted, taxpayer compliance costs should also be minimized. The more complex the tax code, the more time (or money if the taxpayer hires someone to calculate the taxes owed) the taxpayer has to spend to comply with the code. The rise of complex legal instruments to avoid inheritance taxes owes much to both the rate and the complexity of the estate tax. The total costs of administration—both public and private—should be minimized.

Conceptually, a *cost-effective* tax system is one in which tax collections approach 100 percent of the total amount potentially due and administrative and compliance costs are minimized. Although property taxes are unfairly criticized as costing more to administer than income and consumption taxes, they can be practical. In contrast to the base for sales and income taxes, the property tax base is easily identified. The property tax is difficult to avoid. The total cost of property tax administration compares favorably with the costs of administering sales and income taxes when taxpayer compliance costs are considered. Admittedly, administrative costs are relatively high in property taxation, but compliance costs generally are low. The opposite pattern prevails in self-assessed income and consumption taxes. Moreover, compliance costs largely are invisible. Silverstein (1989) calculated that the cost of preparing U.S. income tax returns would be 20 percent of revenues if taxpayers could bill for their time at $10 per hour.

In property taxation, a facet of cost-effectiveness is that the fiscal cadastre constructed during the administration of a property tax constitutes a valuable fund of land information. If up-to-date and publicly available, the information has many governmental and private uses. Satisfying private needs for land and building data can provide a source of revenue to defray part of the costs of administration.

Public Acceptance

Ultimately, *public acceptance* is the cumulative effect resulting from widespread recognition that taxes are necessary and general support for the uses to which tax revenues are put. Citizens must have a sense that the tax system is basically fair and that it neither favors some taxpayers nor is biased against others. There also is acquiescence regarding the level of taxation. Income levels affect perceptions of affordability. In addition, taxpayers object when tax amounts increase significantly, especially when the reasons are not made clear. Administrative features, such as understandability and ease of payment, affect acceptability. Successful public education programs can build public acceptance.

If taxpayers think that their money is being wasted, they are unlikely to make the collection process easier, and tax avoidance and evasion can become major problems.

Chapter 2 Principles, Politics, and the Economies of Taxation   33

Comments such as "the rich can take advantage of loopholes while I can't" indicate that there may be acceptance problems. Note that loopholes are often described in arcane language so that only specialists know of their existence and how to take advantage of them.

Openness and Transparency

Openness and *transparency* contribute to a sense of fairness. Transparency is achieved when the system is understandable. Simplicity improves transparency. Transparency also goes hand in hand with openness. In an open system, taxpayers can easily obtain information, ask questions, lodge appeals, and make payments. Transparency improves accountability and is a characteristic of democratic government.

References

American Heritage Dictionary of the English Language, 4th ed. 2000, http://www.bartleby.com/61/73/P0667300.html (accessed January 3, 2008).

Berenson, B. 1952. *Rumor and reflection*. New York: Simon and Schuster.

Burke, E. 1899. Speech, April 19, 1774, House of Commons, London. First Speech on Conciliation with America: American Taxation, Works, vol. 2 (1899); *The Columbia World of Quotations*, 1996.

Musgrave, R.A., and P.B. Musgrave. 1989. *Public finance in theory and practice*. New York: McGraw-Hill, Inc.

National Conference of State Legislatures. 2007. *Principles of a high-quality state revenue system*, 4th ed. June 2001, http://www.ncsl.org/programs/fiscal/fpphqsrs.htm (accessed February 22, 2008).

Samuelson, P.A., and W.D. Nordhaus. 2001. *Microeconomics*. New York: McGraw-Hill.

Silverstein, M. 1989. "Taxing times: A short-form history of tariffs, levies and other painful payments," *The Chicago Tribune Magazine*, April 9, 1989, page 29.

Smith, A. 1904. *An inquiry into the nature and causes of the wealth of nations*, 5th ed., Edwin Cannan, ed. London: Metheum and Co., Ltd., http://www.econlib.org/library/sith/5mwn.html (accessed December 31, 2007).

Chapter 3
Fundamental Elements of the Property Tax

Property Taxation from a Systems Perspective

Property tax systems reflect the complexities of the political and economic environments of which they are a part. They evolve with changes in the economy and society. Considered systemically, they comprise functions, elements, phases, and linkages. Looking at a property tax system in these different ways can result in a fuller understanding of policy issues and methods for achieving policy goals.

Functionally, a property tax system:
- Identifies and links taxable subjects (taxpayers) and objects (taxable property)
- Produces tax assessments (whether based on value or some other quantity)
- Collects taxes.

The first two activities constitute the assessment component, which determines who is to pay taxes and each taxpayer's share of total taxes. The fiscal cadastre (property tax record system) and any valuation system are parts of the assessment component. The collection component prepares tax statements (bills); receives and accounts for payments; initiates actions to collect overdue taxes, and distributes receipts. There also is a control component, which dictates powers and responsibilities. It provides resources and governs how they are used—in short, how the tax is administered. Quality assurance is an important facet of property tax administration.

Property tax system elements are people, policies, technologies, processes, and data. Whether they are taxpayers, tax administrators, tax recipients, or other stake-holders, people's beliefs, skills, motivations, and experiences help shape property tax policies and procedures. Depending on their perspective and on how an existing property tax system is designed and administered, they may seek to influence the opinions and actions of legislators, who formulate new policies and revise or abandon old ones.

Political leadership is essential in tax reforms, and political leaders often are accused of lacking political will. From a systems perspective, however, a lack of political will can be a sign of a weak case for a proposed change. The tax consequences of a proposed change may not be clear—or may be all too clear, particularly when the "losers" (those who will pay more) are politically stronger than the "winners" (those who will benefit). The costs of the proposed change may be deemed too great in relation to the benefits. The behavior of administrators also is crucial; they can reinforce or hamper policies and reforms. Their skills are essential to effective administration, because they are the ones who apply technologies, design processes, and administer the tax.

Important Legal Issues

Laws give legitimacy to policies and supporting processes. Regulations and court decisions, along with constitutional provisions and statutes, are part of the legal framework for taxation. Although the policy import of a constitutional provision may be self-evident, the intent of a complex statute may not be. For this reason, cases can be particularly important, especially when they consider conflicting policies and laws or new factual situations (Youngman 2006, ix).

Internationally, there are two main legal systems: *common law* and *civil law*. They influence both property rights and the characteristics of property tax laws. The main distinction between the two systems is the relative importance of codified texts of laws versus judicial precedents. Under a civil law system, which originated in Rome and which can be found in continental Europe, the former colonies of European countries, and other places, relatively greater weight is placed on organized written legal texts, or codes. Under common law, which originated in feudal England and which spread to its colonies, including Canada and the United States, relatively greater weight is attached to court decisions. It has been said (with some exaggeration) that under a common law system, something can be done unless it is explicitly prohibited, and under a civil law system, something cannot be done unless it is explicitly allowed. Reviewing cases in U.S. federal courts finds this characterization of American property tax law is not too far off the mark.

Of course, both types of legal systems combine legislatively enacted laws, administratively promulgated regulations, and court decisions. Administrators always have some discretion. Both types of systems also can have un-enforced (and sometimes un-enforceable) laws. It is claimed that a civil law system promotes accessibility by non-lawyers and certainty. However, such systems can be less flexible, which makes adapting to new circumstances difficult. Common law property tax systems tend to have the opposite strengths and weaknesses: by relying more on principles than on detailed rules, they are more flexible. On the other hand, one cannot be as certain about the law in a novel situation until a new decision is rendered.

In the words of Otto Von Bismarck (1867), "Politics is the art of the possible." Both politics and law reflect the tension between ideals and practicalities. As mentioned in Chapter 1, "Introduction to Tax Policy," the ideal of a uniform and universal property tax was defeated in the United States, at least in part, by the practicalities of assessing movable property with nineteenth-century technology. Nevertheless, the principles of universality and, particularly, uniformity can be seen in laws that govern property taxation in the United States today.

The Legal Setting in the United States

Because the United States is a federal country, the bulk of its property tax law has been written by the states. However, the U.S. Constitution influences this body of law in several ways (see Table 3-1). Of paramount importance are the provisions that deal with the powers of taxation of the Federal Government and the states and the provisions that define the rights of citizens. Article I, Section 8, of the 1787 Constitution vests with Congress the power to lay taxes, and Sections 9 and 10 contain limits on direct taxes (they have to be proportional to population) and on taxes on goods in foreign and interstate commerce. (The Sixteenth Amendment, which authorized federal income taxation, excused income taxes from the apportionment requirement. The federal estate tax has been held to be an excise tax, not a property tax [Youngman 2006, 6].) The Tenth Amendment (part of the Bill of Rights) reinforced the principles that the Federal Government has only the powers expressly stated in the Constitution and that the states have broad powers of taxation, including the power to tax property. Nevertheless, Fisher (1996, 38–44) recounts federal efforts to tax property on an ad valorem basis in 1798–1802 and 1812 (both in times of fear of war or actual war). It is worth noting that the Federal Government had a transfer tax based on the value of real property from 1932 until 1968 and that about 40 states now have value-based transfer taxes (Behrens and Gravelle 2005).

Note that local government authority is not directly at issue in the provisions identified in Table 3-1. In the U.S. system, local governments derive their authority from states—this means that local government property tax policies cannot violate state or federal limitations. The shapers of the U.S. federal system were concerned about the proper balance of taxation (and other) powers between the states and the Federal Government.

TABLE 3-1. Federal Constitutional and Statutory Provisions Affecting Taxation and Limiting the States' Powers of Taxation

Measure	What It Does	How It Might Affect Property Taxation
U.S. Constitution, Article I, Section 8	Assigns to Congress the power to lay and collect [federal] taxes.	The enactment of the U.S. Constitution in 1787 did not change the states' basic powers of taxation under the Articles of Confederation.
U.S. Constitution, Commerce Clause (Article I, Section 8, Clause 3; also known as the Foreign Commerce Clause, the Interstate Commerce Clause, and the Tribal Commerce Clause)	Assigns to Congress the power to regulate foreign and interstate commerce.	Precludes states from enacting discriminatory taxes on articles in foreign and interstate commerce. The clause affects property taxes on goods in transit and inventories and has been used to challenge other forms of differential taxation.
U.S. Constitution, Article I, Section 9	Requires, among other things, that federal direct taxes be proportional to state population.	Because under U.S. constitutional law, a property tax is a direct tax, the federal government is effectively precluded from enacting a value-based tax on property without a constitutional amendment, such as that authorizing the income tax.
U.S. Constitution, Import-Export Clause (Article I, Section 10, Clause 2)	Limits state taxes levied on articles in foreign and interstate commerce.	
U.S. Constitution, Privileges and Immunities Clause (Article IV, Section 2; sometimes known as the Comity Clause)	Entitles citizens of each state the "privileges and immunities" of citizens of other states. (A similar clause can be found in the Fourteenth Amendment.) Comity has several meanings. It is the principle by which the courts of one jurisdiction may accede or give effect to the laws or decisions of another. In the United States, comity reflects a federalism principle whereby federal courts give "scrupulous regard for the rightful independence of state governments which should at all times actuate the federal courts."	Can be used by nonresidents to challenge property tax measures that discriminate against out-of-state taxpayers without a valid justification. However, federal courts generally do not take up a case unless the state refuses to act or acts in an otherwise constitutionally dubious manner.
U.S. Constitution, Supremacy Clause (Article VI, Clause 2)	States that federal law is supreme and preempts state law; forbids state courts to disassociate themselves from federal law because of disagreement with its content or a refusal to recognize the superior authority of the source.	Federal Government property cannot be taxed by the states without the federal government's permission (McCulloch v. Maryland 1819).

TABLE 3-1. Federal Constitutional and Statutory Provisions Affecting Taxation and Limiting the States' Powers of Taxation

Measure	What It Does	How It Might Affect Property Taxation
U.S. Constitution, Tenth Amendment (1791)	States that "The powers not delegated to the United States by the Constitution, nor prohibited by it to the States, are reserved to the States respectively, or to the people."	Reinforces the states' broad powers of taxation, including the power to tax property.
U.S. Constitution, Eleventh Amendment (1795)	Provides that "The Judicial power of the United States shall not be construed to extend to any suit in law or equity, commenced or prosecuted against one of the United States by Citizens of another State, or by Citizens or Subjects of any Foreign State."	Immunizes state governments from suits in federal courts unless invidious discrimination is involved.
U.S. Constitution, Fourteenth Amendment (1868)	States (in Section 1) that, "No State shall make or enforce any law which shall abridge the privileges or immunities of citizens of the United States; nor shall any State deprive any person of life, liberty, or property, without due process of law [the Due Process Clause]; nor deny to any person within its jurisdiction the equal protection of the laws [the Equal Protection Clause]"; authorizes Congress to enact enforcement legislation.	The Due Process Clause protects taxpayers from arbitrary taxation. The Equal Protection Clause protects taxpayers from certain discriminatory taxation.
Civil Rights Act of 1871, Section 1983 (United States Code, Title 42, Section 1983)	Provides that: "Every person who under color of any statute, ordinance, regulation, custom, or usage, of any State or Territory or the District of Columbia, subjects, or causes to be subjected, any citizen of the United States or other person within the jurisdiction thereof to the deprivation of any rights, privileges, or immunities secured by the Constitution and laws, shall be liable to the party injured in an action at law, Suit in equity, or other proper proceeding for redress, except that in any action brought against a judicial officer for an act or omission taken in such officer's judicial capacity, injunctive relief shall not be granted unless a declaratory decree was violated or declaratory relief was unavailable. For the purposes of this section, any Act of Congress applicable exclusively to the District of Columbia shall be considered to be a statute of the District of Columbia."	Makes officials like assessors potentially personally liable for their official acts. An injured party may bring a suit in either state or federal court, although the barriers to suit in federal courts are high because of the principle of comity and the provisions of the 1937 Tax Injunction Act.
Tax Injunction Act of 1937 (codified at 28 U.S.C., Section 1341)	Provides that federal courts "shall not enjoin, suspend or restrain the assessment, levy or collection of any tax under State law where a plain, speedy and efficient remedy may be had in the courts of such state."	Limits direct access by taxpayers to federal courts.
Railroad Revitalization and Regulatory Reform Act of 1976 (4-R Act; 45 USC, Section 801) and later, similar enactments protecting interstate trucking firms and air carriers.	Prohibits states from taxing railroads and other transportation carriers more heavily than other commercial and industrial property.	The Eleventh Amendment, comity, and the Tax Injunction Act notwithstanding, allows transportation companies to sue in federal courts in cases of individual discrimination.

Controversial Areas

The U.S. federal system allows the states to experiment in the design of their property tax systems. Taxpayers and other stakeholders sometimes challenge a system feature on constitutional or other grounds, and the courts are the arbiters of these challenges. This section touches on areas of tax policy and administration that the courts have addressed. A particular challenge can involve more than one provision of the Constitution or a statute. The courts may not always neatly address each issue; instead, they may address multiple principles in an undifferentiated matter.

Classification

Despite the principles of universality and uniformity, classification for purposes of property taxation is the norm. By itself, the U.S. Constitution does not preclude non-uniform property taxes. The provisions of state constitutions govern. Although most state constitutions contain requirements that the taxes be imposed uniformly, equitably, or fairly, such standards mean equal treatment within a class of property. Among other things, uniformity requires that the same tax rate be applied to every property in the class. Since U.S. property taxes are value-based, the definition of uniformity can be extended to mean that one tax rate is applied per dollar of property value.

Legislative classifications for tax purposes include differential taxation, exemptions, and other approaches. As suggested in Table 3-1, both the constitution and federal law can be invoked in court challenges alleging unequal or discriminatory treatment under state property tax law or administrative practices. As noted, the courts often have to balance competing interests and principles. Some challenges make their way to the U.S. Supreme Court. There have been numerous challenges of classes inherent in tax legislation and of tax inequalities due to outdated values and the resulting de facto fractional assessment. Some deal with individual claims for relief, and others involve systemic challenges.

Classification schemes are usually upheld if they are rational in some respect (the so-called *rational basis* test). For example, in *Carmichael* v. *Southern Coal & Coke Co.* (1937), the court approved a scheme in which employers with seven employees were classified differently from employers with eight employees. A more recent case is *Fitzgerald v. Racing Assn. of Cent. Iowa* (2003), in which the court held that Iowa could impose higher taxes on landlocked casinos than on casinos located adjacent to waterways. Even if legislative intent is not clear, courts are disinclined to scrutinize closely the legislative reasons for classifications in the tax arena. Legislative or policy-based classifications are generally thought necessary by the judicial system to permit reasonable executive administration of the tax system. The authority to make these classifications is typically delegated to the legislative branch of government. Comity between the branches comes into play when a taxpayer seeks to question the basis for classification, so that judicial deference to legislative decisions can further inhibit the review of tax classifications.

A different result can be achieved, however, when the classification either is or appears to be based on race, color, creed, religion, or other suspect basis. In these cases, much more scrutiny is permitted, and such classifications are routinely overturned. In addition to protected class issues, non-uniform assessment of different property classes can violate the Commerce Clause or the Import-Export Clause. An example of a case in which the classification scheme was held to lack a rational basis and therefore violated the Equal Protection Clause was a New Mexico property tax exemption for Vietnam veterans that depended on when they became a resident of the state (*Hooper v. Bernalillo County Assessor* 1985).

Commerce

The Commerce Clause is considered to be the most important of federal limitations on state taxes, and many challenges of tax law and administration invoke it. As Schoettle (2003, 13) states,

> *Many—maybe all—states attempt to export their tax bill. They do this by structuring taxes so that the economic burden of the tax will be borne by out-of-state taxpayers.*

He identifies two tax-exporting effects: a price/migration effect and a federal offset export (Schoettle 2003, 33). The former occurs when a tax, such as hotel room occupancy tax, is borne by out-of-state residents, and the latter when taxes are deducted from a federal tax return. Implicitly, tax exporting results in tax importing, and measuring the net effect is quite difficult.

Schoettle (2003, 212–252) traces the U.S. Supreme Court's evolving jurisprudence regarding the Commerce Clause and the Import-Export Clause (he also notes that the Due Process Clause is bound up in the commerce jurisprudence in an undifferentiated manner). Early on, the court held that the Commerce Clause, in addition to authorizing Congress to regulate commerce via legislation, contained a negative command known as the dormant Commerce Clause. This prohibited certain state acts even when Congress had failed to legislate on the subject. Beginning with *Brown v. Maryland* (1827), the court held that the Import-Export Clause and the Commerce Clause prohibited a Maryland requirement that an importer obtain a license, because doing so interfered with commerce. Later, the court held that states could not tax interstate commerce in any form (*Leloup v. Port of Mobile* 1888). More recently, the court discarded such a formal rule in recognition of economic realities and other legitimate policy interests. In 1977, it established a four-part test (*Complete Auto Transit, Inc. v. Brady* 1977), as follows:

1. The tax is applied to an activity with a substantial nexus within the taxing state.
2. The tax is fairly apportioned.
3. The tax does not discriminate against interstate commerce.
4. The tax is fairly related to the services provided by the State.

These ideas continue to be refined, and other tests have been developed for taxes other than property taxes.

Exemptions

As widely recognized, exemptions are universal in property taxation. Nevertheless, the definition of the class eligible for exemption can be challenged, because relieving the taxes on one class of property tends to increase the taxes borne by non-exempt classes, thereby creating practical non-uniformity in taxation, especially when tax rates are budget-driven. An Idaho case, *Simmons v. State Tax Commission* (1986), is an instructive example of this phenomenon (Youngman 2006, 23). The *Simmons* case sanctions exemption of 50 percent of the value of owner-occupied residential improvements, up to a limit of $50,000, taking effect in Idaho in 1983 and replacing a previous much smaller homeowner exemption. To maintain revenue, tax rates were increased, increasing the burden on non-exempt property. Table 3-2 illustrates the effect of the exemption before implementation (1982) and after (1983), through hypothetical results of the tax liability on equivalent-value owner-occupied property (eligible for the exemption) and other property (ineligible for the exemption).

TABLE 3-2. Effect of Homeowner Exemption

	Assessed Value	Tax Liability	
		1982	1983
Owner-occupied primary residences eligible for exemption	$100,000	$1,453	$1,085
Other property	$100,000	$1,615	$2,170

Owners of rental property challenged the exemption, alleging that it violated a constitutional requirement that "every person or corporation shall pay a tax in proportion to the value of his, her, or its property" and that "[a]ll taxes shall be uniform on the same class of subjects within the territorial limits of the authority levying the tax." The Idaho Supreme Court rejected the taxpayer's argument that Idaho's constitutional exemption clause, which authorized the legislature to enact exemptions "as shall seem necessary and just," limited the legislature to complete exemptions and did not permit partial exemptions.

An example of a similar exemption argument that was rejected by the U.S. Supreme Court is *Department of Revenue of Oregon v. ACF Industries Inc.* (1994). At issue was whether the prohibition in the 4-R Act of discriminatory state taxation of railroads invalidated specific exemptions for non-railroad property when railroad property did not receive a similar exemption. The court held that Oregon's tax exemptions would run afoul of the 4-R Act's prohibitions only if the exemptions of non-railroad property were so significant that the tax, in effect, singled out railroad property. Because many other taxpayers were taxed along with the railroads, Oregon's tax system was upheld.

In summary, the principle of uniformity does not bar legislatures from differentiating among classes of taxpayers. However, there is an underlying principle that all property is taxable unless specifically exempt and therefore exemptions should be construed narrowly. Uniformity remains important within a class, whether the class is defined as all taxable property or as some broad class as real property, tangible personal property, or intangible personal property. However, de facto classes that result from assessment methods and actions (or inactions) can give rise to uniformity challenges.

Equality

The goal of uniformity in property taxation can be difficult in practice for several reasons. Market value by definition is a hypothetical price, and market conditions cause prices to be volatile. Valuation methods cannot fully replicate the decision-making of market participants, and they inevitably require judgments. Real property is inherently heterogeneous. However, a certain model of a tract house can be more valuable in a good neighborhood than in a less desirable one. Even physically identical things can have different values depending on their circumstances. Prices paid for movable (personal) property depend on the level of trade—the price paid by a wholesaler differs from the price paid by a consumer. Procedural consistency sometimes leads to differences in effective tax rates as measured against sales.

Another difficult challenge arises when appraisals are outdated or when valuation practices have shortcomings. When assessments generally are but a fraction of the legal ratio but a taxpayer (or class of taxpayers) is assessed at a higher ratio than the bulk of properties, what should a court do when confronted with a challenge? Such challenges often have equal protection and due process elements. Should the taxpayer's assessment be raised to the legal level, leaving all other assessments undisturbed? Should all assessments be increased? Should the taxpayer's assessment be lowered to the common level? Clearly, the first option would increase tax unfairness. Although the second option has the advantage of complying with the letter of the law, it has several practical problems: It would be expensive and time-consuming to effectuate. Moreover, doing so would give rise to appeals from other taxpayers. Thus, courts generally recognize that the third option—lowering the taxpayer's assessment to the common level—is the least unpalatable solution.

Such was the decision of the U.S. Supreme Court in *Sioux City Bridge Co. v. Dakota County* (1922). In a case that reached the court after wending its way through the Nebraska appeal and court system, the taxpayer contended that the assessment on portion of an obsolescent railroad bridge across the Missouri River that was in Nebraska was overvalued relative to other real property in the county. The bridge was assessed at approximately its full value, while other property in the county was intentionally assessed at about 55 percent of market value. The state had held that the proper remedy was to raise the assessment on the undervalued property. In contrast, the U.S. Supreme Court held,

> [T]hat such a result as that reached by the Supreme Court of Nebraska is to deny the injured taxpayer any remedy at all because it is utterly impossible for him by any judicial proceeding to secure an increase in the assessment of the great mass of underassessed property in the taxing district. This court holds that the right of the taxpayer whose property alone is taxed at 100 [percent] of its true value is to have his assessment reduced to the percentage of that value at which other are taxed even though this is a departure from the requirement of the statute. The conclusion is based on the principle that where it is impossible to secure both the standard of the true value, and the uniformity and equality required by law, the latter requirement is to be preferred as the just and ultimate purpose of the law.

Although the court held that the taxpayer's Fourteenth Amendment's rights were violated, it held that there must be something more than an error in judgment—"something which in effect amounts to an intentional violation of the essential principle of practical uniformity" (*Sunday Lake Iron Co. v. Wakefield Tp.* 1911). In *Sunday Lake Iron*, the Supreme Court held that a similar degree of assessment discrimination did not violate the Fourteenth Amendment because there was no evidence of intentional discrimination.

Even when a taxpayer has jurisprudence on her or his side, the burden of proving inequity can be difficult and expensive. The burden increases when a challenge is systemic and involves a class of taxpayers. Consequently, there have been more individual challenges than systemic ones. However, Youngman (2006, 19, footnote 51) notes one case in which the plaintiffs were awarded costs.

Two recent Supreme Court cases involving the scope of equal protection provisions as applied in the context of property taxes are *Allegheny Pittsburgh Coal Co. v. Webster County Commission* (1989) and *Nordlinger v. Hahn* (1992). In *Allegheny Pittsburgh Coal Co.*, the court struck down Webster County, West Virginia's, "welcome stranger" method of assessment. The Webster County assessor implemented an assessment scheme in which valuation of property in the county was effectively updated only when there was a sale of property. Thus, newcomers to the county buying property were assessed at full value while established residents were assessed at much less than full value depending on when their property was purchased. The documented disparities were between eight and thirty-five times more burdensome on the recent property owners. The court struck down this scheme as violating equal protection.

However, three years later, the court in *Nordlinger v. Hahn* upheld California's Proposition 13, which institutionalized "welcome stranger" assessment in California. The critical factual difference between the cases was that the California assessment scheme was implemented in compliance with the provisions of the California Constitution inserted by Proposition 13, while the Webster County assessment scheme was unauthorized by, and was contrary to, state law. Although the Supreme Court took pains to distinguish *Allegheny* from *Nordlinger* based on this fact, it is difficult to determine what remains of *Allegheny*, if anything. In other words, did the authority of state law in the California case really remove the equal protection concerns that moved the court to strike down a conceptually identical system in *Allegheny*, or was *Nordlinger* more indicative of a philosophical shift in the court toward reducing the federal judiciary's interference with state sovereignty? The court's recent jurisprudence on the Eleventh Amendment seems to support the latter interpretation.

Procedural Matters

An important principle—weighing on the side of tax administrations—is the need for certainty (or finality) in the determination of assessments and tax obligations. A tax system would fail if taxpayers could indefinitely delay paying the tax by questioning assessments and pursuing other avoidance stratagems. Thus, property tax laws often establish a presumption of correctness that an appellant must overcome. The legislation in Northern Ireland provides a succinct example: "the entry in the valuation list is deemed to be correct until the contrary is proven." (Rates [Northern Ireland] Order 1977) In a number of jurisdictions, however, the pendulum is swinging in the taxpayer's direction. Ontario, Florida, Kansas, and Texas provide examples of instances in which the burden is on the assessor to prove that the assessment is correct (see IAAO 2000).

Key dates and deadlines are important, as are other administrative provisions. A number of important cases focus on jurisdiction (the authority of a court to hear a case), standing (the legal concept that only those parties that actually are involved in a controversy and that suffer an injury have the ability to seek redress), burdens of proof, whether the taxpayer has adequate remedies in state courts, and similar procedural matters.

Even though its text speaks only to suits against a state by citizens of other states, the Eleventh Amendment has been interpreted to restrict federal judicial power in cases in which a citizen of a state sues her or his own state. Until recently, this clause did not have much force because the Supreme Court interpreted it to be subordinate to the Commerce Clause operating through the Supremacy Clause. Congress's power to regulate commerce, in conjunction with the Supremacy Clause, was thought sufficient if Congress chose to override or abrogate the states' Eleventh Amendment immunity from suit; see *Pennsylvania v. Union Gas Co.* (1989). However, the Supreme Court came to a different conclusion with far-reaching implications for federal-state relations in *Seminole Tribe of Florida v. Florida* (1996). The court concluded that, because the Eleventh Amendment was later in time, it altered the balance between the Federal Government and the states as set out in the Supremacy Clause. The result in *Seminole* meant that only amendments that postdated the Eleventh Amendment could be enforced in federal courts. The broadest of these is the Fourteenth Amendment. However, federal jurisdiction is still limited.

In *Rosewell v. LaSalle National Bank* (1981), the U.S. Supreme Court held that the Illinois system that required a taxpayer to pay taxes under protest and that did not require interest to be paid when the taxpayer's suit was successful (which took two years) did not violate the Tax Injunction Act's standard of "a plain, speedy and efficient remedy."

The U.S. Supreme Court also addressed the issue of a possible federal court action by a taxpayer based upon Section 1983 of the Civil Rights Act of 1871 in *Fair Assessment in Real Estate Association v. McNary* (1981). In *McNary*, the court held that a determination that a state taxpayer can recover damages under civil rights provisions because of unconstitutional administration of a state tax system would be fully as intrusive upon state administration of tax laws as equitable actions, which are barred by principles of comity. The court held that state taxpayers alleging unconstitutional administration of a state tax system "must seek protection of their federal rights by state remedies, provided of course that those remedies are plain, adequate and complete and may ultimately seek review of state decisions in the U.S. Supreme Court." Therefore, it appears that taxpayers bringing a Section 1983 action could find it very difficult to reach federal court (*New York State Board of Real Property Services* 1993 and Rothfeld 1994).

How a state discharges its supervisory and equalization responsibilities (discussed under "Administrative Arrangements" below) can raise due process concerns. For example, when a state reviews local assessments and uses direct equalization to alter them, taxpayers whose property changes value are affected. Although few equalization cases have risen to the U.S. Supreme Court, the court has likened equalization to a legislative determination of policy, to which no particular rights of due process of law are attached and over which no particular judicial scrutiny extends (*Bi-Metallic Inv. Co. v. State Board of Equalization* 1915).

From the foregoing, several general conclusions emerge. Measures that benefit one class of taxpayers at the expense of others can be vulnerable to challenge. Administrative practices that favor one group or that discriminates against another also are vulnerable. Although a taxpayer faces legal and procedural difficulties in mounting a challenge, courts and legislatures are slowly reducing such obstacles. Meanwhile, standards such as the *Uniform Standards of Professional Appraisal Practice* (USPAP; The Appraisal Foundation, updated annually) and modern technology are slowly increasing expectations of high-quality assessment performance.

In any event, a well-constructed legal framework states legislative intent, assigns responsibilities, and provides an environment that makes it possible for administrators to carry out property tax policies successfully. The following sections address areas of property tax systems in which policy choices can be made.

Fiscal Arrangements

Three issues are central to the locus of the power to tax property:

- Which government should have the power to tax property?
- Which government should receive property tax revenues?
- How should rates of tax be decided?

When the property tax is a local tax, how to compensate for disparities in local property tax capacity often is of concern.

Powers of Taxation and Revenue Assignments

Where the power to tax property resides depends on the type of government. In unitary systems it resides with the central government; in federal systems it can reside with regional (state or provincial) governments. The government (or governments) with the power writes the laws and makes revenue assignments.

Whether the national government is unitary or federal, questions arise about the degree of autonomy that local governments should possess, particularly with respect to taxes and other revenue sources. In theory, autonomous local governments promote efficiency and accountability.

Rate-Setting Mechanisms

There are two basic approaches to setting nominal property tax rates. The most common approach internationally is to fix rates in legislation. The second approach is to establish a quota or an annual revenue target and to fix the rate accordingly. In practice, many variants and combinations of these approaches have been devised.

Fixed Rates

Fixing rates in legislation has several appeals: First, the legislature remains in firm control (despite rhetoric about local autonomy or control). Fixed rates (or fixed ranges in rates) are comparatively simple to introduce. Taxpayers can readily predict what their tax bills will be. On the other hand, recipient governments have less opportunity to set rates that match their needs or their taxpayers' ability to pay, thereby undercutting efficiency and accountability. Moreover, yields cannot be easily predetermined. Revenue yields become a function of the interplay among allowed rates, the size of the underlying tax base, and the diligence of property tax administrators. Once maximum rates are reached, tax yields are totally dependent on the size of the property tax base. Inflation or infrequent reassessments can diminish revenue in real terms, unless it is possible to index rates.

Budget-Based Rates

When rates are based on budgetary needs, the first step is to determine the amount of revenue desired from the property tax, which in the United States usually is called the property tax *levy*. This levy usually is the difference between planned expenditures and the revenues anticipated from other sources (fees, other taxes, grants from other sectors of government, and so forth). Mathematically, the property tax rate results from application of the following formula:

$$R = \frac{E - NPR}{AV},$$

where R is the rate of tax, E is the total approved budget, NPR is total estimated non-property-tax revenue, and AV is total assessed value. The rate, R, can of course be subject to limits to provide taxpayers with greater certainty about their upcoming tax obligations and to restrain local government spending. Indeed, it is even possible to subject changes in E and AV to limits, as experience in the United States has shown. However, levy and spending limits diffuse accountability. Limits on increases for individual assessments diminish tax equity. Such limits seldom if ever are found in property tax systems in other nations.

Single versus Compound Rates

Property tax rates also can be single or compound (i.e., built up from the rates of overlapping regional and local governments, including general- and special-purpose governments like counties and school districts). Compound rates are common in the United States, where there are tiers of local general-purpose governments and sometimes special-purpose governments as well. Compound rates are comparatively rare outside the United States. In some U.S. states, like Idaho and Illinois, ten or more local government authorities can levy a property tax. Compound tax rates (overlapping governments) tend to blur accountability even though they, at least theoretically, are intended to do the opposite. Few taxpayers have the ability or inclination to monitor multiple local governments.

When Is a Rate Too High or Too Low?

A question when fixing rates in legislation (including setting rate limits and the like) is, When are rates too high or too low? Although this essentially is a matter of judgment, the following factors come into play:

- **The revenues** needed to fund mandated and desired services
- **Affordability**—typical property tax obligations in relation to typical incomes (some public finance experts believe that property taxes in the range of 1–2 percent of income are generally affordable; those with low incomes obviously can afford less)
- **Capitalization** and incidence effects
- **Viability**—the relationship between the costs of administration and the revenues that could be realized at a given rate.

Compensating for Fiscal Capacity Differences

A local government's tax capacity may not match its revenue needs. As a result, national and higher-level regional governments (like provinces and states) often make (equalization) grants to needy local governments to enable them to provide necessary services. Often, the property tax capacity and the effort of a local government influence the size of the grant it is eligible to receive. Along with some Canadian provinces and most U.S. states, this is the case in Denmark. In France, portions of certain grants to local governments are distributed in proportion to tax bases and other portions on the basis of effort. In Switzerland, a canton can make grants when a community taxes at the maximum allowable rate but cannot meet its revenue needs.

Another approach might be termed tax base sharing. In addition to the Twin Cities of Minnesota, other examples of this approach are the special education property taxes in Alberta, Michigan, New Hampshire, and Vermont and the way "rates" (property taxes) on nonresidential property are collected and distributed in the United Kingdom. Although the taxes are collected locally, all revenues are transmitted to the higher-tier government, which then redistributes the revenues to local school districts (or local authorities in the United Kingdom) on the basis of a distribution formula that may consider such things as population.

A more specialized compensation mechanism is payments in lieu of taxes (PILOT). As with variations in the total value of property in each local government, there also are considerable variations in the distribution of tax-exempt properties, and localities with high concentrations of tax-exempt property (such as national capitals) obviously have a diminished property tax capacity. Some of those localities can have an increased demand for certain services (such as protection of government buildings and service to government employees) as well. Some national and state or regional governments compensate for such losses in taxable property by providing PILOT-type grants. Examples can be found in Canada, France, and the United States. Exempt entities, such as universities, can make voluntary payments in lieu of taxes.

Denmark partially avoids the need for payments in lieu of taxes by making central government properties fully liable for the land tax for municipalities and partially liable for the land tax for counties. Similarly, Crown property in the United Kingdom has not been exempt from the nonresidential property tax (the Uniform Business Tax) since 2000. In Estonia, the central government pays land taxes on state-owned forestland (which accounts for about one-third of all land tax revenues).

Grant calculation mechanisms often attempt to ensure that a local government is making full use of its property tax capacity. For example, the government may be required to use the maximum allowable tax rate, and the tax base lost through local-option exemption and relief measures may be disregarded. In the United States, equalization studies that estimate the current market value of taxable property are common.

Administrative Arrangements

Property tax administration embraces (1) supervision and control; (2) fiscal cadastre maintenance, assessment, and often valuation; (3) billing, collection, and accounting for revenues; and (4) appeals. A major issue in the design of a property tax system is the assignment of these administrative responsibilities. As with other features of property tax systems, there are many variations. It is common for these responsibilities to be assigned to different organizations and to different tiers of government. The "orphan" status of the property tax administration and its weak powers to bring about effective coordination among institutions of equal status is a frequent concern. A number of other administrative issues have policy overtones, including the roles of elected officials, private-sector enterprises, and self-assessment and reporting in property tax administration.

Supervision and Equalization

There is a need for a supervisory or control function when overall responsibility for property tax administration is divided among different agencies and tiers of government. Without supervision, some agencies or units of government may fail to carry out their responsibilities properly. When local governments have responsibility for assessment and have considerable latitude in setting tax rates and granting exemptions and relief, safeguards are needed to prevent a few local governments from under-assessing or under-taxing property in the hope of receiving a larger equalization grant from a higher tier of government. These procedures are known generally as assessment equalization and are discussed further in Chapter 7, "Components of Model Property Tax Administrative Systems." The need for equalization arises when a factor, such as taxable value per capita (or as is common in the United States, per-student or average daily attendance in public schools), is used in calculating the amount of the grant. In addition, taxation, supervision, and equalization programs require that documents and data flow smoothly. Lastly, there is a need to guard against corruption.

Because responsibility for property tax administration is highly decentralized in the United States, the supervisory function is highly developed. Some Canadian provinces, including Alberta, also have highly developed supervisory functions, as does the Netherlands. In the U.S. model (Advisory Commission on Intergovernmental Relations 1963; Almy et al. 1978; International Association of Assessing Officers 2003; National Association of Assessing Officers 1941), supervisory agencies typically have four broad, interrelated functions: (1) setting standards and specifications, (2) assisting and counseling local assessors and other property tax officials, (3) monitoring their performance and making other analyses, and (4) enforcing laws and regulations, including equalization. The development of standards and specifications is necessary for effective, uniform administration of property tax laws. Assistance and counseling activities are helpful to, and supportive of, effective local government. Although essential to effective state-level supervision, monitoring and analysis can be perceived by local governments as an intrusion or a threat. Enforcement is contentious and confrontational, with the supervisory agency being in a resented position of power. However, enforcement actions are necessary when local practices do not come up to standards.

A challenge that supervisory agencies face is balancing activities so that the highest level of performance is achieved with the least consumption of resources and the least amount of stress. In other words, the more effectively a state encourages high-level performance and the more effective its assistance activities are, the less onerous its enforcement activities will need to be. In summary, the property tax supervision model combines effective programs for monitoring local conditions and local performance, a strong commitment to assisting when necessary, "counseling" when performance falls below expectations, and enforcing legal standards firmly and consistently. However, application of this model varies considerably. In the United States, local property tax officials are virtually unsupervised in Connecticut, Delaware, and Hawaii. At the other extreme, Maryland and Montana have supplanted local assessors. The remaining states are in between these extremes.

Assessment and Valuation

As used here, the term assessment encompasses all the processes needed to produce a current assessment list, which is a list of properties (or taxpayers) and the factors (such as property use, area, value, eligibility for exemptions, and so forth) that determine property tax liabilities (loosely, the fiscal cadastre). Responsibility for the fiscal cadastre can rest with the central government, be shared, or be given to local governments.

Responsibility for valuation can be a responsibility of the assessment agency, or it can be given to another, nominally independent, valuation agency. In addition, responsibility for the two main property tax valuation activities (the development of valuation models and, second, the application of those models to individual properties) can be given to a single agency, or the responsibility can be divided.

Valuation can be made a responsibility of the central government for several reasons. One is that property tax valuations can be used for other purposes, such as forming part of the base of another tax, for example, as a net wealth tax (Austria, Germany, Spain, and Sweden). Commonly, property tax valuations serve as a default basis for transfer, gift taxes, and inheritance taxes when declared values are lower than property tax values (which, especially when coupled by high transfer tax rates, creates an incentive for taxpayers to understate the actual sale price or value, if there are no countervailing measures that encourage more accurate declarations).

The chief argument for assigning valuation to an independent agency (which is fairly common in British Commonwealth countries) is that it is more difficult to exert political pressure to skew valuations to achieve property tax policy objectives not sanctioned by law. Another argument is that specialized agencies are more likely to develop the expertise needed to value a wide range of properties for a variety of purposes. Disadvantages of independence stem from the fact that specialized valuation agencies often find it difficult to command the resources needed to execute revaluations because they have no direct stake in the outcome. The arguments for assigning valuation to local governments are their closeness to local real estate markets, the greater ease with which taxpayers can hold them accountable, and the government's vital interest in the success of the assessment process.

Billing, Collection, and Enforcement

Responsibility for property tax billing, collection, and enforcement of arrears can be assigned to either the central government or local governments, although other agencies, such as post offices, banks, and utilities, can assist. Administrative capacity, taxpayer convenience, and fiscal interest are factors affecting the assignment.

Often, the recipients of property tax revenues (such as municipalities) want some responsibility for property tax administration. Their interest in being responsible for collection has to do with gaining access to revenues sooner. They also have a direct interest in getting taxpayers to pay their taxes on time and, consequently, often are more willing to take necessary actions to enforce payment of arrears.

Convenience is achieved by having collection points near taxpayers' homes and by allowing payments to be made through the post, banks, the Internet, or other convenient means. Except when the taxpayer lives in another community (or state), local governments can provide convenient collection. Administratively decentralized collection agencies can provide similar convenience.

Appeals

A difference between property taxes and other types of taxes lies with the respective roles of taxpayers and tax administrators. Income and consumption taxes largely are self-assessed. The role of the tax administration is to process taxpayers' returns, evaluate the reasonableness of those assessments, investigate dubious returns, correct erroneous returns, and take actions to compel returns when they are not filed voluntarily. Appeals of income and consumption taxes are rare, occurring only when a taxpayer disagrees with an enforcement action by the tax administration. In contrast, except for some personal property and unit-property assessments, assessors usually determine the taxable base for the property tax, and the review and appeal process gives taxpayers the opportunity to review the reasonableness of their assessments and to challenge them if they so wish. Thus, the appeal process is an integral part of the property tax assessment process, and appeals are common, even welcomed.

In general, appeal processes have a number of hierarchical steps. At the lowest level, the tax administration, an independent body, or both can hear appeals locally. As appeals are taken to higher levels, the hearing body has broader geographic jurisdiction. At the highest level, appeals are to the courts.

Administrative Issues

Funding Property Tax Administration

The resources provided for property tax administration reflect political support for legal, equitable taxation. To achieve political (popular) acceptance, revenue targets, and other goals, the tax administration must have sufficient human and technological resources. Not surprisingly, increasing funding for tax administration relative to other services seldom finds much support. Some tax system failures can be attributed to inadequate funding. A related problem is system features that simply are not cost-effective. Generous property tax relief measures that are complicated to administer are an example. In some countries, residential tax bills are the equivalent to the cost of a package of cigarettes or a few beers. It is almost impossible to administer such taxes in a cost-effective manner. Some countries approach this problem by exempting properties under a certain value or area to achieve administrative efficiency (and to provide a measure of progressivity).

An overall measure of efficiency is the ratio of administrative costs to property tax revenues. The objective is to minimize this ratio without sacrificing fairness. Making meaningful comparisons of administrative efficiency can be difficult. Factors that affect absolute costs and costs per unit of revenue are differences in the coverage of property tax bases, whether taxes are based on area or value, the frequency of revaluations, the extent of automation, and whether there are other uses of valuation and cadastral data. The cost per unit of revenue also depends, in part, on effective tax rates. Other things being equal, the higher the effective tax rate, the lower the administrative cost rate. Another difficulty in analyzing funding (and staffing) is that many governmental budgeting and accounting systems do not permit segregating property tax-related costs from all costs. It also is important to recognize that start-up costs usually are considerably greater than annual operational costs after a system has been working for several years.

For reasons such as these, few statistics on direct expenditures or relative costs are available in the literature. However, administrative costs in the range of 2–5 percent of revenues often are achieved in developed western countries. Ratios in excess of 10 percent are symptomatic of problems. Some property taxes are dysfunctional in that administrative costs are higher than the revenue received—or would be if the tax were administered as required by the law. The problem of administrative costs in excess of revenues can occur in otherwise functional systems when very small properties (especially small items of personal property) must be assessed. It also is worth noting that exemption and relief measures increase administrative costs while tending to decrease revenue.

Institutional Linkages

Property tax administrators depend on data from other agencies. Figure 3-1 depicts some common institutional linkages. Common data dependencies are title records, property transfer information, maps, soil classification data, building and occupancy permits, and business and individual names and addresses. At the same time, other agencies rely on data from property tax administrators.

Figure 3-1. Typical Property Tax System External Linkages

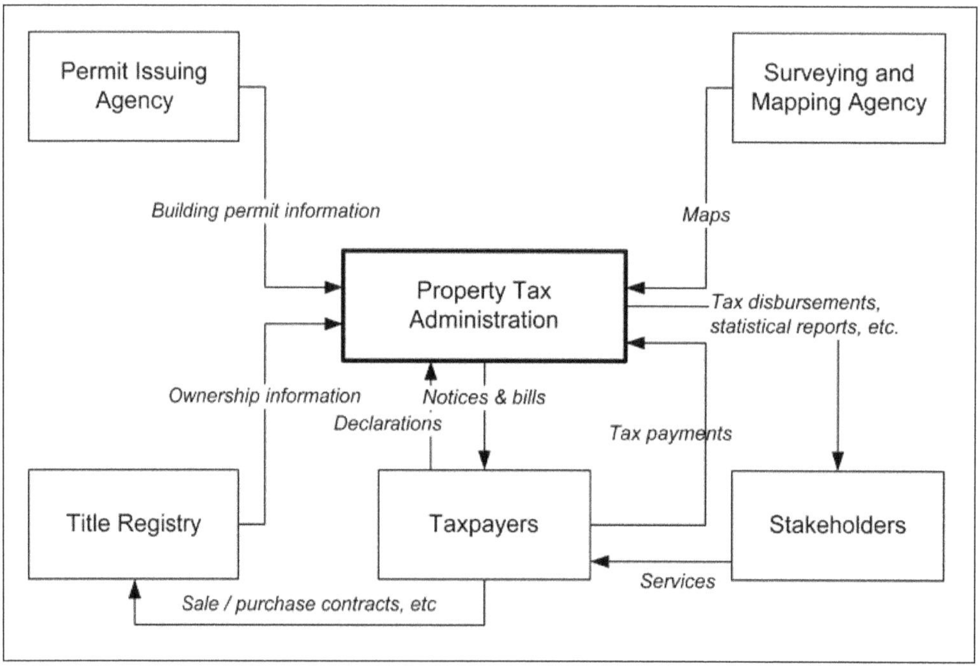

Bureaucratic impediments to the free flow of data are not uncommon. Strategies for reducing or eliminating such problems are integrating computer systems, consolidating functions, and creating interagency groups charged with preventing or solving such problems, such as by developing mutually agreed-upon data standards and transfer protocols. For example, several countries have consolidated land-related functions in a cadastral agency. Title registration commonly is combined with surveying and mapping. Surveying agencies also can be responsible for valuation. However, separating property tax-related activities, such as property attribute data collection and valuation, from activities related to title registration lessens the negative effects of buyers believing that one of the "costs" of title registration is property taxation. When they believe this, they have an incentive not to register ownership changes and to conceal the true nature of transactions, especially sales prices.

Role of the Private Sector in Property Tax Administration

Increasingly, business enterprises provide services once provided by civil servants working for government agencies. Some of these enterprises are quasi-governmental, like Canadian assessment authorities. They rely on fees (or rate surcharges) for the assessment services they provide rather than on budgetary appropriations. Lithuania's state register enterprise is another example. These enterprises insulate assessment from narrow political interference; however, they are not without problems. For example, a government may mandate a service (such as valuation) without providing for adequate compensation. Or such agencies tend to regard the data in their custody as proprietary even though much of it was compiled with public funding in one form or another.

Others are purely commercial enterprises, like North American mass appraisal firms and software vendors. These types of firms also are active in Brazil, Australia, New Zealand, and the Netherlands. Individuals and firms can also be contracted to provide special services. For example, private-sector valuers and real estate agents in England and Wales did about 50 percent of the work involved in assigning residential properties to bands under the residential property tax (the Council Tax). Also noteworthy is the former Conservative government's policy of "competitive tendering," which required local governments to issue bids for services such as property tax collection, even though the existing governmental agencies providing those services also could bid. Other examples are the use of nongovernmental institutions and private firms to help develop valuation methods and land value maps by the Czech and Slovak Ministries of Finance. Similarly, the Estonian National Land Board contracted with private valuers for help during its recent revaluations. Private valuers are used in appeals in Portugal.

Liaison between property tax administrators and associations of valuers and other real estate professionals, such as that between IAAO and The Appraisal Foundation in the United States, is common. These relationships can involve establishment of required professional qualifications, training, testing and certification, and technical assistance.

Self-Assessment

To avoid the expense and controversy associated with the discovery and valuation of real property, some observers have recommended that the property tax be self-assessed like other taxes. The advantages are as follows:

- Considerable data can be collected in a very short time.
- Administrative costs are reduced (while compliance costs are increased).
- With their presumed knowledge of the value of their properties, certainly taxpayers have little cause to dispute their assessments.

The chief disadvantage of self-assessment methods is a lack of accuracy and uniformity in reporting, stemming from a lack of competence and willful acts of evasion, as have been revealed in audits. As with other taxes, it is recognized that without enforcement, a self-assessed property tax would be a "tax on honesty."

To guard against underreporting and undervaluation, advocates of self-assessment recommend that the government be empowered to acquire the property at the declared value. However, this idea would have several defects in practice. First, the penalty (the loss of property) often would be disproportionate to the amount of taxes that should have been paid, especially if the taxpayer made an innocent mistake, such as not knowing the actual value of the property. Second, given the likelihood that the government would have limited liquid assets to acquire property, actual acquisitions would be seen to be arbitrary and unfair. Third, there would be a substantial risk of corruption. Although procedures could be designed to counter these problems (Strasma 1965), in the end little, if anything, would be gained. Consequently, the idea of a pure self-assessed property tax generally is discredited. However, taxpayers commonly are required to supply information needed in the assessment process, especially about the movable property (personal property or chattels) that they own.

Elements of self-assessment are common in many property tax systems. Taxpayer reporting obligations may be only on request, or there may be specific reporting requirements, ranging from required annual declarations of property holdings (including providing the descriptions of those properties) to reporting any changes in ownership or property characteristics. It is common to require taxpayers to disclose prices paid for property and the circumstances of sales. In annual value systems, owners or occupants typically are required to disclose rents paid or received, lease provisions, and, perhaps, expenses paid in maintaining the property. Taxpayers sometimes are required to calculate their assessments and their taxes. In Turkey, the tax return forms provide the rates and adjustment coefficients needed to calculate building values; land rates must be looked up in books that are widely distributed. Businesses in a number of transitional countries must describe and provide the book value of their properties. In some Indian cities with area-based systems, taxpayers calculate their assessments by applying appropriate adjustment coefficients to arrive at tax obligations.

Qualifications of Property Tax Officials

In general, property tax administrators are full-time civil servants. However, elected property tax officials and part-time boards are not unique to the United States. Although board members can be appointed by the property tax administration or appointed by local governments, they sometimes are elected. In France, for example, elected members of local authorities help with data collection. Similarly, members of Swiss cantonal or communal valuation commissions can be elected.

The qualifications of valuers (appraisers) can be an important issue, and international experience varies with respect to the importance of academic preparation, in-service training, and professional credentials. The professionalization of valuers and property tax administrators largely is a twentieth-century development. Internationally, appraisal is a specialty of different professions, including architecture, civil engineering, and surveying. However, knowledge of economics and statistics is now recognized as important. Consequently, academic credentials are important in many countries. Professional designations are important in the United Kingdom and many former English colonies, including the United States. Whatever the path to technical proficiency, there is growing recognition among property tax administrators that the qualifications needed for mass appraisal are different from those for traditional forms of single-property appraisal. These needs may not be appreciated or heeded by professional appraisal organizations.

Low levels of pay in public service are problematic for several reasons. The best staff members likely will leave when they can find better paying jobs elsewhere. A permanently low level of pay is an invitation to corruption. Low levels of pay also can distort the picture of administrative costs, because low levels of pay and competent administration cannot be sustained in the long run.

Basic System Design Features

A property tax system's basic design addresses such issues as the following:

- The person(s) designated as the taxpayer
- How liability for taxation is defined
- The types of property that must be assessed (i.e., are potentially taxable and therefore must be inventoried)
- The unit of assessment (such as the land plot, the property, or the occupancy)
- The basis for apportioning property tax burdens (typically area or value)
- The properties or taxpayers that are eligible for an exemption or relief from at least a portion of ordinary property tax burdens

In practice, there is tremendous diversity in how these issues are addressed.

Who Is Responsible for Paying the Property Tax?

There are two closely related facets of this question: the subjects of the tax and the system for establishing liability for taxation. As used here, the subject of a tax is the person designated as the taxpayer, and the object of the tax is the thing taxed, such as land (see "What Property Is Taxable?" below). However, some writers use the term subject to refer to the thing taxed.

Subjects of Property Taxes

Requiring owners to pay property taxes generally simplifies administration, because there are fewer assessments to be made and because property ownership is more stable than occupancy. This is a sensible choice when the owners of most properties can be readily determined and ownership is widespread. Countries in which ownership often is concealed or is unsettled (as is the case in a number of transitional countries) may adopt a hybrid system: The owner is the taxpayer when the issue has been settled, and the occupant (user) is the taxpayer when (a) ownership has not been determined or (b) when the person has a right to use state-owned (government-owned) property. When more than one person is potentially liable for paying property taxes, the rules for making the determination need to be clear. When occupants are generally liable for paying property taxes, there need to be rules governing the treatment of unoccupied (vacant) properties. A sound policy argument for designating the occupant as the taxpayer, especially when many people live in rented housing, is that more people have a picture of the costs of government, thereby strengthening local government accountability.

Establishing Liability for Taxation

Two systems for determining liability for taxation have been developed. The distinctions are important when past-due property liabilities are enforced. One system holds that the thing that is taxed (the object) is itself liable (in rem taxation). Under this system, the property in question can be confiscated to secure overdue tax obligations, and the owner is only nominally the taxpayer. In rem liability prevails in the United States. Designating non-owners as taxpayers is incompatible with in rem enforcement.

Under the *in personam* taxation system, the person designated as taxpayer is liable. In personam liability is common in the rest of the world and is the most appropriate choice when occupants are taxpayers. Under in personam systems, property owners, occupants, or both can be deemed to be responsible for paying taxes. Under in personam liability, the taxpayer must be found before arrears (delinquencies) can be enforced.

An administrative issue that must be addressed under in personam liability is how to deal with multiple owners or occupiers. The main options are to (1) designate only one person as the taxpayer and (2) assess each person in proportion to his or her interest in the property. The first option simplifies administration and transfers to the property owners or occupants any problems with raising the money needed to pay the taxes. Advocates of the second approach stress its fairness to the part owners or occupiers who pay their share; they have no responsibility for the amounts unpaid by others. (Some laws allow persons who pay property taxes on behalf of another to establish a lien.)

What Property Is Taxable?

The *objects* (or coverage) of a property tax are the types of property that are potentially taxable. The possibilities are some or all categories of real (immovable) property (specifically, land separately, buildings separately, or both as a unit) and of personal (movable) property (also known as chattels). Along with defining the types of property that are taxable, it is necessary to define the unit of assessment.

Movable property can be divided into taxable and nontaxable categories. The categories may be based on physical or functional characteristics (such as machinery and equipment or vehicles). The categories can be based on ownership type (such as business property).

Precise categorization of property as movable or immovable can be difficult in practice. However, when both categories are not taxable, a precise definition of what is taxable is needed. Three types of property are particularly problematic: fixtures, appurtenances, and some industrial plants and machinery. A fixture is an item of movable property attached to real property in such a way that it cannot be removed without causing damage to the real property. An appurtenance is a right that one property owner has over another's property. Industrial plants and machinery such as are found in a chemical plant or oil refinery can be problematic because of their value and because they share characteristics of buildings and portable equipment. Similarly, it is difficult to define buildings and other constructions separately, hence the use of the indefinite term improvements. The distinctions become especially important whenever only one type of property is taxable or when there is a steep differential in taxation. In practice, governments solve such problems by resorting to arbitrary definitions, such as defining specified industrial plants and equipment as real property. However, such definitions can lead to efforts by taxpayers to alter their structures so that they qualify for the category with the lower rate of tax.

When there are separate taxes on land or on buildings, complications also can arise. It is difficult in practice to estimate the market value of each component accurately. (This problem also occurs under unified real property taxes, when the assessor is required to estimate the value of land and buildings separately.) Fundamentally, when land and any buildings are under a single ownership, buyers and sellers set a price for the combined property, not separate prices for the components. When a vacant land plot is sold, the price reflects its readiness for use, which can be the result of invisible improvements, such as tree-cutting and land-grading done long ago. The price also reflects land-use controls. When a building or a unit in a building is sold, its price reflects the value of its location (essentially an element of land value). This makes it difficult to avoid taxing land, even when land is not in private ownership.

Other issues to consider are whether some types of property, such as public rights-of-way and routes of transportation (waterways, state-owned railroads, and streets and roads), should be assessed (included in the fiscal cadastre) when they will not be taxed. This is a common practice, for administrative convenience, partly because there is no market evidence of the value of long-established public routes of transportation. Denmark follows this approach and also does not assess churches and other normally exempt properties. A counterargument is that it is wise policy to know how much the tax base is reduced through exemptions.

There are two considerations in defining the unit of assessment (e.g., an apartment as a parcel of land). First, the unit should correspond to, or be compatible with, the definition of the taxpayer. If the occupant is the taxpayer, the unit can be no greater than the taxpayer's premises (occupancy). Second, when the owner is the taxpayer, the unit of assessment can—and for valuation purposes, should—consist of multiple ownership parcels when they constitute a single economic use.

What Is the Basis of Assessment?

The basis of a property tax is the quantity that is measured or estimated to determine each property's relative share of the total property tax burden. A property tax can be based on a measure of value or on some other basis. As discussed below, there are a number of value and non-value bases. Each has comparative advantages and disadvantages. However, meaningful uniformity in property taxation can be achieved only when effective property tax rates are roughly equal. Uniformity is most easily achieved when market value is the basis of the property tax.

Non-value Bases

The most common non-value property tax systems are those based on land area, building area, or both. Under an area-based property tax system, taxes are determined simply by multiplying a measurement of area by a rate. In general, area-based systems are suitable only as long as revenues are negligible.

Area-based systems have the advantage of being simpler to administer—only area measurements are needed. They are easier to implement, because market data do not have to be collected and analyzed. There is no need for general reassessments. They also are more objective than value-based systems, because area measurements are less contestable than value estimates. On the other hand, area-based property tax systems are quickly perceived to be less fair. Highly desirable properties may pay the same taxes as undesirable properties. Individual assessments bear little relationship to either ability to pay or benefits received, and this reduces public acceptance. These disadvantages of an area-based system can be lessened by the introduction of adjustment coefficients that reflect market factors. However, doing so reduces simplicity and objectivity. Although taxpayers might see this as an advantage, area-based property taxes are less buoyant than value-based systems, unless frequent adjustments are made to rates.

Value Bases

The two main measures of value are *capital value* and *annual rental value*. When the standard of value is *market value*, capital value is the price that would be expected in an open-market, arm's-length sale. Annual rental value is the expected annual rent (or income). Annual value can be expressed on a gross or net basis. On a gross basis, the owner is assumed to be paying all operating expenses; on a net basis, the occupier is assumed to be paying (specified) operating expenses (such as repairs and insurance). Under either basis, actual rentals can be on a different basis, requiring valuers to make adjustments.

A standard of value other than market value can be employed. Such a standard can be current-use value, insurance value, or acquisition price. In practice, when market value is not the basis, tax values usually are described as being notional or normative, and they only accidentally reflect market-value patterns. That is, they simply result from the application of rules, base rates, and adjustment coefficients. Countries with advanced economies usually have systems that are at least nominally based on market values.

Each basis has advantages and disadvantages of a theoretical and practical nature depending on the nature of land tenure patterns and on other features of the property tax system. A system can use more than one basis. For example, agricultural property is taxed on a current-use or soil productivity basis, while urban property is taxed on a market-value basis. Indeed, property tax systems combine value and non-value bases and capital- and annual-value bases. The United Kingdom is an example of the latter; residential property is taxed on a capital-value basis, and nonresidential property is taxed on an annual-value basis.

When market value is the basis for taxation, important issues are the rights to be valued and other valuation assumptions, the valuation (or assessment) date, and revaluation frequency (below). Administration (particularly valuation) is simplified if it is assumed that the taxpayer possesses all private property rights (that is, excluding only the government's right of taxation). Fairness and certainty are served when the law specifies the date (or dates) as of which ownership, property attributes, and value are reflected in assessments. Procedures for updating assessment to reflect later changes also are needed. There are two main ways for dealing with changes in ownership or physical characteristics after the assessment date. One is to ignore the changes until the next tax year. Another is for the assessment or collection agency to prorate taxes according to the fractions of the year before and after the change by issuing supplemental assessments or tax bills. (Even when the change is ignored until the next year, the parties to a sale can prorate taxes in their sale/purchase agreement.)

Revaluation and Reassessment

In dynamic real estate markets, revaluations provide fairness and revenue buoyancy. In theory, each year's property tax obligation bears a predictable relationship to the current value of the property (that is, effective tax rates are approximately equal). This objective is achieved with annual reassessments. Outside North America, annual reassessment programs are rare, although property is revalued annually in the Netherlands. Denmark and Sweden have programs of revaluing categories of property each year so that all are revalued in the course of a revaluation cycle (properties that are not revalued are indexed). Revaluations on a fixed cycle (e.g., every five years) are common. In some countries, it is possible to avoid reassessments indefinitely. Ireland went without a revaluation for nearly a century, and there has not been a revaluation in Germany since the 1960s. However, several countries, including France and Germany, index values in an attempt to bring them into line with current price levels.

When the interval between reassessments is longer than a year, assessments usually are based on price levels and valuation standards (or models) as of the valuation date for the most recent general reassessment. This practice sometimes is known as base-year assessment. It emphasizes procedural consistency over uniformity in effective tax rates, particularly when the current market value differs from the market value in the base year. Market changes are of several types, including

- General changes in price levels in various real property market segments
- Localized value changes related to changes in supply and demand in a particular market segment (such as the market for single-family houses)
- Specific changes to individual properties (e.g., splits and combinations of land parcels, new construction, and demolitions).

A base-year assessment scheme largely ignores the first two categories of change. Fundamentally, a base-year system is incapable of producing an accurate value of a property that did not exist in the base year in a dynamic market. To illustrate this point, what would be the base-year value of a suburban shopping center built years after the base year on what was then rural acreage? An assessor simply cannot recognize any such changes in the supply and demand factors that define real estate markets (e.g., those that led to the development) while preserving the logic of base-year values. The result is assessments based on a non-uniform hodgepodge of factors that reflect value as of various dates. Current-market-value assessment avoids such a predicament.

Before recent technological advances, it was difficult and expensive to complete a revaluation. Politically, the trouble is that the longer the interval between reassessments, the greater the fears of economic, fiscal, and political upheaval when one occurs. Consequently, favored taxpayers resist reassessments. Even the overtaxed may not object strenuously when rising property prices and fixed rates combine to reduce effective tax rates.

Although political and legal thinking may not recognize it, technological advances have made more frequent valuations practical. First, an annual assessment *program* does not require that every assessment be changed every year. Assessments need to be changed only when a property has changed physically or when there is a clear indication based on market evidence that valuations no longer meet level and uniformity standards. This approach requires tax administrators to update the property inventory on an ongoing basis, continually monitor market trends, and update values as necessary. Value updates can be accomplished through indexing, recalibrating existing valuation models, or developing and applying new valuation models, depending on the approach warranted in the circumstances.

Second, changing from occasional revaluation projects to an annual reassessment program offers major benefits. Most important, by maintaining accurate, up-to-date valuations, tax burdens are proportional. Changes in the composition of the tax base are more gradual, and political opposition to revaluations abates. Property owners can more easily predict what their taxes will be, and taxing bodies can better judge their tax capacity. The annual costs of an ongoing reassessment program compare favorably with the annualized costs of periodic revaluations. The value of having an up-to-date property database is an additional benefit.

As is well known, beginning with the enactment of Proposition 13 in California in 1978, a number of U.S. states have enacted programs to eliminate general reassessments altogether and to restrain changes in assessed values in the interest of greater certainty about future property tax obligations at the expense of uniformity. Measures that merely roll back tax rates to prevent large tax windfalls (such as truth-in-taxation laws) have the advantage of greater tax equity.

Strategies for Providing Property Tax Relief

Options

Property tax systems are replete with measures to excuse some categories of taxpayers and properties from taxation altogether and to tax some more heavily than others. There are many ways to do this; see Chapter 6, "Analysis of Selected Property Tax Features."

Differentials (Rate or Ratio Classification)

Differential (or "classified") property tax systems establish different levels of taxation for various property categories, value categories, or types of property owners. They are common. They can be effectuated by applying differential levels of assessment, differential tax rates, differential valuation methods, or a combination. Their ostensible purpose is to shift burdens to those better able to pay, but the real purpose often is to appease voters. Usually, the categories are based on how properties are used, but they can be based on other factors, most notably, the nature of the property (that is, whether the property is land or a building) and the value of the property (or of the taxpayer's property holdings). As noted, the main mechanisms for effectuating differentials are to apply different factors (assessment ratios) to appraised values or to vary tax rates. Different valuation methods also can be used. Sometimes a combination of approaches is used. As the experience in the United States has shown, infrequent reappraisals tend to introduce de facto differentials, because the value trends of different segments of the overall property market often do not have the same direction or rate of change.

Differential tax systems place pressures on tax administrators to classify property properly. When the differentials are steep (say, more than 1:3), differentials can alter how taxpayers use—or appear to use—their properties. Properties with multiple uses create special problems and call for special rules.

Personal Exemptions, Circuit Breakers, Homestead Exemptions, and Similar Relief Measures

Along with differentials, there are many ways to provide relief for residential property taxpayers. These measures can be comprehensive, favoring all residential property, or selective, favoring only the elderly, the disabled, those who provided qualifying military service, or those with lower incomes. An application can be required, and there can be means testing. Relief usually is restricted to the person's principal residence, and only a portion of the assessed value (or area of the property) may be exempted from taxation, providing an element of progressivity in the property tax system. Some such partial exemptions also are rationalized on the basis of administrative practicality, as it often is not economically viable to attempt to collect or enforce property tax obligations on very-low-value properties or from people with very low incomes.

Eligibility criteria and means testing can involve a flat family income limit, such that only persons with incomes below the limit qualify for relief, which diminishes as income rises to the established limit. Another approach is to place limits on the proportion of income that can be taken by property taxes (see the discussion of circuit breakers in Chapter 6 and Table 6-11). Property taxes in excess of the limit can be waived or rebated. In comparison with blanket measures, the aim is to target relief where it is most needed.

Deferrals and Abatements

A number of property tax systems provide for deferring the payment of property taxes on the homes of elderly taxpayers until they die or transfer their property. Some provide for a temporary deferral for any hard-pressed taxpayer without incurring the usual penalties or enforcement procedures. In the former case, unpaid taxes constitute a lien on the property, most or all of which must be repaid when the owner sells the property. The lien may be capped at the value of the property and also may be recovered from the owner's estate. A rather unique approach to repayment has been enacted in North Carolina, where eligible homeowners must pay back only three years of deferred taxes, reflecting the three years immediately preceding a disqualifying event.

Institutional Exemptions

Virtually all property tax systems contain various institutional exemptions. These exemptions are granted to a legal entity, such as a government or qualifying nongovernmental organization, rather than to an individual. Usually institutional exemptions are complete (100 percent) and are of indefinite duration. Initial applications and periodic reapplications can be required.

Incentives

Property tax relief can be provided to encourage some socially or economically desirable activity. Incentives exist for agriculture, forestry, open space preservation, historic property preservation, environmental improvements, new industrial development, housing renovation, and the like. Incentives usually provide only a partial exemption. Except for agriculture, incentives are usually for a limited period, such as five to ten years. When they are of a fixed duration, they often are on a sliding-scale basis; that is, the amount (percentage) of property tax relief is reduced in steps each year until the exemption is completely eliminated. Incentives available to individual properties often require an application, and they can be contractually enforced; that is, they are received only as long as contractual conditions are met. Penalties can be applied when property use is changed.

Disincentives

Although not common, *higher* (as opposed to lower) taxation also can be used as an incentive. Under this approach, property taxes are lowered to the normal level if the desirable activity occurs. Although a number of transitional countries have enacted such measures to encourage the completion of buildings started during the socialist era, it is unlikely that such punitive differentials are effective, especially when demand for the type of building in question is low or nonexistent.

Emergency Relief

Tax relief can be offered on an area-wide basis. The goal is to stimulate property improvements and new development in an area that is economically depressed. Typically, all properties in a designated area have their tax bills capped for a period. Examples of such incentives include enterprise zones in Ireland and the United Kingdom. Special property tax relief can be offered for properties damaged in a natural disaster, such as a flood or earthquake.

Transitional Relief

When a revaluation occurs after a long interval or when a new property tax system is introduced, some taxpayers can experience dramatic increases in their property tax burdens (while others experience commensurate decreases). Because some of the increases can be economically or politically destabilizing, a program to phase in large property tax increases can be desirable. Of course, such temporary property tax relief causes the previously overtaxed taxpayers to continue to bear indirectly the costs of the relief to the formerly under-taxed. Truth-in-taxation laws help keep tax levies steady.

Indirect Relief

Indirect forms of property tax relief include allowing property tax payments to be deducted from income taxes. Interestingly, some countries allow property tax deductions only from the individual income tax (Denmark is an example); others allow it only under the business income tax (France, Germany, and the United Kingdom); while still others make property tax payments generally deductible (the Netherlands, Spain, and the United States). When there is both a personal and corporate income tax but property taxes are deductible from only one, there can be an incentive to transfer property from individuals to businesses (or vice versa) only to take advantage of the deduction.

Spillover Effects and Administrative Considerations

In general, by reducing the property tax base, exemptions and other forms of property tax relief increase the proportional burden on less favored taxpayers and can reduce tax yields (which of course, could be their purpose). For this reason, many property tax systems adhere to the principle that a property is taxable unless it is eligible for a specific exemption. To the extent that property taxes generally influence economic behavior, exemptions can lead to distortions, because they enable owners of exempt property to hold more property than they need. Nevertheless, sound reasons for granting exemptions and other forms of property tax relief exist. Administrative simplicity is the chief rationale for exempting government property (exemptions eliminate the need to "take money from one pocket and put it in another"). Exemption of certain nongovernmental organizations can be rationalized on the grounds that they provide socially worthwhile services that government otherwise might have to provide. Exemptions and relief for residential properties are intended to cushion residents from excessive property tax burdens. Property tax incentives are intended to influence investment decisions and reward certain economic activities. However, the validity of these objectives is often questionable, and the effectiveness of the measures can be limited.

Exemption and relief measures create a policy and administrative dilemma. If exemptions and relief measures are liberally granted, some undeserving taxpayers benefit along with deserving ones, reducing the tax base more than necessary. On the other hand, the more stringent the eligibility criteria are, the more costly administration becomes. Thus, there is a trade-off between the revenue lost from unwarranted exemptions and the increased cost of administration when exemptions are carefully granted.

Exemptions sometimes are granted for reasons of administrative convenience or efficiency. For example, Estonia exempts land that cannot be used economically, which is sensible as long as the conditions that prevent economic use prevail. Several transitional countries (which typically have very low tax rates) do not issue property tax bills when the amount due is small. Denmark and the Netherlands have similar exemptions. Another policy view is that some believe that even the lowest income taxpayer should pay a minimum tax because doing so completes a "social contract." By paying tax, the taxpayer is entitled to hold public officials accountable for their performance. In Australia and New Zealand, in addition to regular property taxes, every property pays what is called a "fixed annual general charge," which is levied at the same amount on every property regardless of use, value, whether entitled to exemption or not. It means that all properties contribute to the tax.

Some types of property can be exempt from ordinary property taxation and taxed on a special basis because they are difficult to value or because it is difficult to assign their value to a particular taxing district. Examples of such properties are telecommunications systems; electricity, gas, water, and other public utility systems; railroads, pipelines, airlines, and the like; and mines. Similarly, extractive resource properties (such as oil wells and mines) can be taxed on the minerals extracted rather than on estimates of the value of un-extracted minerals.

The partial use of an otherwise exempt property for a nonqualifying purpose also poses a dilemma. Should the entire property be taxed; should the nonqualifying use be ignored; or should an exemption be granted to only the part of the property that qualifies? The answer depends on the nature of, and balance between, the qualifying and nonqualifying uses. Although facilities like airports often are exempt, the parts used by businesses, including rental car agencies, shops, and restaurants, can be taxed. They can be assessed and taxed under ordinary rules, taxed as "possessory interests," or subjected to payments in lieu of taxes. Similar considerations arise when a service that otherwise qualifies for an exemption is provided by a for-profit entity (such as a hospital, recreational facility, or cemetery) or when there is a private benefit, such as agricultural land or privately owned historical property.

Important Administrative Provisions

Along with how a property tax is designed, how it is administered is important. Administrative provisions with policy implications are as follows.

Notice and Publicity

Public acceptance of a property tax depends in large part on its transparency. Not only do taxpayers need notice of their assessments and tax obligations, but they also need access to information that will help them judge the fairness of the tax, namely, the assessments of others. Especially when a tax reform is being introduced, when there is a culture of nonpayment, or when tax obligations have not been enforced in the past, comprehensive, effective efforts to explain the rationale for the tax, how it is administered, and taxpayers' rights and responsibilities are needed. Openness goals are achieved when assessment and tax rolls are public and when individual records can be inspected.

Appeal

As noted, a distinguishing feature of most property tax systems is the fact that tax administrators, not taxpayers themselves, initially determine tax obligations, as is the case in self-assessed taxes. In the interest of fairness, taxpayers in such systems need to have an affordable and effective way of challenging assessments that they believe are incorrect or unfair. At the same time, appeal procedures should not open the door to groundless complaints or unduly delay the collection of taxes. Although appeal rights and procedures are well-established in countries like the United Kingdom and the United States, finding the right balance can be difficult in a new system, especially when the level of taxation is low and when traditional appeal systems were designed to meet the needs of self-assessed taxes or authoritarian governments. Perhaps the most important policy issues are as follows:

- *Standing to Appeal.* All appeal systems allow taxpayers (usually including their representatives) to appeal the assessments on their properties. Usually, but not always, their complaint is that the assessment is too high. Opinion varies about whether other taxpayers or stakeholders (such as taxing districts and bond holders in tax increment financing districts) should be able to appeal the assessments on properties that they do not own. Usually their complaint is that an assessment is too low. Whatever their merits, third-party appeals complicate the appeal process.

- *Grounds for Appeal.* The grounds for appeal must be specified to help taxpayers decide whether to pursue an appeal and to guide appeal bodies in their decision-making. The grounds can include the wrong person being designated as the taxpayer, improper classification, an incorrect assessment, an inequitable assessment, and an improper denial of an exemption. Some systems require that the amount of taxes in dispute be sufficiently large.

- *Burden of Proof and Weight of Evidence.* To prevent frivolous appeals, the taxpayer usually must overcome a presumption that the assessment is correct by presenting sufficient evidence. In some systems, including several U.S. states in the case of residential appeals, the burden is on the assessor to prove that the assessment is correct.

Billing, Payment, and Enforcement Provisions

In addition to defining such things as administrative responsibilities and the liability for taxes, contemporary property tax laws attempt to facilitate voluntary payment of tax obligations. They make the rules clear by providing notice, setting out payment procedures, and specifying the actions that can be taken to enforce the collection of delinquent taxes (arrears).

A feature of the property tax that contributes to its unpopularity is the visibility and size of many annual property tax bills. A way to reduce their apparent size is to allow installment and partial payments. Increasingly, tax administrators try other ways to make collection more convenient. Rather than the former requirement that taxpayers appear personally before the tax collector and pay in cash, mailing checks is typical, and some systems allow taxes to be paid by direct debit or credit card. Taxpayers can pay their property taxes along with mortgage and utility bills, or they can pay at banks or at post offices.

Property tax systems provide a variety of measures to make avoiding paying property taxes difficult and expensive. Tax collectors can advance payment deadlines when they believe that the taxpayer or the taxable property will leave the tax district. Penalties and interest charged on late payments provide an incentive to make payments timely, and discounts sometimes are offered for early payments. Of course, interest rates must be higher than market rates for the measures to be effective.

After a stipulated period of delinquency (generally ranging from one to three years), property tax administrators usually have recourse to direct enforcement actions that involve a legal process to force payment of outstanding tax obligations. Typically, a demand for prompt payment is issued. If it is ignored, enforcement begins. In personam enforcement mechanisms are removal and sale of goods, attachments of pay and bank accounts, and imprisonment. In rem mechanisms are the creation of tax liens and confiscation of the real estate. Property tax liens usually have priority over other (private) liens. One problem with in rem enforcement is that the ultimate weapon, confiscation of property, is not proportionate to small arrears, especially when homesteads are involved.

Granting privileges, such as allowing property to be transferred only on proof of payment of property taxes (a tax clearance) and allowing property taxes to be deducted from income taxes, fosters payment of property taxes. In summary, well-designed property tax systems attempt to make it easier and less expensive to pay property taxes than to avoid them.

Other Features

Property tax systems usually contain procedures for dealing with errors and omissions on the part of both taxpayers and tax administrators. Usually there are time limits. There can be penalties.

Conclusions

Upon reflection, the challenge to property tax policy makers in any nation is to make a coherent set of choices. Arguably, this becomes increasingly difficult as systems mature and complexities, such as new incentive and relief measures, are added. As discussed here and in Chapter 6, most measures have bad as well as good points. Measures that solve one policy problem can aggravate another.

The division of the powers of taxation and of tax revenues is likely to be an ongoing area of tension in property tax policy. It is human nature to seek power but not accountability.

References

Advisory Commission on Intergovernmental Relations (ACIR). 1963. *The role of the states in strengthening the property tax.* 2 vols. Washington, DC: ACIR.

Allegheny Pittsburgh Coal Co. v. Webster County Commission, 488 U.S. 336 (1989).

Almy, R., R. Denne, R. Gloudemans, and S. Miller. 1978. *Improving real property assessment: A reference manual.* Chicago: International Association of Assessing Officers.

The Appraisal Foundation. Updated annually. *Uniform standards of professional appraisal practice* (USPAP). Washington, DC: The Appraisal Foundation.

Behrens, J.O. updated by J. Gravelle. 2005. Transfer taxes, real estate. In *Encyclopedia of taxation & tax policy*, 2nd ed. Washington, DC: The Urban Institute Press.

Bi-Metallic Inv. Co. v. State Board of Equalization, 239 U.S. 441, 445; 36 S. Ct. 141, 142 (1915).

Brown v. Maryland, 25 U.S. 419 (1827).

Carmichael v. Southern Coal & Coke Co., 301 U.S. 495 (1937).

Complete Auto Transit, Inc. v. Brady, 430 U.S. 271 (1977).

Department of Revenue of Oregon v. ACF Industries Inc., 510 U.S. 332, 114 S.Ct. 843 (1994).

Fair Assessment in Real Estate Association v. McNary, 454 U.S. 100, 102 S.Ct. 177, 70 L.Ed.2d 271 (1981).

Fisher, G.W. 1996. *The worst tax?: A history of the property tax in America.* Lawrence, KS: University Press of Kansas.

Fitzgerald v. Racing Association of Central Iowa, 539 U.S. 103 (2003).

Hooper v. Bernalillo County Assessor, 472 U.S. 612 (1985).

International Association of Assessing Officers. 2003. *Standard on administration of monitoring and compliance responsibilities.* Chicago: IAAO.

——— 2000. *Property tax policies and administrative practices in Canada and the United States.* Chicago, IL: IAAO.

Leloup v. Port of Mobile, 127 U.S. 640, 648 (1888).

McCulloch v. Maryland, 17 U.S. 316 (1819).

National Association of Assessing Officers. Committee on Assessment Organization and Personnel. 1941. *Assessment organization and personnel.* Chicago: NAAO.

New York State Board of Real Property Services. Office of Counsel. 1993. Opinions of Counsel, Vol. 9, No. 87.

Nordlinger v. Hahn, 505 U.S. 1, 112 S. Ct. 2326 (1992).

Pennsylvania v. Union Gas Co., 491 U.S. 1 (1989).

Rosewell v. LaSalle National Bank, 450 U.S. 503, 101 S.Ct. 1221, 67 L.Ed.2d 464 (1981).

Rothfeld, C. 1994. Section 1983 tax litigation in the state courts. *State Tax Notes* 51: 6.

Schoettle, F.P. 2003. *State and local taxation: The law and policy of multi-jurisdictional taxation.* Newark, NJ: LexisNexis.

Seminole Tribe of Florida v. Florida, 517 U.S. 44 (1996).

Simmons v. State Tax Commission, 111 Idaho 343, 723 P.2d 887 (1986).

Sioux City Bridge Co. v. Dakota County, 260 U.S. 441 (1922).

Strasma, J.D. 1965. *Market-enforced self-assessment for real estate taxes* (LTC Reprint No. 13). Madison, WI: University of Wisconsin, Land Tenure Center.

Sunday Lake Iron Co. v. Wakefield Tp., 247 U.S. 350 (1911).

Youngman, J. 2006. *Legal issues in property valuation and taxation: Cases and materials.* Cambridge, Mass.: Lincoln Institute of Land Policy.

Suggested Reading

Malme, J.H. n.d. *Legal issues in valuation for real property taxation.* Cambridge, MA: Lincoln Institute of Land Policy.

National Association of Assessing Officers. Committee on Principles of Assessment Practice. 1938. *Assessment principles: Final report of the Committee on Assessment Principles.* Chicago: NAAO.

Chapter 4
The Role of Property Tax in Intergovernmental Finance

This chapter describes the distribution of powers in federal governments, focusing in detail on the U.S. federal model for financing the myriad of governments that have developed and been fostered by this system. The chapter addresses the many different sources of state and local government revenue and the policies and administrative issues related to these various revenue forms. A model for the usefulness of each revenue type for financing different levels of government is also suggested. The chapter explores how the property tax best fits into this system and concludes with a discussion of some of the current challenges to both the property tax and other revenue sources, emphasizing school finance issues that have become critical in the United States.

Distribution of Powers
The Case for Multiple Governments

Economic
The economic case for multiple units of government is sometimes called the theory of fiscal federalism. According to this theory, technical features of government goods and services determine the optimal size of government. Those technical features can be divided into xffa (discussed in Chapter 2, "Principles, Politics, and Economics of Taxation"), economies of scale, and variations in demand. Depending upon these technical features, a particular service might best be provided by a town, state, special district, regional government, or national government.

When externalities are important, fiscal federalism argues for having larger units of government provide the service or for using intergovernmental grants to "internalize the externality." A good example is a high-quality education system. When Anytown, U.S. provides an excellent elementary and secondary education, some benefits accrue to citizens of other cities and states. For example, education makes a person more productive in the work force and a better informed citizen, and those benefits accrue to citizens of other cities and states. Anytown citizens do not have an incentive to take those external benefits into account so they tend to spend too little on education. The solution to this externality problem is either to have a larger unit of government, such as the state or national government, provide education or to have the national and state government pay for some portion of Anytown's education system through intergovernmental grants, thus "internalizing the externality."

Economies of scale exist when unit cost falls as the scale of production increases. For example, it is usually more expensive to educate high school students in a school of 100 than in a school of 1,000 (e.g., the per-student cost of educating a student in a small high school may be $14,000, but in a larger high school, $8,000). When economies of scale exist, more centralized production of government goods and services is called for. In states with many small towns, for example, it is customary to have regional high schools or to form school districts that serve more than one town. Other states have made school districts part of county government in order to realize economies of scale.

Finally, variation in demand is important in determining which government should provide a particular good or service. Consider the demand for recreation facilities, such as pools and athletic fields. Some citizens desire them; others do not, and others prefer to join private health clubs. To the extent that preferences vary among the population, decentralized provision of recreation facilities by multiple small governments is called for.

In a pure theory of fiscal federalism, all government goods and services are analyzed according to the extent of their externalities, economies of scale, and variations in demand. For each good or service it could be determined whether it was best provided by a neighborhood, town, state, regional government, or national government. The determination of these technical requirements for all government goods and services might lead to a great many governments, even more than currently exist in the United States. In the practical application of fiscal federalism, however, the cost of operating government and the ability of citizens to monitor their governments must be taken into account. This means that the optimal number of governments is less than that in pure theory.

Political

From a political perspective, the advantage of multiple units of government arises from the importance of checks and balances for limiting government power and preserving citizens' liberty. If there were only a national government, even with three branches to check each other, the liberty of citizens might be jeopardized. In the U.S. system of government, both the national government and states have constitutionally guaranteed power. State governments provide a check on the power of the national government and vice versa. Sometimes the ability of government at one level to check the power of government at another level is called vertical intergovernmental competition. For example, the U.S. Supreme Court ensures that all states give all citizens the right to vote. In this instance the national government curbs state power. One way that states can exercise a check on national power is for governors to reach consensus on a particular policy (e.g., education policy in the No Child Left Behind Act) and use the National Governors' Association to lobby for changes in federal law.

Administrative Assignments—Types of Federalism

Federal versus Unitary Governments

The governmental system in the United States is a federal system. In a federal system, both the state and national (federal) governments possess significant and constitutionally independent powers. In fact, the powers of the states are protected by the Tenth Amendment of the U.S. Constitution, which reads,

> *The powers not delegated to the United States by the Constitution, nor prohibited by it to the States, are reserved to the States respectively, or to the people.*

Not many countries in the world have a truly federal governmental system. In addition to the United States, the countries of Australia, Canada, and Germany have federal governments. Canada's provinces and Germany's länder are the equivalent of U.S. states.

The opposite of a federal government is a unitary government. In a unitary government, states (or local governments) derive their powers from the national government. The system is hierarchical: the power of the national government surpasses that of the states, and the states serve as departments of the national government. France and Great Britain are countries with a unitary system of government.

Number of Governments in the United States

The system of governments in the United States is amazingly complex, fragmented, and decentralized. In addition to the Federal Government and 50 state governments, in 2002 the U.S. Census Bureau counted 87,525 local governments (see Table 4-1).

Australia, Canada, and Germany all have far fewer local governments than the United States. Even after accounting for differences in population, the U.S. local government structure is more fragmented than those in other federal countries. The United States has about 30 local governments per 100,000 people, compared to 5 per 100,000 in Australia, 20 per 100,000 in Germany, and 25 per 100,000 in Canada (Fisher 2007, 129).

Nor is the U.S. governmental structure static. During World War II there were 155,116 local governments. Since that time, there has been a tremendous reduction in the number of school districts as smaller districts have been consolidated into larger ones (the number of school districts has shrunk from 108,579 in 1942 to 13,506 in 2002 (*U.S. Statistical Abstract 2001*, table 413; *U.S. Statistical Abstract 2008*, table 414), and many special districts have been created (the number of special districts has grown from 8,299 in 1942 to 35,052 in 2002). Special districts generally provide a single governmental service such as fire protection, housing, community development, or natural resource functions.

TABLE 4-1. Local Governments in the United States in 2002

Type of Local Government	Number
County	3,043
Municipal	19,429
Town or Township	16,504
School District	13,506
Special District	35,052
Total	87,525

Source: U.S. Statistical Abstract 2007, "Table 415, Number of Local Governments by Type: 2002," http://www.census.gov/compendia/statab/tables/08s0415.pdf (accessed January 17, 2008).

Alternative Theories of Federalism

Various theories of federalism underlie the rationale for the complex governmental system in the United States today.

Dual Federalism

In the theory of dual federalism, the national government and the states have separate sets of responsibilities. For example, the responsibility for the nation's defense belongs to the national government, and the responsibility for education belongs to the states. This was the predominant theory of federalism in the early years of the United States, probably up until the time of President Franklin Roosevelt's New Deal. The metaphor for dual federalism is a layer cake. This model of federalism was appropriate when the role of all governments in society was much more limited than it is today.

Cooperative Federalism

Cooperative federalism recognizes the tremendous interdependence between the Federal Government and state governments. For example, although state governments have the primary responsibility for K-12 education, the Federal Government provides aid for certain educational functions (e.g., special education) and places mandates on state governments to test their students. National defense in an era of concern about terrorism must rely upon state law enforcement as well as on national intelligence agencies and military forces. The theory of cooperative federalism has been the dominant theory among political scientists since the 1930s. The metaphor for cooperative federalism is a marble cake—there is no distinct separation between the chocolate and vanilla layers; the two are swirled together by design.

Coercive Federalism

Coercive federalism has never been a normative theory of federalism (what should be) but has been put forward by some scholars as a description of the unfortunate tendency toward which federal-state relations are heading. Troubling developments are the rise of federal mandates and preemption of state authority. The metaphor for coercive federalism is a pyramid, in which the federal level is at the top, the states are in the middle, and the local level is on the bottom. Elazar (1991, 72), a prominent scholar of federalism, put it this way:

> *To the extent that those involved in governance now conceive of the American federal system as a pyramid with federal, state, and local 'levels,' they have opened the door to the transformation of cooperative federalism into coercive federalism. In any hierarchy, the top is expected to have more authority and power than the middle or bottom.* **Such an arrangement contradicts the basic principles of federalism.** *(Emphasis added.)*

Competitive Federalism

The theory of competitive federalism has been as strongly influenced by economists as by political scientists. This approach is concerned with "government failure," which is the tendency for governments to be insufficiently responsive to their citizens. This approach also takes a benign attitude towards competition among governments, as exhibited by the following quote from Dye (1990, 1–3):

> *All governments, even democratic governments, are dangerous... Democratic political processes alone cannot restrain Leviathan... Among the most important 'auxiliary precautions' the founders devised to control government is federalism, which they viewed as a source of constraint on Leviathan... Federalism is not only competition between the national government and the states, the topic of most modern scholarship on federalism, it is also competition between the states. Indeed, it is also, by extension, competition among the nation's eighty-three thousand local governments.*

State health care policies can be viewed through the prism of competitive federalism. Because the Federal Government has not tackled the problem of the uninsured, state governments have stepped in to fill the gap. Some states, such as Maine, Massachusetts, and Vermont, have pursued comprehensive reforms that aim at universal or near-universal health care coverage. Other states have taken an incremental approach, which focuses on expanding health insurance coverage for children or young adults (Academy Health 2008, 4–5). State policy innovations that are successful make their state a more attractive place to live and work. Successful policy innovations can also be copied by other states.

Not all competition between the states has a positive outcome, however. Many states use tax incentives to influence business location decisions. To the extent to which tax incentive packages are excessively costly, state policy makers are "paying" more for each new job gained than the job is worth. Furthermore, because one state's business location package is likely to be matched by other states, it can be argued that states are playing a "zero sum" game in which the ultimate impact is lower business taxes with no net impact on business location decisions (Kenyon and Kincaid 1991, 22–24).

Local Government—The U.S. Model

It is tempting to apply the various theories of federalism to state-local relations or to conceive of the federal governmental system as including three constitutionally independent types of government: national, state, and local. However, local governments do not have constitutionally given authority like the states. Instead, from a legal perspective, local governments are "creatures of the states," which can be regulated by the state. This theory goes back to *Atkins v. Kansas* (1903), in which Judge Dillon said that cities

> ...are creatures, mere political subdivisions, of the state for the purpose of exercising a part of its powers. They may exert only such powers as are expressly granted to them or such as may be necessarily implied from those granted.

This legal status of local governments is usually referred to as Dillon's Rule.

In fact, there is a great deal of diversity in local governmental authority among the 50 U.S. states. Home rule laws protect local government authority in some states; in others a long tradition of local control gives localities more power in fact than they might have in theory.

Thus, from a practical standpoint, some of the theories of federalism explicitly apply to local governments and others do not. The theories of competitive federalism and fiscal federalism are those most concerned with the role of local governments.

Financing Distributive Powers

Scholars who have examined questions of federalism have reviewed the various taxes and asked, Which type of government is best suited to use this particular revenue source? For example, they have argued that taxes on highly mobile sources should be assigned to central or national governments, while taxes on immobile sources should be reserved for local governments. The implication is that estate and inheritance taxes are best left to central governments, while property taxes are an appropriate source of revenue for local governments. Other considerations are the degree to which a revenue source redistributes income (the more progressive the tax, the better suited it is to central rather than local governments) and the stability of the revenue pattern (the less stable, the more appropriate it is for central than for local governments). These scholars find that user charges can be levied by any type of government. Table 4-2 summarizes the findings from the literature.

TABLE 4-2. Optimal Tax Assignment

Tax	Appropriate Level of Government to Levy Tax
Individual income—generally	C
Individual income—nonprogressive	C or S
Corporate income tax	C
Value-added tax	C
Retail sales tax	S
Excise taxes	C or S
Natural resource taxes	C or S
Customs duties	C
Estate taxes	C
Property taxes	L
User charges	C or S or L
Payroll tax	C or S
Environmental tax	C or S

Note: C = central, S = state, L = local.

Source: Kenyon 1997, 72.

Note that only the property tax and user charges are listed as appropriate revenue sources for local governments. Some federal or state regulations can modify the recommendations in the table, however. For example, for a long time, the federal credit allowed for state estate taxes made it possible for U.S. states to levy taxes on this very mobile tax source.

Government Revenue and Resources

To fund the myriad of governmental functions discussed above, state and local governments have developed and use various revenue sources, which fall into three broad categories: taxes, user fees, and grants. The major difference between a tax and a fee is that taxes, by definition, are paid by a broader segment of the economy than only those who directly benefit from the services provided. When a direct benefit is intended, user fees are the more applicable revenue instrument.

Although the focus of this discussion is intended to be on taxes, there are a variety of ways that the public sector can obtain necessary resources. Four examples of these are common in today's society: voluntary contributions of either money or time, public-sector resources, "taking" of needed resources, and taxation.

First, governments can gain resources through voluntary contributions of either money or time. Parents often volunteer at their children's public schools; individuals serve with little or no compensation on boards and commissions to advise elected officials; and monetary gifts are made to civic artistic enterprises. Nonprofit organizations often serve as "middlemen" between the public and private sectors, and at times, these organizations are given tax incentives to retain their nonprofit status.

Second, in some cases, the public sector owns resources. Some of these resources are geographically limited public goods. In these cases, one person's consumption does not subtract from what is left for other people, and no voluntary price mechanism exists. For example, government parks and national defense are provided for all citizens. With this ownership, the government is able to provide its citizens with services from these resources. At times, government is able to charge for the use of these resources, for example, park entrance fees. Governments can also sell some goods and services that they own. Many jurisdictions have extensive enterprise activity, principally in the realm of public utilities, which generate a product that can be sold to earn revenue. Governments can also charge tuition for state universities and can earn money in the financial markets by investing the cash balances they own. Sometimes, governments are urged to privatize these resources—that is, sell them to the private sector so that the private sector can treat the resources as private goods. In socialist regimes, governments can own all or most of the available resources.

Third, governments can simply "take" the resources they need. This acquisition can be arbitrary, because sometimes this "need" is arbitrary. One example is the use of eminent domain power to acquire property necessary for a government activity. Although government is supposed to compensate for the use of property taken through eminent domain, the value of this compensation is often attacked as being too small and can be viewed as ignoring historical, emotional, or other intangible ties to the property. Another example is government taking an individual's time by requiring jury duty. The token compensation is rarely equivalent to the value of time given.

Finally, and most important for the focus of this text, governments can obtain resources through taxation. "Taxes," said Justice Holmes, "are what we pay for a civilized society" (*Compania General De Tobacos De Filipinas v. Collector of Internal Revenue*). They are necessary when the three preceding ways of obtaining resources do not generate enough to finance the activities that the population deems necessary for government to provide. One of the ongoing—and beneficial—tensions of today's public sector is the question of what to do if the revenue raised by an in-place tax system is not sufficient to cover the desired expenditures. Some would change the tax rates to generate more revenue; others would reduce expenditures to a level that the existing system could finance. The outcome reflects the political desires of the citizens.

Taxes Used by State and Local Governments

The major taxes used by state and local governments are property tax, sales tax, and income tax. Sales tax can be further subdivided into general sales tax (which actually consists of both sales and use taxes as used by U.S. states) and selective sales taxes, which are levied on the sale of specific items, such as tobacco products, gasoline, or liquor. Income tax is further subdivided into individual and corporate income tax.

Chapter 4 ■ The Role of Property Tax in Intergovernmental Finance

Table 4-3 places these taxes into perspective in terms of their relative importance to state and local government. The percentages shown are relative to total state and local tax collections for fiscal year 2005.

TABLE 4-3. State and Local Tax Collection by Source as a Percentage of Total Tax Collections in 2005

State	Property	General Sales	Selective Sales	Individual Income	Corporate Income	Other
Alabama	15.3	30.2	18.8	22.6	3.4	9.6
Alaska	30.3	5.3	8.2	n.a.	20.0	36.2
Arizona	28.0	38.3	9.4	15.5	3.8	4.9
Arkansas	14.6	41.3	12.3	23.3	3.4	5.1
California	23.2	25.6	7.8	29.3	5.9	8.1
Colorado	31.5	28.0	8.3	24.0	2.0	6.1
Connecticut	37.9	17.3	9.8	26.6	3.0	5.3
Delaware	14.8	n.a.	12.4	28.4	7.6	36.8
District of Columbia	26.4	19.7	9.9	26.7	4.6	12.6
Florida	34.1	33.5	16.2	n.a.	3.0	13.2
Georgia	29.9	27.9	9.0	26.7	2.6	4.0
Hawaii	14.8	38.7	13.7	25.0	2.2	5.5
Idaho	27.6	27.0	9.5	24.9	3.4	7.7
Illinois	38.0	17.0	17.0	16.2	4.4	7.4
Indiana	35.8	23.4	10.7	22.6	3.9	3.7
Iowa	34.0	22.3	10.3	23.8	1.9	7.7
Kansas	32.9	26.8	10.1	21.8	2.6	5.6
Kentucky	18.3	21.2	16.7	30.9	3.9	8.9
Louisiana	17.0	39.7	14.0	16.7	2.5	10.1
Maine	41.2	17.9	8.2	24.9	2.6	5.2
Maryland	23.4	12.1	12.0	38.3	3.4	10.8
Massachusetts	36.0	13.5	7.1	33.7	4.6	5.1
Michigan	36.6	22.9	10.5	18.6	5.4	6.0
Minnesota	25.1	20.4	12.2	30.3	4.5	7.6
Mississippi	26.3	34.6	13.3	15.7	3.8	6.4
Missouri	26.9	28.0	12.5	24.9	1.4	6.4
Montana	29.8	n.a.	16.9	26.2	3.6	23.5
Nebraska	31.9	26.8	8.3	21.2	3.0	40.7
Nevada	25.7	33.9	25.1	n.a.	n.a.	15.4
New Hampshire	61.4	n.a.	16.3	1.6	11.0	9.7
New Jersey	45.1	15.4	8.7	19.3	5.2	6.3
New Mexico	14.2	35.5	11.5	17.9	4.0	16.9

(table continued on next page)

TABLE 4-3. State and Local Tax Collection by Source as a Percentage of Total Tax Collections in 2005 (continued)

State	Property	General Sales	Selective Sales	Individual Income	Corporate Income	Other
New York	30.7	19.0	6.2	31.4	6.3	6.4
North Carolina	23.6	22.9	11.6	30.9	4.7	6.4
North Dakota	29.2	22.6	14.7	11.4	3.6	18.5
Ohio	28.7	23.1	7.4	31.4	3.2	6.2
Oklahoma	17.1	29.1	9.5	24.5	1.7	18.1
Oregon	32.1	n.a.	8.7	43.5	3.3	12.4
Pennsylvania	29.1	17.9	11.7	24.9	3.7	12.7
Rhode Island	40.4	18.8	12.1	22.2	2.5	4.1
South Carolina	31.7	25.7	10.2	22.8	2.1	7.6
South Dakota	34.7	39.6	13.8	n.a.	2.3	9.5
Tennessee	24.4	47.3	11.3	1.0	5.0	11.0
Texas	43.8	29.3	15.7	n.a.	n.a.	11.2
Utah	24.5	29.9	11.4	26.4	2.6	5.2
Vermont	41.0	12.2	18.3	19.4	2.7	6.3
Virginia	30.3	14.6	13.0	30.2	2.2	9.7
Washington	28.9	46.3	13.8	n.a.	n.a.	10.9
West Virginia	18.2	19.7	20.1	21.1	8.3	12.5
Wisconsin	36.4	20.1	8.4	25.5	3.7	5.8
Wyoming	33.3	25.5	5.2	n.a.	n.a.	36.0
U. S. Total	30.4	24.0	11.0	22.0	3.9	8.7

Source: Federation of Tax Administrators (www.taxadmin.org/fta/rate/slsource.html (accessed January 17, 2008); based on data from the U.S. Census Bureau.
n.a.= tax not levied.

Changes in Patterns of Local Government Revenue

Much of the focus of this book is on the continual pressure to find alternatives to property tax as a major source of government revenue. Because the property tax largely remains a major funding source for local, rather than state, government in the United States, it is useful to examine changes in the proportional share of local government revenue represented by this tax and to determine whether specific alternatives have been emerging as replacement for the property tax.

Significance of Various Local Government Funding Sources

Figures 4-1 through 4-4 compare major general revenue funding sources for school districts, counties, municipalities, and special districts and show the change in the relative importance of each funding mechanism over a 20-year period (1977–1997).

Although school districts derive almost one-third of their revenue from property taxes, that percentage declined over the 20 years shown in Figure 4-1. The importance of state aid has increased from 40 to 49 percent. Certainly the school funding court cases that have swept the country since 1971 have increased the state's role in providing K–12 education, increased the importance of state aid to school districts, and decreased the importance of the local property tax.

FIGURE 4-1. Major Sources of School Funding, 1977 versus 1997

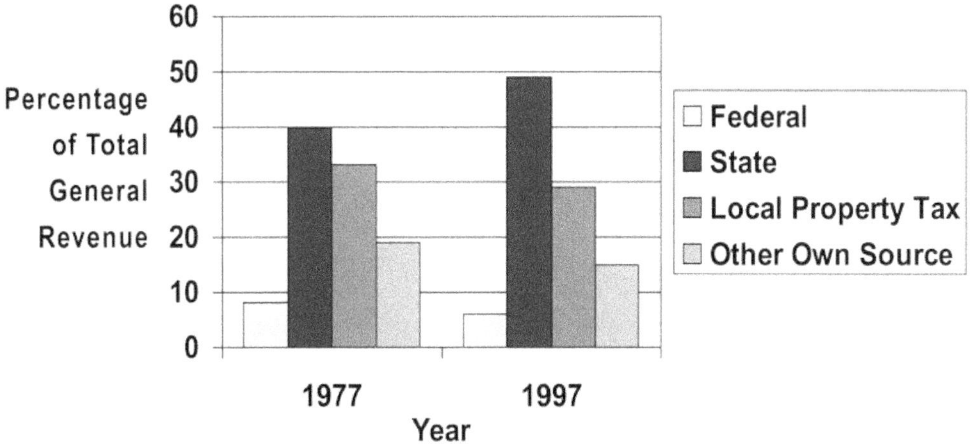

[Bar chart showing Percentage of Total General Revenue by Year (1977 and 1997) for Federal, State, Local Property Tax, and Other Own Source categories.]

The shift from local to state revenue sources can be misleading with respect to reliance on the property tax. Some states have merely replaced locally raised property taxes, established by each school district, with uniform state property tax rates. Hence, it is difficult to ascertain whether property tax reliance for school finance has diminished or whether increased state funding includes a state property tax component. Tax reform in Michigan in 1994, for example, reduced local property taxes for schools, but imposed state property taxes for the same purpose (Wassmer and Fisher 1996). This shifts the level of government responsible for providing the funding and the revenue, but does not eliminate the property tax as a funding source for schools. Similarly, Vermont, New Hampshire, and the province of Alberta have established state- (or province-) level school property taxes. Alternatively, Idaho's 2006 removal of school general property taxes, with replacement by state non-property-tax-generated revenue (including a state sales tax rate increase) represents a true shift away from the property tax (whether state or local)(www.idahostatesman.com/244/story/389526.html).

As shown in Figure 4-2, county governments rely much less heavily on intergovernmental grants and somewhat less heavily on property taxes than school districts. Charges and miscellaneous revenues account for more than a quarter of

FIGURE 4-2. Major Sources of County Funding, 1977 versus 1997

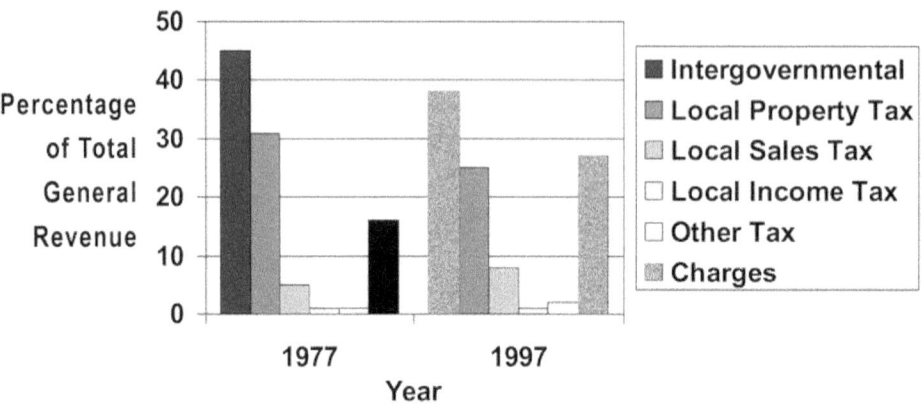

FIGURE 4-3. Major Sources of Municipality Funding, 1977 versus 1997

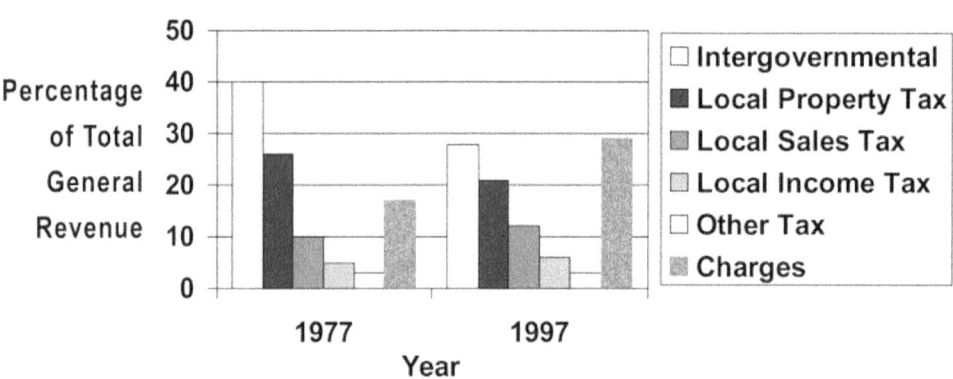

FIGURE 4-4. Major Sources of Special District Funding, 1977 versus 1997

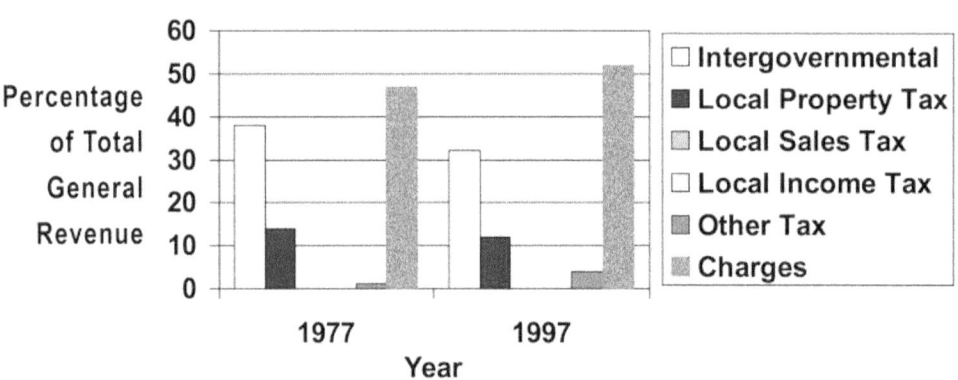

Note: For special districts, funding percentages raised from local sales and income taxes round to zero.

general revenue, and sales taxes account for 8 percent.

Municipalities rely less heavily on intergovernmental grants and property taxes on average than either school districts or counties and more on other taxes and charges; see Figure 4-3. Charges and miscellaneous revenues account for 29 percent of general revenue, sales taxes for 12 percent, and income taxes for 6 percent.

Figure 4-4 shows that more than half of special district revenue is derived from charges and miscellaneous revenues. Intergovernmental grants are also an important source of revenue, contributing about one-third of the total. Property taxes currently account for only 12 percent of special district general revenues.

Regional Variation of Funding Sources

The regions of the country where state and local governments are most reliant on property tax are the New England, the Middle Atlantic, and the Great Lakes states. The South and Far West have the greatest reliance on sales taxation, and the Middle Atlantic states have the greatest reliance upon income taxation. Finally, the highest reliance on user charges for state-local general revenue is in the Southeast and Far West.

Summary of Local Government Revenue Sources

Table 4-4 summarizes the ways in which local governments (taken as a whole) in the United States raise revenue and demonstrates the relative importance of each funding source. Although there are differences in funding sources for specific types of local governments, the significance of the property tax in overall local government finance becomes apparent.

TABLE 4-4. Local Government General Revenue* by Source for FY 2005

State	From State and Federal Governments	Percentage of General Revenue from Own Taxes					Non-Tax Charges and Misc.
		Property Taxes	Sales Taxes	Individual Income Taxes	Corporate Income Taxes	Total from Own Taxes	
U.S. Average	38.9%	27.9%	6.2%	1.8%	0.4%	38.6%	22.5%
Alabama	38.5%	11.3%	12.7%	0.8%	0.0%	28.2%	33.3%
Alaska	40.4%	29.7%	7.0%	0.0%	0.0%	38.0%	21.6%
Arizona	42.7%	23.4%	10.1%	0.0%	0.0%	36.1%	21.2%
Arkansas	57.1%	8.9%	12.4%	0.0%	0.0%	21.8%	21.1%
California	47.0%	17.6%	6.3%	0.0%	0.0%	26.5%	26.4%
Colorado	28.7%	26.4%	14.1%	0.0%	0.0%	42.8%	28.4%
Connecticut	33.1%	55.9%	0.0%	0.0%	0.0%	57.2%	9.8%
Delaware	49.5%	21.4%	0.4%	2.2%	0.0%	30.3%	20.2%
D.C.	34.7%	14.0%	15.7%	14.2%	2.5%	53.0%	12.3%
Florida	30.7%	29.5%	6.3%	0.0%	0.0%	38.1%	31.1%
Georgia	34.1%	27.6%	10.8%	0.0%	0.0%	40.1%	25.8%
Hawaii	20.0%	43.3%	7.8%	0.0%	0.0%	57.7%	22.4%
Idaho	40.5%	27.5%	0.5%	0.0%	0.0%	29.8%	29.7%
Illinois	35.2%	38.3%	6.9%	0.0%	0.0%	46.7%	18.1%
Indiana	36.1%	33.9%	0.4%	2.7%	0.0%	37.6%	26.3%
Iowa	37.1%	31.6%	5.0%	0.6%	0.0%	37.8%	25.0%
Kansas	35.7%	31.5%	7.2%	0.0%	0.0%	39.3%	25.0%
Kentucky	43.1%	18.7%	4.2%	8.0%	0.0%	33.4%	23.5%
Louisiana	38.0%	16.5%	21.4%	0.0%	0.0%	39.3%	22.8%
Maine	31.6%	53.0%	0.0%	0.0%	0.0%	54.0%	14.3%
Maryland	31.9%	25.1%	2.4%	17.3%	0.0%	51.5%	16.6%
Massachusetts	41.3%	43.8%	0.6%	0.0%	0.0%	45.5%	13.1%
Michigan	49.5%	27.5%	0.6%	1.2%	0.0%	30.0%	20.5%
Minnesota	48.2%	22.1%	0.9%	0.0%	0.0%	24.2%	27.6%
Mississippi	45.5%	22.1%	0.7%	0.0%	0.0%	23.7%	30.9%
Missouri	33.5%	26.2%	13.7%	1.7%	0.1%	44.0%	22.6%
Montana	43.0%	31.3%	0.2%	0.0%	0.0%	32.7%	24.3%
Nebraska	30.6%	33.8%	5.5%	0.0%	0.0%	44.9%	24.5%
Nevada	42.3%	20.0%	6.8%	0.0%	0.0%	31.1%	26.6%
New Hampshire	33.4%	54.0%	0.0%	0.0%	0.0%	54.9%	11.7%
New Jersey	32.6%	51.3%	0.2%	0.0%	0.0%	52.5%	14.9%
New Mexico	58.1%	13.2%	11.0%	0.0%	0.0%	25.7%	16.2%
New York	36.1%	26.7%	9.2%	5.3%	3.3%	47.6%	16.2%

(table continued on next page)

TABLE 4-4. Local Government General Revenue* by Source for FY 2005 (continued)

State	From State and Federal Governments	Percentage of General Revenue from Own Taxes					Non-Tax Charges and Misc.
		Property Taxes	Sales Taxes	Individual Income Taxes	Corporate Income Taxes	Total from Own Taxes	
North Carolina	42.5%	22.7%	6.4%	0.0%	0.0%	30.5%	27.1%
North Dakota	41.3%	31.9%	4.2%	0.0%	0.0%	37.1%	21.6%
Ohio	40.6%	26.5%	3.6%	8.1%	0.0%	39.4%	20.0%
Oklahoma	41.0%	18.3%	14.8%	0.0%	0.0%	34.2%	24.8%
Oregon	41.3%	26.7%	2.1%	1.0%	0.0%	34.6%	24.1%
Pennsylvania	41.6%	28.5%	0.9%	6.8%	0.0%	40.0%	18.3%
Rhode Island	33.9%	54.1%	0.3%	0.0%	0.0%	55.7%	10.5%
South Carolina	32.7%	28.0%	2.6%	0.0%	0.0%	33.7%	33.6%
South Dakota	33.7%	34.7%	10.5%	0.0%	0.0%	47.3%	19.1%
Tennessee	33.5%	23.2%	10.3%	0.0%	0.0%	35.7%	30.8%
Texas	29.1%	39.8%	6.9%	0.0%	0.0%	47.8%	23.1%
Utah	38.0%	25.6%	9.8%	0.0%	0.0%	37.4%	24.6%
Vermont	70.1%	16.9%	0.5%	0.0%	0.0%	18.0%	11.8%
Virginia	37.4%	31.6%	8.1%	0.0%	0.0%	44.3%	18.3%
Washington	39.8%	21.2%	9.2%	0.0%	0.0%	34.1%	26.1%
West Virginia	49.1%	23.5%	1.4%	0.0%	0.0%	29.2%	21.7%
Wisconsin	45.3%	35.9%	1.5%	0.0%	0.0%	38.5%	16.1%
Wyoming	39.0%	22.8%	5.7%	0.0%	0.0%	29.9%	31.1%

Sources: U.S. Census Bureau, Tax Foundation.
* General revenue excludes revenue from utilities, liquor stores, and insurance trusts.

Property Taxes

The property tax is the only major tax revenue source levied in every state in the United States and in every Canadian province. As noted in Chapter 1, "Introduction to Tax Policy," the property tax has increasingly become a source of local, rather than state, government revenue. Despite that constriction, as shown in Table 4-3, the property tax remains the single most significant source of state and local tax revenue. This becomes even more apparent when revenue sources for school districts and other units of local government are reviewed (see Figures 4-1 through 4-4). In fact, despite pressure to utilize alternative revenue sources, for own-source tax revenue for local governments, the proportion raised from property tax appears to have stabilized at about 72 percent since 1997.

Issues related to property tax policy and administration are explored in

Chapters 3, "Fundamental Elements of the Property Tax," 6, "Analysis of Selected Property Tax Prescriptions," and 7, "Components of Model Property Tax Administrative Systems." The remainder of this discussion of revenue sources provides a review and oversight of other (non-property) taxes and revenue instruments.

General Sales Taxes

All states except Alaska, Delaware, Montana, New Hampshire, and Oregon levy a general sales tax (in Alaska, the state government does not have a general sales tax, but some local governments do). In many states local governments can also levy a general sales tax, usually collected by the state and returned to the local government. In Illinois, for example, the state collects a 6.25 percent tax, returns 1 percent to municipal governments, and keeps the other 5.25 percent. Also, larger Illinois municipalities with home rule status can levy higher sales tax rates, and the state acts as their collection agent. Similarly, Idaho dedicates specified percentages of state sales taxes to local non-school districts, with different percentages granted to cities, counties, and special-purpose taxing districts.

History

In the United States prior to the 1930s, local government revenues were several times larger than state government revenue, the property tax was a major revenue source for state governments, and there were no general sales taxes. The Great Depression had a major impact on these measures of fiscal structure. Property tax delinquency reached crisis proportions in many states at a time when demands on government were rising rapidly. The Federal Government responded with a number of new grant programs, many of them requiring a matching contribution from the state. Many state governments responded by enacting general sales taxes to match the federal grants and to finance functions, such as welfare, that previously had been paid for by local governments. By the end of the 1940s, state own-source revenues exceeded local own-source revenues, state property taxes had fallen to 3.7 percent, and state general sales taxes had risen to 21.8 percent of total state taxes (Hoffman 2002).

The Sales Tax Base

The sales tax is generally considered a consumption-based tax. As such, it should apply to most if not all consumption purchases including both goods and services. In actual practice, all general sales taxes depart from this consumption ideal in a number of ways. Many retail purchases for consumption are excluded from the base, while many nonconsumption, business-to-business purchases are included.

The specifics of how the tax base is defined vary greatly from state to state, but the typical state or local sales tax is a tax on retail sales of commodities or "tangible personal property." Purchases from outside the state are usually covered by a use tax levied at the same rate as the sales tax. Although in concept the tax should apply only to purchases by final consumers, in practice it applies to many purchases for business use. The tax applies to all commodities except those specifically exempt. The two broad categories of exemptions are business purchases of inputs and exemptions "designed to bring about a distribution of the tax burden that is less regressive" (Due 1999, 308).

Table 4-5 indicates that of the 45 states (46 counting the District of Columbia) with a retail sales tax, 31 exempt groceries, and another 10 subject groceries to a lower (or a local-only rate). The number of states exempting groceries has risen in recent years.

TABLE 4-5. State Sales Tax Rates as of January 1, 2007

State	Tax Rate (%)	Exemptions		
		Food	Prescription Drugs	Non-prescription Drugs
Alabama	4		*	
Alaska	None			
Arizona	5.6	*	*	
Arkansas	6		*	
California[c]	7.25[b]	*	*	
Colorado	2.9	*	*	
Connecticut	6	*	*	*
Delaware	None			
Florida	6	*	*	*
Georgia	4	*d	*	
Hawaii	4	a	*	
Idaho	6	a	*	
Illinois[b]	6.25	1%	1%	1%
Indiana	6	*	*	
Iowa	5	*	*	
Kansas	5.3	a	*	
Kentucky	6	*	*	
Louisiana	4	*d	*	
Maine	5	*	*	
Maryland	5	*	*	*
Massachusetts	5	*	*	
Michigan	6	*	*	
Minnesota	6.5	*	*	*
Mississippi	7		*	
Missouri	4.225	1.225	*	

(table continued on next page)

TABLE 4-5. State Sales Tax Rates as of January 1, 2007 (continued)

State	Tax Rate (%)	Exemptions		
		Food	Prescription Drugs	Non-prescription Drugs
Montana	None			
Nevada	6.5	*	*	
New Hampshire	None			
New Jersey	7	*	*	*
New Mexico	5	*	*	
New York	4	*	*	*
North Carolina[e]	4.25[d]	*	*	
North Dakota	5	*	*	
Ohio	5.5	*	*	
Oklahoma	4.5	a	*	
Oregon	None			
Pennsylvania	6	*	*	*
Rhode Island	7	*	*	*
South Carolina[f]	5	3%	*	
South Dakota	4	a	*	
Tennessee	7	6%	*	
Texas	6.25	*	*	*
Utah	4.75	2.75%	*	
Vermont	6	*	*	*
Virginia	5b	2.5%[b]	*	*
Washington	6.5	*	*	
West Virginia	6	5%	*	
Wisconsin	5	*	*	
Wyoming	4	*,a g	*	
District of Columbia	5.75	*	*	*

Source: Compiled by Federation of Tax Administrators from various sources, www.taxadmin.org (accessed December 31, 2007). Key: * indicates exempt from tax; blank indicates subject to general sales tax rate.

[a] Some states tax food but allow an (income) tax credit to compensate poor households; they are Hawaii, Idaho, Kansas, Oklahoma, South Dakota, and Wyoming.

[b] Includes statewide local taxes of 1.0 percent in California and Virginia and 1.25 percent in Illinois.

[c] Tax rate may be adjusted annually according to a formula based on balances in the unappropriated general fund and the school foundation fund.

[d] Food sales are subject to local sales taxes.

[e] Sales tax rate is scheduled to decrease to 4 percent on 7/1/2007.

[f] Sales tax rate is scheduled to increase to 6 percent on 6/1/2007.

[g] Food sales exempt through 6/30/2008.

Virtually all states exempt prescription drugs, and a minority also exempt over-the-counter medicines. Not shown in the table are a number of other exemptions, such as for clothing, offered by some states. Although the exemption for groceries is defended for making the tax burden less regressive, it comes at great cost in revenue—by some estimates reducing revenue "by as much as 20 percent" (Due 1999, 308).

Exemptions in general, and the groceries exemption in particular, also significantly increase the cost of administering and complying with the sales tax law. State administrators draft complex regulations defining groceries, making distinctions such as for consumption "off-premises" versus "on-premises," or separating non-exempt subcategories such as "snack food" or "soft drinks." The advent of scanners with a computer entry for each inventory item has greatly reduced the cost of enforcing these distinctions at the cash register.

To avoid both the revenue cost and the administrative cost of the groceries exemption, many policy analysts favor an alternative way to avoid excessive tax burden on certain families. As noted in the footnote in Table 4-5, five states do not exempt groceries from the sales tax, but instead offer an offsetting credit against the state income tax that is targeted to low-income families.

There is enormous variation across states in the sales tax treatment of services. Table 4-6 presents a compilation by the Federation of Tax Administrators of the number of distinct types of services subject to tax in each state. It represents a 2007

TABLE 4-6. Number of Services Taxed by Category in Each State in 2007

State	Utilities	Personal Services	Business Services	Computer Services	Admissions/ Amusements	Professional Services	Fabrication, Repair and Installation	Other Services	Total
Alabama	12	2	6	3	10	0	1	3	37
Alaska[a]	0	0	0	0	0	0	0	1	1
Arkansas	16	7	12	1	12	0	11	13	72
Arizona	12	2	7	0	9	0	2	23	55
California	2	2	7	2	1	0	3	4	21
Colorado[a]	4	0	2	1	2	0	3	2	14
Connecticut	10	9	20	6	10	0	10	14	79
Delaware[a]	9	20	33	6	10	9	19	37	143
District of Columbia	13	7	15	6	8	0	12	12	73
Florida	7	4	9	0	14	0	16	13	63
Georgia[a]	10	4	5	2	8	0	1	6	36
Hawaii	16	20	34	8	14	9	18	41	160
Iowa	13	15	18	1	14	0	13	20	94
Idaho	0	3	5	0	11	0	6	4	29
Illinois	12	1	1	1	0	0	1	1	17
Indiana	7	4	3	2	3	0	1	4	24
Kansas	10	11	9	1	13	0	15	15	74

(table continued on next page)

TABLE 4-6. Number of Services Taxed by Category in Each State in 2007 (continued)

State	Utilities	Personal Services	Business Services	Computer Services	Admissions/ Amusements	Professional Services	Fabrication, Repair and Installation	Other Services	Total
Kentucky	11	2	4	0	6	0	4	1	28
Louisiana	10	8	5	3	9	0	13	7	55
Maine	9	1	6	0	3	0	4	2	25
Maryland	5	3	13	1	11	0	4	2	39
Massachusetts	9	1	4	0	1	0	2	1	18
Michigan	12	2	7	1	1	0	1	2	26
Minnesota	15	7	12	2	13	0	6	11	66
Mississippi	10	5	8	3	11	0	13	22	72
Missouri	8	1	2	2	10	0	0	3	26
Montana	12	0	0	0	2	0	0	4	18
Nebraska	14	9	14	3	12	0	13	12	77
Nevada	0	1	4	0	7	0	2	4	18
New Hampshire[a]	6	1	0	2	0	0	0	2	11
New Jersey	12	5	16	1	6	0	15	19	74
New Mexico	16	20	32	8	14	9	18	41	158
New York	4	4	13	1	6	0	14	15	57
North Carolina	10	4	5	0	9	0	1	1	30
North Dakota	6	1	4	2	11	0	0	2	26
Ohio	8	12	14	5	3	0	12	14	68
Oklahoma	9	3	4	1	10	0	0	5	32
Oregon	0	0	0	0	0	0	0	0	0
Pennsylvania	9	5	16	1	1	0	15	8	55
Rhode Island[a]	10	1	6	3	4	0	3	2	29
South Carolina	4	6	7	4	10	0	1	3	35
South Dakota	14	19	28	8	13	5	18	41	146
Tennessee[a]	11	10	7	3	12	0	13	11	67
Texas	12	10	14	8	12	1	10	16	83
Utah	7	8	6	0	11	0	15	11	58
Vermont	9	2	5	2	11	0	2	1	32
Virginia[a]	1	3	4	0	1	0	4	5	18
Washington	16	20	33	8	13	9	16	43	158
West Virginia	6	17	26	4	13	1	13	25	105
Wisconsin	11	11	8	3	14	0	14	15	76
Wyoming	10	6	6	2	6	0	16	12	58
Total Number in Category	16	20	34	8	15	9	19	47	168

[a] State did not respond, 2004 data reported.
Source: Federation of Tax Administrators, "FTA Survey of Services Taxation—Update," *By the Numbers*, July 2008.

Chapter 4 ▪ The Role of Property Tax in Intergovernmental Finance

update to 2004 and 1996 survey data. Since 2004, the most significant change was in New Jersey, which enacted legislation that expanded the number of services taxed from 55 to 74. (Note that this table covers both general and selective taxes. Most of the states with no general sales tax are counted as taxing at least some services. Oregon is the sole exception.)

Almost all states tax some types of utilities; personal services; business services; admissions and amusements; and fabrication, repair, and installation services. The 2004 update found that thirty-four different types of business services are taxed in one or more states. The 2004 survey also noted that only seven states tax any type of professional services, and only eight different types of professional services are taxed. As of 2007, a total of 168 distinct types of service are taxed by at least one state. Obviously, states having no general sales tax, like Oregon, do not tax services, although they may tax some services separately, such as hotel occupancy and automobile rental. Alaska taxes only one service, but municipalities or boroughs may tax various services. At the other extreme are Delaware (143), Hawaii (160), New Mexico (158), South Dakota (146), and Washington (158), which tax services quite broadly.

The sales tax is intended to be a tax on consumption, although it is often not applied in this way in many states. From the standpoint of tax policy, the sales tax base should include all retail purchases, but not intermediate sales from one business to another. The taxation of business inputs leads to what is known as the cascading of taxes (taxes levied at multiple stages on the same product) and creates incentives for the provision of services by employees within a firm rather than from outside providers. For example, if janitorial services are taxed, a small firm that does not need a full-time janitor would pay taxes on the payments to the service provider, while a large firm employing its own janitor would not be taxed. Almost all states exempt direct ingredients used in production, but many tax a variety of other business inputs. In addition, goods and services exported to other states should not be taxed, but retail goods and services imported into the state should be taxed.

Using this as a guideline, consumer services should clearly be part of the sales tax base. These would include such things as entertainment, auto and home repairs, dry cleaning, home cleaning services, funeral services, health club fees, legal services provided to consumers, financial services provided to consumers, health services, rent, educational fees, and so on. For a variety of reasons (usually based on equity), health care, rent, and education are seldom taxed even though, conceptually, they belong in the base.

Some of these activities are already partially taxed indirectly because the service providers currently pay sales tax on their inputs. For example, dry cleaners pay sales tax on their equipment purchases and supplies. For this reason, the imposition of a tax on services may not provide as much extra revenue as expected because a portion of services is already taxed.

Most services provided to business would not be taxed using these guidelines, including accounting, advertising, legal, and consulting services. This leads to the result that similar services may be either taxed or untaxed depending on who receives the services. For example, services by an attorney for an individual such as tax and estate planning would be taxed, but planning for a business would be exempt.

Note also that state and local sales tax payments usually are not deductible for federal income tax purposes (since 1986). Therefore, rarely is any of the sales tax burden on individuals shifted to the Federal Government.

In recent years, the problem of the taxation of sales by out-of-state vendors has become a major issue; this is discussed below.

Sales Tax Rates

The retail sales tax typically has a uniform rate. The second column of Table 4-5 shows the statewide rate in each state. In California, Illinois, and Virginia, this includes a statewide local tax. For states with a sales tax, the range in the statewide sales tax rate is from 2.90 percent in Colorado to 7.25 percent in Tennessee. The median statewide rate has been climbing and is more than 5.0 percent at present.

State rates should not be viewed in a vacuum as some relative measure by which to differentiate sales tax burdens in various states. Thirty-two states permit local governments, usually municipalities, the option to adopt a local sales tax. Sometimes the option is limited to cities of a certain size. Sometimes the tax revenue is earmarked to particular services such as regional mass transit. Almost always the tax base definition is the same as that for the statewide tax and the state acts as collection agent for local governments. Local rates can vary considerably between localities and can be quite high. In Colorado, for example, the extremely low 2.9 percent statewide rate is offset by add-on local rates, which can be as high as an additional 4.5 percent. Table 4-7 shows typical uses of local sales taxes by indicating the magnitude of those levied in the largest city in each state. The highest combined state and local rate shown is 9.25 percent in Memphis, Tennessee.

Sales Tax Policy Issues

There are a number of issues or concerns that arise in the policy analysis of state and local taxation of retail sales.

Regressivity

A tax is regressive when its burden is a larger percentage of the income of low-income than high-income families. The sales tax is regressive because low-income people spend a larger part of their income on taxable commodities than do high-income people, who typically save more and spend relatively more on nontaxable services. As already noted, most states attempt to reduce the regressivity of the sales tax by exempting groceries, prescription drugs, or other "necessities." One problem is that an across-the-board exemption for groceries also includes many luxury products

Chapter 4 — The Role of Property Tax in Intergovernmental Finance

TABLE 4-7. State and Local Sales Tax Rates in the Largest City in Each State

City	State	Total Rate	State	City	County	School	Transit
Memphis	TN	9.25	7.0		2.25		
New Orleans	LA	9.0	4.0	3.5		1.5	
Seattle	WA	8.8	6.5	0.85	0.25		1.2
Chicago	IL	8.75	6.25	1.0	0.75		0.75
Los Angeles	CA	8.50	6.25	1.0	0.25		1.0
New York City	NY	8.375	4.0	4.0			0.375
Oklahoma City	OK	8.375	4.5	3.875			
Houston	TX	8.25	6.25	1.0			1.0
Phoenix	AZ	8.1	5.6	1.8	0.7		
Birmingham	AL	8.0	4.0	3.0	1.0		
Little Rock	AR	7.5	6.0	0.5	1.0		
Charlotte	NC	7.5	4.5		2.5		0.5
Las Vegas	NV	7.5	2.0		3.0	2.25	
Denver	CO	7.2	2.9	3.5			0.8
Jacksonville	FL	7.0	6.0		0.5		0.5
Atlanta	GA	7.0	4.0		1.0	1.0	1.0
Minneapolis	MN	7.0	6.5	0.5			
Jackson	MS	7.0	7.0				
Omaha	NE	7.0	5.5	1.5			
Philadelphia	PA	7.0	6.0		1.0		
Providence	RI	7.0	7.0				
Kansas City	MO	6.975	4.225	1.5	0.750		0.5
Albuquerque	NM	6.75	5.0	1.50	0.25		
Columbus	OH	6.75	6.0		0.5		0.25
Salt Lake City	UT	6.6	4.75	1.0	0.35		0.5
Fargo	ND	6.5	5.0	1.5			
Wichita	KS	6.3	5.3		1.0		
Bridgeport	CT	6.0	6.0				
Des Moines	IA	6.0	5.0			1.0	
Louisville	KY	6.0	6.0				
Detroit	MI	6.0	6.0				
Newark	NJ	6.0	6.0				
Sioux Falls	SD	6.0	4.0	2.0			
Boise	ID	6.0	6.0				
Burlington	VT	6.0	6.0				
Charleston	WV	6.0	6.0				
Cheyenne	WY	6.0	4.0		2.0		
Washington	DC	5.75	5.75				
Milwaukee	WI	5.6	5.0		0.6		
Indianapolis	IN	5.0	5.0				

(table continued on next page)

TABLE 4-7. State and Local Sales Tax Rates in the Largest City in Each State (continued)

City	State	Total Rate	State	City	County	School	Transit
Boston	MA	5.0	5.0				
Baltimore	MD	5.0	5.0				
Portland	ME	5.0	5.0				
Columbia	SC	5.0	5.0				
Virginia Beach	VA	5.0	4.0	1.0			
Honolulu	HI	4.0	4.0				
Unweighted Average		6.72	5.23				
Median		6.75	5.15				

Source: Government of the District of Columbia, Tax rates and tax burdens in the District of Columbia—A nationwide comparison 2006, http://www.taxadmin.org/fta/rate/DC_tax_burden_2006.pdf (accessed January 17, 2008).

consumed by high-income people. A smaller number of states address the regressivity problem more directly by having an offsetting credit administered under the income tax and often targeted to low-income families.

Border Effects and Out-of-State Sellers

A large percentage of the American population lives near a state border. A state with a higher sales tax rate than its neighbor can cause residents to do their shopping across the border and lose revenue. Ideally the use tax imposed on purchases outside the state would take care of this, but, with the exception of automobiles, for which registration of new purchases is required, and large corporate purchases, which are picked up in the auditing process, use taxes are very difficult to collect.

A major threat to state revenue systems has emerged in recent years with the increased dollar volume of remote purchases—goods bought by mail order or over the Internet. (An entire issue of the *National Tax Journal* [Vol. 53, No. 4, Part 3, December 2000] was devoted to the important topic of "The Taxation of Electronic Commerce.") State tax administrators are seeking ways of cooperating to avoid some of the revenue loss from this change in consumption patterns. The problem cannot be understated and is succinctly summarized in Figure 4-5, reprinted here in its entirety from the prestigious, and usually serious, *National Tax Journal* (December 2000, 1389).

FIGURE 4-5. Tax Tunes: "The Day the Sales Tax Died" by Billy Hamilton, Deputy Comptroller, State of Texas*

> *(Sung to the tune of "American Pie." Apologies to Don McLean.)*
>
> *A long, long time ago,*
> *I can still remember*
> *How the sales tax used to make me smile.*
> *I can't remember if I cried*
> *When I watched as the ACEC† fried,*
> *But something touched me deep inside*
> *The day the sales tax died.*
> *And we were singin'*
> *Bye, bye to the sales tax pie*
> *Tied our budget to the levy*
> *But the levy ran dry*
> *And Budget Committee chairs*
> *Were heaving dot.com sighs*
> *The day the sales tax died.*

*Reproduced with permission of National Tax Journal (Hamilton 2000).
†ACEC refers to the Advisory Commission on Electronic Commerce, which was created by the Congress to make tax policy recommendations

Issues relating to the tax treatment of sales over the Internet are conceptually identical to those from catalog and telephone sales. Sales from out-of-state vendors are legally subject to taxation at the same rate as if they were purchased within the state. If the vendor does not collect the tax, the buyer is required to pay a use tax of an equal amount. The problem is that most buyers do not pay the use tax, and state and local governments are limited in their ability to collect the tax.

Remote vendors who have nexus (a substantial presence) in a state are required to collect the sales tax. Vendors who do not have nexus are not required to do so. This creates a problem for state and local governments in terms of lost tax revenue (which will grow in magnitude over time as the Internet develops). It also creates problems for local merchants and remote vendors with nexus, because they face a competitive disadvantage in regard to remote sellers that do not collect taxes. For example, in most states, even though a major bookstore like Barnes & Noble might sell books over the Internet, the company would be expected to collect sales taxes on these sales because it also has "bricks and mortar" stores. This is not the case with an online retailer like Amazon.com, because it has no such stores.

States would like all remote vendors to collect sales taxes. Currently they are not required to do so because of a series of court rulings. To deal with this problem, a number of states have formed the Streamlined Sales Tax Project to find ways to improve the collection of sales taxes. Currently more than 40 states are participating in the project (see www.streamlinedsalestax.org). The goal is to simplify sales tax administration to make collection less burdensome. The hope is that this will lead to more voluntary compliance, as well as to possible changes at the federal level that will mandate the collection of the tax by vendors.

On November 22, 2002, the steering committee for the project issued the Streamlined Sales Tax Agreement. Some of the key features of the agreement are as follows:

- *Uniform definitions.* State legislatures are still given broad latitude to create exempt sales; however, participating states have agreed to use common definitions for items such as food, clothing, and drugs.
- *Rate simplification.* Participating states will, with two exceptions, agree to impose only one rate on all sales. The two exceptions are for sales of food and drugs. Local rates are limited to one rate per jurisdiction.
- *State administration of local taxes.* Participating states must administer city and county taxes. (Currently, the six resort cities in Idaho administer their own taxes.)
- *Uniform sourcing rules.* Most states impose the tax rate of the jurisdiction to which goods are delivered. Some states, however, impose the tax of the jurisdiction of the seller. Participating states will use the destination-sourcing rule. (This has kept at least two states, Kansas and Washington, from enacting the enabling legislation.)
- *Simplified exemption administration for use- and entity-based exemptions.* Under this goal, sellers would not be liable for uncollected tax. In addition, states will have a uniform exemption certificate.
- *Uniform audit procedures.* Sellers that participate in one of the certified Streamlined Sales Tax System technology models will face limited audit exposure.
- *State funding of the system.* States will assume responsibility for funding some of the technology models.

The member states are hoping that Congress will enact legislation requiring remote sellers to collect and remit tax for participating states even if the seller does not have nexus with all the states. It is also possible that remote sellers will voluntarily start collecting sales taxes if the administrative burden is reduced.

At the time this book was being written (early 2008), 18 states had laws that were fully in compliance with the Streamlined Sales and Use Tax Agreement, while four additional states either were in substantial compliance or were expected to be in compliance by January 2008 (www.streamlinedsalestax.org/govbrdstates.htm, last accessed June 30, 2008).

Revenue Elasticity

The two dimensions of revenue elasticity are cyclical and trend. Over the business cycle, sales tax revenues tend to be more stable than the major alternative, income taxes, because goods consumption varies less than income. On the other hand, longer term growth in incomes and living standards leads to greater consumption of nontaxed services, so sales tax revenues grow less than incomes.

Political Acceptability

Increases in the sales tax often encounter less political resistance than increases in other revenue sources. Sales taxes are less visible than other taxes because they are paid in small increments. There are no large annual or semiannual bills, as with the property tax, and no complicated forms to fill out, as with the income tax.

Individual Income Tax

Seven states have no individual income tax. Two other states tax only dividend and interest income. Some local governments tax income, but the number that do is far smaller than the number that tax sales.

History

In the colonial period, several colonies levied "faculty" taxes. These taxes were based on the estimated earning ability of tradespeople and others who had skills that represented income-earning ability not related to ownership of property. In the nineteenth century, several states had locally administered income taxes on the books, but they were poorly administered and fell out of practice.

Hawaii adopted an income tax in 1901. In 1911, Wisconsin adopted and successfully administered a state income tax, and by the end of the decade, eight other states had followed. The modern *federal* income tax was adopted after the approval of the Sixteenth Amendment in 1913. Six states adopted a comprehensive individual income tax in the 1920s, and sixteen in the 1930s. Eleven states have adopted the tax since 1940. Only one state, Alaska, has repealed the tax after adopting it.

The Individual Income Tax Base

With the exception of the seven states with no income tax and the two states that tax only investment income, the state income tax is applied comprehensively to wages, salaries, and most other sources of income. (Local income taxes, where they exist, usually have a much narrower base.) All but four states conform their taxes to key federal income tax concepts. (See Federation of Tax Administrators, "State Personal Income Taxes: Federal Starting Points," www.taxadmin.org/fta/rate/inc_stp.html [accessed January 17, 2008].)

In 26 states, the calculation of the taxable base starts with federal adjusted gross income (AGI). This amount is adjusted in various ways as required by constitutional law or state policy. For example, the Federal Government does not tax interest from state and local government bonds, and the states cannot tax interest from federal bonds. Income earned from work or property in another state may or may not be subject to state tax. Some states differ from the Federal Government in the extent to which they tax pension or Social Security benefits. Other states depart from the federal list of deductible expenditures. A few states do not allow itemized deductions at all and have only a standard deduction. Some states conform to federal income definitions of a year or two earlier—either for administrative timing reasons or to avoid the revenue impact of recent federal changes. Eight states avoid specifying exclusions, deductions, or personal exemptions and simplify things by starting with federal taxable income. State taxable income is specified as income minus deductions minus personal exemptions. Two states, Rhode Island and Vermont, reduce their role even further by simply specifying the state tax as a percentage of the federal tax.

Unlike the sales tax (in most cases), state and local income tax payments (as well as property taxes) are deductible for federal income tax purposes for taxpayers who itemize. Itemization is most likely for high-income taxpayers, homeowners (because of the deduction for mortgage interest), and residents of high state and local income and property tax states. Therefore, some of the burden is shifted to the federal treasury. Note that the issue of deductibility has become somewhat more problematic since, beginning with tax year 2004, taxpayers are permitted to choose between deducting state and local sales tax or state and local income tax payments. This is expected to be of limited applicability, as the change was intended mostly to level the playing field between states that have income taxes and those that do not but rely on sales tax. In general, in states with state and local income taxes, the total of these taxes paid by most taxpayers will exceed the amount deductible under the sales tax option.

State Individual Income Tax Rates

Table 4-8 shows the major elements of each state's individual income tax rate structure. The table indicates seven states have no income tax, two states have a tax on interest and dividends only, and two states tax a percentage of the federal tax. All other states have some combination of personal exemptions, standard deductions, or credits that create a "zero tax bracket"—an exempt amount of income that shields low-income individuals or families from the state income tax. In Connecticut, for example, a single individual starts paying taxes when his or her taxable income exceeds the personal exemption amount of $12,750. (In states with a standard deduction, not shown in the table, or a personal credit, the calculation is different, but still results in an effective "zero tax bracket.") Most states have a progressive rate-bracket structure on top of the tax-exempt amounts of income—low rates on low incomes, higher rates on higher incomes. Continuing the previous example, a single individual in Connecticut pays a 3.0 percent tax rate on the next $10,000 of income and a 5.0 percent tax rate on

Chapter 4 ■ The Role of Property Tax in Intergovernmental Finance

income greater than $22,750. Connecticut has just two tax brackets. Six states have a flat tax with a single rate bracket. The other states have from three to as many as ten tax brackets.

As shown by the tax-exempt amounts and the rate brackets in Table 4-8, there is a great deal of variation across states in the degree of progressivity in the individual income tax. One final feature of state tax law has the effect of reducing the degree

TABLE 4-8. Tax Year 2007 State Individual Income Tax Rates as of Jan. 1, 2007

State	Tax Rates		# of Brackets	Income Brackets		Personal Exemption			Federal Tax Deductible
	Low	High		Low	High	Single	Married	Child	
Alabama	2.0	5.0	3	500	3,000	1,500	3,000	300	X
Alaska				No State Income Tax					
Arizona	2.59	4.57	5	10,000	150,000	2,100	4,200	2,300	
Arkansas	1.0	7.0	6	3,599	30,100	22	44	22	
California	1.0	9.3	6	6,622	43,468	91	182	285	
Colorado	4.63		1	Flat Rate		None			
Connecticut	3.0	5.0	2	10,000	10,000	12,750	24,500	0	
Delaware	2.2	5.95	6	5,000	60,000	110	220	110	
Florida				No State Income Tax					
Georgia	1.0	6.0	6	750	7,000	2,700	5,400	3,000	
Hawaii	1.4	8.25	9	2,400	48,000	1,040	2,080	1,040	
Idaho	1.6	7.8	8	1,198	23,964	3,400	6,800	3,400	
Illinois	3.0		1	Flat Rate		2,000	4,000	2,000	
Indiana	3.4		1	Flat Rate		1,000	2,000	1,000	
Iowa	0.36	8.98	9	1,343	60,436	40	80	40	X
Kansas	3.5	6.45	3	15,000	30,000	2,250	4,500	2,250	
Kentucky	2.0	6.0	6	3,000	75,000	20	40	20	
Louisiana	2.0	6.0	3	12,500	25,000	4,500	9,000	1,000	X
Maine	2.0	8.5	4	4,550	18,250	2,850	5,700	2,850	
Maryland	2.0	4.75	4	1,000	3,000	2,400	4,800	2,400	
Massachusetts	5.3		1	Flat Rate		4,125	8,250	1,000	
Michigan	3.9		1	Flat Rate		3,300	6,600	3,300	
Minnesota	5.35	7.85	3	21,310	69,991	3,400	6,800	3,400	
Mississippi	3.0	5.0	3	5,000	10,000	6,000	12,000	1,500	
Missouri	1.5	6.0	10	1,000	9,000	2,100	4,200	1,200	
Montana	1.0	6.9	7	2,300	14,500	1,980	3,960	1,980	
Nebraska	2.56	6.84	4	2,400	27,001	106	212	106	
Nevada				No State Income Tax					

(table continued on next page)

TABLE 4-8. Tax Year 2007 State Individual Income Tax Rates as of Jan. 1, 2007 (continued)

State	Tax Rates		# of Brackets	Income Brackets		Personal Exemption			Federal Tax Deductible
	Low	High		Low	High	Single	Married	Child	
New Hampshire	State Income Tax is Limited to Dividends and Interest Income only.								
New Jersey	1.4	8.97	6	20,000	500,000	1,000	2,000	1,500	
New Mexico	1.7	5.3	4	5,500	16,000	3,400	6,800	3,400	
New York	4.0	6.85	5	8,000	20,000	0	0	1,000	
North Carolina	6.0	8.0	4	12,750	120,000	3,400	6,800	3,400	
North Dakota	2.1	5.54	5	30,650	336,550	3,400	6,800	3,400	
Ohio	0.649	6.555	9	5,000	200,000	1,400	2,800	1,400	
Oklahoma	0.5	5.65	7	1,000	10,000	1,000	2,000	1,000	
Oregon	5.0	9.0	3	2,750	6,851	159	318	159	
Pennsylvania	3.07		1	Flat Rate		None			
Rhode Island	25% Federal Tax Liability								
South Carolina	2.5	7.0	6	2,570	12,850	3,400	6,800	3,400	
Tennessee	State Income Tax is Limited to Dividends and Interest Income only.								
Texas	No State Income Tax								
Utah	2.3	6.98	6	1,000	5,501	2,550	5,100	2,550	
Vermont	3.6	9.5	5	30,650	336,551	3,400	6,800	3,400	
Virginia	2.0	5.75	4	3,000	17,000	900	1,800	900	
Washington	No State Income Tax								
West Virginia	3.0	6.5	5	10,000	60,000	2,000	4,000	2,000	
Wisconsin	4.6	6.75	4	9,160	137,411	700	1,400	700	
Wyoming	No State Income Tax								
Dist of Columbia	4.5	8.7	3	10,000	40,000	2,400	4,800	2,400	

Source: Federation of Tax Administrators, "State Individual Income Taxes," http://www.taxadmin.org/fta/rate/ind_inc.html (accessed January 19, 2008). Note: The source tables have extensive explanatory footnotes that are not repeated here.

of progressivity. Eight states have full or partial deductibility of federal tax payments from their state taxable income. Because the federal rate structure is progressive, this disproportionately reduces the effective tax burden on high-income taxpayers.

Individual Income Tax Administration

Income taxes are inherently more difficult to administer than sales taxes. However, the existence of the federal income tax simplifies state administration. The calculations and data required to complete the return can involve a number of different sources of income and require many difficult decisions. American income taxes are self-reported; that is, each taxpayer is responsible for filing a return and paying the tax.

Administrative agencies provide forms, instructions, and assistance. Agencies also check all returns for completeness and arithmetic consistency and target a fraction of returns for office audit and a smaller fraction for field audit.

Most state income tax administrators work closely with the federal Internal Revenue Service (IRS). Most state tax returns start with either adjusted gross income, taxable income, or amount of tax from the same taxpayer's federal tax return. The cost of record-keeping and compliance with federal tax law is enormous, but the extra cost of filling out a state tax return at the same time is much less. States also piggyback on federal withholding and reporting requirements imposed on employers and financial institutions.

Withholding is an important feature of the income tax. The perceived cost of the income tax is reduced by automatic withholding of smaller amounts from each paycheck. The annual accounting of the total amount of tax on one line of the return may be less noticeable than the amount of a check written at the same time for the balance due. Indeed, taxpayers with large refunds are more likely to be happy that they are getting something back than resentful at the size of the interest-free loan they, in effect, made to the state treasury.

Issues of Income Tax Policy

Income taxes are more closely related to ability to pay than sales or property taxes are. State income taxes introduce an element of progressivity into state and local tax systems that are otherwise regressive. Income taxes can raise a great deal of revenue relative to the administrative costs, and tax collections grow with a growing economy.

The administration of a state income tax is easier the more closely state tax law conforms with federal tax law; however, conformity with federal income tax concepts has a cost for the state. The federal tax is riddled with special treatments—exclusions, deductions, credits, deferrals—for many good and many bad reasons. (These are called *loopholes* if *someone else* gets them, and *important incentives* or *equitable adjustments* if *we* get them.) The cumulative effect of these numerous special treatments is to cause distortions, inefficiencies, horizontal inequities, vertical inequities, and either revenue losses for the government or higher tax rates on the income that is left to be taxed.

Federal conformity also makes a state's revenue vulnerable to political shifts that take place outside their jurisdiction—a change in the federal tax law changes state income tax collections or forces the states to bear the administrative cost of administering a different tax. In the past several presidential elections, especially in Republican primaries, there have been proposals for radical reform in federal income tax law. Some have proposed eliminating the federal income tax altogether and substituting some type of consumption tax. There have been proposals for various types of flat tax structures: taxation of business income at the source in a way that exempts the return to new saving, a broader tax base with fewer deductions, and a single-rate bracket above a low-income exempt amount.

Local individual income taxes are sometimes proposed as an alternative to local property taxes. They are, for the most part, not widely used. Although local individual income taxes are used by about 4,000 local governments in 11 states, from a national perspective such local income taxes constitute only 4.6 percent of local government tax revenue. Local sales taxes, on the other hand, constitute 11.2 percent of local government tax revenue, the lion's share of which is property tax (72.3 percent). Local income taxes can create competitiveness problems with surrounding areas that are often more serious than those associated with property tax. As a result, local income taxes are usually constrained to low rates and narrow bases, usually labor income only. Local income taxes have many of the same problems as property taxes in reinforcing resource disparities among jurisdictions.

Corporate Income Taxes

Forty-five states and the District of Columbia levy a corporate income tax. However, the imposition of corporate taxes at the state level is problematic. There is no doubt that businesses benefit from and impose costs on government. The problem is that costs and benefits are not limited to businesses organized as corporations, and there seems to be little correlation among costs, benefits, and profits earned. Indeed, it could be argued that an unprofitable business is more apt to impose certain costs on government than a profitable one.

All taxes nominally imposed on businesses are necessarily passed on to people in different economic roles—customers, suppliers, employees, and owners. A logical tax policy would tax all businesses, not just those organized as corporations, to pay the costs that businesses impose and would tax the owners and employees on the income derived from or taken out of the business.

Most tax experts do not believe there is a strong case for the separate taxation of corporations if measures are taken to ensure that all the profits of corporations are fully taxed under the individual income tax. A full integration of the corporate and individual tax would require every dollar of corporate profits to be allocated to shareholders, regardless of whether the profits are actually distributed in the form of dividends. Current federal tax law does not do this, so there is some justification for the separate corporate tax.

The corporate income tax remains an important source of federal and state revenue. Politically it is appealing because corporations are perceived as rich and able to bear taxes directly. Even if the economic impact of the tax is shifted to people in their roles as customers or employees, they are often unable to perceive such indirect burdens.

Most states rely to some extent on the federal tax law definition of taxable income. The second and third columns of Table 4-9 show the tax rates and brackets of the corporate income taxes in each state. Most states have a flat rate, but 13 states have a graduated rate structure. The flat rates or top rates range from 4.0 percent to 10 percent; the great majority fall in the 6.0–9.0 percent range. States have a wide variety of credits and exemptions for corporations that build new facilities or create jobs in the state. Several states have lowered corporate income tax rates in recent years. Texas is replacing its corporate income tax with a gross receipts tax beginning in 2007.

The allocation of the income of multistate corporations is a major policy concern. Most states use some combination of three factors—sales, property, and payroll—to allocate a share of national profits to one state. A corporation would calculate the in-state share of each of these factors: in-state sales divided by total sales (s/S); in-state property values divided by total property values (v/V); in-state payroll divided by total payroll (p/P). The traditional allocation was equal one-third weighting for each of the

TABLE 4-9. State Corporate Income Tax Rates and Apportionment Factors in 2007

State	Tax Rates (%)	Number of Brackets	Tax Brackets Lowest	Tax Brackets Highest	Apportionment Factor
Alabama	6.5	1	Flat Rate		3 Factor
Alaska	1.0–9.4	10	10,000	90,000	3 Factor
Arizona	6.968	1	Flat Rate		60% sales; 20% property and payroll
Arkansas	1.0–6.5	6	3,000	100,000	Double-weighted sales
California	8.84	1	Flat Rate		Double-weighted sales
Colorado	4.63	1	Flat Rate		3 Factor/Sales & Property
Connecticut	7.5	1	Flat Rate		Double-weighted sales/Sales
Delaware	8.7	1	Flat Rate		3 Factor
D. C.	9.975		Flat Rate		3 Factor
Florida	5.5	1	Flat Rate		Double-weighted sales
Georgia	6	1	Flat Rate		90% sales; 5% property and payroll
Hawaii	4.4–6.4	3	25,000	100,000	3 Factor
Idaho	7.6	1	Flat Rate		Double-weighted sales
Illinois	7.3	1	Flat Rate		Sales
Indiana	8.5	1	Flat Rate		60% sales; 20% property and payroll
Iowa	6.0–12.0	4	25,000	250,000	Sales
Kansas	4	1	Flat Rate		3 Factor
Kentucky	4.0–7.0	3	50,000	100,000	sales
Louisiana	4.0–8.0	5	25,000	200,000	Double-weighted sales
Maine	3.5–8.93	4	25,000	250,000	Double-weighted sales
Maryland	7	1	Flat Rate		Double-weighted sales/Sales
Massachusetts	9.5	1	Flat Rate		Double-weighted sales/Sales
Michigan	1.9% "Single Business (Value-Added) Tax"				92.5% Sales, 3.75% Property & Payroll
Minnesota	9.8	1	Flat Rate		78% Sales, 11% Property & Payroll
Mississippi	3.0–5.0	3	5,000	10,000	Accounting/3 Factor
Missouri	6.25	1	Flat Rate		3 Factor/sales
Montana	6.75	1	Flat Rate		3 Factor
Nebraska	5.58–7.81	2		50,000	Sales

(table continued on next page)

TABLE 4-9. State Corporate Income Tax Rates and Apportionment Factors in 2007 (continued)

State	Tax Rates (%)	Number of Brackets	Tax Brackets Lowest	Tax Brackets Highest	Apportionment Factor
Nevada	No State Corporate Income Tax				
New Hampshire	8.5	1	Flat Rate		Double-weighted Sales
New Jersey	9	1	Flat Rate		Double-weighted Sales
New Mexico	4.8-7.6	3	500,000	1 million	Double-weighted sales
New York	7.5	1	Flat Rate		80% sales; 10%property and payroll
North Carolina	6.9	1	Flat Rate		Double-weighted sales
North Dakota	2.6-7.0	6	3,000	30,000	3 Factor
Ohio	5.1-8.5	2		50,000	60% Sales, 20% Property & Payroll
Oklahoma	6	1	Flat Rate		3 Factor
Oregon	6.6	1	Flat Rate		Sales
Pennsylvania	9.99	1	Flat Rate		Triple-weighted sales
Rhode Island	9	1	Flat Rate		Double-weighted sales
South Carolina	5	1	Flat Rate		Double-weighted sales/Sales
South Dakota	No State Corporate Income Tax				
Tennessee	6	1	Flat Rate		Double-weighted sales
Texas	4.5		Flat Rate		Sales
Utah	5		Flat Rate		3 Factor/Double-weighted sales
Vermont	6.0-8.5	4	10,000	250,000	Double-weighted. sales
Virginia	6	1	Flat Rate		Double-weighted sales
Washington	No State Corporate Income Tax				
West Virginia	8.75	1	Flat Rate		Double-weighted sales
Wisconsin	7.9	1	Flat Rate		80% sales; 10% property and payroll
Wyoming	No State Corporate Income Tax				

Source: Federation of Tax Administrators, "Range of State Corporate Income Tax Rates," http://www.taxadmin.org/fta/rate/corp_inc.html; "State Apportionment of Corporate Income," http://www.taxadmin.org/fta/rate/corp_app.html (accessed January 17, 2008).

Note: The source tables have extensive explanatory footnotes that are not repeated here.

three factors. In recent years, intense lobbying by firms with high in-state shares of property or payroll has led to state apportionment formulas that rely much more heavily on sales. Most states now double-weight sales with weights of one-half for sales, one-fourth for property, and one-fourth for payroll. Four states have gone all the way to a sale-only allocation formula for assigning profits to a single state. The last column of Table 4-9 shows the apportionment factors for the corporate income tax in each state. Although Washington does not have a corporate income tax per se, its business and occupations (B&O) tax operates as a gross receipts tax and is paid by many of the same entities that would otherwise pay corporate income taxes.

Both federal and state corporate tax receipts are declining in importance relative to other tax sources. This is the result of a long-term decline in profits as a share of income as well as the increasing use of avoidance techniques by companies to shift their tax obligations to other states or nations with lower (or zero) tax rates.

The administrative problems of *local* government corporate income taxation are formidable, and with the exceptions of New York City and the District of Columbia, there are no such taxes.

Selective Sales Taxes

Unlike general sales taxes, which are levied on a broad range of sales, selective sales taxes or excise taxes are levied on the sale of specific items such as cigarettes, gasoline, or liquor. Sometimes selective sales taxes are grouped in subcategories based on the nature of the product being taxed or the relationship between the tax and government expenditures. Sumptuary taxes, colloquially referred to as sin taxes, are intended to discourage the sale of specific items, such as alcoholic beverages or tobacco products. Benefit-based taxes are levied on certain items and earmarked for a related expenditure category. For example, gasoline taxes are often dedicated to state highway funds or local road maintenance funds. Privilege taxes include taxes levied on businesses and occupations for the privilege of engaging in the business. Some selective sales taxes are mere revenue sources and do not fit neatly under any of these subheadings. Some selective sales taxes could be placed under multiple headings. For example, public utility taxes could be considered both a benefit tax compensating for the uses of city streets and rights-of-way and as a business privilege tax.

Sumptuary Taxes

Sumptuary taxes have a long and controversial history. Today taxes on liquor and tobacco are fixtures in the tax structure of U.S. state and local governments. Although these taxes are often characterized as taxes designed to discourage behavior associated with social costs, that is too narrow a view. There are two other reasons why taxing these items is politically attractive. First, the purchase of cigarettes or alcohol is very inelastic to changes in price. Thus increasing the price of, say, cigarettes by imposing a higher tax does not alter the quantity purchased very much and does not have an adverse impact on the tax base. Second, taxing a behavior that is socially discouraged diminishes the political impact of those who protest higher tax rates.

Taxes on Alcoholic Beverages

A few states, such as Iowa, still operate state liquor stores, with a monopoly on the sales of distilled spirits. (Recall that the receipts of state liquor stores are *excluded* from general revenue as measured by the U.S. Bureau of the Census.) In other states, such as Nebraska, liquor is sold in privately run stores and subject to excise taxes. An excise tax on liquor sales in Nebraska and a markup of liquor prices in state-run stores in Iowa could be similar in magnitude and economic impact, but they are not reported in the same place in official cross-state comparisons.

States differ in how they tax alcoholic beverages. Often there are different laws dealing with distilled spirits, wine, and beer or other malt beverages. In addition, there are special license fees or privilege taxes on establishments serving or selling liquor. Alcohol taxes are usually *unit* taxes based on the volume or alcohol content of the beverage, not on the price. Because the physical volume consumed does not grow along with incomes or prices, liquor tax collections often decline over time relative to other sources of revenue.

Two factors contribute to alcohol taxes being regressive in burden:

- Low-income people happen to spend a larger fraction of their income on alcoholic beverages.
- Low-income people do buy lower priced products, but the unit or per-bottle tax is a larger fraction of the price of those goods.

The demand for alcoholic beverages is relatively inelastic to changes in price, so the tax does not achieve its sumptuary purpose of reducing consumption. Instead, it provides revenue to pay some of the costs imposed on the government or society by those who overindulge. The border effect problem is also important. Because liquor is light in weight in relation to its value, shopping across the border by consumers or importation by smugglers is a common problem for states with a high tax rate.

Tobacco Taxes

Many of the same issues are involved in the taxation of cigarettes and other tobacco products. Cigarettes are commonly taxed at a fixed rate per pack. Table 4-10 shows that state rates range from a low of 7.5 cents per pack in South Carolina to a high of $2.575 per pack in New Jersey. Six states allow municipal or county governments to levy additional tax; this ranges from 1 cent per pack in Alabama and Tennessee to a whopping $1.50 per pack in New York City. Notwithstanding the extreme regressivity of cigarette taxes, they have proven to be very popular with state legislatures struggling with revenue shortfalls in recent years. In 2002 after income tax and general sales tax collections declined sharply, 18 states and New York City increased their cigarette tax rates.

Other tobacco products, such as cigars, smoking tobacco, and chewing tobacco, are often taxed under separate statutes, sometimes on their wholesale or retail price. In general, these products are a minor source of revenue.

Gambling Taxes and Other Gaming Revenues

Gambling is a growing source of revenue in many states. Some revenue is derived from taxes and fees levied on private gambling enterprises such as casinos and tracks, while

TABLE 4-10. State Excise Tax Rates on Cigarettes as of January 1, 2007

State	Tax Rate (cents per pack)	Rank	State	Tax Rate (cents per pack)	Rank
Alabama[a]	42.5	40	Nebraska	64	31
Alaska[c]	180	7	Nevada	80	26
Arizona	200	4	New Hampshire	80	26
Arkansas	59	33	New Jersey	257.5	1
California	87	24	New Mexico	91	23
Colorado	84	25	New York[a]	150	13
Connecticut	151	11	North Carolina	35	44
Delaware	55	36	North Dakota	44	39
Florida	33.9	45	Ohio	125	16
Georgia	37	41	Oklahoma	103	19
Hawaii[c]	160	10	Oregon	118	18
Idaho	57	34	Pennsylvania	135	15
Illinois[a]	98	22	Rhode Island	246	2
Indiana	55.5	35	South Carolina	7	51
Iowa	36	42	South Dakota	53	38
Kansas	79	28	Tennessee[a,b]	20	48
Kentucky[b]	30	46	Texas	141	14
Louisiana	36	42	Utah	69.5	30
Maine	200	4	Vermont	179	8
Maryland	100	20	Virginia[a]	30	46
Massachusetts	151	11	Washington	202.5	3
Michigan	200	4	West Virginia	55	36
Minnesota[d]	123	17	Wisconsin	77	29
Mississippi	18	49	Wyoming	60	32
Missouri[a]	17	50	Dist. of Columbia	100	20
Montana	170	9	U. S. Median	80.0	

Source: Federation of Tax Administrators, "State Excise Tax Rates on Cigarettes," www.taxadmin.org/fta/rate/cigarett.html from various sources (accessed January 17, 2008).

[a] Counties and cities may impose an additional tax on a pack of cigarettes in Alabama, 1¢ to 6¢; Illinois, 10¢ to 15¢; Missouri, 4¢ to 7¢; New York City, $1.50; Tennessee, 1¢; and Virginia, 2¢ to 15¢.

[b] Dealers pay an additional enforcement and administrative fee of 0.1¢ per pack in Kentucky and 0.05¢ in Tennessee.

[c] Tax rate is scheduled to increase to $2.00 per pack on July 1, 2007 in Arkansas and to $2.00 on September 30, 2007 in Hawaii.

[d] An additional 25.5 cent sales tax is added to the wholesale price of a tax stamp (total $1.485).

other revenue comes from state-run activities such as lotteries. Gambling revenues vary widely from state to state, and the activity is spreading to more states. There are issues relating to American Indian-owned casinos that are part of a broader set of questions about the taxation by states of American Indian enterprises.

Benefit-Based Excise Taxes

Benefit-based excise taxes tie very closely and obviously with the item being taxed and are used to provide a service related to that item.

Motor Fuel Taxes

The leading example of benefit-based selective sales taxes is the tax on motor fuel. Along with vehicle license taxes, motor fuel taxes have long been a major source of funds for building and maintaining highways in the United States. The taxes collected are earmarked to a specific public expenditure (roads) that will benefit the subset of citizens (drivers) who pay the tax. Thus the tax is like an indirect price paid for the use of particular government services—less direct than charges for the use of toll roads but still highly correlated.

Motor fuel taxes are usually levied on a per-gallon basis. Table 4-11 shows the range of gasoline fuel excise tax rates in 50 states and the District of Columbia, as well as the extra tax levied by the Federal Government. Basic gasoline excise taxes that are earmarked to the state highway fund range from a low of 4 cents per gallon in Florida to a high of 34 cents per gallon in Washington, with a median of 20 cents per gallon. About half the states levy additional taxes earmarked to other purposes such as vehicle inspections or environmental cleanup. When these are added in, combined gasoline tax rates range from a low of 8 cents per gallon in Alaska to a high of 34 cents per gallon in Washington, with a median of 21 cents per gallon. Table 4-11 indicates ten states in which motor fuel is also subject to all or a part (in the case of Delaware) of the general sales tax.

Taxes for diesel fuel are similar to those for gasoline, but in some states diesel fuel is taxed at a higher rate than gasoline to allow for the higher mileage obtained from this fuel. Motor fuel taxes are collected from the fuel wholesaler or distributor and passed on by the retailer. Some states have lower rates for gasohol or ethanol blends. There are usually exemptions or refunds for fuel used for nonhighway purposes such as agriculture.

Often the state gasoline tax is shared with local government. Typically statutory formulas based on factors such as miles of road and population are used to distribute a portion of the state tax to local governments for use in highway construction and maintenance. Local governments in a number of states also can levy additional gasoline taxes.

Because the motor fuel tax is usually levied on a per-gallon basis, it is inelastic to changes in prices or an increase in state incomes. Frequent rate increases may be necessary to maintain the tax relative to other sources of revenue, but because the proceeds of the fuel tax are earmarked, debate about tax rates often is linked to highway policy rather than general budgetary concerns. A few states have formulas linking tax rate changes to average fuel prices or to some measure of the need for highway construction and maintenance.

TABLE 4-11. Motor Fuel Excise Tax Rates as of January 1, 2007

State	Gasoline			Notes
	Excise Tax	Additional Tax	Total Tax	
Alabama	16.0	2.0	18.0	Inspection fee
Alaska	8.0		8.0	
Arizona	18.0		18.0	
Arkansas	21.5		21.5	
California	18.0		18.0	Sales tax applicable
Colorado	22.0		22.0	
Connecticut	25.0		25.0	
Delaware	23.0		23.0	Plus 0.5% GRT
Florida	4.0	11.3	15.3	Sales tax added to excise
Georgia	7.5	7.7	15.2	Sales tax added to excise
Hawaii	16.0		16.0	Sales tax applicable
Idaho	25.0		25.0	
Illinois	19.0	1.1	20.1	Sales tax add., environmental and Leaking underground storage tank (LUST) fee
Indiana	18.0		18.0	Sales tax applicable
Iowa	21.0		21.0	
Kansas	24.0		24.0	
Kentucky	18.3	1.4	19.7	Environmental fee
Louisiana	20.0		20.0	
Maine	26.8		26.8	
Maryland	23.5		23.5	
Massachusetts	21.0		21.0	
Michigan	19.0		19.0	Sales tax applicable
Minnesota	20.0		20.0	
Mississippi	18.0	0.4	18.4	Environmental fee
Missouri	17.0	0.55	17.55	Inspection fee
Montana	27.0		27.0	
Nebraska	27.1	0.9	28.0	Petroleum fee
Nevada	24.0	0.805	24.805	Inspection and cleanup fee
New Hampshire	18.0	1.625	19.625	Oil discharge cleanup fee
New Jersey	10.5	4.0	14.50	Petroleum fee
New Mexico	17.0	1.875	18.875	Petroleum loading fee
New York	8.0	16.6	24.6	Sales tax applicable, petroleum tax
North Carolina	29.9	0.25	30.15	Inspection tax
North Dakota	23.0		23.0	
Ohio	28.0		28.0	Plus 3 cents commercial
Oklahoma	16.0	1.0	17.0	Environmental fee
Oregon	24.0		24.0	

(table continued on next page)

TABLE 4-11. Motor Fuel Excise Tax Rates as of January 1, 2007 (continued)

State	Gasoline			Notes
	Excise Tax	Additional Tax	Total Tax	
Pennsylvania	12.0	19.2	31.2	Oil franchise tax
Rhode Island	30.0	1	31.0	LUST tax
South Carolina	16.0		16.0	
South Dakota	22.0		22.0	
Tennessee	20.0	1.4	21.4	Petroleum tax and environmnetal fee
Texas	20.0		20.0	
Utah	24.5		24.5	
Vermont	19.0	1.0	20.0	Petroleum cleanup fee
Virginia	17.5		17.5	
Washington	34.0		34.0	0.5% privilege tax
West Virginia	20.5	11.0	31.5	Sales tax added to excise
Wisconsin	29.9	3.0	32.9	Petroleum inspection fee
Wyoming	13.0	1	14.0	License tax
District of Columbia	20.0		20.0	
Federal	18.3	0.1	18.4	LUST tax

Source: Federation of Tax Administrators, "Motor Fuel Excise Tax Rates," www.taxadmin.org/fta/rate/motor_fl.html (accessed January 17, 2008).

Note: The tax rates listed are fuel excise taxes collected by distributors/suppliers/retailers in each state. Additional taxes may apply to motor carriers. Carrier taxes are coordinated by the International Fuel Tax Association. The source tables have extensive explanatory footnotes that are not repeated here. See original for extensive notes and additional columns for diesel fuel and gasohol. "Additional" taxes are mostly for "environmental" or "inspections" purposes. Not shown here are local government tax rates or special rates for gasoline blended with ethanol.

The border problem can be important, especially when motorists have easy access to filling stations in neighboring states. In the case of interstate trucks, states have combated this problem by prorating taxes on a mileage basis regardless of where the fuel was purchased. This requires a separate administrative system that can be combined with other highway transportation regulations.

In addition to the selective excise on motor fuels, some states, as shown in the last column of Table 4-11, also levy the normal sales tax on purchases. The rationale for this is that the motor fuel tax is a benefit tax for roads, and the sales tax is a general ability-to-pay tax on consumption.

Other Benefit Taxes

In recent decades, there has been an increase in the use of selective taxes on hotel and motel rooms and restaurant meals with the proceeds earmarked for improving and promoting tourist facilities. This is an area of some controversy, especially when the funds have been used to provide subsidies to sports stadiums, thus enriching team owners and millionaire athletes.

Other examples of benefit taxes are taxes on phone service to support 911 emergency phone systems and taxes on the sale of agricultural products earmarked to promote those products.

Privilege Taxes

There are a large number of privilege taxes. Corporate franchise taxes are levied against corporations for the privilege of doing business in the corporate form. Many taxes levied against businesses are justified as privilege taxes. Not all of these taxes are excise taxes. Many are levied at flat rates. Some are based on profits, the number of employees, space occupied, or the amount of capital employed. The taxes do not usually account for a significant portion of overall state and local government revenue, but in some regions of the country, they are an important source of local government revenue.

Utility franchise taxes are levied by many local governments, especially municipalities. Often they are levied as part of an agreement in which the municipality grants the utility company the exclusive right to use the streets and other rights-of-way to install and maintain lines or pipes. Usually the tax is levied as a percentage of the receipts from the sale of the utility's services within the city.

User Fees and Charges

State and local governments receive own-source revenue from many sources other than the taxes discussed above. Many of these are not taxes.

Revenue is received from many municipal enterprises such as airports, hospitals, golf courses, or trash collection; states charge tuition for public universities, as do counties or other local governments for junior colleges. Many of these services could have been provided by the private sector, but for some reason local and state governments have chosen to provide them. User fees that pay all or part of the cost of these services reduce wasteful use by the public, give government an indication of the level of public demand, and are equitably linked to the benefit received.

User fees can be a way for state and local governments to tap additional resources when political or economic factors limit their tax options. In general, user fees escape much of the scrutiny that taxes undergo in regard to fairness issues such as progressivity. In a sense, it is a way to move the debate from tax issues to one of prices. Seldom is there a concern with the regressivity or progressivity of goods in the private sector that are allocated by price.

Special assessments are often levied against property that adjoins public facilities such as streets, sewers, or sidewalks. The assessments are usually based on the value added to the property by the improvement. Assessments are often administered with the property tax and may be mistakenly called taxes. Impact fees are similar, but are levied over a wider area such as entire new subdivision.

Governments, especially local governments, receive miscellaneous income in the form of interest on funds held, rent from property owned, and revenue from gifts and donations.

Intergovernmental Revenue

In federal systems, governments share revenue in various ways. This section examines several such systems, including intergovernmental grants, PILOTs, and indirect aid through the tax code.

Intergovernmental Grants

Federal grants-in-aid are an important source of financing for state and local governments. State grants (and federal grants passed through the states) are an important source of financing for local governments. On average, almost 40 percent of local government revenue is derived from either federal or state grants, but this varies considerably by state depending upon which functions are provided by the state and whether local governments have the option to levy income or sales taxes. Intergovernmental grants come in several types.

Categorical Grants
Categorical grants are grants given for a specific purpose. State grants to local school districts for transportation or vocational education are examples.

Block Grants
Block grants are grants given for a certain category of expenditure. Not as restrictive as categorical grants, they have broader goals, more discretion, and fewer administrative requirements. However, block grants are not as flexible as general revenue sharing (see below). The Temporary Assistance to Needy Families (TANF) grants from the Federal Government to the states are an example of block grants.

General Revenue Sharing
General revenue sharing is the most flexible form of aid from the recipient's point of view. Revenue-sharing money can typically be used for a wide range of purposes. The federal General Revenue Sharing program was repealed, leaving block grants as the most flexible form of aid from the Federal Government to state and local governments.

Matching versus Lump-Sum Grants
Another important distinction among the various grant programs is whether they are matching grants or lump-sum grants (this further distinction can apply to either categorical or block grants). Matching grants pay a certain fraction of the expenditure

of the recipient government. State school building aid might contribute 40 percent of the cost of school district building projects, for example. This stipulation effectively changes the price of building a school, making it 40 percent less expensive than it would otherwise be. Lump-sum grants have no such price effects. A lump-sum school building aid program, for example, might allocate $10 million for each school district engaging in a program of school construction. No cost sharing is involved.

Open-Ended versus Close-Ended Grants

Matching grants can be either open-ended or close-ended. With an open-ended state grant of 40 percent for school construction, for example, the state pays the school district for 40 percent of any construction, no matter how great. A close-ended grant places a cap on the total amount of the grant. In this example, a close-ended grant might stipulate that the state pays for 40 percent of school construction up to a maximum of $20 million for any school district.

School Aid Grants

In turn, there are several common formulas for general school aid grants from state to local governments. Although not typically labeled as such, these grants could be considered a form of block grant.

Foundation Grants

Foundation grants are the most common type of general state aid for education, and the type most recommended if the goal is to provide an adequate education for all children. Foundation grants are so named because they set the same foundation level of spending per pupil for all districts to guarantee a basic level of education. State aid per pupil is the difference between the foundation amount of spending and a local contribution. The local contribution is often equal to some common statewide tax rate times the district's property tax base. Since the local contribution is inversely related to a district's property tax base, higher state aid is provided to districts with lower fiscal capacity, and lower state aid is provided to districts with higher fiscal capacity.

There are a number of variations on the basic form of foundation grant. Foundation levels can be modified to take into account differences in wage costs among districts or differences in education costs. In addition, sometimes the common tax rate included in the local contribution is mandated, and sometimes the common tax rate is only suggested. Finally, the local contribution can depend on community income in addition to the property tax base.

Guaranteed Tax Base Grants

A second type of aid formula, more popular in the 1970s and 1980s, is the guaranteed tax base (GTB) grant. Under this type of grant, the state matches local education spending at a rate that varies inversely with the district's fiscal capacity. GTB grants are best suited to achieving a form of taxpayer equity to make per-pupil spending in a district dependent only on the tax rate a district is willing to levy, not on the district's tax base. GTB grants are not as well suited as foundation grants to guaranteeing an adequate education for all children.

Flat Grants

Flat grants provide a certain level of state support per pupil or per some other unit of need. Fewer states use flat grants than either GTB or foundation grants. Hawaii does not rely on general state aid for education, but uses full state funding. Table 4-12 shows the number of states that use each type of school aid formula.

TABLE 4-12. Formulas for State Aid to Education in 2003

Type of Formula	Number of States
Foundation	30
Guaranteed tax base (GTB)	3
Foundation plus GTB	10
Flat grant	3
Other grant combinations	3
Full state funding	1

Sources: Yinger 2004, 337; State of Washington Web site.

PILOT (Payments in Lieu of Taxes)

The term PILOT (or PILT) refers broadly to a payment made to a state or local government in place of a property tax that would otherwise be assessed on tax-exempt property. A closely related term, services in lieu of taxes (SILOT), refers to in-kind services provided to a government in place of taxes on a tax-exempt property. These payments reflect only a portion of the money that would be collected at the full tax rate.

Federal PILOT/PILT Policy

The United States and Canada have PILOT/PILT programs in which the Federal Government makes payments to state governments for nontaxed land owned by the Federal Government. The U.S. law governing these PILOTs/PILTs was first passed in 1976. These payments are dispersed annually by the U.S. Department of Interior according to the formula set out in the law based on the amount of land, population, and other factors. Canada administers a parallel program through Public Works and Government Services Canada under its Payments in Lieu of Taxes Act.

State Policies

Just as the Federal Government makes payments in lieu of taxes to states, some states make payments in lieu of taxes to local governments where state-owned property is tax-exempt. New Hampshire gives municipalities authority to negotiate "voluntary payment in lieu of taxes from otherwise fully or partially tax exempt properties."

Massachusetts makes payments to towns in its watershed region, as well as for park and conservation land. The state also makes payments to towns with private land under current use for intervals of at least ten years. The State of Connecticut has a unique policy of making annual payments to local governments to offset loss in taxes from private colleges, general hospitals, and freestanding chronic disease hospitals that are tax-exempt. State law sets the current reimbursement rate at 77 percent of the property tax assessment on the property if it were not exempt.

Indirect Aid through the Tax Code

The Federal Government provides aid to state and local governments through the federal tax code in two important ways: the exemption of interest on state and local bonds from taxation, and federal deductibility of state and local taxes. Interest exemption is valuable because state and local governments can issue debt at lower interest rates than otherwise necessary. Investors find tax-exempt bonds attractive as long as the rate of return to tax-exempt bonds is no lower than the after-tax rate of return of taxable bonds.

In addition, individuals can deduct individual income, real estate and personal property taxes if they itemize deductions on their federal income tax returns. Beginning in 2004, individuals can deduct general sales taxes paid instead of income taxes if they so choose. The benefit from tax deductibility increases with the individual's marginal tax bracket. A person in the 15 percent tax bracket can receive $150 in federal tax savings for every extra $1,000 in state and local taxes deducted ($1,000 × 0.15); a person in the 31 percent tax bracket receives $310 for every extra $1,000. Federal tax deductibility makes either state or local property or income taxation more palatable than selective sales taxation or fees since neither is a deductible item. Tax deductibility directly benefits the individual receiving the tax deduction, but it indirectly benefits the state or local government by making it somewhat easier to raise taxes or increase spending. The benefits of tax deductibility are reduced for those taxpayers subject to the alternative minimum tax.

Other Intergovernmental Fiscal Issues

In addition to intergovernmental revenue sharing-mechanisms, governments affect each other financially through mandates and legal requirements.

Mandates

Mandates are federal regulations that impose costs on state and local governments. There are several types of mandates, but a few of the most important are as follows:

- *Direct orders* to implement some federal standard, such as the federal laws on special education that require the state to provide a free and appropriate education to all handicapped children, including an individualized education plan for each child. These orders have a direct impact on the budgets of school districts and also on the budgets of states because states typically pay for a portion of school district costs.

- *Cross-cutting requirements* attached to certain federally funded programs such as the National Environmental Policy Act requirement to submit environmental impact statements for certain projects.
- *Crossover sanctions* that impose penalties in one area to obtain compliance in another, such as the requirement to comply with the 21-year-old drinking age requirement or risk losing some portion of a state's highway funds.

The increasing burden of mandates has become very controversial in recent years. Mandates introduce inefficiencies in the system of government because the Federal Government can obtain credit for solving a problem at the same time that it shifts costs to state and local governments. The cumulative burden of mandates also can threaten the financial health of less-well-off state and local governments.

Rules of the Game

A final category of mechanisms that affect state and local finances is constitutional provisions, laws, and regulations of the Federal Government or state governments.

Note that there is a wide range of state policies that restrict local property taxation. They come in the following forms (and are discussed in more detail in Chapter 6):

- *Truth-in-taxation provisions.* Truth-in-taxation provisions require advertisements and public hearings on proposed rate increases.
- *Limitations on assessment increases.* These force increases in statutory rates in order to increase revenues.
- *General revenue limits.* These set the maximum revenue that can be raised from all sources by a jurisdiction.
- *Property tax levy limits.* These set the maximum revenue that can be raised from the property tax by a jurisdiction.
- *Specific property tax rate limits.* These set a maximum rate that can be applied against the assessed value of property by one type of government or for one type of service.
- *Overall property tax rate limit.* These set a maximum rate that can be applied against the assessed value of property, taking into account all local governments.

Probably the most well-known state limitation on local property taxation is Proposition 13, enacted in 1978 in California. This property tax limitation is particularly complicated. Property taxation is limited to 1 percent of assessed value, and assessments can rise by no more than 2 percent per year, unless the house is sold, at which time it can be reassessed at market value. According to Fischel (2001), these stringent restrictions on taxation have turned California's local property taxes into de facto state taxes.

At least one scholar has argued that state limitations on property taxes may have gone too far:

> ...state governments and voters have imposed so many restrictions on local access to the tax that it has become crippled beyond recognition. In many states a combination of property tax limitation measures, homestead and elderly exemptions and credits, and classification of property—among other restrictions—has hampered the ability of local governments to finance their expenditures with property tax revenues. (McGuire 2001)

States also affect local taxing powers in a significant way by allowing or disallowing local general sales and income taxes. General sales taxes are more frequently allowed than are income taxes. Sometimes a specific sales tax base is required, and often restrictions are placed on permissible rates. Pennsylvania is the state where the majority of local governments levying income taxes are located; cities, boroughs, townships, and school districts are allowed to levy income taxes on wages and compensation.

Problems and Challenges

Tax policy makers face many challenges in trying to craft workable, acceptable systems through which to fund government. Although some of these challenges are of a legal or technical nature, many are becoming more pronounced as a result of the global economy and increased global mobility. This section explores challenges faced by policy makers when they decide on a tax structure. Four current issues of major concern are reviewed: tax competition, taxation of the service sector of the economy, taxation of remote sales and business activity, and school equalization.

Tax Competition and Jurisdictional Issues

Competition among states for economic development presents a number of problems for tax policy. Businesses seeking to build new facilities or to expand compare the tax structures of different locations and often seek incentives to locate in one place versus another. Granting such preferences creates inequities with other businesses in the same locale. Competition with other states or cities might constrain tax policy makers from making changes that might be desirable for other reasons, such as increasing revenue or reducing regressivity.

Politicians in many states and localities face the dilemma that the sales tax and selective excise taxes on items such as cigarettes are often more popular sources for additional revenue as compared with increases in income taxes or property taxes. Politicians, however, are constrained in the use of these taxes because increases can create tax-induced border differentials for retailers. The smaller the jurisdiction, the more important these considerations become.

Growing Importance of the Service Sector of the Economy

The increasing consumption of services, as opposed to goods, has already been noted for its negative impact on the sales tax base over time. Few states have responded with a meaningful increase in the coverage of services. This trend also affects state corporate tax collections because many service providers are organized as partnerships or sole proprietorships, rather than corporations. Also, the trend to increase the sales factor in state income apportionment formulas can have a differential impact on goods-producing and service-producing corporations.

Unlike many complex tax issues, this is a problem for which a solution is relatively easily attainable given the political will. The extension of the sales tax to services presents few conceptual or administrative problems. However, there are powerful political forces associated with service providers opposing such changes. One approach is to extend the sales tax to consumer services while lowering the overall tax rate. The change will be revenue neutral in the short run, but will increase the elasticity of the sales tax in the long run.

Growing Importance of Remote Sales and Multistate Businesses

The negative impact on sales tax revenues of the increase in sales by remote vendors has already been noted. Federal policies have contributed to the problem. An important U.S. Supreme Court case, *National Bellas Hess v. Illinois State Department of Revenue* (1967), defined nexus (what constitutes sufficient presence in a state to require a vendor to collect a tax) quite narrowly. Recent attempts by state interests to get federal laws to redress this, especially in response to the growing problems with Internet sales, have been unsuccessful.

The trend toward remote sales is associated with the increasingly national and international scope of business activity in general. This larger trend has exacerbated the problem of allocating the income of multistate or multinational corporations among states. The broader the scope of a corporation, the more opportunities it has to game the system and allocate a larger share of its income to no-tax or low-tax states.

Unfortunately, this is a problem that cannot be solved by state and local governments alone. As noted above, states can contribute to the solution by simplifying the structure and administration of their sales tax systems. However, federal action is required to deal fully with the problems.

Equalization Issues

Equalization refers to a process by which governments attempt to create a level playing field regarding some aspect of taxation or governmental finance. Chapter 7, "Components of Model Property Tax Administrative Systems," discusses more fully the equalization of assessed values used as an underpinning for property taxation. This type of equalization is designed to prevent inequitable distribution of the property tax burden due to over- or under-assessment of different types of property or different geographic areas in comparison to a statutory or otherwise established standard. Alternatively, equalization can be related to the availability of multiple funding sources and the need to provide a uniform basic level of service. Two common uses of equalization in the United States are school funding and revenue sharing.

School Funding and Equalization

In the United States, school funding comprises a mixture of mostly state and local revenue sources. Figure 4-6 demonstrates the proportion of revenue derived from various sources for school funding for fiscal year 2005.

The proportion of revenue derived from each level of government can be further analyzed by state, as shown in Table 4-13.

Although there is considerable variance between states, local revenue sources are significant in every state except Hawaii and Vermont. Of locally generated revenue, 65 percent is raised from property taxes.

Uniformity versus Wealth

A goal of state financing for public education in many states has been to provide a uniform base amount of per-pupil funding for each school district. State grants to schools constitute a major funding source. However, because many school systems rely heavily on local property, often with uniform rates (or millage) for school property tax purposes, this increases the difficulty in providing uniform base funding amounts since in each state there are property-rich and property-poor districts. Such richness is different and distinct from income-based wealth.

Nevertheless, school districts with high taxable property value per pupil have the potential to raise more revenue from a given tax rate than districts with a low taxable property value per pupil. Where uniform property tax rates are used, such wealth differences can translate into disparities in funding available for education in each school district. States have dealt with this problem in different ways. In Idaho, for example, until 2006 when the state eliminated most local property tax funding of basic levels of education, there were two types of equalization used. First, a nominally uniform property tax levy rate was adjusted upwards when assessments were lower than the statutorily required level of assessment (see Chapter 7 for examples of indirect equalization of this type). This prevented districts from applying an otherwise uniform rate that would have raised too little property tax because of low assessments rather than less underlying property wealth. Second, after adjusting for assessment practices, the state paid more to school districts that had less property-related wealth (i.e., assessed value) and less to school districts that were "richer" in terms of assessed property value per pupil. The goal was to couple state and local revenue resources to provide uniform base amounts per pupil regardless of ability to raise property tax.

FIGURE 4-6. Percentage Distribution of Total Public Elementary-Secondary School System Revenue in 2004–2005

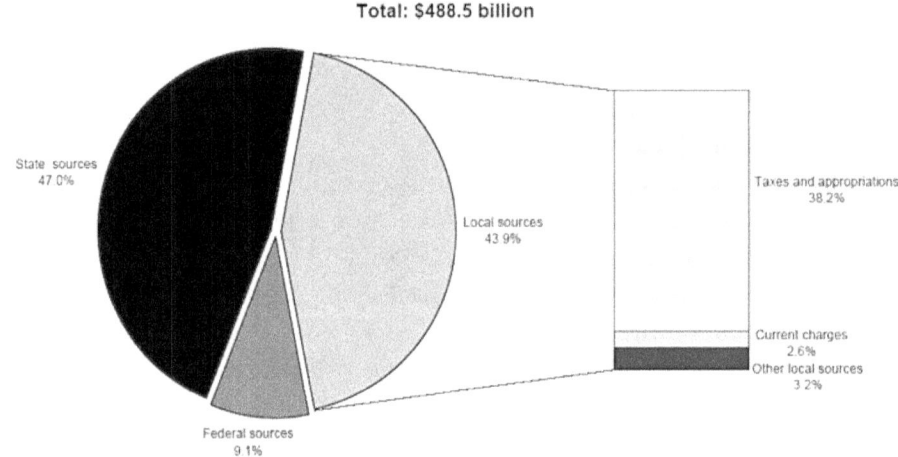

Source: U.S. Census Bureau, "Public Education Finances 2005," Figure 1, http://ftp2.census.gov/govs/school/05f33pub.pdf (accessed January 17, 2008).

Chapter 4 ■ The Role of Property Tax in Intergovernmental Finance

TABLE 4-13. Percentage Distribution of Elementary-Secondary Public School System Revenue by Source and State in 2004-2005

Geographic Area	Total	Federal Sources		State Sources		Local Sources			Changes
		Total*	Compensatory (Title 1)	Total*	Formula Assistance	Total[1]	Taxes and Parent Gov. Contribution	Other Local Gov.	
United States	100.0	9.1	2.3	47.0	31.9	43.9	37.1	1.1	2.6
Alabama	100.0	11.3	3.6	55.2	46.1	33.5	13.6	10.3	5.4
Alaska	100.0	18.9	2.7	54.9	46.1	26.1	20.5	-	2.6
Arizona	100.0	12.0	2.7	44.4	37.8	43.6	33.4	3.0	2.8
Arkansas	100.0	11.3	2.9	75.6	46.7	13.2	7.1	0.1	3.8
California	100.0	11.9	3.6	58.0	34.1	30.1	22.3	0.6	1.4
Colorado	100.0	6.9	1.9	43.1	40.0	50.1	40.4	0.2	4.9
Connecticut	100.0	5.2	1.6	37.2	16.2	57.6	51.8	4.1	1.6
Delaware	100.0	7.7	2.2	64.8	45.2	27.4	22.9	-	1.3
District of Columbia	100.0	15.1	4.3	-	-	84.9	84.0	-	.8
Florida	100.0	10.0	2.5	42.8	16.1	47.1	37.5	-	4.0
Georgia	100.0	9.3	-	43.8	37.6	46.8	40.2	1.3	3.4
Hawaii	100.0	10.4	1.7	87.4	63.2	2.2	-	0.1	1.1
Idaho	100.0	10.7	2.5	57.0	43.8	32.3	28.0	-	1.8
Illinois	100.0	8.7	2.5	34.1	19.8	57.2	52.4	0.2	2.3
Indiana	100.0	6.2	1.6	45.9	39.0	47.9	39.1	0.6	3.2
Iowa	100.0	8.2	1.4	46.0	42.2	45.8	40.6	0.1	2.8
Kansas	100.0	8.5	2.2	65.9	45.6	35.7	27.5	2.1	2.6
Kentucky	100.0	11.9	-	57.3	36.6	30.8	26.6	0.4	2.1
Louisiana	100.0	14.1	4.3	46.7	43.9	39.2	35.7	0.4	1.0
Maine	100.0	8.9	2.0	40.1	28.3	61.0	48.1	0.3	1.9
Maryland	100.0	6.8	1.7	37.7	21.7	55.5	51.1	-	2.8
Massachusetts	100.0	5.9	1.7	42.2	24.7	51.8	41.6	6.3	1.9
Michigan	100.0	8.3	2.3	60.1	52.7	31.6	26.7	0.1	2.8
Minnesota	100.0	6.2	1.2	69.6	52.8	24.2	14.3	1.5	4.6
Mississippi	100.0	15.2	4.6	53.9	51.0	30.9	23.8	0.3	2.9
Missouri	100.0	8.4	2.2	44.0	25.3	47.6	37.7	2.2	4.4
Montana	100.0	14.9	3.5	45.0	36.5	40.1	25.2	8.5	4.0
Nebraska	100.0	10.5	1.4	31.1	23.3	58.5	50.3	0.7	4.3
Nevada	100.0	7.4	1.7	59.2	19.5	33.4	28.0	-	3.3
New Hampshire	100.0	5.6	1.3	39.2	35.8	55.2	51.2	0.4	2.2

(table continued on next page)

FIGURE 4-6. Percentage Distribution of Total Public Elementary-Secondary School System Revenue in 2004–2005 (continued)

Geographic Area	Total	Federal Sources		State Sources		Local Sources			Changes
		Total*	Compensatory (Title 1)	Total*	Formula Assistance	Total¹	Taxes and Parent Gov. Contribution	Other Local Gov.	
New Jersey	100.0	4.2	1.1	41.9	15.3	53.9	46.4	0.9	2.4
New Mexico	100.0	16.1	3.8	70.5	61.4	13.4	10.3	-	1.6
New York	100.0	7.2	2.6	43.9	25.0	48.9	44.8	0.5	.8
North Carolina	100.0	10.1	-	58.0	56.0	31.9	27.9	-	2.8
North Dakota	100.0	16.1	3.8	36.9	28.0	47.0	37.5	1.4	4.7
Ohio	100.0	7.3	-	42.9	35.5	49.8	42.0	0.5	4.5
Oklahoma	100.0	13.9	4.2	49.9	32.8	36.2	26.0	2.7	5.2
Oregon	100.0	10.0	3.0	49.0	45.7	41.0	30.4	3.3	3.0
Pennsylvania	100.0	8.1	2.2	35.6	20.3	56.2	51.1	0.7	1.8
Rhode Island	100.0	7.7	2.3	39.5	33.1	52.8	51.0	-	1.3
South Carolina	100.0	10.1	2.5	44.8	10.9	45.1	34.1	1.9	3.6
South Dakota	100.0	16.8	3.5	33.4	28.2	49.8	43.5	1.2	3.0
Tennessee	100.0	11.6	3.0	43.7	40.9	44.7	29.6	7.7	6.4
Texas	100.0	10.9	3.0	34.6	27.3	54.5	49.7	.2	2.3
Utah	100.0	10.3	1.5	54.4	26.5	35.3	29.8	-	2.2
Vermont	100.0	7.6	2.1	87.2	74.1	5.2	0.6	0.1	1.6
Virginia	100.0	6.9	1.7	40.7	31.8	52.4	49.0	-	2.2
Washington	100.0	8.7	2.2	61.3	45.1	30.0	23.6	0.1	3.3
West Virginia	100.0	12.2	3.6	59.7	34.9	28.1	25.0	0.3	1.2
Wisconsin	100.0	6.0	1.7	50.5	44.2	43.5	38.3	1.0	2.5
Wyoming	100.0	9.4	2.5	51.8	35.0	38.8	27.1	8.9	1.4

*Includes amounts not shown separately.

Source: U.S. Census Bureau, "Public Education Finances 2005," Table 5, http://ftp2.census.gov/govs/school/05f33pub.pdf (accessed January 17, 2008).

Revenue Sharing and Equalization

Revenue sharing is any process by which one level of government distributes revenue raised at that level to another level of government. Revenue shared in this way constitutes intergovernmental revenue, using U.S. Census Bureau parlance. This is discussed in greater detail in Chapter 5, "Tax Analysis"; Table 5-1 shows that, in 2005, states received 24.9 percent of their total revenue from intergovernmental revenue, mostly from the Federal Government. Local governments in the U.S. received 34.5

percent of their revenue from intergovernmental revenue, mostly from states.

Various formulas are used to distribute state revenue to local governments. Such formulas commonly rely on factors such as population, highway miles, or taxable value to provide a rational basis for the distribution. Equalization comes into play when taxable value is used as the basis for the revenue distribution. If assessed values are higher or lower than is proper according to state laws or other standards, distributions are inaccurate. Since many such distributions are "zero sum games," in which local governments "win" or "lose" at the expense of other local governments, a system that levels the playing field as much as is practical maintains the rationale and basic perception of fairness important to retain the revenue-sharing system. Using equalized assessed values, instead of nominal assessed values, helps to accomplish this goal.

Summary

This chapter has provided a broad overview of federalism and fiscal federalism, especially with respect to how these concepts have been implemented in the United States. In addition to the interrelations between different levels of government, various funding mechanisms in common use have been described, and the advantages and challenges of each mechanism have been explored. Finally, some of the major systemwide challenges, including tax competition, remote sales, and school equalization, have been reviewed. Although property tax policy was not the major focal point, an important goal of this chapter was to create an awareness of the many issues involved with any decision regarding governmental funding sources, emphasizing the fact that alternative revenue sources are not without significant policy and administrative challenges.

References

Academy Health. 2008 (January). *State of the states: Rising to the challenge,* http://www.statecoverage.net/publications.htm (accessed August 6, 2008).

Atkins v. Kansas, 191 U.S. 182 (1903).

Compania General De Tobacos De Filipinas v. Collector of Internal Revenue. 275 U.S. 87.

Due, J.F. 1999. Retail sales tax. In *The encyclopedia of taxation and tax policy*, J.J. Cordes, R.D. Ebeland, J.G. Gravelle, eds.Washington, DC: The Urban Institute Press.

Dye, T.R. 1990. *American federalism: Competition among governments.* Lexington, MA: D.C. Heath.

Elazar, D. J. 1991. Cooperative federalism. *Competition among states and local governments: Efficiency and equity in American federalism.* Washington, DC: The Urban Institute.

Fischel, W. 2001. *The homevoter hypothesis.* Cambridge, MA: Harvard University Press.

Fisher, R.C. 2007. *State and local public finance,* 3rd ed. Mason, OH: South-Western College Publishing.

Hamilton, B. 2000. The day the sales tax died. *National Tax Journal* 53 (4):1389.

Hoffman, D. 2002. *Facts and figures on government finance,* 36th ed. Washington, DC: Tax Foundation.

Kenyon, D.A. 1997. Tax policy in an intergovernmental setting: Is it time for the U.S. to change? In *Intergovernmental fiscal relations (recent economic thought),* R.C. Fisher, ed. New York: Springer.

Kenyon, D.A., and J. Kincaid, eds. 1991. *Competition among states and local governments.* Washington, DC: The Urban Institute.

McGuire, T.J. 2001. Alternatives to property taxation for local government. In *Property taxation and local government finance: Essays in honor of C. Lowell Harriss,* W.E. Oates, ed. Cambridge, MA: Lincoln Institute of Land Policy

National Bellas Hess v. Illinois State Department of Revenue, 386 U.S. 753 (1967).

Wassmer, R.W., and R.C. Fisher. 1996. An evaluation of the recent move to centralize the finance of public schools in Michigan. *Public Budgeting and Finance* 16 (3): 90–112.

Yinger, J, ed. 2004. *Helping children left behind: State aid and the pursuit of educational equity.* Cambridge, MA: MIT Press.

Chapter 5
Tax Analysis

Tax analysis involves research designed to determine the effects of the tax structure or any proposed changes to the existing tax structure. Three types of effects are explored in this chapter: revenue effects, taxpayer effects, and economic effects. This chapter does not include expenditure analysis. Although expenditures can mitigate or alter tax incidence, they occur through a largely independent series of decisions and are not properly part of tax policy, which focuses on revenue inputs.

Approaching the Analysis

Before effects of the tax structure can be analyzed, the fundamental principles of analysis must be understood. This is true whether the analysis involves review of the underlying tax structure or review of available data to estimate costs and effects of current or proposed policies. Analyzing the effects of tax policy involves several preliminary steps.

Defining the Problem

First, the question must be clearly defined. The prevailing characteristics of a particular audience can influence understanding of the question, and it is critical to isolate the goal of the analysis at the outset. Is the question, "Are property taxes in the city high?" Or is the question, "Do homeowners in the city pay higher property taxes than homeowners in comparable cities?" The methods used and data needed for the analysis can change considerably depending on the precise nature of the question.

Identifying the Level of Precision

The second step involves ascertaining the level of precision needed in the answer. For example, legislative policy makers often care about how much a proposed exemption will cost: $1 million or $10 million or $100 million. It may be possible to estimate the effect of the exemption with the precision necessary to provide such order-of-magnitude information, despite data limitations that preclude any greater degree of precision (i.e., with the underlying data the analyst cannot state that the cost will be $1.5 million, but can estimate it will be closer to $1 million than to $10 million).

Collecting Data

The third step is collection of the data necessary for the analysis. Except when the most basic questions are asked, the analysis probably will extend beyond the limits of the available data. For example, in answering questions about a proposed exemption of machinery and equipment, the analyst often finds that some equipment is categorized as real, rather than personal, property and thereby loses its identity in the database. Since it may still be subject to the proposed exemption, it becomes a source of error in the analysis. While it is not always possible to quantify this type of error or errors related to definitions that are arguable or subjects for future litigation, assumptions and sources of potential error must be identified and explained as part of the analysis.

Using Positive versus Normative Approaches

Although there are many ways to approach analysis, the underlying agenda or bias of the analyst always must be clearly stated to avoid deception. Analysis can therefore be approached either positively or normatively.

A positive statement is based purely on fact and contains no value judgments. An example of a positive statement is, "If homeowners move in and out of a neighborhood with the same exact homes and if acquisition value is used for assessment, different homeowners will pay different property taxes on similar properties for the same local services." A normative statement relies on some form of value judgment. An example of a statement requiring an assessor's value judgment is, "Acquisition value assessment is preferred (or not preferred) to market value assessment." Although all tax policy premises are debatable, the analyst may be predisposed toward a particular conclusion. Normative statements make such predisposition more apparent.

Those who analyze property tax policy should try to keep advocacy within the positive realm. When making normative statements in offering policy advice, analysts should acknowledge that this is their opinion and it cannot necessarily be supported by the facts alone. Beyond knowing this distinction between positive and normative statements, analysts should make sure that the normative statements they do make are accurate. This requires that analysts know the specifics of the law and the policy-making practices in their jurisdiction that relate to the tax being analyzed and, to the extent possible, to other taxes that also may be affected by proposed policy changes.

Finally, an effective policy advocate needs to think like a policy analyst. A policy problem should be defined without including a specific solution in the statement of the problem. An example of how to appropriately define a policy problem would be,

"The revenues of local governments in the United States are less than what it costs to provide the goods demanded from them." An inappropriate way to define this policy problem is, "Local governments should raise local property tax rates to cover their shortfalls in revenue." This second statement clearly includes a value judgment and assumes the answer to the policy problem is within the statement that defines it.

Once a policy analyst has defined a policy problem in an appropriate manner, he or she should suggest specific alternatives or solutions. For instance, for the problem of shortfalls in local government revenues, solutions could include higher local property taxes, sales taxes, fees, and more efficient, low-cost methods to get the job done. Another solution could be making citizens more aware of the true cost of local government services in the hope that their demand for them will decrease and so will the shortfalls. Once reasonable alternatives have been suggested, they can be evaluated by the policy analyst based on an agreed-upon set of criteria equally applied to each alternative. If raising local property taxes is identified as the preferred solution to a revenue shortfall, the policy analyst is better able to justify his or her choice in a more normative manner.

Types of Analyses

Policy analysis falls into three broad classifications: descriptive studies, forecasts, and analytical studies.

Descriptive Studies

Descriptive studies provide factual or legal information or data. Examples of questions such studies are designed to answer are as follows:

- How much income tax was collected in a given year?
- How has the amount collected been changing over the past five years?
- What is the largest monetary tax credit claimed?
- What are the basic qualifications for the senior citizen property tax relief program?
- What is the property reappraisal cycle?

Descriptive studies can provide a basis for additional analysis or basic understanding of the effects of tax policies. Such information can also be useful in providing general information to the public and to policy makers.

Forecasts

Forecasts involve predictions or estimates of the effects of existing tax policy or of proposed changes to tax policy. Forecasts can be short term (perhaps 1–2 years) or long term. Forecasts often involve multiple elements, including effects on revenue, effects on burden (how high or low the taxes are expected to become), effects on subpopulations of taxpayers (i.e., business versus residential property or high-income people versus low-income people), and effects on different regions or economic sectors (i.e., whether the rural development tax credit program is likely to inordinately limit economic development in urban areas). In making a forecast of the effects of a tax policy change, the analyst must take into account (or report any failure to account for) any interactive effects, as well as nominal effects. For example, it may be relatively easy to forecast the amount of money needed to fund schools by substituting sales tax for current funding based on property tax. However, since, for individuals, property tax is deductible from income for federal income tax purposes and sales tax (usually) is not, the overall burden of state and local taxes will rise with respect to individual after-tax income. In addition, some income that remained with individuals and therefore remained in a given state would go to the Federal Government and potentially be lost to the economy of that state and to individuals who may not realize as much savings from lower property taxes.

Tax changes often produce behavioral effects, depending on demand elasticity. A typical goal of higher tobacco taxes, for example, is to curtail the use of the product. There is an expectation therefore that demand for tobacco is at least somewhat elastic and will be reduced by higher taxes. The extent to which demand is elastic affects the forecast as well, since, given any demand elasticity, doubling the tax rate probably will not double the revenue. Forecasts of tax rate effects on revenue that fail to consider demand elasticity can be considerably overstated, either on the high or low side, depending on whether the analysis assumes tax rate increases or decreases.

Principles and Techniques of Revenue Forecasting

Among the multiple reasons to forecast revenues accurately, two stand out. If revenues for the budget are underestimated, then expenditures will be held unnecessarily low. Yet if revenues are overestimated, mid-year budget reductions may very well be necessary and are likely to be ad hoc rather than carefully analyzed. Blom and Guajardo (2001) expand on the following discussion.

Forecasting Issues

Because there are multiple revenue sources for jurisdictions and because different revenue streams have different levels of stability, the first step in the process is to determine which revenues should be focused on. It is probably not worth a great deal of effort to spend significant resources attempting to forecast an erratic revenue source that constitutes a very small percentage of the total budget.

Once the budget for forecasting revenues has been determined, the following process can be used. For a one-year forecast, begin with the current year, specify the necessary assumptions (typically population and economic growth), and then "grow" the revenue by multiplying the current year by the growth factor. This generates the forecast. It is important to check the results after the forecasted year is complete to ensure that the assumptions were correct. For short-term forecasting, it is feasible to take macroeconomic projections for the region (say, forecasted income growth) and then, using tax elasticity calculations, form forecasts of the percentage increase in tax revenue. However, macroeconomic forecasts have little validity beyond a year or so.

Long-term (five-year) forecasts follow a slightly different process. More formal models tend to be used; assumptions must be based on long-term data; and the process should generate formal feedback so the model is continuously refined. The technique should be sophisticated enough so that "what-if" scenarios can be developed and the budgetary implications analyzed over a period of time.

Qualitative Techniques

Qualitative forecasting techniques do not use statistical analysis to reach revenue projections; rather, these techniques use human judgments. These techniques assume that experience, historical information, and the recognition of environmental changes provide the best revenue estimates. Qualitative techniques involve mathematical computations; however, they often do not clearly identify the underlying factors and assumptions. Further, each forecaster may have a unique process for making his or her judgments.

Examples of qualitative techniques are as follows:

- *Naïve forecasting.* Historical relationships will hold constant, and thus this year's revenue is a constant function of last year's revenue.

- *Consensus forecasting.* Collective agreement by a group of knowledgeable finance department individuals projects this year's revenues.

- *Expert forecasting.* Collective agreement by a group of knowledgeable individuals outside of the finance department (economists, demographers, market researchers, and so on) projects this year's revenues.

- *Delphi forecasting.* In this multiple-step revenue projection method, predictions of expert individuals are reconsidered after other expert individuals comment on the forecasts.

All these qualitative methods are easy to learn and are very useful when historical data (which are necessary for quantitative techniques) are not available, the revenue source is unstable, and there is a limited amount of time to make the projection. However, because sometimes they are dependent on personal biases, lack rigor, and are not standardized, they can lead to less realistic forecasts.

Quantitative Techniques

Quantitative techniques are used to estimate revenues by using statistical techniques. These techniques attempt to discover historical statistical relationships between the particular revenue source and relevant factors, such as past revenue yields, population, and economic growth. This relationship is used to predict future revenue yield. As long as this relationship does not change, the projections can be quite accurate. However, if there are changes in the relationships, the projections are likely to be wrong. Quantitative methods require carefully stated assumptions concerning the data and the form of the relationships.

Examples of quantitative techniques are as follows:

- *Trend analysis.* This year's revenue is based on the historical trend (not only on last year's revenue) of the particular revenue source.

- *Time series forecasting.* This year's revenue depends on data collected at equally spaced time intervals (similar to trend analysis) corrected for serial correlation and seasonal variations.

- *Regression analysis.* This year's revenue is forecasted by using an estimated regression that calculates the historical relationship between the particular revenue and a variety of independent variables.

- *Econometric forecasting.* This year's revenue is forecasted by using a complex model of several regression equations so that feedback and multiple sources of information can be used.

Quantitative techniques allow checking the accuracy of the underlying assumptions, ensure a consistent methodology, and minimize the subjective judgments of any particular individual. However, these techniques consume a good deal of time, can be cumbersome, require knowledge of statistical techniques, and are heavily dependent on the accuracy of historical data, much of which will be decades old. They can also depend on the accuracy of the underlying econometric assumptions.

In conclusion, a good revenue-forecasting system incorporates both qualitative and quantitative techniques. The goal is to establish a consensus on the forecast among all the players—legislatures, executive agencies, and, at times, even private-sector lobbyists. This consensus helps minimize political disputes about the forecast and thus keeps the budget process on track. Once this consensus is reached, it should be used to develop and adopt the operating budget. Because of the importance of the revenue projections, government should compare actual to projected revenues consistently. In general, the more sensitive the revenue source is to changes in demand and economic conditions, the more closely that source should be monitored.

When the actual revenue collected differs from the projected revenues in a consistent manner, the forecasters should examine why there is a variance and, if necessary, change the revenue forecast to account for the incorrect assumptions, changes in demand, or changes in other economic conditions. The updating of the forecast should follow the steps discussed in the introductory paragraphs of this chapter. Finally, this updating should occur only after the assumptions have been carefully examined and economic conditions have changed in a known manner. Budget adjustments based on these revised forecasts should be based on whether the local government can reasonably expect the differential to continue. Major budget changes based on short-term anomalies should not be undertaken.

Government budget officers are not always interested in putting forward the most likely revenue outcome as the official revenue estimate. Often they may purposely underestimate revenue to provide more flexibility. Overestimating revenue is a more serious problem than underestimating revenue because overestimating results in the need for painful mid-year reductions. In addition, conservative revenue estimates provide fiscal discipline in the appropriation process for legislatures and local government bodies.

Analytical Studies

Analytical studies focus on multiple effects of tax policy and proposed changes. Such studies attempt to combine elements of economic analysis with tax analysis. Analytical studies review such issues as the following:

- *Behavioral changes.* Will an increase in liquor taxes lower consumption and thereby not raise revenue a commensurate amount?
- *Incidence or shifting.* Who will bear the ultimate economic burden of the tax (or policy)? Is the policy progressive or regressive in its effects?
- *Subpopulations.* How will the tax or policy affect different income groups, geographic regions, industries, and the like?
- *Economic effects.* How will business or personal locational decisions be affected? How will infrastructure needs be met?

In addition, analytical studies often address income elasticity, the expected or actual rate of change in tax revenue given different changes in underlying income.

Sources of State and Local Taxes and Other Revenues

The property tax is only one of many revenue sources for state and local governments. Table 5-1 shows details on the many different revenue sources for state and local governments, combined and separately, for the entire United States in FY 2005 (July 1, 2004 through June 30, 2005). This is part of a much longer table on the U.S. Census Bureau Web site, which includes considerable detail on the expenditure side of state and local government budgets. The groupings in the table are defined as follows:

- *General revenue* is all government revenue except the categories shown at the bottom of the table:

- revenue from government-operated public utilities
- government-operated liquor store revenue
- unemployment compensation, employee retirement, workers' compensation, or other government trust funds.

- *Intergovernmental revenue* is "received from other governments as grants-in-aid, shared revenues, payments in lieu of taxes, or a reimbursement for the performance of services for the paying government" (Hoffman 2002).

- *Own-source revenue* is all general revenue except intergovernmental revenue and includes
  - taxes
  - current charges
  - miscellaneous general revenue.

The bottom of Table 5-1 shows that state and local governments raise a grand total of $2.5 trillion from all sources. The state and local government sectors are roughly the same size, at $1.6 trillion and $1.3 trillion, respectively. (Note that these add up to more than the combined total because of double-counting state transfers to local government.) Intergovernmental revenue grants are an important source of revenue: state governments receive 23.6 percent of their total revenue from the Federal Government, and local governments receive 30.6 percent of their total revenue from their state governments (it is not shown in the table, but most of this is in the form of state aid to local school districts).

TABLE 5-1. State and Local Government Finances by Level of Government, 2004-2005

Description	State and Local Government		State Government		Local Government	
	$ Millions	% of Total	$ Millions	% of Total	$ Millions	% of Total
Intergovernmental Revenue	438,156	17.4%	408,449	24.9%	451,495	34.5%
From federal government	438,156	17.4%	386,027	23.6%	52,129	4.0%
From state government	0	0.0%	0	0.0%	399,366	30.6%
From local government	0	0.0%	22,422	1.4%	0	0.0%
General Revenue from Own Sources	1,582,770	62.7%	873,869	53.4%	708,901	54.2%
Taxes	1,096,385	43.5%	648,111	39.6%	448,273	34.3%
Property	335,678	13.3%	11,349	0.7%	324,329	24.8%
Sales and gross receipts	383,264	15.2%	311,434	19.0%	71,830	5.5%
General sales	262,955	10.4%	212,907	13.0%	50,048	3.8%
Selective sales	120,309	4.8%	98,527	6.0%	21,782	1.7%

(table continued on next page)

TABLE 5-1. State and Local Government Finances by Level of Government, 2004-2005 (continued)

Description	State and Local Government		State Government		Local Government	
	$ Millions	% of Total	$ Millions	% of Total	$ Millions	% of Total
Motor fuel	35,770	1.4%	34,570	2.1%	1,200	0.1%
Alcoholic beverage	5,145	0.2%	4,732	0.3%	413	0.0%
Tobacco products	13,337	0.5%	12,917	0.8%	420	0.0%
Public utilities	22,551	0.9%	11,023	0.7%	11,529	0.9%
Other selective sales	43,506	1.7%	35,286	2.2%	8,220	0.6%
Individual income	240,930	9.5%	220,255	13.4%	20,676	1.6%
Corporate income	43,138	1.7%	38,691	2.4%	4,447	0.3%
Motor vehicle license	19,654	0.8%	18,221	1.1%	1,433	0.1%
Other taxes	73,720	2.9%	48,162	2.9%	25,558	2.0%
Charges and Miscellaneous General Revenue	486,386	19.3%	225,758	13.8%	260,628	19.9%
Current charges	308,254	12.2%	122,800	7.5%	185,455	14.2%
Education	89,469	3.5%	68,334	4.2%	21,135	1.6%
Institutions of higher education	75,856	3.0%	67,190	4.1%	8,666	0.7%
School lunch sales (gross)	6,500	0.3%	22	0.0%	6,479	0.5%
Hospitals	79,369	3.1%	29,131	1.8%	50,238	3.8%
Highways	10,034	0.4%	6,228	0.4%	3,806	0.3%
Air transportation (airports)	14,471	0.6%	1,042	0.1%	13,430	1.0%
Parking facilities	1,627	0.1%	33	0.0%	1,594	0.1%
Sea and inland port facilities	3,393	0.1%	987	0.1%	2,406	0.2%
Natural resources	3,355	0.1%	2,347	0.1%	1,008	0.1%
Parks and recreation	7,978	0.3%	1,360	0.1%	6,618	0.5%
Housing and community development	4,892	0.2%	575	0.0%	4,317	0.3%
Sewerage	31,250	1.2%	39	0.0%	31,211	2.4%
Solid waste management	12,960	0.5%	466	0.0%	12,494	1.0%
Other charges	49,456	2.0%	12,259	0.7%	37,197	2.8%
Miscellaneous General Revenue	178,131	7.1%	102,958	6.3%	75,173	5.8%
Interest earnings	58,246	2.3%	31,375	1.9%	26,871	2.1%
Special assessments	6,295	0.2%	752	0.0%	5,543	0.4%
Sale of property	2,813	0.1%	1,042	0.1%	1,771	0.1%
Other general revenue	110,778	4.4%	69,789	4.3%	40,988	3.1%
General Revenue	2,020,926	80.1%	1,282,318	78.3%	1,160,396	88.8%
Utility revenue	113,792	4.5%	14,627	0.9%	99,165	7.6%
Liquor store revenue	6,082	0.2%	5,212	0.3%	870	0.1%
Insurance trust revenue	382,205	15.1%	335,634	20.5%	46,572	3.6%
Total Revenue	2,523,006	100.0%	1,637,792	100.0%	1,307,002	100.0%

Source: U.S. Census Bureau, Governments Division, "Table 1. State and Local Government Finances by Level of Government and by State: 2004-05," http://www.census.gov/govs/estimate/0500ussl_1.html (accessed Jan. 21, 2008).

The property tax is the principal source of local revenue (24.8 percent in FY 2005, up from 23.9 percent in FY 1999), but is a relatively small source of states' revenue (0.7 percent). State governments rely principally—and roughly equally—on individual income taxes (13.4 percent) and general sales taxes (13.0 percent). These two sources of revenue are much less important to local governments (1.6 percent and 3.8 percent, respectively). While there may have been political pressure to reduce property taxes, tax collection figures do not show this happening through FY 2005. This is true in total dollars (unadjusted for inflation, total local property taxes increased 42 percent in comparison to 1999, a 6 percent annual rate of increase) and as a proportion of local government revenue.

These U.S. Census Bureau definitions and categorizations of state revenue structures are widely used. The Bureau of Economic Analysis of the U.S. Department of Commerce, however, uses a different system for reporting the state and local government sector in its national income and product accounts. Some states and counties use still different definitions in their reporting. Analysts therefore need to be especially careful in mixing or interpreting data from multiple sources.

Analysis of Revenue Trends

Table 5-2 shows total revenue and the major components for selected fiscal years from 1927 to 2005. Total revenue for all state and local governments in the United States grew from $7,838 million in 1927 to $2,523 billion in 2005. So much has happened

TABLE 5-2. State and Local Government Revenue for Selected Years

Year	Total Revenue ($ millions)	Own-Source General Revenue ($ millions)	Taxes ($ millions)	Consumer Price Index (1999 = 1.0)	Population (thousands)	Personal Income ($ billion)	Real Total Revenue (millions of 1999 $)	Real Total Revenue ($ per capita)	Total Revenue (per $1000 personal income)
1927	7,838	7,155	6,087	0.1042	119,038	85.3	75,225	632	92
1938	11,058	8,428	7,605	0.0846	129,825	68.6	130,725	1,007	161
1948	21,613	15,389	13,342	0.1443	149,188	211.1	149,742	1,004	102
1959	53,972	38,929	32,379	0.1750	177,830	394.0	308,450	1,735	137
1969	132,153	95,397	76,712	0.2202	202,677	780.8	600,159	2,961	169
1979	404,934	268,115	205,514	0.4357	225,055	2,081.5	929,402	4,130	195
1989	953,517	660,020	468,647	0.7440	246,819	4,599.8	1,281,634	5,193	207
1999	1,794,557	1,163,836	815,777	1.0000	273,828	7,786.5	1,794,557	6,554	230
2005	2,523,006	1,582,770	1,096,385	1.1722	296,507	10,239.2	2,152,431	7,259	246

Note: Revenue is for fiscal years, and the CPI, population, and personal income numbers are for calendar years or are based on July 1 figures.

Sources: Revenue and population, Hoffman 2002, updated to 2005 using U.S. Census Bureau Web site (http://www.census.gov); consumer price index, U.S. Department of Commerce, Bureau of Economic Analysis (http://www.bea.doc.gov). note the series starts in 1929 and that is the number used for 1927; personal income, U.S. Department of Labor, Bureau of Labor Statistics (http://stats.bls.gov).

during this 78-year period that it would not be a meaningful comparison, for example, to look at the ratio of these two numbers and say that revenues increased 322-fold. In responsibly analyzing the impact of taxes over time, it is necessary to make certain adjustments.

First, there has been considerable price inflation—the consumer price index (CPI) column shows that prices rose tenfold for this period. The "current dollar" total revenue numbers can be adjusted for inflation by dividing by the price index; the resulting "real" numbers show what total revenue would be if prices had been at 1999 levels in all previous decades. Even given limited inflation during the period since 1999, 2005 dollars must be adjusted downward by 17 percent to reflect 1999 dollars.

Second, the population of the United States more than doubled. Dividing by population gives a per-capita amount, which is much more suitable for comparisons over time. Real total state and local government revenue per capita increased tenfold, from $632 in 1927 to $7,259 in 2005.

The third major change over this nine-decade period is an increase in real standard of living, as reflected in the enormous growth in personal income. It is common in comparing revenue burdens over time or across states to divide by personal income and to calculate taxes or other revenues per $1,000 of personal income. (Note that because personal income grows with both population and prices, it is not necessary to *also* adjust for those.) By this measure, total state and local government revenue per $1,000 of personal income increased from $92 in 1927 to $246 in 2005—a factor of about 2.7 to 1. So there is a significant increase in the burden of state and local government over the long term that is not explained by the technical adjustments for population, prices, and income, but it is not nearly as dramatic as would be suggested by a naive comparison before these adjustments are made.

The reason for the remaining growth has not been fully explained. However, it may be related to the increasing importance of transfer expenditures by government and by slower rates of productivity growth in government services as compared with the private economy. Practices and procedures for government services like schools, firefighting, courts, and police have not changed as dramatically as those in manufacturing over the years, possibly because they are more labor intensive. It may be that they are intrinsically not amenable to efficiency-enhancing advances like those in manufacturing, or it may be that the incentive structure in the government sector does not promote such advances.

The other long-term trend shown in Table 5-2 is a decrease in the share of revenue from taxes relative to other sources. In 1927, state and local government tax collections were 78 percent of total revenue ($6,087 million in collections versus $7,838 million in revenues), but in 2005 taxes represented only 43 percent of the total ($1,096,385 million versus $2,523,006 million). Utility and insurance revenue, intergovernmental transfers, and charges all increased in relative importance during the last century.

Often there is confusion about some of the terminology used in tables such as Table

5-2. One of the most important terms in use is "total personal income," or "personal income," defined by the U.S. Bureau of Economic Analysis as follows:

> ... income received by persons from all sources. It includes income received from participation in production as well as from government and business transfer payments. It is the sum of compensation of employees (received), supplements to wages and salaries, proprietors' income with inventory valuation adjustment (IVA) and capital consumption adjustment (CCAdj), rental income of persons with CCAdj, personal income receipts on assets, and personal current transfer receipts, less contributions for government social insurance.
>
> The personal income of an area is the income that is received by, or on behalf of, all the individuals who live in the area; therefore, the estimates of personal income are presented by the place of residence of the income recipients. (http://bea.gov/bea/glossary/glossary_c.htm)

Measurement of Tax Burden

Although it is a somewhat separate issue from revenue projection and analysis, tax burden and, in particular, perception of tax burden can lead to legislative and economic decisions that affect revenue and revenue forecasts. Tax burden is defined as the economic costs of or losses resulting from the imposition of a tax. It can be viewed from the perspective of the overall tax system and the burden this system places on the overall economy. Tax burden and analysis of tax burden are frequently confused with tax incidence and analysis of tax incidence. The principal difference is that tax incidence views the distribution of the tax burden with respect to specific sectors of the economy and specific subgroups of the population of all taxpayers. For example, it may be correct to state that taxes in a particular state are $1,000 per person (per capita) or, perhaps, 10% of total income. While that may correctly depict the overall tax burden, it does not answer several important questions, such as the following:

- How much of the tax is on business versus individuals?
- How much of the tax is on high-income versus low-income taxpayers?
- How much of the tax is on residents versus nonresidents?
- How much of the tax is borne by the agricultural sector versus the industrial sector?

These questions all relate to the incidence of the tax. The question of incidence can become very complex; that is, initial incidence may be borne by the business community, yet ultimately transferred to individuals in the form of lower wages or loss of jobs. This interaction between economic sectors can alter the ultimate economic incidence of a tax far beyond the nominal or initial incidence. Most tax burden and incidence analyses examine initial incidence only. Nevertheless, the analyst must recognize and acknowledge the potential for a far different ultimate economic incidence.

As a starting point toward understanding tax burden, it is useful to be informed about state and local revenue structures and the size of the public sector as a whole. Much of the information that enables this analysis is compiled by the U.S. Census Bureau. Informational tables generated and updated by the Census Bureau are frequently reworked and presented in alternative formats by other entities. Many U.S. state tax and economic research agencies maintain tax research units that recompile census data, much of which is then placed on agency Web sites or is otherwise available in state agency publications. Entities commonly relied on for informational tables and tax burden examples are

- Federation of Tax Administrators
- Department of Finance and Revenue of the District of Columbia
- Minnesota Department of Revenue
- Idaho State Tax Commission.

Comparison of Fiscal Structures

Citizens, business groups, or policy makers are often interested in comparing the structure and level of taxation and other revenues in their jurisdiction with those of other jurisdictions. The fairness, economic efficiency, and other effects of tax policy will depend on the level of taxes relative to those in another state. When comparing revenue structures of states, it is usually advisable to examine the combined state and local government sector. Otherwise, cross-state variations in the way responsibility for performing services and levying taxes is divided among state and local governments can produce misleading results. For example, local government tax burdens are very low in Hawaii; however, elementary and secondary education is solely a responsibility of the Hawaii state government. In addition to divisions of responsibility, tax structures differ as well, and analysis of state taxes apart from local taxes can misrepresent these structural differences. For example, in Idaho, local governments have very limited authority to levy sales taxes, and none has authority to use local income taxes. This concentrates tax collections for these two types of taxes at the state level and tends to overstate Idaho's tax burden in comparisons of state-level taxes.

The unique status of the District of Columbia can add confusion to fiscal comparisons between states in the United States. In many ways the District of Columbia resembles a state fiscally; for instance, it uses all three major taxes—income, sales, and property taxes—and, unlike most localities in the United States, even levies corporate income taxes. But the district is most definitely *not* a state. The U.S. Census Bureau conventions for compiling and reporting fiscal data always consider the District of Columbia to be a local government. Because tax collections in the district tend to be significant and few other local governments use corporate income taxes, the local proportion of this and some other taxes can appear overstated and the analyst must be aware of this anomaly.

Comparison of Overall Revenue Burdens

Table 5-3 shows total state and local government revenues for each of the 50 states, the District of Columbia, and the entire United States. Examining the second column—total revenue—is not very meaningful because of cross-state variations in population and income. There are two standard ways of presenting cross-state comparisons.

Table 5-3. Total State and Local Government Revenue, Population, and Personal Income by State, FY 2004-2005

State	Total Revenue ($ millions)	Population (thousands)	Personal Income ($ millions)	Total Revenue per Capita $	Rank	Total Revenue per $1,000 Personal Income $/1000	Rank
United States	2,523,006	296,507	9,982,781	8,509		253	
Alabama	33,606	4,548	130,818	7,389	38	257	24
Alaska	11,334	663	22,936	17,089	1	494	1
Arizona	41,135	5,953	171,143	6,910	47	240	34
Arkansas	18,877	2,776	72,667	6,801	49	260	21
California	380,477	36,154	1,301,152	10,524	5	292	9
Colorado	38,930	4,663	169,876	8,348	22	229	39
Connecticut	30,584	3,501	162,596	8,737	16	188	50
Delaware	7,638	842	30,202	9,074	8	253	26
District of Columbia	9,327	582	29,994	16,024	2	311	5
Florida	135,339	17,768	584,217	7,617	34	232	38
Georgia	60,293	9,133	273,349	6,602	51	221	46
Hawaii	11,000	1,273	42,652	8,639	19	258	23
Idaho	10,004	1,429	39,480	6,999	44	253	25
Illinois	100,447	12,765	452,141	7,869	29	222	45
Indiana	43,792	6,266	191,417	6,989	45	229	40
Iowa	23,250	2,966	92,711	7,840	31	251	27
Kansas	19,921	2,748	88,110	7,249	41	226	43
Kentucky	28,044	4,173	114,880	6,721	50	244	31
Louisiana	35,848	4,507	124,157	7,953	28	289	10
Maine	11,346	1,318	40,022	8,607	20	284	13
Maryland	45,327	5,590	227,528	8,109	25	199	49
Massachusetts	61,507	6,433	273,644	9,561	6	225	44
Michigan	81,370	10,101	325,985	8,056	26	250	28
Minnesota	45,464	5,127	188,232	8,868	14	242	33

(table continued on next page)

TABLE 5-3. Total State and Local Government Revenue, Population, and Personal Income by State, FY 2004–2005 (continued)

State	Total Revenue ($ millions)	Population (thousands)	Personal Income ($ millions)	Total Revenue per Capita $	Rank	Total Revenue per $1,000 Personal Income $/1000	Rank
Mississippi	21,092	2,908	71,241	7,252	40	296	7
Missouri	41,340	5,798	177,150	7,130	42	233	37
Montana	7,438	935	26,456	7,957	27	281	15
Nebraska	15,883	1,758	56,969	9,034	10	279	16
Nevada	18,953	2,412	83,252	7,857	30	228	42
New Hampshire	8,924	1,307	48,426	6,829	48	184	51
New Jersey	77,812	8,703	372,795	8,941	12	209	47
New Mexico	16,650	1,926	52,261	8,645	18	319	3
New York	231,011	19,316	758,121	11,960	4	305	6
North Carolina	64,824	8,672	261,528	7,475	37	248	29
North Dakota	5,240	635	19,175	8,257	23	273	17
Ohio	102,601	11,471	359,549	8,945	11	285	11
Oklahoma	24,552	3,543	103,176	6,929	46	238	35
Oregon	32,393	3,639	114,263	8,902	13	283	14
Pennsylvania	103,730	12,405	424,320	8,362	21	244	30
Rhode Island	9,729	1,074	37,335	9,062	9	261	20
South Carolina	33,277	4,247	116,993	7,835	32	284	12
South Dakota	5,825	775	24,684	7,517	35	236	36
Tennessee	43,686	5,956	179,345	7,335	39	244	32
Texas	163,057	22,929	716,147	7,112	43	228	41
Utah	19,186	2,490	65,606	7,704	33	292	8
Vermont	5,393	622	19,978	8,665	17	270	18
Virginia	56,859	7,564	275,706	7,517	36	206	48
Washington	57,586	6,292	222,437	9,152	7	259	22
West Virginia	14,739	1,814	46,925	8,125	24	314	4
Wisconsin	48,430	5,528	180,706	8,761	15	268	19
Wyoming	7,931	509	18,333	15,588	3	433	2

Source: U.S. Census Bureau, "State Government Finances," http://www.census.gov/govs/www/state.html (accessed January 22, 2008).

Dividing by population yields total state and local government revenue per capita. By this measure, Alaska ranks first, with $17,089 in revenue per capita. Every state is different, but the fiscal structure of Alaska is very, very different—the tax burden on Alaskan residents is actually extremely *low*, and this large total comes overwhelmingly from "miscellaneous general revenue" from the oil and gas industry. The next highest ranked "state" in per-capita revenue is the District of Columbia, which of course is not a state at all and has the fiscal responsibilities of a large central city. Wyoming ranks third and, like Alaska, receives a considerable proportion of its revenue from its extensive mineral wealth. Discounting these special cases, the total state and local government revenue per capita ranges from a high of $11,960 in New York to a low of $6,602 in Georgia, a ratio of less than 2:1.

Dividing by income yields a measure of the burden of state and local government revenue relative to the ability to pay taxes. The usual convention is to present this as per $1,000 of personal income. Again discounting Alaska and Wyoming, the range is from $319 per $1,000 of personal income for New Mexico to $184 in New Hampshire.

It is interesting to look at similarities and differences in the rankings on the two different measures. For example, New York is a high tax state by either measure; New Hampshire is a low tax state by either measure; Connecticut, which has higher-than-average income, is a fairly high tax state per capita but a very low tax state relative to income; New Mexico, with lower-than-average income, has a per-capita burden near the U.S. average, but a high burden relative to income.

These measures of burden are not necessarily normative standards for judging states. For example, there is no reason that every state should attempt to behave like the average state. An unusually high or low burden may signal a problem for a particular state, but it may also simply reflect the voters' choice for a particular tax and expenditure mix. Some areas may prefer high taxes along with high levels of government services while others may not.

Also, note that personal income shown in Table 5-3 does not exactly match personal income shown in Table 5-2. This discrepancy occurs because Table 5-2 is based on calendar-year income statistics, while Table 5-3 is based on FY 2004–2005. Differences of this type abound in the mass of statistical information that describes various aspects of the U.S. economy. Analysts must note such discrepancies and provide explanations when possible.

Relative Reliance on Different Sources of Revenue

States also differ in their choice of, or access to, different revenue sources. Columns 2, 3, and 4 in Table 5-4 show the division of total revenue in three major categories. Connecticut at 75.8 percent is at the top in terms of the share coming from own-source revenue, below average in the share coming from federal grants, and at the bottom in its 9.7 percent reliance on utility, liquor store, and insurance trust receipts. Wyoming at 53.8 percent is at the bottom in reliance on own-source taxes and charges, at the top in intergovernmental revenue, and near the bottom in utility, liquor store, and insurance trust revenues. The last column looks at state government own-source revenue as a percentage of combined state plus local government own-source revenue. Discounting the District of Columbia, the range is from a high of 84.3 percent in Vermont, where revenue-raising is concentrated at the state level, to a low of 43.6 percent in New York, where revenue-raising is concentrated at the local level.

Table 5-5 subdivides own-source revenue into the major types of taxes. Reliance on taxes (as opposed to charges and miscellaneous revenues) for own-source revenue ranges from a high of 81.6 percent in Connecticut to a low (discounting Alaska) of 57.5 percent in South Carolina. The overwhelming majority of states rely on taxes for 65–75 percent of own-source revenue. Property tax reliance varies enormously—from 8.9 percent in Alabama, Delaware, and New Mexico to 43.5 percent in New Hampshire. Four states—Delaware, Montana, New Hampshire, and Oregon—have no general sales tax (Alaska is not included in this grouping because certain boroughs and municipalities levy sales tax), while Tennessee relies on the general sales tax for 30.8 percent of own-source revenue. Most states receive less than 10 percent of own-source revenue from selective sales taxes (refer to Table 5-1

TABLE 5-4. Distribution of Total State and Local Government Revenue by State, 2004–2005

State	Percentage of Total State and Local Government Revenue That Is:			State Share of:
	General Own-Source Revenue	Intergovernmental Revenue from Federal	Utility, Liquor Store and Insurance Trust Revenue	State and Local General Own-Source Revenue
United States	62.7%	17.4%	19.9%	55.2%
Alabama	60.0%	22.1%	17.9%	58.0%
Alaska	64.2%	22.5%	13.3%	76.5%
Arizona	62.1%	20.0%	17.9%	54.5%
Arkansas	62.0%	23.0%	15.1%	74.7%
California	56.6%	14.3%	29.0%	55.4%
Colorado	63.4%	13.1%	23.5%	45.9%
Connecticut	75.8%	14.5%	9.7%	63.1%
Delaware	71.5%	15.5%	13.0%	79.0%
District of Columbia	56.7%	30.2%	13.1%	0.0%
Florida	67.2%	15.6%	17.2%	48.1%
Georgia	65.7%	17.5%	16.8%	51.0%
Hawaii	69.0%	17.9%	13.1%	80.1%
Idaho	64.2%	18.8%	17.0%	61.2%
Illinois	65.1%	15.3%	19.6%	51.7%
Indiana	72.9%	16.4%	10.7%	54.9%
Iowa	64.7%	18.8%	16.5%	56.3%
Kansas	67.9%	17.1%	15.1%	54.2%
Kentucky	63.2%	21.8%	15.0%	69.5%
Louisiana	61.5%	21.9%	16.7%	59.4%
Maine	63.5%	23.3%	13.2%	62.3%
Maryland	70.0%	16.6%	13.4%	56.6%
Massachusetts	64.9%	15.0%	20.1%	65.3%

(table continued on next page)

TABLE 5-4. Distribution of Total State and Local Government Revenue by State, 2004–2005 (continued)

State	Percentage of Total State and Local Government Revenue That Is:			State Share of:
	General Own-Source Revenue	Intergovernmental Revenue from Federal	Utility, Liquor Store and Insurance Trust Revenue	State and Local General Own-Source Revenue
Michigan	64.9%	17.4%	17.7%	62.4%
Minnesota	66.2%	16.1%	17.8%	63.9%
Mississippi	55.9%	28.4%	15.7%	59.8%
Missouri	61.4%	20.7%	17.9%	53.3%
Montana	57.6%	26.9%	15.5%	65.5%
Nebraska	60.4%	16.8%	22.8%	55.1%
Nevada	69.3%	11.8%	18.9%	52.3%
New Hampshire	68.2%	18.2%	13.6%	54.2%
New Jersey	71.7%	13.7%	14.6%	54.8%
New Mexico	58.6%	25.6%	15.9%	73.3%
New York	62.7%	19.8%	17.5%	43.6%
North Carolina	61.4%	20.2%	18.4%	58.9%
North Dakota	62.5%	25.0%	12.5%	65.3%
Ohio	58.5%	16.7%	24.8%	55.5%
Oklahoma	62.1%	21.1%	16.8%	63.6%
Oregon	55.8%	16.2%	28.0%	57.0%
Pennsylvania	62.4%	18.6%	19.0%	57.8%
Rhode Island	62.1%	21.6%	16.3%	63.2%
South Carolina	61.7%	21.3%	17.0%	56.3%
South Dakota	54.1%	23.5%	22.3%	55.8%
Tennessee	56.3%	20.8%	22.9%	54.7%
Texas	63.4%	17.8%	18.9%	47.8%
Utah	61.5%	16.8%	21.7%	63.2%
Vermont	65.1%	24.4%	10.5%	84.3%
Virginia	71.4%	12.2%	16.4%	59.1%
Washington	58.9%	14.5%	26.6%	57.7%
West Virginia	59.7%	24.0%	16.2%	75.3%
Wisconsin	61.2%	14.7%	24.2%	60.5%
Wyoming	53.8%	34.5%	11.7%	55.5%

Source: U.S. Census Bureau, "State Government Finances," http://www.census.gov/govs/www/state.html (accessed January 22, 2008).

for a list of the subcategories); the highest reliance on this source is Nevada at 17.3 percent (mostly, of course, gambling taxes). Reliance on individual income taxes ranges widely—from seven states with none (this grouping excludes Tennessee and New Hampshire, which have taxes related to income but limited to individuals' interest and dividend income, rather than wage and salary income) to 28.8 percent in Maryland. Reliance on corporate income taxes ranges from four states with zero to Alaska with 8.1 percent and New Hampshire with 7.8 percent. All but five states rely on motor vehicle license and all other taxes combined for less than 15 percent of own-source revenue; the highest is 24.2 percent in Delaware, a favored location for business incorporations, which result in franchise tax collection.

TABLE 5-5. Distribution of State and Local Own-Source General Revenue by State, 2004–2005, as Percentage of General Revenue from Own Sources

State	Total	Property	General Sales	Selective Sales	Individual Income	Corporate Income	Motor Vehicle License and Other	Charges and Miscellaneous
United States	69.3%	21.2%	16.6%	7.6%	15.2%	2.7%	8.2%	30.7%
Alaska	40.5%	12.3%	2.2%	3.3%	0.0%	8.1%	15.2%	59.5%
Arizona	71.8%	20.1%	27.5%	6.7%	11.2%	2.7%	6.3%	28.2%
Arkansas	68.9%	10.0%	28.5%	8.4%	16.0%	2.4%	7.3%	31.1%
California	68.0%	15.8%	17.4%	5.3%	19.9%	4.0%	7.1%	32.0%
Colorado	63.5%	20.0%	17.8%	5.3%	15.3%	1.3%	6.3%	36.5%
Connecticut	81.6%	30.9%	14.1%	8.0%	21.7%	2.5%	6.4%	18.4%
Delaware	60.0%	8.9%	0.0%	7.4%	17.1%	4.6%	24.2%	40.0%
District of Columbia	81.2%	21.5%	16.0%	8.1%	21.7%	3.8%	10.7%	18.8%
Florida	65.8%	22.4%	22.1%	10.7%	0.00%	2.0%	11.7%	34.2%
Georgia	69.4%	20.7%	19.3%	6.2%	18.5%	1.8%	5.1%	30.6%
Hawaii	72.8%	10.8%	28.2%	10.00%	18.2%	1.6%	6.1%	27.2%
Idaho	65.1%	18.0%	17.6%	6.2%	16.2%	2.2%	8.5%	34.9%
Illinois	75.2%	28.6%	12.8%	12.7%	12.1%	33%	8.0%	24.8%
Indiana	66.9%	23.9%	15.7%	7.1%	15.1%	2.6%	5.0%	33.1%
Iowa	64.5%	22.0%	14.4%	6.6%	15.4%	1.2%	7.9%	35.5%
Kansas	69.4%	22.9%	18.6%	7.0%	15.2%	1.8%	7.1%	30.6%
Kentucky	69.2%	12.7%	14.7%	11.5%	21.4%	2.7%	9.0%	30.8%
Louisiana	64.9%	11.0%	25.8%	9.1%	10.9%	1.6%	9.3%	35.1%
Maine	72.4%	29.9%	13.0%	5.9%	18.0%	1.9%	6.9%	27.6%
Maryland	75.3%	17.6%	9.1%	9.0%	28.8%	2.5%	10.5%	24.7%
Massachusetts	72.0%	25.9%	9.7%	5.1%	24.3%	3.3%	5.4%	28.0%
Michigan	66.9%	24.5%	15.3%	7.0%	12.4%	3.6%	6.1%	33.1%
Minnesota	69.7%	17.5%	14.2%	8.5%	21.1%	3.1%	7.5%	30.3%
Mississippi	63.5%	16.7%	22.0%	8.4%	10.0%	2.4%	7.8%	36.5%
Missouri	68.5%	18.5%	19.2%	8.6%	17.0%	0.9%	7.2%	31.5%
Montana	63.5%	23.3%	0.0%	10.7%	16.6%	2.3%	15.1%	36.5%

(table continued on next page)

TABLE 5-5. Distribution of State and Local Own-Source General Revenue by State, 2004-2005, as Percentage of General Revenue from Own Sources (continued)

State	Total	Property	General Sales	Selective Sales	Individual Income	Corporate Income	Motor Vehicle License and Other	Charges and Miscellaneous
Nebraska	68.6%	21.9%	18.4%	5.7%	14.5%	2.1%	9.2%	31.4%
Nevada	68.9%	17.7%	23.3%	17.3%	0.0%	0.0%	14.0%	31.1%
New Hampshire	70.9%	43.50%	0.0%	11.6%	1.1%	7.8%	9.1%	29.1%
New Jersey	76.3%	34.4%	11.7%	6.6%	14.7%	4.0%	5.7%	23.7%
New Mexico	62.3%	8.9%	22.1%	7.2%	11.1%	2.5%	12.8%	37.7%
New York	76.7%	23.6%	14.6%	4.7%	24.1%	4.8%	5.3%	23.3%
North Carolina	68.6%	16.2%	15.7%	8.0%	21.2%	3.2%	7.7%	31.4%
North Dakota	64.8%	18.9%	14.6%	9.5%	7.4%	2.3%	15.7%	35.2%
Ohio	69.5%	20.0%	16.1%	5.2%	21.8%	2.2%	7.1%	30.5%
Oklahoma	66.1%	11.3%	19.2%	6.3%	16.2%	1.1%	14.7%	33.9%
Oregon	61.5%	19.7%	0.0%	5.4%	26.7%	2.0%	9.8%	38.5%
Pennsylvania	71.0%	20.7%	12.7%	8.3%	17.7%	2.6%	11.9%	29.0%
Rhode Island	74.5%	30.1%	14.0%	9.0%	16.5%	1.9%	5.2%	25.5%
South Carolina	57.5%	18.2%	14.8%	5.8%	13.1%	1.2%	6.7%	42.5%
South Dakota	66.7%	23.2%	26.4%	9.2%	0.0%	1.6%	10.3%	33.3%
Tennessee	65.0%	15.8%	30.8%	7.4%	0.6%	3.3%	10.6%	35.0%
Texas	66.9%	29.3%	19.6%	10.5%	0.0%	0.0%	10.3%	33.1%
Utah	61.9%	15.2%	18.5%	7.1%	16.3%	1.6%	6.2%	38.1%
Vermont	73.3%	30.1%	9.0%	13.4%	14.3%	2.0%	7.1%	26.7%
Virginia	68.1%	20.7%	10.0%	8.8%	20.6%	1.5%	8.8%	31.9%
Washington	67.7%	19.6%	31.4%	9.4%	0.0%	0.0%	10.1%	32.3%
West Virginia	63.0%	11.5%	12.4%	12.7%	13.3%	5.3%	11.5%	37.0%
Wisconsin	72.3%	26.3%	14.5%	6.1%	18.5%	2.6%	7.5%	27.7%
Wyoming	62.6%	20.9%	16.0%	3.2%	0.0%	0.0%	24.1%	37.4%

Source: U.S. Census Bureau, "State Government Finances," http://www.census.gov/govs/www/state.html (accessed January 22, 2008).

Comparison of Overall Tax Burdens

Table 5-5 shows that, from a national perspective, state and local governments have made different decisions about the degree of their reliance on particular taxes for providing revenue. While there are various ways to demonstrate the effects of these differences, it is useful analytically to standardize as many differences between states as possible and then examine differences in use of specific taxes from this perspective. Tables 5-6, 5-7, and 5-8 are excerpts from tax burden studies prepared by the Idaho State Tax Commission since FY 1979 and updated as often as new census data become available (generally annually, lagging the calendar by about two years). The tables rely

Chapter 5 ■ Tax Analysis

on a systematic approach that standardizes for differences in total personal income and population. They rank states on the basis of tax capacity determined by applying the U.S. average tax rate as a percentage of total personal income or per capita to each state's income or population. Actual tax collections in each state are then divided by this "capacity" to determine each state's "tax effort."

Tables 5-6 and 5-7 show total personal income-based tax capacity and tax effort for each state and the District of Columbia for FY 2005 using this methodology

TABLE 5-6. Property Tax Burden by State Based on Total Personal Income for FY 2005

State	Personal Income FY 2005 ($ millions)	State & Local FY 05 Property Tax Revenue ($ millions)	Tax Capacity Potential Tax Coll. ($ millions) (avg. rate pers. inc.)	Underutil. Potential: (overutil.) ($ millions) (C4 - C3)	Avg. Actual Tax Rate: Col. 3 ÷ Col. 2 (% of inc.)	Tax Effort: % of Tax Capacity Utilized (C3 ÷ C4)	Rank: Based on Tax Effort
United States	9,982,781	335,678.0			3.36%		
Alabama	130,818	1,792.3	4,398.9	2,606.5	1.37%	40.7%	51
Alaska	22,936	892.3	771.2	(121.1)	3.89%	115.7%	14
Arizona	171,143	5,126.1	5,754.8	628.7	3.00%	89.10%	29
Arkansas	72,667	1,172.3	2,443.5	1,271.2	1.61%	48.0%	49
California	1,301,152	34,058.3	43,752.2	9,693.9	2.62%	77.8%	39
Colorado	169,876	4,940.4	5,712.2	771.8	2.9t%	86.5%	33
Connecticut	162,596	7155.6	5,467.4	(1,688.2)	4.40%	130.9%	8
Delaware	30,202	485.8	1,015.6	529.7	1.61%	47.8%	50
Dist. of Col.	29,994	1,135.5	1,008.6	(127.0)	3.79%	112.6%	15
Florida	584,217	20,389.1	19,644.7	(744.5)	3.49%	103.8%	21
Georgia	273,349	8,214.5	9,191.5	977.0	3.0t%	89.4%	28
Hawaii	42,652	818.2	1,434.2	616.0	1.92%	57.1%	46
Idaho	39,480	1,153.8	1,327.5	173.7	2.92%	86.9%	32
Illinois	452,141	18,690.1	15,203.6	(3,486.6)	4.13%	122.9%	11
Indiana	191,417	7,639.0	6,436.5	(1,202.5)	3.99%	118.7%	12
Iowa	92,711	3,302.3	3,117.5	(184.8)	3.56%	105.9%	19
Kansas	88,110	3,090.4	2,962.8	(127.7)	3.5t%	104.3%	20
Kentucky	114,880	2,246.9	3,862.9	1,616.0	1.96%	58.2%	45
Louisiana	124,157	2,429.4	4,174.9	1,745.5	1.96%	58.2%	44
Maine	40,022	2,152.0	1,345.8	(806.2)	5.38%	159.9%	2
Maryland	227,528	5,594.4	7,650.8	2,056.4	2.46%	73.1%	41
Massachusetts	273,644	10,341.1	9,201.5	(1,139.6)	3.78%	112.4%	16
Michigan	325,985	12,918.9	10,961.5	(1,957.4)	3.96%	117.9%	13
Minnesota	188,232	5,250.9	6,329.4	1,078.6	2.79%	83.0%	34
Mississippi	71,241	1,967.4	2,395.5	428.1	2.76%	82.1%	36
Missouri	177,150	4,695.5	5,956.8	1,261.3	2.65%	78.8%	38

(table continued on next page)

TABLE 5-6. Property Tax Burden by State Based on Total Personal Income for FY 2005 (continued)

State	Personal Income FY 2005 ($ millions)	State & Local FY 05 Property Tax Revenue ($ millions)	Tax Capacity Potential Tax Coll. ($ millions) (avg. rate pers. inc.)	Underutil. Potential: (overutil.) ($ millions) (C4 - C3)	Avg. Actual Tax Rate: Col. 3 ÷ Col. 2 (% of inc.)	Tax Effort: % of Tax Capacity Utilized (C3 ÷ C4)	Rank: Based on Tax Effort
Montana	26,456	997.4	889.6	(107.8)	3.77%	112.1%	17
Nebraska	56,969	2,101.8	1,915.6	(186.2)	3.69%	109.7%	18
Nevada	83,252	2,320.8	2,799.4	478.6	2.79%	82.9%	35
New Hampshire	48,426	2,650.3	1,628.4	(1,022.0)	5.47%	162.8%	1
New Jersey	372,795	19,196.6	12,535.5	(6,661.1)	5.15%	153.1%	4
New Mexico	52,261	863.1	1,757.3	894.2	1.65%	49.1%	48
New York	758,121	34,150.0	25,492.3	(8,657.6)	4.50%	134.0%	7
North Carolina	261,528	6,449.6	8,794.1	2,344.4	2.47%	73.3%	40
North Dakota	19,175	619.9	644.8	24.9	3.23%	96.1%	23
Ohio	359,549	11,974.0	12,090.1	116.1	3.33%	99.0%	22
Oklahoma	103,176	1,718.6	3,469.4	1,750.7	1.67%	49.5%	47
Oregon	114,263	3,563.0	3,842.2	279.2	3.12%	92.7%	26
Pennsylvania	424,320	13,390.5	14,268.0	877.5	3.16%	93.8%	25
Rhode Island	37,335	1,819.4	1,255.4	(564.0)	4.87%	144.9%	5
South Carolina	116,993	3,738.8	3,934.0	195.1	3.20%	95.0%	24
South Dakota	24,684	730.1	830.0	99.9	2.96%	88.0%	31
Tennessee	179,345	3,894.4	6,030.6	2,136.2	2.17%	64.6%	42
Texas	716,147	30,275.7	24,080.9	(6,194.8)	4.23%	125.7%	10
Utah	65,606	1,792.5	2,206.1	413.6	2.73%	81.3%	37
Vermont	19,978	1,056.4	6/1.8	(384.6)	5.29%	157.2%	3
Virginia	275,706	8,390.00	9,270.8	880.8	3.04%	90.5%	27
Washington	222,437	6,637.3	7,479.6	842.3	2.98%	88.7%	30
West Virginia	46,925	1,008.4	1,577.9	569.5	2.15%	63.9%	43
Wisconsin	180,706	7,796.0	6,076.4	(1,719.7)	4.31%	128.3%	9
Wyoming	18,333	890.7	616.4	(274.3)	4.86%	144.5%	6

Source: Idaho State Tax Commission, Comparative tax potential: Tax burden in Idaho and the United States, fiscal year 2005, http://tax.idaho.gov/pdf/publications/TaxBurdenReports/2005TaxBurdenStudy.pdf

and results for property taxes and for overall state and local taxes, respectively. Table 5-8 demonstrates per-capita tax capacity and effort in a similar way.

While these tables are useful in analyzing overall tax burdens or burdens relative to specific tax types, care must taken in interpreting this information. Results can be distorted by anomalous tax collection patterns (e.g., an audit that results in a one-time large payment by a major taxpayer; a significant up- or downturn in mineral prices in states heavily dependent on taxes on extractive industries), so they should be reviewed for long-term patterns, rather than specific-year rankings. Tables of this type also do *not* reflect the following important considerations:

- The incidence of the tax in question (i.e., which group pays or how progressive the tax is)
- Whether the state's business climate or prospects for economic growth are good or bad
- Whether the state's revenue needs are higher or lower than those of the average state.

TABLE 5-7. Overall Tax Burden by State Based on Total Personal Income for FY 2005

State	Personal Income FY 2005 ($ millions)	State & Local FY 05 Total Tax Revenue ($ millions)	Tax Capacity Potential Tax Coll. ($ millions) (avg. rate pers. inc.)	Underutil. Potential: (overutil.) ($ millions) (C4 - C3)	Avg. Actual Tax Rate: Col. 3 ÷ Col. 2 (% of inc.)	Tax Effort: % of Tax Capacity Utilized (C3 ÷ C4)	Rank: Based on Tax Effort
United States	9,982,781	1,096,384.7			10.98%		
Alabama	130,818	11,686.7	14,367.5	2,680.8	8.93%	81.3%	48
Alaska	22,936	2,947.0	2,519.0	(428.1)	12.85%	117.0%	7
Arizona	171,143	18,331.1	18,796.2	465.1	10.71%	97.5%	28
Arkansas	72,667	8,053.9	7,980.9	(73.1)	11.08%	100.9%	21
California	1,301,152	146,616.9	142,902.4	(3,714.5)	11.27%	102.6%	17
Colorado	169,876	15,680.8	18,657.1	2,976.3	9.23%	84.0%	47
Connecticut	162,596	18,896.8	17,857.5	(1,039.3)	11.62%	105.8%	11
Delaware	30,202	3,277.4	3,317.0	39.7	10.85%	98.8%	25
Dist. of Col.	29,994	4,297.2	3,294.1	(1,003.1)	14.33%	130.5%	3
Florida	584,217	59,863.9	64,163.1	4,299.2	10.25%	93.3%	39
Georgia	273,349	27,486.1	30,021.2	2,535.1	10.06%	91.6%	41
Hawaii	42,652	5,523.7	4,684.3	(839.4)	12.95%	117.9%	5
Idaho	39,480	4,182.5	4,336.0	153.4	10.59%	96.5%	31
Illinois	452,141	49,138.5	49,657.5	519.0	10.87%	99.0%	23
Indiana	191,417	21,337.1	21,022.9	(314.2)	11.15%	101.5%	18
Iowa	92,711	9,704.9	10,182.2	477.3	10.47%	95.3%	35
Kansas	88,110	9,385.5	9,676.9	291.4	10.65%	97.0%	30
Kentucky	114,880	12,261.8	12,617.0	355.2	10.67%	97.2%	29
Louisiana	124,157	14,302.0	13,635.9	(666.1)	11.52%	104.9%	15
Maine	40,022	5,219.7	4,395.5	(824.2)	13.04%	118.7%	4
Maryland	227,528	23,899.1	24,988.8	1,089.8	10.50%	95.6%	34
Massachusetts	273,644	28,757.0	30,053.7	1,296.7	10.51%	95.7%	33
Michigan	325,985	35,295.2	35,802.1	507.0	10.83%	98.6%	27

(table continued on next page)

TABLE 5-7. Overall Tax Burden by State Based on Total Personal Income for FY 2005 (continued)

State	Personal Income FY 2005 ($ millions)	State & Local FY 05 Total Tax Revenue ($ millions)	Tax Capacity Potential Tax Coll. ($ millions) (avg. rate pers. inc.)	Underutil. Potential: (overutil.) ($ millions) (C4 - C3)	Avg. Actual Tax Rate: Col. 3 ÷ Col. 2 (% of inc.)	Tax Effort: % of Tax Capacity Utilized (C3 ÷ C4)	Rank: Based on Tax Effort
Minnesota	188,232	20,956.6	20,673.0	(283.6)	11.13%	101.4%	19
Mississippi	71,241	7,490.7	7,824.3	333.6	10.51%	95.7%	32
Missouri	177,150	17,374.3	19,455.9	2,081.6	9.81%	89.3%	43
Montana	26,456	2,722.7	2,905.6	182.9	10.29%	93.7%	38
Nebraska	56,969	6,586.2	6,256.7	(329.5)	11.56%	105.3%	14
Nevada	83,252	9,043.6	9,143.4	99.8	10.86%	98.9%	24
New Hampshire	48,426	4,319.8	5,318.5	998.8	8.92%	81.2%	49
New Jersey	372,795	42,557.4	40,943.2	(1,614.2)	11.42%	103.9%	16
New Mexico	52,261	6,069.3	5,739.7	(329.7)	11.61%	105.7%	12
New York	758,121	111,107.6	83,262.6	(27,845.0)	14.66%	133.4%	1
North Carolina	261,528	27,307.1	28,723.0	1,415.9	10.44%	95.1%	36
North Dakota	19,175	2,121.4	2,105.9	(15.4)	11.06%	100.7%	22
Ohio	359,549	41,714.8	39,488.4	(2,226.3)	11.60%	105.6%	13
Oklahoma	103,176	10,073.1	11,331.6	1,258.5	9.76%	88.9%	44
Oregon	114,263	11,107.0	12,549.2	1,442.2	9.72%	88.5%	45
Pennsylvania	424,320	46,019.3	46,602.0	582.7	10.85%	98.7%	26
Rhode Island	37,335	4,499.6	4,100.4	(399.2)	12.05%	109.7%	8
South Carolina	116,993	11,800.6	12,849.0	1,048.4	10.09%	91.8%	40
South Dakota	24,684	2,103.8	2,711.0	607.1	8.52%	77.6%	51
Tennessee	179,345	15,993.1	19,697.0	3,703.8	8.92%	81.2%	50
Texas	716,147	69,133.9	78,652.6	9,518.8	9.65%	87.9%	46
Utah	65,606	7,304.0	7,205.4	(98.6)	11.13%	101.4%	20
Vermont	19,978	2,574.8	2,194.1	(380.6)	12.89%	117.3%	6
Virginia	275,706	27,659.2	30,280.2	2,621.0	10.03%	91.3%	42
Washington	222,437	22,974.0	24,429.7	1,455.7	10.33%	94.0%	37
West Virginia	46,925	5,550.7	5,153.6	(397.1)	11.83%	107.7%	10
Wisconsin	180,706	21,403.5	19,846.5	(1,557.0)	11.84%	107.8%	9
Wyoming	18,333	2,671.9	2,013.4	(658.4)	14.57%	132.7%	2

Differences in Fiscal Capacity, Need, and Effort

The differences across states in the level of taxes are due to differences in conditions that affect the cost of delivering state and local government services, differences in access to taxable resources, and political choices about the degree of effort made to use those resources to provide services. Following the lead of earlier researchers at the now defunct U.S. Advisory Commission on Intergovernmental Relations (ACIR), Robert Tannenwald (1999), an economist at the Federal Reserve Bank of Boston, attempted to separately estimate these reasons for cross-state fiscal differences. These measures of fiscal capacity, need, and effort (see Table 5-9) used the data described above as well as other data, but were more subjective and extended beyond the simple reporting of facts. Tannenwald's analysis involved establishing various fiscal measures derived from the characteristics and behavior of the various states often used as normative standards.

TABLE 5-8. Per-Capita Overall Tax Burden by State for FY 2005

State	July 1, 2005 Population (millions)	Overall Tax Revenue ($ millions)	Per-Capita Tax Capacity ($)	Tax Effort Per-Capita: Tax Capacity Index	Rank: Based on Tax Effort
United States	296.507	1,096,384.7			
Alabama	4.548	11,686.7	16,818.21	69.5%	51
Alaska	0.663	2,947.0	2,452.49	120.2%	7
Arizona	5.953	18,331.1	22,012.25	83.3%	35
Arkansas	2.776	8,053.9	10,263.65	78.5%	45
California	36.154	146,616.9	133,686.07	109.7%	13
Colorado	4.663	15,680.8	17,243.32	90.9%	28
Connecticut	3.501	18,896.8	12,944.43	146.0%	3
Delaware	0.842	3,277.4	3,112.48	105.3%	15
Dist. of Col.	0.582	4,297.2	2,152.22	199.7%	1
Florida	17.768	59,863.9	65,700.89	91.1%	27
Georgia	9.133	27,486.1	33,769.16	81.4%	39
Hawaii	1.273	5,523.7	4,708.16	117.3%	8
Idaho	1.429	4,182.5	5,285.33	79.1%	43
Illinois	12.765	49,138.5	47,202.32	104.1%	17
Indiana	6.266	21,337.1	23,169.66	92.1%	26
Iowa	2.966	9,704.9	10,965.53	88.5%	31
Kansas	2.748	9,385.5	10,161.83	92.4%	25
Kentucky	4.173	12,261.8	15,428.92	79.5%	41
Louisiana	4.507	14,302.0	16,666.62	85.8%	32
Maine	1.318	5,219.7	4,874.34	107.1%	14
Maryland	5.590	23,899.1	20,668.49	115.6%	9
Massachusetts	6.433	28,757.0	23,788.46	120.9%	6

(table continued on next page)

TABLE 5-8. Per-Capita Overall Tax Burden by State for FY 2005 (continued)

State	July 1, 2005 Population (millions)	Overall Tax Revenue ($ millions)	Per-Capita Tax Capacity ($)	Tax Effort Per-Capita: Tax Capacity Index	Rank: Based on Tax Effort
Michigan	10.101	35,295.2	37,349.54	94.5%	24
Minnesota	5.127	20,956.6	18,956.98	110.5%	12
Mississippi	2.908	7,490.7	10,754.66	69.7%	50
Missouri	5.798	17,374.3	21,437.99	81.0%	40
Montana	0.935	2,722.7	3,456.35	78.8%	44
Nebraska	1.758	6,586.2	6,501.10	101.3%	19
Nevada	2.412	9,043.6	8,919.89	101.4%	18
New Hampshire	1.307	4,319.8	4,832.18	89.4%	30
New Jersey	8.703	42,557.4	32,181.37	132.2%	5
New Mexico	1.926	6,069.3	7,121.66	85.2%	33
New York	19.316	111,107.6	71,423.14	155.6%	2
North Carolina	8.672	27,307.1	32,067.88	85.2%	34
North Dakota	0.635	2,121.4	2,346.56	90.4%	29
Ohio	11.471	41,714.8	42,414.80	98.3%	23
Oklahoma	3.543	10,073.1	13,102.48	76.9%	46
Oregon	3.639	11,107.0	13,455.34	82.5%	37
Pennsylvania	12.405	46,019.3	45,870.87	100.3%	20
Rhode Island	1.074	4,499.6	3,969.74	113.3%	10
South Carolina	4.247	11,800.6	15,703.75	75.1%	47
South Dakota	0.775	2,103.8	2,865.26	73.4%	48
Tennessee	5.956	15,993.1	22,022.37	72.6%	49
Texas	22.929	69,133.9	84,782.03	81.5%	38
Utah	2.490	7,304.0	9,208.43	79.3%	42
Vermont	0.622	2,574.8	2,301.38	111.9%	11
Virginia	7.564	27,659.2	27,970.38	98.9%	21
Washington	6.292	22,974.0	23,265.36	98.7%	22
West Virginia	1.814	5,550.7	6,707.88	82.7%	36
Wisconsin	5.528	21,403.5	20,439.40	104.7%	16
Wyoming	0.509	2,671.9	1,881.37	142.0%	4

An index of fiscal capacity was constructed by asking what own-source revenue could each state raise if it had a representative tax system, that is, if it applied the *national* average tax rate to its *own* amounts of each of the major sources of taxes and charges—property values, retail sales, personal incomes, corporate incomes, alcohol sales, gasoline sales, tobacco sales, vehicle licenses, oil or mineral extractions, and so on. The second column of Table 5-9 shows Tannenwald's estimates of an index of fiscal capacity for FY 1995–1996. Montana (with an index of 99), Nebraska (99), Vermont (99), and Virginia (101) are very close to the national average of 100 in their combined access to income, property, sales, and other potential sources of state and local government revenue. The richest state in terms of fiscal capacity is Nevada, with 141 percent of the national average access to sources of revenue. The poorest state in terms of fiscal capacity is Mississippi, with an index of only 72.

An index of fiscal need can be constructed by the "representative expenditure system" approach. First, the researcher must "identify and define categories of state and local governmental outlays whose level of spending within a state is significantly influenced by factors other than population" (Tannenwald 1999, 13). Second, these categories are linked to a "workload" variable: elementary and secondary education to the number of pupils, highway spending to vehicle-miles traveled, or welfare spending to poverty counts, for example. The 30 percent of spending in categories for which a workload assignment cannot be made are linked to population. Third, an adjustment is made for cross-state variations in wages and other input costs. Finally, a calculation is made of how much a state would spend *if* it chose to provide the national average levels of service per pupil, per mile traveled, per low-income

TABLE 5-9. Indexes of Fiscal Capacity, Need, and Effort by State, 1995–1996

State	Fiscal Capacity	Fiscal Need	Fiscal Comfort	Tax Effort
United States	100	100	100	100
Alabama	83	104	79	83
Alaska	127	102	124	116
Arizona	94	105	90	93
Arkansas	81	100	81	92
California	103	110	94	101
Colorado	114	90	126	82
Connecticut	129	102	126	115
Delaware	121	89	135	90
District of Columbia	126	126	100	141
Florida	110	96	104	90
Georgia	96	104	92	95
Hawaii	120	90	134	104
Idaho	90	100	90	92
Illinois	110	101	109	97
Indiana	97	92	105	88
Iowa	97	89	108	98
Kansas	96	95	101	99
Kentucky	84	101	93	99
Louisiana	88	109	81	86
Maine	89	88	100	113
Maryland	108	95	113	100
Massachusetts	116	93	125	104

(table continued on next page)

TABLE 5-9. Indexes of Fiscal Capacity, Need, and Effort by State, 1995–1996 (continued)

State	Fiscal Capacity	Fiscal Need	Fiscal Comfort	Tax Effort
Michigan	98	101	97	100
Minnesota	107	94	113	113
Mississippi	72	110	65	102
Missouri	97	92	105	87
Montana	99	98	101	79
Nebraska	99	88	112	99
Nevada	141	94	150	73
New Hampshire	118	84	141	74
New Jersey	116	95	122	114
New Mexico	85	115	74	102
New York	109	104	105	141
North Carolina	92	95	97	94
North Dakota	97	96	101	89
Ohio	96	97	99	100
Oklahoma	84	104	80	92
Oregon	103	91	113	85
Pennsylvania	95	93	102	102
Rhode Island	91	89	102	117
South Carolina	85	101	85	89
South Dakota	95	96	100	79
Tennessee	92	102	90	79
Texas	91	108	85	90
Utah	92	95	97	89
Vermont	99	90	111	100
Virginia	101	96	105	89
Washington	104	95	109	104
West Virginia	78	100	78	99
Wisconsin	97	89	109	117
Wyoming	127	101	126	74

Source: Tannenwald 1999.

person, and per capita. The third column of Table 5-9 is just such an index of fiscal need. The workload measures and state wage costs combine such that West Virginia has a level of need for state and local government services just equal to the national average of 100. The highest need for revenue to support standard service levels is in the District of Columbia (126) and the lowest is in Nebraska (88).

The capacity and need measures can be combined into a single measure of relative fiscal disparity. Tannenwald used the ratio of fiscal capacity to fiscal need to construct what he called an index of fiscal comfort. Nevada is doubly advantaged by high capacity and low need and has a fiscal comfort index of 150 percent of the all-state average. Mississippi is doubly disadvantaged by low capacity and high needs and has a comfort index of only 65. The District of Columbia has high needs offset by high capacity and ends up at the national average of 100. South Dakota ends up at 100 with low capacity divided by equally low needs.

Finally, this method can be used to calculate a measure of tax effort, "the ratio of each state's actual tax collections to the taxes it would have collected under the representative tax system" (Tannenwald 1999, 20). The result is shown in the last column of Table 5-9. Nevada (73) and Wyoming (74) are lowest in terms of what they actually collected compared with their representative tax bases. New York (141) and the District of Columbia (141) have made the highest tax effort. California (101), Michigan (100), Ohio (100), Maryland (100), Kentucky (99), Nebraska (99), Kansas (99), and West Virginia (99) all make about average effort.

The earlier discussion stressed the usefulness of looking at tax burdens over time or across states "per $1,000 of personal income." That was a simpler measure of tax effort, because personal income per capita is a simpler measure of tax capacity.

Other Fiscal Measures and Information Sources

Several other measures of fiscal burdens are often used in making comparisons among states and localities. The Minnesota tax incidence studies (http://www.taxes.state.mn.us/legal_policy/research_reports/content/incidence.shtml) break down tax burdens in that state by income class. The study focuses only on the state of Minnesota and does not provide comparable information for all states. The Government of the District of Columbia compiles an annual publication, *Tax Rates and Tax Burdens in the District of Columbia—A Nationwide Comparison*, which details state and local tax burdens for households of different income level for Washington, D.C., and 50 other cities around the nation.

In both of these studies and other similar ones, a number of assumptions must be made about the incidence of taxes to determine who actually bears the burden. The results are highly sensitive to these assumptions. There is also considerable controversy about the shifting process in regard to the property and corporate income tax. There are also questions about what proportion of state and local sales taxes can be exported.

Studies that purport to measure state and local tax burdens on business present even more challenging issues because of the need to determine who actually bears the ultimate burden of business taxes. The shifting and incidence issues, as well as the capitalization of burdens in asset values, make these studies very difficult to interpret and potentially unreliable. In addition, it is sometimes difficult to accurately or consistently classify taxpayers as business or residential. One of the most difficult assignment issues is what to do with small residential housing complexes that are used for non-owner-occupied housing. Most conventions assign complexes containing four or fewer housing units to the residential sector, but this distinction may not adequately reflect business use and business taxes may be understated. The analyst must state and the user must understand such underlying assumptions.

Despite the analytical difficulties of which the user must be aware, tax burden and incidence studies that are well documented provide valuable information to policy makers and to the public. Both the Minnesota tax incidence studies and the District of Columbia study attempt to analyze at least the initial progressivity or regressivity of each state's (or the largest city's) tax structure. The Minnesota study does this by showing the taxes paid by individual taxpayers in various income deciles (i.e., lowest 10 percent, 10–20 percent, and so on). If individuals in low-income deciles pay higher amounts as a percentage of their income, a tax is considered regressive. The District of Columbia study ranks the 51 cities used in the analysis in terms of an index of progressivity.

At the time this text was being prepared, a project jointly sponsored and conducted by the Lincoln Institute of Land Policy and George Washington University was under way with the goal of reinstating the data compilations and analysis previously provided by the ACIR. When completed, the planned replacement publication and Web site should fill a significant gap and become a valuable resource to tax analysts.

Observations on Tax Burden and Incidence

As pointed out earlier, the need for services and, concomitantly, the acceptability and availability of taxes to pay for these services differ from state to state and place to place within states. Hence, tax burdens may appear to be high, but may be quite acceptable given a high demand for services. Tax incidence may similarly appear to be high on certain segments, but this too may be acceptable given a state's political and economic culture. As an example, note that in Table 5-9, property taxes in Wyoming are high in national comparisons based on income. Nominally, in terms of the size of the overall economy in Wyoming as measured by total personal income, this means a high property tax brden. However, much of the tax is paid by minerals industries, so the incidence of the property tax in Wyoming on residences cannot be determined from this analysis and can be mistakenly assumed to be high.

State legislators often are concerned about tax incidence. However, there may be a tendency to confuse burden with incidence. Rate restrictions or reductions, for example, can reduce an overall high tax burden. Such a change ordinarily affects only the magnitude of the tax, not its incidence. If the goal is to reduce the proportion of tax being paid by one sector (such as low-income homeowners), additional or alternative mitigating means must be employed. Commonly, this is done through exemptions and tax credits. Some specific exemptions and credits are discussed more fully in Chapter 6, "Analysis of Selected Property Tax Features."

Analysis of Effects of Taxes

As discussed throughout this chapter, there are many ways to observe and analyze the effects of taxes. For example, there is the effect on individuals, such as homeowners, and the effect on wages and business decisions. Moreover, initial and long-term effects and behavioral effects must be taken into account. This section delves further into the issue of tax incidence and explores some of the theoretical and economic effects of taxes. In addition, the effect of taxes and of tax changes on revenue produced must be understood. This issue is addressed in the section on tax elasticity.

Effects of Taxes in Relation to Tax Base

In analyzing the effects of taxes, it is important to understand the nature of the tax base. There are essentially three tax bases: income, consumption, and wealth. All have arguments in their favor, and all have significant theoretical and practical problems. All are used somewhere in the tax system, and all have been adjusted by exclusions from the base. These exclusions are often determined by political expediency or practical administrative problems rather than economic analysis. However, the greater the amount of deductions, the higher the tax rate must be to raise the same amount of revenue. Specific taxes developed to utilize specific tax bases are analyzed in Chapter 4, "Role of Property Tax in Intergovernmental Finance."

The best conceptual definition of income is the amount of consumption added to the change in net worth that a household realizes over a period of a year. This is a measure of the money value of the net increase to an individual's power to consume during a period. Of course, income is not measured this way in the United States; rather, all the income that the household (or corporation) receives is measured. There are several institutional imperfections in this method. These imperfections are often theoretical in nature and are solved by political decision-making. Examples of these imperfections are the handling of changing inflation rates, accurate counting of income-in-kind, determination of the value of services provided by a member of the taxed unit (e.g., how should the value of a stay-at-home spouse be counted?), income averaging, and the imputed rent on owner-occupied housing. The national government and state governments are the primary users of the income tax; local governments rarely use it.

Consumption as a tax base is justified on two grounds. First, households should be taxed on what they take from society (i.e., their consumption). Second, consumption is easier to measure than income or wealth, so it should be taxed. However, the consumption tax base in the United States varies from state to state (and within some states, from jurisdiction to jurisdiction). For example, in most states, for equity reasons food and medical supplies are not taxed. Housing consumption is not taxed. In many states, few services are taxed, but in some states many services are taxed. Some types of e-commerce are taxed. Cigarettes and alcohol tend to be taxed heavily, partially because demand for these products is believed to be inelastic (i.e., a large price increase will not lead to a large quantity decrease) and partially because they are easy to justify as "sin" goods and so should be taxed to modify smokers' behavior and lessen the use of cigarettes. Consumption taxes can be ad valorem (i.e., based on the value) or per unit (sometimes called excise taxes). The national government has only a few excise taxes; they are primarily a tax of the state and local levels of government. However, many of the proposals of the Bush administration, by exempting large amounts of savings from the personal income tax, are actually moving toward a national consumption tax.

Net worth, which should be defined as the value of all the taxpayer's assets less the value of all the taxpayer's liabilities, is probably the best measure of the well-being of the household. It can be argued that a household with $10,000,000 in the bank that is generating $500,000 in income is "better off" than a wage earner working for $500,000 or a consumer spending $500,000. But, as in the two above measures of tax bases, there are some serious problems in defining net worth. For example, how is human capital measured using this concept? Or, personal property can be easy to hide (one example is jewelry). In the past, it has often been difficult to convince homeowners that allowing the tax assessor to wander through their homes to examine their furnishings is a good idea. Thus, the current property tax in the United States is not a net wealth tax. Further, there is some property that does not generate a realized cash flow until it is sold, so that the tax is paid out of the income flow, raising potential equity questions. For business, these problems are multiplied.

In each of the above cases, limiting the base results in a smaller base, thus requiring the rate to be higher to collect the same amount of revenue. As discussed in Appendix D on the behavioral effects of taxes, it is better to have a broader base and lower rates than vice versa. Care must be taken when instituting exemptions from the tax base.

There is one final concept that alters the tax base and thereby relates to tax analysis: tax expenditures. Tax expenditures are the value of an exemption/deduction in the tax base. For example, mortgage interest is a deduction in the federal income tax. Those who are paying mortgages can take advantage of this deduction and pay less tax. This saving in taxes is conceptually equivalent to the government giving that amount to the household. This is called a tax expenditure. Tax expenditures exist for all three bases, and tax reform often tries to eliminate the more egregious of these expenditures. Table 5-10 illustrates a few examples of the type and magnitude of various tax expenditures. However, these estimates should be treated cautiously, because they assume no change in behavior of the recipient of the tax expenditure. For example, the calculation of the tax expenditures associated with the mortgage interest deduction assumes that there will be no change in the number of homes purchased (a person needs to purchase a home to take advantage of the deduction) or that there will be a change in their price if the deduction were no longer allowed.

TABLE 5-10. Examples of Tax Expenditures

Type of Expenditure	Years	$ Millions
U.S. Income Tax Expenditures[a] Individual Retirement Account Property tax deduction Total charitable deduction Employer contributions to medical insurance premiums Capital gains on residence Capital gains Step-up basis of capital gains on death	2003-2007	94,200 97,800 223,800 480,600 107,600 293,900 155,500
Oregon Property Tax Exemptions[b] Charitable, literary, and scientific Religious organizations	1997-1999	45.2 63.0
Arizona Sales Tax Exemptions[c] Legal services Telemarketing bureaus Computer system design Temporary help Auto repair shop Hair, nail, skin care Sale of stocks and bonds Prescription drugs and eyeglasses Food Lottery tickets	2000-2001	92.7 12.1 31.6 67.5 87.9 13.7 92.7 143.0 431.1 13.6

[a] *Source:* Budget of the U.S. Government. 2002. Table 6-1. Estimates of total income tax expenditures. In Fiscal year 2003. Analytical perspectives. Washington, D.C.: Government Printing Office, pp. 99-101.
b Source: Oregon Department of Revenue. Research and statistical report 1999-2001. pp. 10-16.
c Source: Arizona Department of Revenue, Office of Economic Research and Analysis. The revenue impact of Arizona's tax expenditures, FY 2000 2001.

Initial versus Ultimate Incidence of Taxes

The incidence of any tax indicates who pays the tax. Only people pay taxes—that is, people pay taxes in their roles as income earners, consumers, and property owners (most people are in all three of these roles). Thus, comments such as "corporations pay taxes" are somewhat meaningless. Nevertheless, tax incidence is important, and analysts should understand some of the underlying principles and potential distortive factors.

Incidence of Property Tax

Analysis of property tax incidence is complex because owners of certain classes of property can pass taxes on to consumers of goods and services, thus increasing or lessening the ultimate incidence on a regional basis. For example, assume that computer manufacturers are classified so that they pay a higher proportional share of property tax. To the extent that the price of their product is not constrained by the global market for computers, the additional tax is passed on to computer purchasers. If few of these purchasers are local, the tax is exported and the regional incidence of the tax diminishes. The opposite occurs if many of the consumers are local. Adding to the complexity of this process, the manufacturer may become less competitive and lower employee wages or benefits, thus shifting some of the tax incidence to wage earners and their economic community.

Much of the incidence debate on the property tax centers on a largely outdated and spurious assumption that the tax is inherently regressive.

While there are many theoretical debates about this aspect of the property tax, most economists conclude that the tax as a whole may be slightly progressive or neutral and more like a price or benefit tax. For example, it is suggested that ownership of capital assets increases with income, providing a progressive component. In addition, exemptions or provisions such as circuit breakers have been widely enacted and usually serve to reduce an element of perceived regressivity within the property tax. Finally, there is a benefit view of the tax that suggests that people are mobile, selecting their homesites in part because of the services that are available and for which they are willing to pay. The concept of regressivity or progressivity does not apply to the property tax if it is indeed a benefit tax.

Much of this mobility and benefit tax argument dates from the work of Charles Tiebout, who in 1956 published his "homevoter" hypothesis that desired levels of taxes and services influence individual locational decisions. Under this hypothesis, homeowners become consumers of services and "shop" for the services they prefer, as opposed to simply voting in the local political process.

There is an ongoing debate about whether the property tax is regressive for defined segments of the taxpaying population who have limited ability to pay at certain times of their lives. For example, the tax may represent a disproportionately high share of income for older persons or others now on fixed incomes but formerly with greater income with which to pay the tax. This "lifetime" nonregressive nature of the tax of course misses the snapshot view of regressivity in the present for such a group. Circuit breakers and other possible solutions to this problem are discussed in Chapter 6.

Although it is important for assessing officers to understand that such complex economic interrelationships exist, analysis provided to the public or policy makers should be limited to studying initial incidence, the first stage of any tax shifting that is likely, and how it changes the tax burden.

The burden of the tax reflects the initial incidence as well as the magnitude of the tax. Although burden can be expressed in many different ways, assessing officers can analyze property taxes (1) with respect to shares of the tax paid by different classes of property and different strata within each class, (2) by the tax shifts resulting from administrative practices or legislative proposals, and (3) by the magnitude of the tax with respect to income or other bases. Analysis can also be done to demonstrate how proposed tax policy changes will affect any of these aspects of property tax burden.

Technical Issues Related to Tax Incidence

Technical issues related to analyzing property tax incidence and effects of taxation, including behavioral effects, are covered in more detail in Appendixes A through E. The specific topics in these appendixes are as follows:

- *Appendix A* examines the question of the supposed regressivity of the property tax.

- *Appendix B* examines the economic effects of property taxation, with respect to economic development, and discusses alternative property tax system approaches along these lines.

- *Appendix C* examines legal versus economic incidence and provides examples based on sales tax, Social Security tax, and land tax.

- *Appendix D* differentiates between partial and general equilibrium analysis, emphasizing the long-term effects of taxes. This appendix also discusses behavioral effects, including shifts in consumption, savings, and work choices that may result from taxes.

- *Appendix E* examines criteria for evaluating effects of taxes, in terms of economic efficiency, ability to pay (horizontal and vertical tax equity), and balance.

Tax Elasticity

Elasticity measures the change in tax revenues collected as the base changes. It can be formally described as the percentage change in tax revenues divided by the percentage change in the base. However, it is almost never used in this sense; rather, it is more often used as the percentage change in tax revenues divided by the percentage change in income. In this way, the elasticities of different taxes can be directly compared. Two hypothetical examples of the use of elasticity measures are as follows:

- An elasticity of 1.2 means that for every 10 percent increase in income, taxes collected will increase by 12 percent.

- An elasticity of 0.8 means that for every 10 percent increase in income, taxes collected will increase by 8 percent.

The elasticity of a tax is principally affected by the established tax policies and laws; for example, an income tax can be designed to collect proportionally more than income increases by instituting higher rates for high-income taxpayers. Sales tax elasticities are often estimated to be less than 1, while income tax elasticities are usually greater than 1. Tax elasticity is sometimes used in defining the extent of progressivity in the tax system. With some caveats, an elasticity greater than 1 usually implies a progressive system. An elasticity of 1 is a proportional system, while an elasticity of less than 1 often implies a regressive system. Finally, the concept of elasticity is often used in forecasting tax revenues. Econometric models can forecast income growth, which then can be employed using elasticities, to predict tax revenue growth. Table 5-11 shows examples of income elasticity.

Example A in Table 5-11 is a tax that is not dependent on income, and therefore neither more nor less revenue will be collected regardless of the underlying income. In other words, the behavior, in terms relative to generating the tax (i.e., buying a product or using a service), is not expected to change given higher or lower income. A frequent example is electricity.

TABLE 5-11. Examples of Income Elasticity

Example	Change in Income (%)	Change in Taxes (%)	Income Elasticity
A	10	0	0.0
B	10	5	0.5
C	10	10	1.0
D	10	15	1.5

Elasticities can also be computed around rate, with a rate elasticity of 1.0 meaning that a 1 percent change in tax rate should result in a 1 percent change in tax revenue. When tax rate increases are expected to lead to behavior changes, usually in the form of less demand for whatever is being taxed, rate elasticities are less than 1.0. This is especially important to recognize when the revenue implications for tax rate increases are being forecast. Table 5-12 shows examples of rate elasticity.

TABLE 5-12. Examples of Rate Elasticity

Example	Change in Tax Rate (%)	Change in Tax Collections (%)	Rate Elasticity
A	10	0	0.0
B	10	5	0.5
C	10	10	1.0
D	10	15	1.5

Conclusions

Taxes have highly complex effects on people and on the economy. Nominally, taxes are part of the revenue structure and can be analyzed in terms of revenue sufficiency and compared in terms of the amounts raised under different tax structures. Operationally, taxes place a burden on people who pay them and on the economy. A major function of tax analysis is to determine the magnitude and incidence of this burden—in other words, how much is to be paid by whom. Analysis is complicated by the fact that the ultimate payers and costs often differ from the initial, nominal payers and effects. Analysts must note limitations in analysis of initial effects of taxes or proposed changes in tax structure. In addition, although analysts may be unable to address ultimate tax effects, the existence of such complexity and possible effects should be noted to the extent practical.

Finally, analysts should not assume the correctness of underlying perceptions about taxes. A fundamental flaw in any analysis of property tax, for example, is the often-stated but erroneous presumption that the tax is regressive. Analysts should challenge such assertions by providing the best and most up-to-date discussions of any premise. Analysts should also attempt to parse questions whenever possible. For example, the property tax regressivity issue can be restated more correctly to indicate that, while the tax itself is not regressive, its incidence on certain taxpayers under certain circumstances can produce such an effect. In this way, proposals to change tax structures can be refined to accomplish particular goals without broader changes with unintended side effects.

References

Blom, B., and S.A. Guajardo. 2001. *Revenue analysis and forecasting.* Chicago, IL: Government Finance Officers Association.

Government of the District of Columbia. *Tax rates and tax burdens in the District of Columbia—A nationwide comparison 2006,* http://www.taxadmin.org/fta/rate/DC_tax_burden_2006.pdf (accessed January 17, 2008).

Hoffman, D., ed. 2002. *Facts and figures on government finance,* 36th ed. Washington, DC: Tax Foundation.

Minnesota Department of Revenue. "Minnesota Tax Incidence Studies, Who Pays Minnesota's Household and Business Taxes," http://www.taxes.state.mn.us/legal_policy/research_reports/content/incidence.shtml (accessed January 24, 2008).

Tannenwald, R. 1999. Fiscal disparity among the states revisited. *New England Economic Review* . (Boston: Federal Reserve Bank of Boston) (July/August):3–25, http://www.bos.frb.org/economic/neer/neer1999/neer499a.htm (accessed January 24, 2008).

Tiebout, C.M. 1956. The pure theory of local expenditures. *Journal of Political Economy* 64:416–424; as found in Fisher, R.C. 2007. *State and local public finance,* 3rd ed. Mason, OH: Thomson South-Western.

Chapter 6
Analysis of Selected Property Tax Features

The property tax is established and utilized in many different ways in the United States and in other nations. This chapter explores some of the key principles and features of property tax systems and discusses arguments in favor of and against various approaches to the property tax, in particular, the base (value) against which the tax is levied. Included in this discussion are model systems, focusing on taxation and effects on taxation rather than on assessment practices and administration, which are covered in Chapter 7, "Components of Model Property Tax Administrative Systems." Valuation system options are presented next, and the chapter concludes with a discussion of exemptions and tax relief mechanisms.

The taxation system establishes the methods by which the magnitude and distribution of the property tax are determined. The valuation portion of this system is responsible for the distribution of the property tax. Assuming the system is based on market value, the accuracy and professionalism of the assessment system are paramount in creating equitable distribution of the property tax burden. Beyond and distinct from the assessment process, however, the actual magnitude of the property tax on an overall basis is determined by largely independent taxing districts. While the valuation process is discussed in some detail in Chapter 7, taxation systems that provide the framework for tax district budgeting and therefore help determine the magnitude of the property tax are discussed next.

Key principles of model property tax systems are discussed at length in Chapter 3, "Fundamental Elements of the Property Tax." However, it is worth restating some of the fundamentals before delving into a discussion of the major types of systems.

In 2005, as noted in Chapters 1, "Introduction to Tax Policy," and 4, "Role of Property Tax in Intergovernmental Finance," 28 percent of local government general revenue and 72 percent of tax revenue were derived from property tax, making this tax source the predominant tax in local government finance. Although revenue alternatives are available, none enjoy the widespread use or provide the stable revenue stream within the political and legal control of local governments as does the property tax. At least one noted scholar, Brunori (2003), has stated bluntly that the "...only revenue source capable of ensuring a strong and vibrant local government is the property tax."

The ideal property tax system is visible and understandable. Although the assessor determines the distribution of the tax by establishing and updating the base value against which rates are computed, the overall magnitude of the tax must be clearly tied to the taxing units of government that will be spending the revenue.

Budget- versus Rate-Driven Systems

On the taxation side, property tax systems generally fit into one of two categories, rate-driven or budget-driven. In both systems, a tax rate, expressed variously as mills (dollars per $1,000 assessed value) or as percentages of assessed or market value, is multiplied by the assessed value of each taxable parcel to determine the tax amount. The portion of the tax generated by the part of the overall tax rate that represents the rate for a particular taxing district (i.e., city, county, school, fire protection, and so on) is distributed to that district. The sum of all these distributions represents the total property tax revenue for all the districts.

In a *rate-driven system*, the rate is fixed (although slight changes may be permitted), and therefore the budget of the taxing district is not known until the assessed values have been determined. Thus, the formula is

$$assessed\ value \times levy\ rate = property\ tax$$

Rate-driven systems have the advantage of a degree of tax certainty and predictability given stable markets with little year-to-year change in underlying property values. Such systems also enable taxing districts to more or less automatically obtain more revenue when new improvements are constructed and especially when significant new property developments, such as large commercial or industrial sites, are built. Except in these situations, however, rate-driven systems have the disadvantage of separating the determination of the amount of money needed to provide any particular service from the service provider (i.e., taxing district). So the assessor often appears to be the budget officer for the taxing district because the determinant of the property tax revenue is the assessed value and increases in value increase the property tax component of the budget for the taxing district. Similarly, when there is a downturn in the market, in a rate-driven system budgets must decrease, regardless of any underlying need for continuing services, even during economic downturns.

An alternative, and preferred, approach is the *budget-driven system*, in which the taxing district first establishes a budget (in dollars) to be raised from property tax. Assessed values are determined independently, and the levy rate floats (usually within some limits) to produce the necessary revenue. The formula for this system is

$$budget\ \$ \div assessed\ value = levy\ rate$$

The budget-driven system distributes the property tax burden on the basis of the proportional share of total (district-wide) assessed value represented by each taxable parcel. To the extent the underlying valuation system permits this value to be current market value, the tax burden distribution reflects wealth indicated by current property values and responds quickly to changes in this distribution of wealth. Table 6-1 demonstrates the two systems. The table assumes the 2007 property tax rate is 0.0125, based on a $5,000 budget divided by $400,000 in assessed value. The table also assumes that, absent the assessed value increase, the taxing district does not increase its budget, because that is what it needs to operate.

TABLE 6-1. Budget- versus Rate-Driven Property Tax Systems

Parcel	2007 Assessed Value ($)		2007 Property Tax ($)	2008 Property Tax ($)		Change in Property Tax Related to Rate-Driven Budget System ($)
	2007	2008		Rate-Driven	Budget-Driven	
A	100,000	200,000	1,250	2,500	2,222	+278
B	100,000	100,000	1,250	1,250	1,111	+139
C	100,000	100,000	1,250	1,250	1,111	+139
D	100,000	50,000	1,250	625	556	+69
Totals	400,000	450,000	5,000	5,625	5,000	+625

With a fixed rate, the increase in overall assessed values generates more property tax revenue in 2008 for the taxing district shown in Table 6-1. The proportional shares paid by each parcel change relative to the proportions represented by the new value, so the distribution is "correct" in terms of the underlying value. However, the additional revenue generated was strictly a result of the increased value of the property and not clearly related to any external, service-related decision by the taxing district receiving the revenue. Note too that under the rate-driven option the 12.5 percent increase in budget reflects exactly a 12.5 percent increase in assessed value. The budget-driven system also proportionally redistributes the tax burden in comparison to the underlying value. The difference is that in the budget-driven system, market value changes, in and of themselves, do not alter the overall tax collections. What would have happened to the budget of the taxing district if assessments had remained the same or decreased? Table 6-2 shows how taxpayers and taxing districts are affected by assessment changes in rate-driven and budget-driven systems.

Table 6-2 demonstrates another advantage of the budget-driven system: its responsiveness to economic change that affects the proportion of underlying property value represented by each property. The property tax system should not be set up to automatically force value-related increases or decreases into taxing district budgets simply because assessed value changes (assuming no new construction or annexation). However, the system should be responsive to selective changes in value that alter the proportional distribution of value and, therefore, should alter the distribution of the property tax. This is exactly what happens in the third example of the budget-driven system (shown later in Table 6-4).

TABLE 6-2. Contrasting Rate- and Budget-Driven Tax Systems

Situation	Rate-Driven System	Budget-Driven System
Assessed values decrease 10 percent for all property.	Taxing districts receive 10 percent less revenue from property tax.	Levy rates rise by the mathematical inverse (about 11 percent) of the value decrease. The same overall amount of property tax revenue is generated.
Assessed values increase 10 percent for all property.	Taxing districts receive 10 percent more revenue from property tax.	Levy rates fall by the mathematical inverse (about 9 percent) of the value increase. The same overall amount of property tax revenue is generated.
One-half of all property (weighted by total assessed value) increases in assessed value by 10 percent, while the other half experiences no assessed value change.	Taxing districts receive 5 percent more revenue from property tax, but properties with the 10 percent increases in assessed value pay 10 percent more, while other parcels pay the same amount as in the prior year.	Levy rates fall by about 5 percent and the same amount of overall revenue is generated, but properties with the 10 percent value increases pay about 5 percent more property tax, while properties with no change in value pay about 5 percent less property tax.

By divorcing dollars needed to fund services from the budgeting process of taxing districts, rate-driven property tax systems provide fertile ground for reappraisal-related revenue windfalls, for which there is no specific, service-related justification. Also, the budgeting process is not as visible and transparent as in budget-driven systems, where the taxing district must establish the desired amount. Rate-driven systems are even more problematic when markets are volatile or when market value (or underlying taxable value) increases rapidly. Consider a reappraisal to current value following many years of use of fixed (or relatively fixed) base-year values: the ensuing windfall to taxing districts and sticker shock to taxpayers can be detrimental to the long-term sustainability of the property tax as a revenue source and to market value as an underpinning for the tax base.

The IAAO *Standard on Property Tax Policy* (2004) strongly discourages rate-driven systems. Furthermore, usually there are a large number of taxing districts serving a given property. In rate-driven systems in the United States nearly every district has a limit on the rate it can charge. With the exception of California and a few similar systems, the *overall* rate that can be charged to a single parcel generally is not capped, however, and this can result in very high rates (more than double average rates) in select localities and tends to negate any constraint that might otherwise be imposed by district rate limits.

Alternatives to Strict Budget- or Rate-Driven Systems

Most systems in place in the United States include elements of both budget- and rate-driven systems. Often, these hybrid systems consist of the following components:

- Rate limits by taxing district
- Dollar (budget) limits by taxing district in the form of allowable annual percentage increases in budget
- Additional dollar allowances for service-related changes, such as annexation or new construction
- Escape clauses, permitting additional dollar allowances for specified purposes (i.e., bonds, special projects, and so on) with voter or administrative body approval required.

Typically, school districts are required to provide equal local support in terms of property tax dollars raised per student. This translates into uniform, equalized levy rates for general purposes and for the distribution of state aid to school districts (see Chapter 4 for a broader discussion of this issue).

Truth-in-Taxation Systems

In recent years, many states have modified their property tax systems, adding or increasing public notice requirements when property tax budgets (or sometimes rates) are to be raised more than a nominal amount or percentage. So-called "truth-in-millage" or "truth-in-taxation" notification requirements are in addition to normal budget publication requirements and usually include

- Large visible advertisements or individual notification of each property owner
- Explanations of what the increase probably will mean to a typical taxpayer
- Information on public hearing dates and locations.

Some truth-in-taxation programs include procedures for rolling back unacceptable increases. In general, by making tax increases more visible to taxpayers, systems of this type have served to constrain property tax increases. There is some evidence that truth in taxation systems work best when highly individualized (rather than generic) notices are developed. The credibility of a truth-in-taxation system is tenuous and may be lost if generic notices suggest, for example, a 5 percent increase in taxes to typical taxpayers, while individual parcels with large, reappraisal-related, assessed-value increases experience 25 percent tax increases.

As of 1999, 20 U.S. states and 1 Canadian province indicated they were using truth-in-taxation systems (IAAO 2000). Although most states enacting truth in taxation have continued to use this system, at least one (Idaho) found the constraints insufficient (and the generic notices confusing) and legislatively repealed the program in favor of strict budget increase constraints three years after initial implementation.

Valuation System Basis

Regardless of the drivers in the budget–revenue system, there must always be an underlying valuation against which to apply levy rates. Property taxes by definition are ad valorem, or based on and in proportion to the underlying value of the property being taxed. Although this value may deviate from market value or from current market value, the most fair and most understandable basis for the tax is current market value. The IAAO *Standard on Property Tax Policy* (2004) goes further along these lines, and part of the lead paragraph in Section 4.2.1 is worth quoting here:

> *In a dynamic economy, property values constantly change. Values in one area may increase, whereas those in another may decrease or stabilize. Property taxes then shift to areas with increasing wealth as measured by property value. Only a system requiring current market value acknowledges these changes in local economies and the distribution of property-related wealth.* (IAAO 2004, 13)

Economic and legal definitions of market value can be found throughout appraisal literature (e.g., the IAAO *Glossary for Property Appraisal and Assessment* [1997]). This chapter, however, examines the policy implications of the use of market value and current market value as an underpinning for the property tax, rather than the derivation of market value through appraisal or other means.

Alternatives to Current Market Value

Internationally, alternative systems tend to relate to market value indirectly. Israel, for example, uses schedules that establish rates per unit of area and that vary depending on location and other factors. Japan incorporates floor space and employee salaries. Some Canadian provinces adjust values annually to reflect current market value, while others do so only during reappraisals, in effect establishing base years (Youngman and Malme 1994).

In the United States the following alternatives are most common:

- *Base-year appraisal.* Property is appraised as of a given date, and typically, values are not adjusted until the base year is changed.
- *Cyclic reappraisal.* Property is reappraised on a regular cycle. Depending on this cycle, a proportionate share of parcels is reappraised and updated each year. For parcels not reappraised in a particular year, there is no adjustment in values.

- *Frozen valuation.* Property is appraised as of a given date, as with base-year appraisals, but a limited annual change is permitted for all parcels (2–5 percent ranges are common). This is also known as *value constraint.*

- *Acquisition value.* Appraisals of selling parcels are adjusted to reflect sale price at time of sale. Nonselling parcels may be permitted a small annual increase, generally in the same range as with frozen valuation systems.

By reducing the number of properties to be reappraised each year, these alternative valuation systems can reduce administrative overhead. The major advantage to the property owner is greater predictability of the amount of tax, at least for tax changes related to value changes. However, by deviating from market value that, in principle, is guided by economic conditions, each of the alternative systems creates groups of winners and losers. Ultimately, this means less equity in terms of a tax rooted in changing wealth as measured by the changing target of the market value of property.

Policy advantages and disadvantages of current market value as a basis for property tax systems are outlined in Table 6-3.

TABLE 6-3. Advantages and Disadvantages of Current Market Value

Advantages	Disadvantages
Reflects dynamics of economic changes—tax burden shifts as distribution of property-based wealth changes.	Property wealth may not be directly related to ability to pay the tax—may be difficult for those on limited income to pay.
Identifies property as a measure of wealth that is untaxed by other means.	Tax is on unrealized capital gains as well as initial value.
Maintains objectivity—value is determined by and rooted in open market.	Because current market value may be subject to economically driven fluctuations, the tax may not be predictable.
Can be understood by the public—facilitates checks and balances through appeals.	

Controls on the Distribution of the Property Tax Burden through Valuation System Alternatives

Although the advantages of current market value reflect sound economic principles, the disadvantages cannot be dismissed lightly. Various controls, such as tax credits and specialized exemptions that target specific issues or affected groups can be implemented. These controls are discussed later in this chapter. However, certain types of controls, such as those involving underpinnings to the property tax that differ from current market value, reflect the alternative value systems just described. The following discussion focuses on the effects of systems that artificially constrain assessed value changes, meaning that market-driven changes are not fully permitted. Rather than those value constraint systems, such as base year and cyclic reappraisal, that are rooted in administrative appraisal and assessment concerns, the discussion is limited to constraints imposed because of political and tax policy considerations.

Value Constraints

An increasing number of U.S. states have statutorily imposed constraints on the amount by which assessed values can increase in a given year. In 1999, only 16 states reported such limits. In a paper on the effect of such constraints, Dye and McMillen (2007) cite a 2006 analysis indicating that 20 states and the District of Columbia now impose constraints on value increases. Constraints typically restrict assessed value increases to no more than 5–10 percent per year, provided that market value assessment would dictate greater increases. Regardless of the type of constraint, stated increase limits are only that, and assessed values are never permitted to be increased greater than market value. In all but three (Arizona, Minnesota, and Oregon) of the states with value constraints, assessed value is reset at market value upon sale (Sexton 2007).

Table 6-4 demonstrates the effect of constraining assessed value growth with a 5 percent cap on annual increases in value. The parcels shown in this table are assumed to be the only ones in a small taxing district that needs to derive $5,000 from 2008 property taxes. Changes in market value are presumed to be a result of shifting economic conditions that affect each parcel differently, not physical changes in the property.

In the example shown in Table 6-4, the most economically advantaged parcel (A) has a large property tax reduction that the 5 percent cap shifts to the comparatively disadvantaged parcels.

Chapter 6 — Analysis of Selected Property Tax Features

TABLE 6-4. The Effect of Assessed Value Change Constraints on Property Tax Distribution

Parcel	2007 Assessed Value ($)	2008 Assessed Value ($) Without Constraint	2008 Assessed Value ($) With 5% Constraint	2008 Property Tax ($) Without Constraint	2008 Property Tax ($) Given Constrained Value	Change in Property Tax Caused by Constraint ($)
A	100,000	200,000	105,000	2,222	1,479	-743
B	100,000	100,000	100,000	1,111	1,408	+297
C	100,000	100,000	100,000	1,111	1,408	+297
D	100,000	50,000	50,000	556	704	+148
Total*	400,000	450,000	355,000	5,000	5,000	0

Comments on Value Constraints

The IAAO *Standard on Property Tax Policy* (2004) argues strongly against use of such constraints in Section 5.4.3. It is worth reprinting that section verbatim:

> *Limits that constrain changes in assessed or appraised value of property may appear to provide control but actually distort the distribution of the property tax, destroying property tax equity and increasing public confusion and administrative complexity. Owners whose properties are increasing in value more rapidly than the permitted rate of increase (say, 5 percent) receive a windfall at the expense of those whose properties are decreasing in value or are increasing at lower rates. In effect, valuation increase limits result in lower effective property tax rates for owners of desirable property and higher effective property tax rates for owners of less desirable property. Similarly, when state funds are distributed to school districts or other taxing jurisdictions based on taxable property value (indirect equalization), funding will tend to shift from poorer areas to wealthier areas with rapid appreciation—an illogical and undesirable result. Legislators and the public should be made aware of the inequities resulting from valuation increase limits and be actively discouraged from pursuing such limitations. Any other control is preferable.* (IAAO 2004, 23)

Value constraints create the most distortion in horizontal equity, because there is no underlying system basis, such as market value, whereby equally situated properties are expected to pay equal (or proportionately equal) taxes. Vertical equity issues are less certain, because it can be argued that owners of low-value properties may have lower income and tend to be less mobile. If that is the case, these properties would be subject to slower turnover and tend to return to full market value less frequently given value increase constraints (Sexton 2007). Studies that focus more on vertical inequity of assessments, disregarding the owner's income, have had mixed results.

The outcome depends on whether potential appreciation is greater in high- or low-value properties. At least one study, using data from two Idaho counties, found greater appreciation in high-value properties and therefore worsening assessment regressivity (and thereby vertical inequity) given value increase caps (Dornfest 2005). In the Idaho study, the effect was particularly pronounced in residential property in the county that experienced a high rate of increase in market value (the median assessed value of homes increased 28 percent in one year). In this case, taxes clearly would have been shifted from high-value homes to low-value homes, had value constraints been in place.

In addition to creating winners and losers on the basis of a politically chosen value increase limit as a dividing line, recent research conducted independently in Minnesota and Idaho (among others) indicates a deceptive attribute of such systems (Dornfest 2005; Minnesota Department of Revenue 2007). It may be obvious that taxpayers with market-driven increases larger than the constraint point (say, 5 percent) are winners, while those with lower assessed value increases (or even decreases), based on market value, tend to be losers. However, it is not at all intuitively obvious that there is a third group of taxpayers. Some properties actually pay *higher* taxes with constrained assessed values than without the constraint. In other words, the properties have lower values and owners have every reason to believe they are benefiting as a result of the value increase constraint. Nevertheless, they pay more property tax with the constraint than without it. This occurs, in the words of the Idaho-based research report, "...because value increase caps are most effective (reducing taxes the most) for the typically small number of properties that otherwise would be subject to the greatest increases" (Dornfest 2005). This effect can be demonstrated by observing the tax change in Parcel C in Table 6-5.

TABLE 6-5. Constrained Values That Result in Tax Increases for Certain Properties with Lower Assessed Value Increases

Parcel	2007 Assessed Value ($)	2008 Assessed Value ($)		2008 Property Tax ($)		Change in Property Tax Caused by Constraint ($)
		Without Constraint	With 5% Constraint	Without Constraint	Given Constrained Value	
A	100,000	200,000	105,000	2,174	1,458	-716
B	100,000	100,000	100,000	1,087	1,389	+302
C	100,000	110,000	105,000	1,196	1,458	+262
D	100,000	50,000	50,000	543	694	+151
Totals*	400,000	460,000	360,000	5,000	5,000	0

*Totals may not add due to rounding.
Source: Dornfest 2005.

Note in Table 6-5 that Parcel C has a 2008 assessed value that is $5,000 lower than what its assessed value would have been without the 5 percent value increase constraint. Yet Parcel C paid $262 more in taxes than it would have without any constraint, because of the large benefit gained by Parcel A. Because real-world situations contain far greater numbers of parcels and complex distributions of value changes dictated by economic markets, taxpayers are not aware of such distortions and are led to believe they are winners when, in fact, they are losers. This situation violates the precept of a transparent tax.

Acquisition Value

Every alternative to the market value system adds economic distortions and shifts the property tax burden. Acquisition value systems were part of Proposition 13, a major tax revolt in California in 1978. Since its passage, Proposition 13 has been extensively analyzed and litigated all the way to the U.S. Supreme Court. In addition to limiting most property tax rates to 1 percent of value, Proposition 13 amended the California Constitution to limit assessed valuation increases to the lesser of 2 percent per year or the rate of inflation. However, in most cases, upon sale of the property the purchase price becomes the new taxable value (O'Sullivan, Sexton, and Sheffrin 1995).

Because of the length of time the California acquisition value system has been in place and the amount of inflation in property values, studies conducted in 1995 show that it is common for identical, adjacent parcels to differ legally in assessed value by 500 percent (O'Sullivan, Sexton, and Sheffrin 1995). Recent movers and first-time home buyers tend to pay much higher property taxes, while senior citizens, by reason of length of time in one house, pay lower taxes. In the business sector, there is a competitive disadvantage for new businesses, which must own property to conduct their business enterprise. In their analysis, O'Sullivan et al. (1995) suggest that this practice is "…not sound tax policy and has no policy rationale."

Because of the provisions of acquisition value systems that tend to place more property tax burden on recent movers, there have been questions about whether such systems violate the Equal Protection Clause of the Fourteenth Amendment to the U.S. Constitution. California's system is in accordance with California law and its state constitution. This system was upheld and deemed to be within the rights of a state to set tax policy by the U.S. Supreme Court in *Nordlinger v. Hahn,* a case involving a residential property owner in 1992.

The IAAO *Standard on Property Tax Policy* (2007) recommends against the use of systems, such as acquisition value, that distort the economic realities of the property tax. Instead, when social or political goals make it desirable to prevent the full economic burden of the tax from falling on particular groups, such as low-income or older homeowners, the standard recommends alternative programs, such as circuit breakers, which target relief to selected groups. Such alternatives are also discussed and recommended in a recent article from the Lincoln Institute of Land Policy (Youngman and Malme 2005).

Acquisition Value in California—A Case Study

In California, under Proposition 13, the assessed value of property cannot increase by more than 2 percent per year until the property is sold, at which time it is reassessed at its full market value, usually the selling price. Until the early 1990s, inflation in real estate generally exceeded 2 percent per year, creating a widening gap in property taxes between homes bought more recently and those owned for many years. However, from 1991 through 1995, California experienced a severe recession. Property values fell throughout the state, dropping as much as 30 percent in many places. Although the decline in property values helped to eliminate some of the inequities in the property tax system, reducing the gap between market value and assessed value, it also placed a tremendous strain on California's understaffed and underfunded county assessor's offices. As property values fell, residents and businesses throughout the state inundated county assessors with appeals for reassessment.

When the voters passed Proposition 13 in 1978, assessments were rolled back to the property values that prevailed in 1975, the initial base year for all existing properties in the state. When property is sold, it is reassessed and assigned a new base year. As long as housing price inflation exceeds 2 percent per year, properties with more recent base years are assessed closer to market value than properties with older base years. The base year is the key piece of information needed to estimate the disparity between market value and assessed value, which Sheffrin and Sexton (1998) define as the *disparity ratio*. Once the base year of a property has been identified, the disparity ratio can be calculated by dividing the market value of the property by its assessed value in the preceding year. Sheffrin and Sexton did this for properties sold in Los Angeles and San Mateo counties in 1990–1991 and in 1995–1996, the years bracketing the recession. The analysis involved about 8 million property records for Los Angeles County and 1.4 million for San Mateo County, with base years running from 1975 to 1996.

Figure 6-1 shows the distribution of disparity ratios for single-family, owner-occupied homes in Los Angeles County that had a base year of 1975 and that were sold in 1995–1996. The median disparity ratio for all these homes is 3.84. This means that an average new home buyer in Los Angeles today pays almost four times the basic property tax as a resident who has been in his or her home since 1975. The disparity between market and assessed value was much greater in 1991, when the median disparity ratio for 1975 base year property was 5.19, or 26 percent higher than in 1996. The decline in the disparity ratio was a direct consequence of the recession and falling real estate prices.

Chapter 6 Analysis of Selected Property Tax Features   **177**

FIGURE 6-1. Disparity Ratios for Properties in Los Angeles County: 1975 Base Year

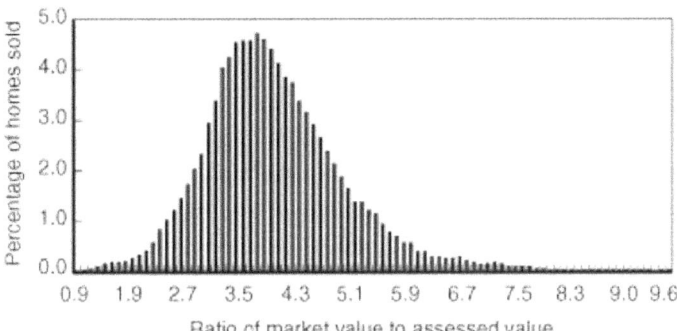

The fraction of 1975 base-year property also decreased substantially during this period. In 1991, 43 percent of all properties in Los Angeles County had 1975 base years. By 1996, the number had fallen to 33 percent. Two primary factors contributed to this decline. First, some of the 1975 base-year properties were sold and thus assumed later base years. Second, new construction increased the total number of properties, reducing the percentage of 1975 base-year properties. The 1975 base-year percentages are key statistics because they are the most important source of property tax disparities. The median disparity ratio in all base years after 1980 currently falls below 1.3, and a 30 percent difference between assessed and market values is not unusual in states using a market-value-based rather than an acquisition-value-based property tax system. In other words, the inequity of the post-Proposition 13 tax system is not that serious in the case of properties with base years after 1980.

Whether inequities in the property tax system will continue to be reduced through turnover and new construction depends largely on two factors. The first is property appreciation. If housing inflation again begins to exceed 2 percent per year on a sustained basis, inequities will increase. The second factor is the stock of 1975 base-year housing. Whether the owners of these properties sell or pass the properties on to their children or grandchildren (and thereby maintain the base year) will largely determine whether the number of such properties—those with the greatest disparities—decreases over time.

Before 1991, the assessor's job was relatively easy. For the majority of properties, it was simply a matter of adjusting the previous year's assessed value upward by 2 percent or the rate of inflation, whichever was smaller. However, between 1991 and 1996, hundreds of thousands of property owners who believed that the market value of their property had fallen below the base-year value filed appeals for reassessment. Under Proposition 8, a constitutional amendment passed by California voters in 1978, such properties must be reviewed and reassessed each year until the market value again exceeds the factored base-year value (base year value plus 2 percent for each subsequent year). If an appeal is not resolved within two years, the assessor is obligated to enroll the property at the value claimed by the owner of the appeal (which may be artificially low).

At the same time that hundreds of thousands of appeals were being filed, assessors' budgets were being cut. In 1992 and 1993, at the peak of the recession, the governor reduced the state's financial obligations to schools by shifting $3.4 billion in property tax revenues from local agencies to schools through the Educational Revenue Augmentation Fund. This shift led to a significant reduction in counties' share of property tax revenues, which continues to this day. For example, Alameda County saw its revenue share decline from 40 percent to 16 percent, and Orange County keeps only about 5 cents of every property tax dollar collected in the county. The state enacted certain measures to help counties enhance their property tax administration, including a temporary loan program that enabled assessors' offices to hire additional staff, but many counties were still working through a backlog of appeals cases several years later.

Although property values have more than fully recovered, property tax administration problems remain. Because the counties' share of property tax revenues is so small, they have little incentive to spend their scarce budgetary dollars on staffing and modernizing assessors' offices at the expense of other county services. One solution to the budgetary problems would be to ensure that all recipients of property tax revenue pay the assessor's administrative costs in proportion to the revenue they receive. This was the essence of a bill passed in 1990, SB 2557. However, in 1991, schools were exempted. According to the allocation of property tax revenues in 1995–1996, schools received more than 53 percent of all property tax revenues. Thus, under this proposal, the state would pay 53 percent of property tax administration costs on behalf of schools. However, relieving counties of some of the administrative costs does not provide them with the incentives for thorough and accurate assessments that come with having a larger stake in the outcome—namely, property tax revenues. A better (but politically difficult) solution would be to shift property tax revenues back to counties as their primary source of revenue.

Note that California's Proposition 13 imposed not only acquisition value limits on the property tax system but also an overall cap on property taxes of 1 percent of taxable value, the basis of which is acquisition value as described. This cap effectively prevented tax shifting through rate increases that would otherwise have occurred when taxable values were constrained. By combining a strict tax rate cap with a strict valuation increase cap, Proposition 13 restricted total property taxes as well as property tax (base) growth to a far greater extent than elsewhere in the United States; this exacerbated the revenue shortage effects described above.

Chapter 6 Analysis of Selected Property Tax Features

This section has discussed various methods by which property taxes commonly are controlled. Since every property tax prescription includes both revenue and valuation aspects, controls tend to focus on these facets of the property tax. Tables 6-6 and 6-7 summarize the three major controls that have been reviewed: budget increase limits, levy rate limits, and valuation increase limits. Table 6-6 presents characteristics and advantages of these controls, while Table 6-7 presents disadvantages.

TABLE 6-6. Characteristics and Advantages of Property Tax System Controls

Budget Increase Limits	Levy Rate Limits	Valuation Increase Limits
Limit taxing district budgets to specified annual percentage increase.	Limit maximum levy rate, regardless of how much property tax is raised.	Constrain assessed value increases.
Usually contain provisions for additional services needed by newly constructed or annexed property.	Are effective when assessments are stable over time.	Provide protection to parcels most affected by value appreciation.
Prevent reappraisal-driven windfalls.	Provide early warning of reappraisal-driven tax increases.	
Place responsibility for magnitude of property tax increase on taxing district.	Depending on number of overlapping taxing districts, may provide overall maximum rate.	

TABLE 6-7. Limitations and Disadvantages of Property Tax System Controls

Budget Increase Limits	Levy Rate Limits	Valuation Increase Limits
Do not usually control tax shifting or prevent large increases to individuals in response to isolated assessed value increases.	Fail to control reappraisal-related windfalls when assessed values rise rapidly.	Shift property tax burden to property with less appreciation or economically depressed areas.
May not provide sufficient flexibility for taxing districts to fund special needs; escape clauses are needed.	Force taxing district to reduce spending when assessed values decline.	Increase complexity and lessen understandability of property tax system.
Ceilings on increases become floors unless provisions for recapturing unused portions of allowable increases are included.	Shift apparent responsibility for tax increases from taxing district to assessor.	Reduce uniformity and equity, moving the property tax away from the ad valorem system it was originally conceived to be.
	Should be coupled with budget increase limits or truth in taxation to be effective.	

Site Value Taxation

Another idealistic system of property taxation, first espoused by Henry George in 1879, is the site value tax, also known as two-rate or split-rate property tax. In the purest form of the site value tax, *only* land rent or the unimproved value of land is taxed. The rationale is that the supply of land largely is fixed, so the value of each tract of land essentially derives from the actions of society, not the individual landowners. Because it could not be avoided in a well-administered tax system, a tax on land value would be economically neutral. Through land taxes, governments would recoup part of the value created by society, and land prices would be driven down.

On the other hand, a tax on the value of buildings and other improvements tends to penalize construction and discourage the optimal development of land. Several countries, including a number of British Commonwealth countries, Denmark, and Estonia, have property taxes under which only land rent or land value is taxed or is taxed more heavily than buildings. Convincing empirical evidence of the theoretical advantages of site value taxation has been difficult to find. This may be partly because it is politically difficult to garner support for the extremely high tax rates needed for the incentive effects to be strong. Fiscally, potential property tax revenue yields are lessened when only land is taxed. Administratively, there are practical problems in assigning land values when most sales are of improved properties. Economically, market participants may be able to stymie the sort of development patterns envisaged by city plans and land assessments.

Although the theoretical benefits of site value taxation may not be attainable, the rationale for the tax clearly argues against taxing land *less heavily* than buildings. In practice, when site value taxation has been implemented, it is in this fashion. A recent example is Pittsburgh, Pennsylvania, which for a time beginning in 1979, taxed land at about five times the rate of structures (Fisher 2007). The Pittsburgh experiment ended in 2001, following a court-ordered reassessment (Brunori 2003).

When there are separate taxes on land or on buildings, complications also can arise. It is difficult in practice to estimate the market value of each component accurately. Fundamentally, when land and any buildings are under a single ownership, buyers and sellers set a price for the combined property, not separate prices for the components. When a vacant land plot is sold, the price reflects its readiness for use, which may be the result of invisible improvements, such as clearing of trees and grading of the property done long ago. When a building or a unit in a building is sold, its price reflects the value of its location (essentially an element of land value). This makes it difficult to avoid taxing land, even when land is not in private ownership.

Chapter 6 ■ Analysis of Selected Property Tax Features

Classification Systems

Systems of classification, such as differentials or fractional assessment ratios, are designed to lower the taxable value and thereby lower the effective tax rate for selective (favored) classes of property. Although the effect is similar to providing a partial exemption, there is no application process for the property owner, unless there is a requirement to prove qualification to be assigned to a particular favored class of property.

Ostensibly, classification is less distortive than systems that artificially constrain the appraisal process, because market value appraisal usually is permitted. Once the appraisal is completed, a given fractional ratio is applied and the taxable value computed based on this ratio. Occasionally, classification is accomplished by altering the rate of tax that applies to a particular class of property.

Classification shifts taxes from favored to unfavored classes, as demonstrated in Table 6-8, which assumes the tax rate has already been established at 2 percent of the assessed value.

TABLE 6-8. Effect of Classification on Individual Property Taxes

Class of Property	Appraised Value ($)	Ratio (%)	Assessed Value ($)	Property Tax ($)
Residential	100,000	25	25,000	500
Commercial	100,000	50	50,000	1,000
Vacant land	100,000	70	70,000	1,400
Agricultural	100,000	20	20,000	400

Although limited use of classification can provide desired protections and lessen the effects of reappraisal or rapid market-driven value increases on classes with lower ratios, systems with numerous classes, each with its own fractional ratio, add complexity and make the true effect of the various ratios difficult to ascertain. In addition, classification invariably includes aspects of discrimination, which can be legally proscribed. The federal Railroad Revitalization and Regulatory Reform (4-R) Act of 1976 (codified at 49 U.S.C. § 11501), for example, prohibits classification schemes that favor commercial and industrial property over railroads. Subsequent acts extend this protection to interstate trucking firms and air carriers.

As with exemptions, classification that favors protected classes is usually overturned. In addition, in a 1989 West Virginia decision (*Allegheny Pittsburgh Coal Co. v. Webster County Commission* 1989), the U.S. Supreme Court found that "welcome stranger" assessments, in which higher values are placed on property owned by the most recent owner, constituted de facto classification (in West Virginia, the classification scheme was implemented by the local assessor without express statutory authority). This was deemed unconstitutional under the equal protection provisions of the Fourteenth Amendment to the U.S. Constitution. The subsequent 1992 ruling in *Nordlinger v. Hahn* indicated that such assessment does not violate equal protection, provided it does not single out a federally protected group, is authorized by law, and is not simply administrative practice.

As a final caution, classification tends to obscure the effective tax rate, which must be determined against a constant base value (usually market value) for valid comparison between locations and jurisdictions. In Table 6-8, as an example, the effective tax rate for residential property is 0.5 percent, while the effective rate for commercial property is 1.0 percent. Hence, the 2 percent nominal rate applied to each parcel's taxable value effectively is not uniform.

Targeted Controls on Property Taxes—Individuals

In virtually every property tax system, specialized controls have been developed to lessen the impact of the property tax on certain groups of taxpayers. The design and effects of various broad controls, such as value increase constraints and application of different fractional assessment ratios through classification, have already been described. Most of these controls tend to be less oriented toward specific situations, and none is based on identified need or individualized criteria (although there are elements of individualized criteria found within acquisition value systems that base taxable value largely on value as of the purchase date). Various criteria are established, with controls tending to fall into the following categories:

- Exemptions
- Deferrals, circuit breakers, and tax credits

Exemptions

In principle, all property is taxable unless expressly exempt. In establishing tax policy, every policy-making body has granted exemptions for several broad purposes, as outlined in Table 6-9.

Exemptions are considered most supportable when they shift taxes away from tax-supported entities that would otherwise need to increase taxes to pay their own taxes. Following this principle, governmental buildings and schools are nearly always exempt in the United States and Canada.

Aside from administratively necessary exemptions, it is recommended that exemptions should be granted only if they benefit "...a substantial segment of the affected population and...similar properties and similarly situated taxpayers are accorded the same treatment" (IAAO 2004).

TABLE 6-9. Purpose and Examples of Property Tax Exemptions (Full or Partial)

Purpose of Exemption	Common Examples
Satisfy legal considerations or prohibitions	U.S. Federal Government property
Avoid taxing tax-supported functions	State and local government property
Encourage specified use	• Historic property • Educational property • Religious property • Charitable property • Primary residential property
Facilitate economic or public objectives	• Agricultural land • Formerly contaminated property
Ease administrative burden associated with assessment	• Business inventory • Household goods • Livestock • Personal property

Although many are supportable, exemptions narrow tax bases (sometimes resulting in revenue losses), shift property taxes from favored to nonfavored property, and raise tax rates. Costly administrative mechanisms and court battles about definitions and eligibility also can occur. Although the effect of one exemption may be quantifiable, the effect of numerous overlapping exemptions is difficult to ascertain, and the effect on originally favored groups may be to lessen their exemption by the granting of additional exemptions to other groups. Exemptions often create hidden or de facto tax expenditures, and benefits and costs should be analyzed. Because the underlying exemptions may apply broadly, tax expenditures can reduce revenue substantially. Many states attempt to quantify and publish these effects. See, for example, California state and local tax expenditure studies found at www.dof.ca.gov/Research/Research.php.

Three types of exemptions are in common use: partial exemptions, full exemptions, and de facto exemptions.

Partial Exemptions

Partial exemptions reduce the otherwise taxable value of property, but do not completely relieve the property tax. Partial exemptions apply mostly to residential and agricultural property, but also can be applicable to select components of industrial and commercial property. Most partial exemptions take one of the following forms:

- Subtraction of fixed dollar amount from assessed value
- Subtraction of percentage of assessed value
- Subtraction of hybrid amount determined using dollars and percentages of value
- Use of constrained valuation techniques, such as agricultural use value

- Removal of specified personal property components from value
- Removal of intangible value components.

As examples, in 1999, 34 states and 3 provinces indicated that agricultural property was favored through lower assessed values determined using use value methodology; 27 states and 1 province indicated having partial exemptions for residential property (IAAO 2000). Some states that tax business machinery and equipment do not tax intangible components of such equipment or the software used to operate the equipment.

To prevent unanticipated broadening of these exemptions, some states require initial and periodic applications and may restrict eligibility of taxpayers or property. For example, residential "homestead exemptions" typically apply only to a primary residence (home) and a limited amount of associated land. Residential property exemptions may also include age or income criteria. Farmland that is developed for other uses within a specified period may be required to pay penalties based on value exempted under farm use classification. Such paybacks commonly are known as *greenbelt* laws.

When exemptions involve alternative, non-market-based calculations of taxable value, they are inherently more difficult to understand, the tax-shifting or revenue loss aspects of the exemptions can be clouded, and the overall transparency of the property tax system is reduced.

Full Exemptions

The U.S. Constitution prohibits taxation of property owned by the Federal Government. Most states have chosen to extend this full exemption to property owned by state and local governments and to property used for publicly beneficial purposes. Table 6-10 shows the five most common full exemptions in the United States and Canada based on a 1999 survey (IAAO 2000).

TABLE 6-10. Common Full Property Tax Exemptions in the United States and Canada in 1999

Type of Property	Number of States with Exemption	Number of Provinces with Exemption
Charitable organizations	44	6
Educational organizations	45	7
Government	46	7
Hospitals	33	7
Religious organizations	41	9

De Facto Exemptions

The difficulties and political sensitivities of assessment administration sometimes result in lower assessed values, even when favored treatment is not statutorily allowed. At least 43 states and 4 provinces tax some personal property, most notably, business machinery and equipment. Most personal property is reported by the owner, and few assessing jurisdictions have the resources to thoroughly audit these reports. Hence, missed personal property receives a de facto exemption.

Similarly, assessment of residential property is politically sensitive. Ratio studies often indicate greater under-assessment of this class in comparison with legal requirements. If not corrected through equalization or other means, such under-assessment also constitutes de facto exemption. Statutorily provided partial exemptions are more visible and are preferred.

Controls on Exemptions

The following list provides several methods for controlling exemptions and for reviewing exemptions to ensure the effects are understood and the exemptions themselves are still valid.

- Construe each exemption narrowly.
- Have specific criteria for eligibility.
- Place burden of proof on claimant.
- Review exempt property frequently to ensure criteria are still met.
- Incorporate sunset provisions in statutory exemptions to ensure periodic review by policy makers.
- Track amount of value that is exempt under each provision and number of parcels receiving exemption.
- Determine amount of taxes shifted or lost, and track these amounts over time.

There are also state and federal constitutional legal controls on exemptions. Although state legislators generally have broad authority to grant exemptions, discrimination against protected classes can result in overturning of an exemption.

Property Tax Deferrals, Circuit Breakers, and Tax Credits

This final section about controlling property taxes explores specific mechanisms for reducing individual property taxes, usually with regard to property used for residential purposes and by individuals with limited means for paying the tax. Three methods are described here: property tax deferrals, circuit breakers, and tax credits. Table 6-11 shows common features of these tax relief programs.

TABLE 6-11. Features of Property Tax Deferrals, Circuit Breakers, and Credits

Deferrals	Circuit Breakers	Tax Credits
Permit accumulating lien in lieu of tax payments.	All or portion of property tax is paid by state through state-funded credits or replacement funding for property tax-supported units of government.	Reduce income tax liability for expenses related to property tax.
Require satisfaction of lien upon sale or settlement of estate.	Unlike exemptions, there is no property tax shift because of availability of state replacement funding.	May be based on actual property tax or imputed amount for renters.
Lien includes interest but not penalty.	There are no liens and no repayment provisions.	May be dollar or percentage based.
State may provide replacement funds until lien is satisfied.	Usually targeted to low-income, older, or disabled people.	Usually targeted to low-income people.
Tend to be used infrequently because of negative connotations of lien.	Relief usually based on sliding scale inversely related to income. Fixed-dollar scale or scale based on percentage of tax may be used.	Most effective if established as refundable credit to be paid even if no income tax liability exists.
	Usually applies to renters and homeowners meeting income and status criteria.	

Circuit breakers are the most widely used of these tax relief mechanisms. The name derives from an analogy with electric circuit breakers, which shut off electricity in response to overloads (Gold and Liebschutz 1996, 68–79). Depending on the precise definition used for the term *circuit breaker*, various sources agree that such programs function as tax credits (often applicable to both homeowners and renters) or sliding-scale homestead exemptions that decrease as income increases. In addition, circuit breaker programs usually are state-funded (as described in table 6–11) and are available in 34–36 U.S. states (Baer 2003; National Conference of State Legislatures 2002). However, with any of these programs, effectiveness and penetration into (use by) the target group are related to several factors, including awareness, ease of application, understandability, and participation stigma. For a more complete analysis of property tax relief programs, see Baer (1998).

As an alternative to ongoing tax credits, states frequently provide one-time credits or tax refunds, often to homeowners. A recent example is found in the state of Montana; Figure 6-2 is a reprint of a page from the Montana Department of Revenue Web site describing this program.

FIGURE 6-2. Montana Web Page Describing a $400 Property Tax Refund

- $400 per-household property tax refund applies to real estate property taxes paid on a homeowner's primary residence in 2006. If less than $400 was paid in 2006, homeowners can sum their real estate property taxes paid on their primary residence owned and occupied for at least 7 months in 2005 and 2004 to reach the $400 total.
- **Applications will be available in late August.** Applications will be mailed to homeowners, will be available online on the State of Montana's website www.mt.gov, and will be available in public places such as county courthouses and public libraries.
- The Department of Revenue will begin processing applications **September 1, 2007.**
- Homeowners must apply for the refund by **December 31, 2007.**
- Homeowners must have owned and occupied the home as their primary residence for at least 7 months in 2006.
- The refund applies to real estate property taxes paid on a person's home including multi-unit dwellings, manufactured homes, mobile homes and trailers.
- The refund does not apply to renters.
- Only one claim may be made with respect to each primary residence.
- The refund is not considered to be taxable income if you used the "standard deduction" for the 2006 tax year. The refund is considered to be taxable income if you reported your personal property taxes as "itemized deductions" for the 2006 tax year. In that case, the refund should be reported as income for the year in which you receive the refund check (either 2007 or 2008).

Abatements and Tax Increment Financing (TIF)

Property tax abatements and TIFs are specialized, geographically focused property tax incentives that promote economic development. In the case of abatements, property taxes are forgiven or reduced for a specified period of time. When a TIF is used, property in the area continues to pay property tax at the underlying rate, but a portion of the tax, usually generated by new development in the area, is diverted from the taxing districts to be used for infrastructure and other amenities within a specified development area.

Both systems help lessen start-up costs for new business enterprises. However, the infrastructure needs of taxing districts can increase because of the new enterprises, and sufficient additional revenue may not be obtainable because of the abatement or revenue diversion. This is especially true with a TIF, which more often is established for lengthy or indeterminate periods. Table 6-12 delineates major advantages and disadvantages of these systems.

TABLE 6-12. Advantages and Disadvantages of Tax Abatements and TIFs

Advantages	Disadvantages
Abatements and TIFs encourage development in depressed areas by lessening start-up costs.	Development may be artificially induced and may not be economically sustainable.
TIFs provide funding for development or infrastructure within development area.	Abatement does not provide funding for new infrastructure.
Abatements and TIFs are preferred over classification and limits on assessment increases.	There may be competitive disadvantages for existing businesses that did not enjoy abatement or use TIF.
TIFs may permit bonding or other types of financial leverage, so all up-front costs are not immediately payable.	Property taxes can be shifted to properties outside the development area, particularly if development would have occurred without the incentive.
	Separate record-keeping requirements add to administrative complexity and burdens.

It is sometimes difficult to ascertain whether development would have occurred without the existence of a TIF. Nevertheless, when a TIF is allowed, the tax base is narrowed, and tax shifting occurs. Table 6-13 demonstrates this effect, assuming that a fire protection district needs $500,000 to provide fire protection services to both existing property and the new development. Parcel A is a new manufacturing firm within the TIF. The land that the manufacturing improvements are built on was formerly owned by a municipal redevelopment agency and was exempt. The other parcels are within the same area, but predate the area's designation as a TIF region.

In either case, the fire district receives the funding it considers necessary. However, existing taxpayers pay to subsidize the new firm. Although the new company also pays at a higher rate, its contribution to projects within the development area is in proportion to its share of the overall assessed value within this area. Suppose, for example, the new firm necessitated new sewer and water lines, which cost $166,667. Without the TIF, the company might have had to pay this full amount. With the TIF, three-fourths of the amount is paid by other parcels.

Chapter 6 ■ Analysis of Selected Property Tax Features

TABLE 6-13. Tax Shifting as a Result of a TIF

Parcel	Assessed Value ($ millions)	Tax Rate (%) for Fire Protection with TIF	Taxes Paid with TIF in Place ($)	Tax Rate (%) for Fire Protection without TIF	Taxes Paid without TIF in Place ($)	Taxes Shifted due to TIF ($)
A (new manufacturing firm within TIF)	25.0	0.667	166,667	0.500	125,000	41,667
B	25.0	0.667	166,667	0.500	125,000	41,667
C	25.0	0.667	166,667	0.500	125,000	41,667
D	25.0	0.667	166,667	0.500	125,000	41,667
Subtotal—available for fire protection levy rate calculation	75.0	0.667	500,000	0.500	500,000	NA
Total	100.0	0.667	666,667	0.500	500,000	166,667

The tax shifting demonstrated in Table 6-13 occurs only given a budget-driven underlying tax system. If the tax rate to be levied by the fire district were locked in place, there would be no tax shifting in the form of higher rates, but the fire district would suffer a revenue loss.

Tax incentives, such as abatements and TIFs, operate under the premise that they tip the scales in favor of business locational decisions and therefore encourage economic development. Many factors other than property tax tend to influence such decisions, and ascribing a cause-and-effect relationship to property tax incentives is at best suspect and sometimes counterintuitive. As an example, a study commissioned by the New York Legislature found that property taxes on certain residential property in which, presumably, company managers would be living could be more significant in terms of business locational decision making than property taxes on business property (New York Legislative Commission 1984).

Summary

This chapter has explored general principles that apply to the property tax, particularly as it is used in the United States. It has focused largely on the underpinnings of the tax and suggested strongly that the basis for the tax should be current market value, with the proviso that carefully crafted exemptions and limitations be employed to make the tax more predictable and less of a burden on those least able to pay. Some of the basic principles that should underlie every tax type have been presented, notably, transparency and accountability, thus the strong argument for the model of budget- rather than rate-based systems.

Recently there have been trends in the United States away from current market value, and these have also been explored, along with reasons for these trends, examples of alternative systems, and economic and practical arguments against non-market-value-based systems. Ultimately, decisions about the basis for the property tax are made in the political arena. The goal here is to inform the process so that decision makers are aware of the various arguments and considerations and understand that today's apparently obvious solution can lead to tomorrow's entrenched problem.

References

Allegheny Pittsburgh Coal Co. v. Webster County Commission, 488 U.S. 336 (1989).

Baer, D. 2003. *State programs and practices for reducing residential property taxes.* Washington, DC: AARP Public Policy Institute.

———. 1998. A*wareness and popularity of property tax relief programs.* Washington, DC: AARP Public Policy Institute.

Brunori, D. 2003. *Local tax policy.* Washington, DC: The Urban Institute Press.

Dornfest, A.S. 2005. Effects of taxable value increase limits, fables and fallacies. *Journal of Property Tax Assessment and Administration* 2 (4):5–15.

———. 2003. Overcoming property tax demons and mysteries. *Fair and Equitable* 1 (1):10–17.

Dye, R., and D. McMillen. 2007. Surprise! An unintended consequence of assessment limitations. *Land Lines* (Lincoln Institute of Land Policy) 19 (4) (October), http://www.lincolninst.edu/pubs/PubDetail.aspx?pubid=1260 (accessed March 4, 2008).

Fisher, R.J. 2007. *State and local public finance*, 3rd ed. Mason, OH: South-Western College Publishing, pp. 363–364.

Gold, S.D. and D.S. Liebschutz. 1996. *State tax relief for the poor*, 2nd ed. Albany, NY: Nelson Rockefeller Institute of Government.

International Association of Assessing Officers (IAAO). 2007. *Standard on property tax policy.* Chicago, IL: IAAO.

———. 2000. *Property tax policies and administrative practices in Canada and the United States.* Chicago, IL: IAAO.

———. 1997. *Glossary for property appraisal and assessment.* Chicago: IAAO.

Chapter 6 Analysis of Selected Property Tax Features **191**

Minnesota Department of Revenue, Tax Research Division. 2007. *Limited market value report: 2006 assessment year, taxes payable 2007,* http://www.taxes.state.mn.us/legal_policy/research_reports/content/2007_lmv_report.pdf (accessed March 4, 2008).

National Conference of State Legislatures. 2002. *A guide to property taxes: Property tax relief.* Denver, CO: NCSL.

New York Legislative Commission on the Modernization and Simplification of Tax Administration and the Tax Law. 1984. I*nterstate business locational decisions and the effect of the state's tax structure on after tax rates-of-return of manufacturing firms.*

Nordlinger v. Hahn, 505 U.S. 1, 112 S. Ct. 2326 (1992).

O'Sullivan, A., T.A. Sexton, and S.M. Sheffrin. 1995. *Property taxes and tax revolts: The legacy of Proposition 13.* New York: Cambridge University Press.

Sexton, T. A. 2007. The increasing importance of assessment limitations as a means of limiting property taxes on homeowners. Paper given at Lincoln Institute of Land Policy, George Washington Institute of Public Policy, Property Tax Policy Roundtable. Washington, DC, October 5, 2007.

Sheffrin, S.M., and T.A. Sexton. 1998. Proposition 13, the recession and the tax assessor's dilemma. *Research Brief* (Public Policy Institute of California, San Francisco, CA) (September) issue 14, http://www.ppic.org/content/pubs/rb/RB_998SSRB.pdf (accessed January 31, 2008).

Youngman, J.M., and J.H. Malme. 2005. Stabilizing property taxes in volatile real estate markets. *Land Lines* (Lincoln Institute of Land Policy) 17 (3) (July):5–7, http://www.lincolninst.edu/pubs/PubDetail.aspx?pubid=1040 (accessed March 4, 2008).

Chapter 7
Components of Model Property Tax Administrative Systems

> *Practically, the general property tax as actually administered is beyond all doubt one of the worst taxes known to the civilized world.*
> —Edwin R. A. Seligman, 1895 (1925, 62)

Although administrative advancements have been made, an enduring area of concern has been property tax administration. Fundamental criteria for evaluating property tax systems are discussed in Chapter 2, "Principles, Politics, and Economics of Taxation." The focus in this chapter is on *administrative* criteria. The following general criteria seem appropriate:

- Laws are carried out (but see "Administrative Policy Setting," below)
- Administration is evenhanded
- Administration is cost-effective.

The specific features of a cost-effective system for administering a recurrent property tax of course depends on the nature of the tax and its setting; therefore, there is no single "model." This chapter focuses on processes commonly found in a broadly based, value-based property tax. Matters considered include the following:

- Does the property tax administration have sufficient resources?
- Is the staff of the property tax administration well-managed?
- Have all assessable properties been discovered, accurately described, and linked to a taxpayer? Alternatively, have all persons legally liable for paying the property tax been identified, and have their taxable property holdings been identified?
- If the tax is value-based, are values in line with legal requirements and is the valuation system capable of producing accurate, supportable valuations? ("Appraisal" and "valuation" are used synonymously in this chapter.)
- Have properties been classified correctly for purposes of taxation?
- Have exemptions or other forms of relief been administered correctly?
- Have procedures for finalizing assessment rolls, issuing assessment notices, and issuing tax bills been complied with?

- Are appeals heard in a timely manner, and are they disposed of appropriately?
- Are past-due tax obligations monitored and appropriate enforcement actions taken?
- Are tax receipts properly accounted for and distributed?
- Are the information needs of taxpayers and other stakeholders met?

Along with technical matters, this chapter discusses standards for evaluating performance and traits of administrators that may be needed for effective performance. Increasingly, standards of practice come into play. The literature identifies generally accepted practices. In the United States, the *Uniform Standards of Professional Appraisal Practice* (USPAP; The Appraisal Foundation, updated annually) and especially Standard 6, "Mass Appraisal," are important. Most of the standards promulgated by IAAO are relevant. In addition, the International Valuation Standards Committee (IVSC) has taken notice of the requirements of mass appraisal. In addition to these standards, this chapter draws upon such IAAO textbooks as *Assessment Administration* (Johnson, Bennett, and Patterson 2003), *Property Appraisal and Assessment Administration* (Eckert, Gloudemans, and Almy 1990), and *Improving Real Property Assessment: A Reference Manual* (Almy et al., 1978). Works providing a more basic treatment of property tax administration include Dillinger (1991) and Keith (1993).

Preferably, a standard statement is sufficiently explicit that it is a simple matter to determine whether it is appropriate and met in a particular circumstance. Alas, such is not the case. Many standards statements are in the nature of policy statements, and considerable judgment is required to determine compliance. They typically reflect the view of providers of valuation and assessment services, not the views of consumers, especially those who must pay for performance. The value at risk may not be considered. Another issue in measuring administrative performance in property taxation is developing practical and meaningful productivity and performance measures. Another is finding a balance between procedural consistency and valuation accuracy or, at least, cogent, defensible analysis in support of valuation models and performance.

Administrative Arrangements, Practices, and Issues

Who Should Do What?

As noted in Chapter 3, "Fundamental Elements of the Property Tax," property tax administration embraces (1) supervision and control; (2) fiscal cadastre maintenance, assessment, and often valuation; (3) billing, collection, and accounting for revenues; and

(4) appeals. A longstanding issue has been the extent to which powers, responsibilities, and accountability for such functions should be decentralized. At the heart of the debate is the notion of *subsidiarity*. Subsidiarity is a federalism principle that states that matters ought to be handled by the smallest (or the lowest) competent authority. Looked at another way, subsidiarity can be defined such that a central authority has only a subsidiary function, performing only those tasks that cannot be performed effectively at a more immediate or local level. Subsidiarity is the heart of the Tenth Amendment to the U.S. Constitution and is enshrined in the 1992 Treaty of Maastricht on the European Union. Subsidiarity also is an important element of the Council of Europe European Charter of Local Self-Government.

Administration of property taxes in the United States is especially highly decentralized, and an ongoing issue is where responsibility for assessment should be located. The policy debate chiefly has to do with the viability of small or sparsely populated town and township assessment districts. Table 7-1 summarizes the arguments made in favor of more and less centralized assessment. Perhaps because the ultimate issue is one of power, the issue is an emotional one. Although most of

TABLE 7-1. Arguments for Centralized and Decentralized Assessment Administration

For More Centralized Assessment	For Highly Decentralized Responsibility for Assessment
1. Larger districts are more economical; they enjoy economies of scale.	1. Local governments have a greater stake in property taxes than states and hence are more likely to attend properly to assessment administration.
2. Larger districts have a greater ability to command the necessary resources, especially appraisal expertise.	2. Local officials have more intimate knowledge of local conditions and resident taxpayers.
3. Larger districts increase the uniformity of assessment within a class through the consistent application of standards and practices over a broad area.	3. Smaller districts are more responsive to the needs of taxpayers, enhancing accountability, especially when the assessor (or board of assessors) is elected.
4. The larger the district, the more likely it would encompass a real estate submarket and the greater the pool of data needed to estimate values.	4. Taxpayers find decentralized administration more convenient.
5. The larger the assessment district, the fewer the occasions in which a single property would lie in more than one district (the greater the opportunity to assess each property as a unit).	5. Smaller districts avoid the concentration of political power that could accrue to the head of a large assessment agency.
6. The fewer the districts, the easier supervision and equalization would become.	6. The status quo is fine.

the arguments have a grain of truth, most are difficult to prove. It also is possible to advance counterarguments to many. For example, there is only limited evidence that larger districts are more cost-effective. At the same time, many taxpayers question whether small districts provide greater accessibility or accountability.

Nevertheless, some critics have gone straight to a solution without much analysis. Jens Peter Jensen, author of *Property Taxation in the United States* (1931) favored counties (Almy 1982, 76). The Advisory Commission on Intergovernmental Relations (ACIR) in its landmark study, *The Role of the States in Strengthening the Property Tax,* preferred that states assume responsibility for assessment administration (1963, vol. 1, p. 14), but it recognized that states may not be prepared to do that (only Maryland and Montana currently are responsible for assessment). Consequently, the ACIR recommended that

> *The geographical organization of each State's primary local assessment districts should be reconstituted, to the extent required, to give each district the size and resources it needs to produce a well-ordered overall structure that makes successful State supervision feasible. No assessment district should be less than countywide ....* (ACIR 1963, vol. 1, p. 15)

This recommendation echoes the IAAO's (then the National Association of Assessing Officers, or NAAO) policy in 1938:

> *The local assessment district should be large enough in area and taxable resources to permit the employment of one full-time assessor and at least one assistant.* (National Association of Assessing Officers, Committee on Principles of Assessment Practice, p. 11)

The inability to attract and compensate a technically competent assessor was the chief concern of the committee. Other concerns were false economies associated with forcing assessors to do clerical work, limited opportunities for professional development, and inabilities to afford maps and equipment. Among the advantages of larger assessment districts that the committee envisaged were fewer owners with properties that spanned assessment district boundaries and, significantly, easier equalization. The committee was dismissive of the two arguments in support of small districts: the assessor's greater familiarity with the properties in the district and the tendency of larger organizations to be "bureaucratic." Undercutting the first argument was the recognition that economies and property markets were not confined to the boundaries of small assessment districts; the committee believed specialized appraisal skills and systematic analyses were more important than general familiarity with properties. The committee argued that excessively bureaucratic behavior was not an inevitable consequence of assessment district enlargement. The committee (NAAO 1938) supported central assessment of certain properties, such as utilities (p. 15), and opposed overlapping assessment districts, that is, situations in which a property is assessed by more than one district (p. 16).

The Committee on Principles of Assessment Practice did not attempt to specify what a minimal assessment district should be, doubtless because "taxable resources" would change over time and would vary with effective tax rates as well as value. A later NAAO committee, the Committee on Assessment Organization and Personnel (1941), revisited the question of an appropriate jurisdictional framework for assessment administration. It also was concerned about districts that were too small to provide economically accurate, uniform assessments, noting that 88 percent of the nation's 26,300 primary assessment districts had populations less than 5,000 (p. 44), and 96 percent of township districts were in this size category.

The Committee on Assessment Organization and Personnel made five recommendations regarding primary local assessment districts (NAAO 1941, 46–59). The third of these was essentially the same as the recommendation of the Committee on Principles of Assessment Practice quoted above. The fourth recommendation was, "The assessment district should not be so large that the flexibility required to adapt the assessment process to special cases is not lost." The fifth recommendation outlined the following five options when a state's existing jurisdictional framework could not be assured of producing quality assessments at low cost:

1. Two or more small governmental units that perform assessment functions could cooperate to form a single assessment district.
2. Two or more small governmental units that perform assessment functions could be consolidated to form a single governmental unit.
3. The assessment function could be transferred to an existing governmental unit whose area includes that of two or more of the units now performing the function.
4. The assessment function could be transferred from townships and small municipalities to their counties while large municipalities could be separated from or consolidated with their counties.
5. An exceptionally large assessment district could decentralize its operations by establishing branch offices in charge of deputies to whom a large measure of authority and responsibility has been delegated by the assessor—a model that has been followed in Maryland and Montana.

Reflecting the makeup of IAAO, the committee viewed state assumption of responsibility for assessment administration as an unlikely and not necessarily desirable outcome (NAAO 1941, 106–108).

The second recommendation of the Committee on Assessment Organization and Personnel, in stating that

the political subdivision performing the assessment function should be one which engages in other important governmental activities and which finances itself in large measure out of property tax receipts, raised the important question of fiscal interest in property tax administration (NAAO 1941, 18). That is, should all taxing districts have a say in how the assessment function is managed and should they help fund assessment operations? This issue may not have received the attention it deserves (recognizing, of course, that taxpayers ultimately bear the costs of assessment administration). However, in Iowa and Texas, boards representing taxing districts have a say in the budget and staffing for assessment administration (the same is true of the governing boards of Canadian assessment corporations). In *Assessment Practices: Self-Evaluation Guide*, the IAAO explicitly linked minimal property tax levies with minimally sized assessment districts (IAAO 2003a, 8).

It also is important to recall (from Chapter 2) that *responsibility* for a function should not be confused with *performance* of the function. Responsibility for assessment, for example, could be centralized, while the workers that carry out the work are decentralized. Or responsibility could be decentralized, while the work is contracted (even to a state agency). The questions are, (1) Is the current system effective and efficient? and (2) Is there a way to improve performance?

Figure 7-1 depicts how responsibility for assessment is assigned by state in the United States. The main patterns are identified in the legend, and the number of states using each pattern is displayed in parentheses. The number of assessment districts in each state is displayed in the map. In total, there are 12,724 assessment districts in the United States.

FIGURE 7-1. Responsibility for Original Assessment in the United States

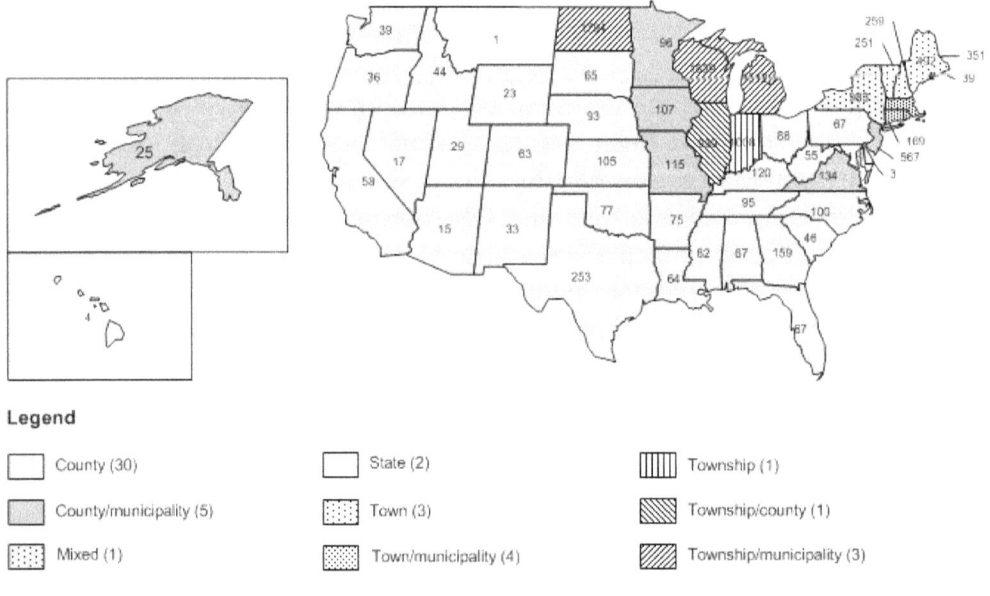

Source: IAAO 2000.

Especially in highly decentralized states, the need for state supervision and equalization has been recognized since the late eighteenth century (Silverherz 1936, 3). Notably, the states with the fewest assessment districts, Delaware and Hawaii, have no supervisory function; see the section on "Supervision and Equalization," below.

Administrative Policy Setting

How a tax is administered always has policy consequences. Administration can support legislated policy, or it can undercut it—in effect substituting a de facto set of policies for the legislated ones. Administrators' efforts to carry out legislated policies also can be thwarted if, for example, they are given insufficient resources. Administrators may be the first to realize unintended consequences of a policy. However, their roles in policy debates and policy formulation vary considerably in practice. Arguably, however, their views on administrative policy matters would merit hearing.

Administrators can face a number of policy dilemmas. Sometimes property tax laws resemble a closet full of clothes. Alongside new, functional clothes can hang some that are outmoded and worn out. It would be foolish to enforce all laws equally, especially when there are time and resource constraints. But it would be foolhardy to enforce only the laws that the administrator agreed with. (Presumably, rules of statutory construction would give precedence to later acts.)

Perhaps foremost among administrative practices that have policy consequences is infrequent reappraisals. When assessors are denied the resources and political support needed to reassess frequently enough to maintain or keep assessments in line with current market values or to comply with legal reassessment schedules, a de facto shift in fiscal responsibility takes place. In effect, in addition to being responsible for how property tax obligations are apportioned, the assessor becomes responsible for the amount of revenue that can be raised in a given rate structure. In effect, taxing bodies are denied the benefits of a buoyant tax base. This power shift is greatest when there are constraints on raising rates. Of course, infrequent reassessments also create groups of favored and unfavored taxpayers. The same is true of selective reassessment of only recently sold properties (so-called sales chasing or "welcome stranger" assessing) and of other "spot assessing" practices.

Perhaps because carrying over assessments from year to year is in violation of an assessor's oath to assess property fairly at a uniform percentage of market value, assessors sometimes personalize challenges from taxpayers who believe they have been discriminated against. They are asked, "Would you sell the property for its assessed value?" There is a tendency to obfuscate: information about property characteristics and current market values is not made readily available and valuation methods are not explained (perhaps because they cannot be). In any case, fractional assessments have been described as the "graveyard of assessors' mistakes" (Shannon 1967).

Effective Management

Fundamentally, management is the art of effectively and efficiently getting work done through people. The work to be done, of course, depends on the requirements of the property tax system and on the duties of the office in question. Formalized management structures are more important in large agencies than in small ones. Good habits may suffice in a small agency. A large one needs to devote considerable resources to proper management. However, anyone with management responsibilities benefits from knowledge of sound practices and procedures. Taxpayers and stakeholders also benefit from well-managed tax offices.

Planning and Budgeting

Effective managers strive to obtain adequate resources and use available resources wisely. In addition to wasting resources, poor administration can cause tax equity to suffer, result in decreased revenue, and erode public acceptance of the property tax and confidence in governance generally.

Planning

Planning is a key aspect of sound management. Property tax administrators engage in three types of planning: strategic planning, annual work planning, and—when necessary—project planning. Plans communicate management's vision of things to be accomplished in the future. Plans lay the foundation for budget requests. They provide a basis for organizing work, measuring progress, and evaluating performance.

Plans that affect more than one person are written. Good written plans briefly address such issues as (1) why the work in question is to be performed, (2) the estimated quantity of work to be performed, (3) production standards for repetitive activities, (4) estimated personnel requirements, (5) estimates of other resource requirements, and (6) the schedule of tasks and projects. After initial adoption, plans are adjusted as needed to reflect changing circumstances, including limitations on available funding.

Strategic plans help organizations shape their future, particularly in times of change or dissatisfaction with the current situation. Strategic planning focuses on reinforcing strengths and eliminating weaknesses. Strategic planning clarifies expectations and standards. It assigns responsibilities. Strategic plans are broad in scope and extend three to five years into the future. Strategic planning sets the stage for operational planning. There are many strategic planning models. The key to successful strategic planning is an ongoing commitment by political leaders and top managers to realizing plans.

Annual operational plans support the strategic plan, and they are tied to the annual budget cycle. They recognize the cyclical nature of property tax administration. Preferably, the annual operational plan addresses all major aspects of property tax administration. It contains information about objectives, activities and tasks, workloads, measures of performance, and resource requirements. Project plans are similar to an operational plan, except that they concentrate on a single general objective or a set of closely related objectives (i.e., "a project"). The period covered by a project plan depends on how long it takes to accomplish the project.

Estimating Resource Requirements and Budgeting

Obtaining sufficient resources often is an important management challenge in property tax administration (as discussed in Chapter 3). Funding requests are more persuasive when plans and budgets are coordinated and when budgets are based on the results to be achieved, rather than on the previous budget or merely the funds needed to maintain the existing staff and other customary expenditures. Results-oriented budgets also strengthen accountability and protect against arbitrary reductions in funding. Many factors affect funding requirements, including workloads or required outputs, inputs or resource requirements, and the wage levels and the costs of other goods and services. Output estimates depend on workloads, standards of performance, and productivity rates. Inputs include skills and technologies.

The chief purpose of public-sector budgeting historically has been financial control. Although this remains an important purpose, budgets can be used to improve governance in other ways, such as helping to realize service goals and improve managerial productivity. To achieve these other purposes, the focus of budgets must shift from the goods and services that may be purchased (so-called line-item or object classification budgeting) to how well programs (like real estate tax administration) are managed (performance budgeting) or to what is achieved (program budgeting).

When there is more than one way to carry out a governmental function, performance budgeting essentially focuses on minimizing the cost of each unit of output. Program budgeting, in contrast, focuses on maximizing gains in benefits associated with each activity that is part of a program. Because advanced budgeting models can be difficult and expensive to implement, governments usually focus on incremental spending. This has led to presenting budgets for different service-level packages, such as current, reduced, and increased service levels. Service-level packages allow budget decision-makers to select the package that best fits the government's overall spending priorities.

Even if line-item budgeting is required, elements of program and performance budgeting can be incorporated in budget requests. This helps budget decision-makers understand the rationale for a request and the consequences of not granting it. The annual budget process also provides an opportunity to report on the accomplishments and goals of the property tax administration. The presentation of budget requests benefits from good communications skills (whether written or oral), and negotiation skills may be needed as well.

Many factors affect resource needs. The most important resource requirement is an adequate staff. Major factors include (1) the simplicity of the property tax system,

(2) how the size of the assessment district and its economy affects workloads, (3) the time available, and (4) available technology, including staff skills, as these affect productivity rates. See the IAAO *Standard on Facilities, Computers, Equipment, and Supplies* (2002) for information on infrastructure needs.

Employee selection—finding the right person for each job—is an important management responsibility. Successful administration of a property tax requires a range of people skills and technical skills. Formal education, past experience, and specific training can help ensure that the staff responsible for tax administration has the requisite skills. A much debated question is the minimum educational and professional qualifications of valuers and other property tax officials. Table 7-2 provides some guidelines on required knowledge and skills. Mandatory requirements are discussed under "Supervision and Equalization," below.

Another management challenge is obtaining levels of compensation commensurate with the responsibilities and skills required of each position. In order for a property tax administration to compete successfully for qualified employees, pay levels need to be commensurate with levels offered in the marketplace.

Work Management

As discussed further on, effective management and quality assurance both encompass many practices and procedures. Additional information on them can be found in the textbooks and standards identified in the list of references. Ratio studies, an essential quality assurance tool, are discussed in the section "Ratio Studies," further on.

TABLE 7-2. Overview of Required Job Skills for Tax Administration Staff

Area of Responsibility	Knowledge/Skill Requirement	Importance
Management and supervision	• Knowledge of legal responsibilities • Planning, budgeting, and human resource management • Written and oral communications	• Very important • Very important • Very important
Land and building description and measurement	• Knowledge of the technical requirements in the law • Knowledge of basic geometry and map reading • Knowledge of property classification requirements • Drafting and mapping skills • General knowledge of the real estate tax	• Very important • Very important • Very important • Important • Important
Record handling	• Knowledge of declaration processing, register-building and maintenance procedures, and record security procedures • General knowledge of the real estate tax	• Very important • Important
Payment receipt and processing	• Knowledge of payment-processing procedures • General knowledge of the real estate tax	• Very important • Important

Organization

Property tax administration can have three organizational dimensions: between tiers of government (intergovernmental), within a tier of government, and within an agency. At the agency level, well-developed organizational designs consider the nature of activities, the volume of work, the skills required, and realistic production rates. In larger agencies, responsibility for carrying out policies and procedures is appropriately delegated. Effective organization of tasks and jobs increases efficiency. Efficiency is obtained when subordinates are accountable to only one superior and when gaps and overlaps in areas of authority are minimized. Efficiencies often can be obtained by specialization. Specialization can occur along functional, property type, and geographic lines (often in combination). Optimal organizational designs provide challenging career paths and opportunities for job enrichment.

Well-managed property tax agencies have a written organization plan that documents, with charts and statements, the responsibilities of each job and organizational unit. These documents formalize the agency head's delegation of work and depict lines of communication. Good managers always are alert to organizational problems, such as work bottlenecks, tasks that are not performed because everyone assumes someone else is responsible for them, and duplication of work (beyond that necessary for quality control). If problems arise, they consider whether reorganization can provide a lasting solution.

Managing People

Managers use their interpersonal skills to direct the talent and energy of workers to achieve the organization's goals, including its quality goals. Managers do this by knowing their subordinates, recognizing the power of self-motivation, delegating authority, encouraging teamwork and participation, expecting and rewarding excellence, and taking appropriate steps to correct unsatisfactory performance. Aspects of human resource management are the following:

- *Internal communications.* A major management challenge is effective internal communications and an emotionally healthy workplace.

- *Performance evaluations.* Employees benefit from frequent, fair performance evaluations. Good managers acknowledge good performance and counsel employees when problems are identified.

- *Corrective actions.* Rules should be administered firmly but fairly. Lax compliance with reasonable rules reduces productivity and morale. In cases of persistent or seriously unsatisfactory performance, disciplinary measures encourage desired behaviors. In general, disciplinary measures are progressive, beginning with the least severe and with dismissal being the ultimate option.

- *Development.* Although most employees improve their skills by their own efforts, managers have an organizational responsibility for employee development. They use education, training, counseling, and performance reviews to identify talents and help employees grow in their positions and to become eligible for promotion.

Good managers realize that no behavior takes place in isolation, that behavior can rarely be attributed to a single cause, and that every action sets off a chain of reactions.

Quality Assurance

Public acceptance of property taxes depends in large measure on the perception that the taxes are fair. The perception of fairness is reinforced when data are accurate, valuations appear accurate and uniform, and all taxpayers are treated without prejudice or favoritism. Quality assurance has to do with the practices, procedures, and systems that managers install to achieve legal and fair taxes. Of course, available resources affect the level of quality that can be obtained, and under-investment in property tax administration is not uncommon. Nevertheless, good management builds into every task a concern for quality. An organizational culture of ethical behavior, public service, and excellence ensures high-quality work. In short, public acceptance of the property tax depends greatly on the performance of every member of the staff of the property tax administration.

The IAAO textbook *Assessment Administration* (Johnson, Bennett, and Patterson 2003) contains an excellent treatment of quality assurance. Some of the program options not covered in other chapters are listed below. A major quality assurance tool is the ratio study, which is described in the section below on "Ratio Studies." Another tool, a performance audit, is discussed under "Supervision and Equalization" (such an audit can, of course, be commissioned locally).

Professional Ethics

Questionable or unethical conduct jeopardizes the integrity of property tax administration. Valuation and property tax administration can present situations in which ethical guidance may be needed. The property tax administration's managers should require all property tax officials to comply with formal ethical standards.

Standards of Performance

Standards of performance include effectiveness targets and rules designed to ensure uniform treatment. Related work includes developing and maintaining procedural manuals, valuation manuals, and valuation standards, such as land unit values.

Efficiency targets or production standards are needed for planning and budgeting and for evaluating performance. Although experience from other property tax systems can provide useful information, it is better to develop standards locally to account for the factors that affect production. Statistics on how time is used and on work accomplishments are needed to develop standards.

Documented Rules and Procedures

Property tax administration involves many complicated tasks. Documenting the proper way of doing any regularly performed task enhances consistency and facilitates training. An important procedural document is a data collection manual. This manual explains how to measure structures and select the most appropriate choice from among the codes available for each property characteristic. The manual contains well-written and specific definitions of property characteristics, illustrated with examples and pictures.

Data Edits

The completeness and accuracy of recently collected data can be evaluated in several ways:

- Samples of properties collected by each data collector can be re-collected by a supervisor or senior data collector. Any problems are reviewed with the data collector, and any corrections are made. This technique is especially useful when data collectors are new to the job, when they have a history of problems, or when new data collection methods are introduced.

- Data entry software can incorporate edits that require the data being entered to be consistent with allowable entries (such as requiring only specified alphabetic or numeric characters) and entries that are consistent with the data entered in other fields. Similar edits can be performed after data entry. Apparent problems are noted in a report as error or warning messages.

- It is important to send field personnel into an area only after they have been briefed about the types of property they should expect to encounter. Careful control of production, good public relations with the citizens in the area, and coordination of law enforcement are all critical steps necessary for successful data collection. It is easier to correct problems in the field than to send a field person back later.

- Property owners can be sent a computer-generated report sometimes known as a "data mailer." This report contains the data for key property attributes as they currently are listed in the property record. The owner is asked to return the mailer to the assessor's office confirming or correcting the data. Any corrections are verified in a follow-up inspection.

Security Procedures

Security procedures restrict access to manual and computerized records to protect confidentiality, prevent loss of records, and prevent unauthorized changes in records. They protect against disasters. They also minimize opportunities for corruption (such as by rotating work assignments and by designing procedures that prevent an individual from making and concealing an error). They help fix responsibility for work by establishing "audit trails."

An audit trail is a record of changes made to a record. It identifies who made the change (or the computer terminal used to make the change), when the change was made, and what was changed. An audit trail makes it easier to recover from errors. It also makes it possible to isolate responsibility for making errors or for failing to correct them. In turn, the cause of the problem can be identified. Mistakes happen, but patterns of mistakes identify more serious system problems.

Ratio Studies

In a market-value-based property tax, a ratio study is the most effective means of evaluating the accuracy of appraisals (Gloudemans 1999 and IAAO 2007). They are used by assessors to evaluate in-place and proposed assessment, by supervisory agencies (as discussed under "Supervision and Equalization" below), and by taxpayers and appeal bodies in assessment discrimination claims. They have been used since about 1880 (Silverherz 1936, 5; U.S. Bureau of the Census 1975, 7). This section provides an overview of ratio studies; more detail can be found in the *Standard on Ratio Studies* (IAAO 2007) and in the *Standard on Mass Appraisal of Real Property* (IAAO 2008).

In a ratio study, ratios (R) of appraised values or assessments (A) to independent indicators of market value or sales (S) are calculated, as in the following formula:

$$R = A/S.$$

For example, if a property is valued at $148,000 and sold for $154,000, the sales ratio would be

$$R = A/S - 148{,}000/154{,}000 - 0.961.$$

That is, the appraisal is 96 percent of the sale price.

In a ratio study, sales ratios are calculated for all the sales deemed usable, and patterns in the ratios are examined. There are two principal concerns:

1. *Level.* How close is the typical ratio to 1.00, or 100 percent of market value?
2. *Uniformity.* How close are the individual ratios to the typical ratio?

Statistics describing the general level of the ratios (such as the mean and median) and describing uniformity (such as the coefficient of dispersion and coefficient of variation) are calculated for a variety of strata (groups of properties).

The main steps in a ratio study are to (1) assemble the data, (2) determine the study groups (strata), (3) make statistical analyses, (4) evaluate results, and (5) report the results.

Data Assembly
This is the most labor-intensive phase of a ratio study; it embraces the following steps:

- *Collecting raw sales data.* Ideally, buyers and sellers would be required to file a declaration stating the price, terms, and circumstances of each sale. Other sources of sales can be used. Key data are computerized; quality checks are made.

- *Screening the sales to determine whether a particular sale should be used in the ratio study.* Recall that only open-market, arm's-length sales provide reliable evidence of market values. Family sales, foreclosure sales, and the like often do not. More controversially, sales that produce extremely high or low sales ratios are excluded; these are called outliers.

- *Matching the sale price with an appraisal (assessment).* In doing this, it is important to determine whether the property that was sold essentially is the same as the property that was assessed. A sale can take place any day of the year, while assessments are as of a single date. If significant physical changes to a property took place between the two dates, the sale cannot be used to evaluate the quality of the assessor's appraisal.

- *Making necessary adjustments to reported sales prices.* Sometimes adjustments to actual sales prices are warranted to make the evaluation of assessments fairer. If a sale included significant movable property that was not considered in the real property assessment, the estimated value of the movable property should be subtracted from the sale price. When the seller helps the buyer finance the purchase, the price agreed to may include the value of the financing as well as the value of the real estate. Such distortions should be removed. Finally, if real estate prices are rising or falling significantly over the period of sales used in the ratio study, the sales prices that occurred well before or after the date of the analysis should be adjusted to the price level on that date to better reflect what the property would have sold for on that date.

After these steps have been completed, the sales file is ready for analysis.

Stratification
Recalling that the real estate market is naturally segmented and that different methods can be used to value different types of property, a better picture of valuation performance can be obtained if different subsets of property are studied separately; this is called *stratification.* Common subsets (strata) are the main types of property— residential, commercial, industrial, agricultural, and vacant land.

Data Analysis
After data assembly and stratification, analysis can begin. The data in Table 7-3 are used to show how ratio study statistics are calculated. As previously noted, the

statistics calculated in ratio studies mainly deal with the *level* of value (assessment) and the *uniformity* of values. Level of value is measured by a *measure of central tendency*, such as the *median*, the common *arithmetic mean*, and the *weighted mean*. There are several aspects to uniformity. If the question is whether two

TABLE 7-3. Sample Sales Data

ID No.	Valuation	Sale Price	Ratio
61	$99,200	$772,000	0.128
3	28,000	59,250	0.473
16	54,110	99,000	0.547
20	36,320	63,300	0.574
27	50,560	70,500	0.717
29	61,360	78,000	0.787
33	58,080	69,000	0.842
68	182,000	153,000	1.190
57	160,000	129,600	1.235

or more groups of property are valued uniformly, measures of central tendency are compared. If the question is whether all the properties *in* a group are valued uniformly, a *measure of variability* is calculated. The *coefficient of dispersion* (COD) is the chief measure used. Sometimes, the concern is whether high-value properties and low-value properties are valued uniformly. The *price-related differential* (PRD) is used here. Another area of statistical inquiry is whether the primary statistics described below can be considered *reliable*.

Median

The median ratio is the middle sales ratio when the ratios are arrayed in order of magnitude. When the total number of sales is even, the median is the arithmetic mean of the two middle-most ratios. In Table 7-3, the sales ratios in column 4 have already been arrayed from lowest (0.128) to highest (1.235). The middle ratio (the median) is that of the fifth sale (ID no. 27), which is 0.717. If the sale with ID no. 57 were not in the sample, the median would be the average of the ratios of sales 20 and 27, which would be 0.646 ([0.574 + 0.717]/2). The value of the median is unaffected by the values of the ends of the array. For this reason, the median generally is the preferred measure of central tendency when the quality of a reassessment is being evaluated.

Arithmetic Mean

The arithmetic mean is the sum of the individual ratios divided by the number of ratios. If the nine ratios in Table 7-3 were added, they would total 6.491, the average of which would be 0.721. Although not evident from this small sample of nine sales, the value of the mean is strongly affected by the values of the extreme ratios. Hence, it is not relied upon in sales ratio studies.

Weighted Mean

The weighted mean ratio is the sum of the appraisals (assessments) divided by the sum of the sales prices. In Table 7-3, the sum of appraised values (column 2) is 729,630, and the sum of the sales prices (column 3) is 1,493,650. Dividing the first by the second results in a ratio of 0.488. As shown in Table 7-3, this ratio is heavily influenced by sale 61, which sold for $772,000. This dollar-weighting feature makes the weighted mean the preferred measure of central tendency when the objective is to estimate to total market value of a district (as in indirect equalization, discussed in the next section).

Coefficient of Dispersion

The COD measures the average percentage deviation of individual ratios from the median ratio. It is calculated by (1) subtracting the median from each ratio, (2) taking the absolute value (negative signs are ignored) of the differences, (3) summing these values, (4) dividing by the number of ratios to obtain the average absolute deviation, (5) dividing by the median, and (6) multiplying by 100 (to express the results in percentage terms). Table 7-4, which is derived from Table 7-3, illustrates the calculations in steps 1 through 3. Dividing the sum of the deviations (2.331) by 9 produces an average absolute deviation of 0.259. Dividing this by the median of 0.717 equals 0.361, which when multiplied by 100 equals a COD of 36.1. The lower the COD, the more uniform the appraisals are.

TABLE 7-4. Calculation of the Coefficient of Dispersion

ID No.	Ratio	Ratio Median	Absolute Value
61	0.128	-0.589	0.589
3	0.473	-0.245	0.245
16	0.547	-0.171	0.171
20	0.574	-0.143	0.143
27	0.717	0.000	0.000
29	0.787	0.070	0.070
33	0.842	0.125	0.125
68	1.190	0.472	0.472
57	1.235	0.517	0.517
Sum			2.331

Price-Related Differential
The PRD is the mean ratio divided by the weighted mean ratio. The PRD of the nine ratios in Table 7-1 is 1.477 (0.721/0.488). PRDs close to 1.0 signify uniform appraisals. If the PRD is much above 1.0 (as is the case here), high-value properties tend to be valued at a lower percentage of value than low-value properties. This is known as assessment regressivity. PRDs much below 1.0 signify progressivity.

Evaluation of Results
When a sample of sales is small, when it does not represent the total makeup of the total assessment roll well, and when the variation in sales ratios is great, ratio study statistics may not reliably portray the quality of appraisals. The same is true when ratio study statistics have been manipulated by adjusting appraisals so that they approximate sales prices (so-called sales chasing) or by selecting only sales with "good" ratios (*cherry picking*). Analysts should consider such possibilities before drawing conclusions about the quality of valuations based on ratio study statistics.

Reporting
The final step in a ratio study is to report the results. What is reported depends on the purpose of the study and the audience. More detail is required when the audience includes non-specialists. It often is helpful to compare observed performance with standards of performance.

Computer Support

Computer support is a virtual necessity in property tax administration. Computers store cadastral and tax records, increase analytical capabilities, perform routine calculations, and produce reports, including assessment notices and tax bills. They facilitate access to data and increase data security, especially from disasters like fire. Advanced computer-assisted mass appraisal (CAMA) systems facilitate market research; support all three approaches to value; identify comparable properties, including comparable sales; and assist with quality assurance. The best are tightly integrated with financial management (tax administration), document and other image managements systems, and geographic information systems (GIS). Increasingly, Internet applications provide taxpayers and others with access to information and data.

CAMA System Features
Well-designed CAMA and assessment administration systems have the following functional capacities:

- *Efficient data management.* Data management is the heart of a CAMA or tax administration system. Increasingly, they are based on general-purpose relational database management systems (RDBMS). In any case, the system provides for efficient data entry, editing, retrieval, and query.

- *Multiyear processing.* Under multiyear processing at least two assessment data files are maintained, a current-year file and a next-year file, which starts out as a copy of the current-year file. Changes in properties and ownership occurring after the assessment date are made to the working draft of the next year's roll rather than being held in abeyance until year end. Being able to promptly update assessment records for changes in properties and ownership smoothes workloads, reduces data ambiguities, and enables better quality control.

- *Work flow management.* Especially in large property tax offices, computerized routines help managers monitor work progress and compare it with planned progress. A management information system (MIS) quantifies the total workload associated with each major routine activity (e.g., properties inspected and permits processed), the work that has been done, and the work that remains. Completion dates are projected, and the plan is revised as necessary.

- *Reporting and data transfer.* The system facilitates the production of reports on the status of routine activities and in response to ad hoc questions. It facilitates the transfer of data into and out of the system.

- *Building perimeter sketching.* Modern CAMA systems support perimeter sketches that check for closure and calculate areas used in analysis and application of valuation models.

- *Building permit tracking.* The system allows assessors to track building permits from issuance to completion, so new construction and renovations are reflected in the fiscal cadastre in a timely fashion.

- *Statistical analysis tools.* The CAMA system incorporates, or provides an easy interface with, a wide range of statistical tools including graphics. These tools enable assessors to perform ratio studies easily, develop regression models, and so on.

- *Land valuation.* The system facilitates the development and application of land value models using one or more recognized methods (particularly direct sales analysis). The system stores land base rates and adjustment factors in tables so that land value estimates can be automatically calculated. The system allows users to select the unit of comparison (e.g., area, frontage, or the parcel or lot as a unit). The system permits adjustments for size, depth, and important location factors.

- *Support of all three main valuation methods.* The CAMA system provides for the application of all three approaches to value (described later).

- *Multiple value estimates and overrides.* Property records provide for recording multiple value estimates (based on different valuation methods). There are codes or other methods for identifying the selected value estimates. The valuer is able to override model-generated value estimates and record her or his estimate when none of the estimates is acceptable.

- *Comparable property selection.* An automated routine is preferable for identifying comparable properties and sales. When only a few properties are involved, sorting properties or sales by key comparability criteria can be sufficient. When the number of sales (or properties) in the type or location in question exceeds a few dozen, a routine for identifying the *most* comparable properties is necessary. Such routines weight differences among multiple criteria (Gloudemans 1999, 201).

- *Appeal case tracking and management.* Appeal case tracking and management systems assist in scheduling appeals, tracking the status of outstanding appeals, and ensuring that appeal decisions are properly implemented. The systems also provide management-level information, such as lists of appeals grouped by status (e.g., rejected, no change, valuation change, pending), statistics on the tax base at risk, and so forth. The system is able to access the assessment database to obtain information on ownership, property attributes, and valuation. It creates a record of each appeal case, containing such information as property identification, appellant, date of appeal, value in dispute, date of hearing, disposition of appeal, date of decision, and adjusted valuation if a change is approved. Appeal results are added to the assessment record. In these ways, the documentation involved in the appeal process is integrated with corresponding information on property from the assessment rolls.

- *Photographs and document images.* Superior systems incorporate digital photographic images of properties and links to images of relevant documents.

Use of GIS in Valuation

A GIS provides capabilities for displaying and analyzing data spatially. A GIS database normally includes graphic (map) data and attribute data. Although GISs have existed for several decades, the technology only recently has become inexpensive enough to be used in valuation for property tax purposes. (The literature on GIS is large; good introductory works include Bernhardsen [1992] and Urban and Regional Information Systems Association and International Association of Assessing Officers [1999].)

A GIS can be used in at least five ways (the last two of which are discussed under "Immovable Property Valuation," below): (1) to select properties of interest and highlight them on a map and produce reports, (2) to produce special maps needed for a mass valuation project, (3) to produce thematic maps to support valuation analyses, (4) to identify groups of property that share common market characteristics (cluster analysis), and (5) to evaluate how distances from a property to important geographic features affect the value of the property. These capabilities have uses beyond the immediate needs of property tax administrations, and a number of these administrations are attempting to sell services or products as a strategy for recovering some of their investments in staff training, computer systems, and data maintenance.

- *Selection of properties of interest.* A GIS allows users to identify on a map the properties that possess attributes selected by the user. For example, the user could ask for a map that displays all the properties in a specified land use category that sold in the last year. Similarly, the user could ask for all properties within 1 km of a particular property that recently sold.

- *Work maps.* Traditional paper-based (or other similar medium) cadastral maps are like rectangular tiles. Their size and scale generally were fixed. When a valuer wanted to study a street or area that spanned more than one map, it was difficult to make a conveniently sized map of the area of interest. (The parts of the maps that were needed would have to be cut out and glued together.) In a GIS database, the map of a territory exists as a single continuous "sheet" whose dimensions and scale can be changed at will. Moreover, in a GIS, it is possible to select only properties that share certain characteristics, such a fronting on a street or being in an identified market area, and to produce a map of only those properties in a convenient scale.

- *Thematic maps.* GIS has thematic mapping capabilities. Thematic (choropleth) maps allow data (such as average sale prices) to be displayed geographically (such as by land value zone). Usually data can be color-coded.

Although a property tax can be effectively administered without a GIS, it would be wise to consider development of a GIS eventually. In particular, it would be unwise to commission the production of *new* paper-based maps (see "Cadastral Mapping," further on in this chapter).

Supervision and Equalization

The need for supervision and equalization in decentralized property tax administration was first recognized in the United States in the late eighteenth century (Silverherz 1936, 3). The main elements of supervision programs were identified in Chapter 3. Table 7-5 identifies some of the more common supervisory activities. The choices are akin to an à la carte menu. Each state chooses activities based on perceived needs and available resources, which change over time. The IAAO *Standard on Administration of Monitoring and Compliance Responsibilities* (2003b), *Standard on Property Tax Policy* (2004b), and *Standard on Ratio Studies* (2007) offer not wholly congruent advice on which activities should be undertaken and how.

Standards and Specifications

Standards and specifications guide both local assessors and supervisory agencies, facilitate the transfer of data, and provide an objective basis for measuring local administrative performance and for deciding whether to take equalization and enforcement actions. They can be contained in legislation, regulations, or guidelines, which can be compiled in an assessor's manual.

TABLE 7-5. Examples of Supervisory Activities in Tax Administration

Setting Standards and Providing Specifications	Providing Assistance	Monitoring Performance	Taking Corrective Action
Rules and regulations generally	General advice	General oversight (routine field visits and ad hoc complaint investigations)	Roll approval (without which taxes cannot be levied)
Appraisal performance (ratio study standards)	Manuals (procedural, appraisal, and legal) and standard forms	Ratio studies	Reappraisal orders
Revaluations (frequency and inspection standards)	Professional development (courses and designation programs)	Procedure audits	Direct equalization
Technical proficiency (course completion and testing standards)	Appraisals (advisory and assumption of responsibility for industrial, utility, and similar properties)	Roll review (ranging from abstracts to electronic copies of rolls)	Financial penalties
Forms, codes, and data	• Computer system design and information technology (IT) services • Aerial photography and mapping products and services • Financial assistance (with and without strings attached)	Competency testing	Indirect equalization

Appraisal Accuracy (Ratio Study) Standards

Arguably, the legal assessment standard is the most important standard. It, however, is not an absolute standard—it is the ideal. Appraisal performance (ratio study) standards provide a framework for deciding whether assessments effectively comply with the legal standard. Usually, the actual level of valuation must be within a certain distance from the legal level. Often uniformity standards are established. COD standards require assessment districts to achieve CODs at or below a specified value, which may vary by class of property in keeping with the *Standard on Ratio Studies* (IAAO 2007). PRD standards usually set a performance range based on the IAAO standard. Failure to meet the standards can trigger enforcement actions.

Re-inspection and Reappraisal Standards

States often accompany valuation accuracy standards with specific reappraisal requirements. The IAAO *Standard on Property Tax Policy* (2004b) recommends an annual reappraisal program. Under such a program, the assessor continuously monitors valuation accuracy using ratio studies and property market developments often for the purpose of establishing factors for adjusting sales prices for date of sale. When values change significantly for any segment of the property market or when accuracy standards are no longer met, the assessor decides on an appropriate course of action. Small deviations from performance standards can be handled by simple indexing, often referred to as *trending*. More substantial deviations require recalibrating valuation models or larger scale valuation projects. States also may require assessors to develop plans for re-inspecting properties to help ensure that they are accurately described. Professional standards recommend re-inspections at least every four to six years.

Appraiser Qualifications

Another strategy for improving valuation accuracy and, hence, property tax equity is to increase the technical proficiency of assessing officers. Most U.S. states have established qualifications for assessors and appraisers who work in, or for, assessors' offices, or both. The requirements can specify courses of study, continuing education requirements, testing requirements, and experience requirements. Education and testing requirements often vary with the perceived difficulty in valuing property in the assessment district. Parcel counts and total valuation can be used as a surrogate for difficulty. New Jersey has taken the unusual steps of abolishing elected assessors and of requiring assessors to be college graduates.

Forms, Codes, and Data Formats

States have long set standards designed to ensure that assessors have the information needed to carry out their duties properly and to ensure that data transmitted to the state were in a standard format. These objectives originally were achieved by prescribing forms or by requiring locally developed forms to be approved. With computerization, states began to set standards for record formats and coding data. Often those standards were embedded in computer systems developed by the state for local use. Such standards setting practices indirectly promotes consistency in policy and practices. They facilitate transmission of information electronically and analysis of that information.

Technical Assistance

Technical assistance activities run the gamut from informally providing advice on request to the more technical options listed below.

Legal Opinions and Interpretations

Wisely, most supervisory agencies attempt to keep local officials advised of changes in laws and regulations. They can offer interpretations of law as well.

Manuals, Bulletins, and Newsletters

In print or on Web sites, most supervisory agencies maintain manuals, issue bulletins, and publish periodicals. Manuals vary widely in scope. Some contain only appraisal information, but many recommend procedures as well. In addition to reference works, assessors need information on developments that affect them.

Education and Training

In conjunction with technical proficiency standards, supervisory agencies provide or support training. Assessors also can be required to attend annual conferences.

Computer Services

Supervisory agencies sponsor the development of CAMA systems and other property-tax-related systems. They can also host systems and provide services. Usually, use of software or services is discretionary.

Valuation Assistance

Supervisory agencies provide valuation assistance in a variety of ways, ranging from mere advice to assuming responsibility for certain types of property. Supervisory agencies may provide field staff for revaluations or for actually managing revaluation projects. About 30 states provide direct on-site valuation assistance. About 23 states assist with property inspections. Tennessee and West Virginia are examples of states that routinely provide revaluation assistance. Arizona helps with mass appraisal model building. Most states assume responsibility for valuing railroad, utility, and similar property. Oregon, Wisconsin, and other states value industrial property.

Cadastral Mapping

Some states assist with cadastral mapping. Assistance ranges from providing specifications to actually making maps and providing aerial photography. They also foster use of GIS.

Public Relations

An important aspect of every property tax administrator's job is increasing awareness of property tax systems, answering questions, and maintaining good public relations. State agencies often produce publications and handouts that assessors can provide taxpayers. Some go further and work with assessors in media relations and provide video materials.

Financial Aid

To provide incentives for more accurate appraisals or to compensate for a lack of local fiscal capacity, states furnish funding for such activities as reappraisals, property inventory maintenance, and system improvements. Sometimes the aid is in the form of a loan.

Performance Monitoring

Supervisory agencies employ a range of techniques to monitor the performance of local property tax officials. They range from informal, unstructured visits by field staff to local assessors to rigorous performance audit programs, of which ratio studies and procedural audits are the main components. Although routine visits allow supervisory agency personnel to form general, subjective opinions of the quality of assessments and assessment practices in the districts visited, Silverherz (1936, 15) recognized the inherent limitations of brief visits and advocated ratios studies for their objectivity. Nearly all North American supervisory agencies now conduct ratio studies (Dornfest and Thompson 2004), and they are used in other property tax systems to evaluate the quality of appraisals.

Of course, ratio studies also have their limitations when sales samples are too small or nonrepresentative to permit sound conclusions or when property is not assessed on a market value basis. In such situations, procedural audits can shed light on the accuracy of assessments. If the assessor's systems and procedures conform to legal requirements and professional standards, the resulting values can be presumed to be accurate reflections of the underlying market values. While ratio studies provide evidence that appraisals do not meet accuracy standards, they do not provide direct evidence of the cause of the problems. Procedural audits can pinpoint the most likely causes. If they incorporate data audits, procedural audits can buttress statistical findings that an assessor practices sales chasing, cherry-picking, and other strategies to manipulate ratio study data to skew ratio study results. When a supervisory agency administers payments to local assessment districts for assessment-related work, such as field inspections, data and procedural audits can ensure that the work that was paid for was, in fact, done. Finally, both the auditor and the audited can use the results of a procedural audit to identify strengths and weaknesses in current operations, design improvements, and build a case for investments in new systems and procedures.

Procedural audit practices have not been studied as closely as ratio study practices, and apart from general auditing standards (United States Government Accountability Office 2007), there are no standards for property tax procedural audits. Nevertheless, there is growing interest on the part of supervisory agencies, and at least 20 conduct some form of procedural audits (Dornfest and Thompson [2003] identify 27 states that responded positively to questions about procedural audits). An examination of current procedural audit programs suggests the following design options:

- *Purpose.* Although ensuring compliance with laws and regulations usually is the main purpose, the audits may also be designed to encourage improvements in practices by recognizing promising innovations and best practices. Massachusetts and New York attempt to ensure that reappraisal projects conform to standards *before* they are completed. Alberta wants to move in this direction.

- *Jurisdictional coverage.* The program may be designed to review every assessment jurisdiction during a cycle of one or more years. Alternatively, only selected jurisdictions may be audited based on one or more triggering mechanisms, such as a reappraisal, noncompliance with assessment accuracy or practice standards (usually the noncompliance must be serious and repeated), an emerging issue, or a serious complaint about assessment practices.

- *Comprehensiveness.* At one end of the spectrum, the procedural audit program may examine virtually every facet of an assessor's operations (real property assessment, personal property assessment, exemption administration, and the like). At the other, a single area, such as use-value assessments, may be examined. Most programs fall between the extremes.

- *Methodology.* An audit may be in-depth, involving a combination of interviews, detailed documentation of work processes, analysis of computer system documentation, data completeness and accuracy audits, and the like. More commonly, the audit is cursory, involving completing a questionnaire or checklist.

- *Timing.* Often the audit takes place after an assessment has been completed. Occasionally an attempt is made to audit work in progress (such as a reappraisal) in hopes of improving the outcome.

The main impediments to a procedural audit program are the time and expense of the audits (both the auditor and the audited agency must devote time to the audit). The timeliness of reporting unsatisfactory assessment practices can be an issue when taxes already have been assessed on the basis of the deficient practices. A problem may already have been addressed by the time it is pointed out.

Another issue is the credibility of the audits, especially if the audited jurisdictions believe they have been unfairly singled out or if the auditors are perceived to be incompetent. Addressing such concerns can lead to another: finding the right balance between objectively verifiable findings (which may address trivialities) and subjective judgments about, say, whether high-value investment properties are appraised consistently and fairly. Comprehensive audits obviously require greater skills and more time. Yet they usually are most revealing. Audits based on surveys and checklists have advantages of being quick and easy to make, but they offer the fewest insights and nuances.

Another monitoring technique is to require local assessment districts to furnish the supervisory agency with an electronic copy of the assessment roll and the property characteristics data upon which assessments are based. (Traditionally, only abstracts of rolls have been required.) Having assessment data in digital form allows the supervisory agency to rigorously test whether assessment practices are evenhanded or whether groups like recently sold properties are singled out. Arizona, Florida, New York, and Utah are among the states that require assessors to submit digital copies of sales files and assessment rolls for use in the states' enforcement and equalization programs. Alberta has a system called ASSET (Assessment Shared Services Environment) that allows the province and all participating municipalities to examine assessment and sales data.

Equalization and Other Corrective Actions

Equalization is a loosely used term in assessment administration. Here it is *not* the process by which individual assessments are adjusted on a case-by-case basis as a result of appeals (discussed later). Equalization is a process by which a supervisory (or oversight) or review agency adjusts initial assessments as determined by local assessors to ensure that the assessments *overall* (not individually) are at the legal level of assessment or are uniformly assessed. In addition to ensuring that legal requirements are met, equalization ensures that taxes levied by districts that span more than one assessment district are more fairly apportioned. Similarly, partial exemptions have similar tax benefits across the jurisdiction of the equalization agency.

Direct Equalization

Equalization adjustments can be made before initial assessments are used to determine property tax liabilities as illustrated in Table 7-6; that is, each individual initial assessment is adjusted. This form of equalization often is known as *direct* equalization.

As shown in Table 7-6, the property tax assessment (column 5) is the product of the first four columns. The initial assessment is determined by the local assessor. After the supervisory agency makes a determination of the level of assessment in the assessment district (or type of property) by using a ratio study and if it finds that the actual level of assessment differs sufficiently from the legal level of assessment (which is assumed here to be 100 percent), it orders local tax officials to adjust initial assessments by the equalization factor (1.25 in this case) to produce equalized assessed values ($125,000 in this case) that overall are at (or nearer) the legal standard. The equalization factor is the reciprocal of the overall ratio (or 1/0.8 in this case). Without the application of the equalization factor—and assuming that the property tax rate would not change—the property taxes in this example would have been $1,500 (column 1 multiplied by column 4). Rather than adjusting assessments in the manner shown in Table 7-6, tax rates can be adjusted in an analogous manner; this can be done when there is a state- or provincial-wide property tax.

TABLE 7-6. Illustration of Direct Equalization on a Single Property

Initial Assessment	Equalization Factor	Equalized Assessed Value	Nominal Property Tax Rate	Property Tax
$100,000	1.25	$125,000	0.015	$1,875

Table 7-7 illustrates the effects of direct equalization by property class on the tax base of an entire assessment district. This example is based on the following assumptions: (a) the taxes to be raised are fixed at $20 million; (b) all property types are legally required to be assessed at full market value (the level should be 100 percent); and (c) the initial assessments (column 2) and the computed levels of assessment (column 3) are as shown.

As shown in Table 7-7, residential and vacant properties are under-assessed and industrial properties are over-assessed. Column 5 shows how taxes would be distributed among classes without equalization. Column 6 shows how taxes would be distributed after equalization (the factors would be 1.33, 1.0, 0.8, and 2.0, respectively). Table 7-8 illustrates a further point: the difference between effective tax rates before and after equalization (recalling that in Table 7-7, the nominal tax rate was 1 percent).

TABLE 7-7. The Effect of Equalization on the Distribution of Property Taxes

Class of Property	Total Assessed Value ($ millions)	Computed Level of Assessment (%)	Equalized Assessed Value ($ millions)	Taxes without Equalization ($ millions)	Taxes after Equalization ($ millions)
Residential	600	75	800	6.00	7.02
Commercial	600	100	600	6.00	5.26
Industrial	600	125	480	6.00	4.21
Vacant	200	50	400	2.00	3.51
All Classes	2,000	NA	2,280	20.00	20.00

In Table 7-8, the effective tax rates are taxes as a percentage of equalized assessed value (the differences in effective tax rates after equalization are due to rounding). Note that even though commercial property is correctly assessed in the example, that class of property would bear more than its fair share of taxes without equalization. The same types of results in Tables 7-7 and 7-8 would obtain if, instead of property use classes, the analysis were of assessment districts within a school district, townships within a county, or counties within a state. Table 7-8 illustrates another point: fractional assessment can have a fiscal consequence; that is, if the 1 percent nominal rate were a tax rate limit, total taxes could be as high as $22.8 million (instead of the $20 million in Table 7-7). Thus, assessors can assume an unintended local fiscal-policy-setting role if unchecked by supervision and equalization (of course, favored taxpayers in the local assessment district may approve of this role). In a similar vein, equalization agencies assume a fiscal policy role when they directly equalize to a common level legally authorized class differences in assessment level, as is the case in Illinois.

TABLE 7-8. Effect of Equalization on Effective Tax Rates

Class of Property	Effective Tax Rate without Equalization	Effective Tax Rate with Equalization
Residential	0.75	0.875
Commercial	1.00	0.877
Industrial	1.25	0.877
Vacant	0.50	0.878
All Classes	0.877	0.877

Direct equalization does not address over- and under-assessment within a class or stratum and therefore cannot improve uniformity within the class or stratum of property being equalized, because every assessment in the stratum is adjusted by the same factor. Thus, it is not a substitute for effective valuation procedures, frequent reappraisals, and local review and appeal procedures. If direct equalization is applied before local appeals, the result gives taxpayers and appeal bodies better cues about which properties should be reduced on appeal (Almy et al. 1978, 398, 403-404).

Regardless of uniformity considerations, by overriding local assessment decisions, direct equalization can arouse political tensions. For this reason, caution is advised when ordering direct equalization (or reassessment orders, discussed next). The IAAO *Standard on Ratio Studies* (2007) recommends a high burden of proof for the equalizing agency.

Reassessment Orders

Some supervisory agencies have authority to address intra-district or class non-uniformity by ordering a reassessment of either the entire district or classes of properties that are found to be over- or under-assessed. The orders may have to be complied with before local taxation can proceed or they may take effect the next tax year. If the reassessments produce the desired results, reassessment orders are a more powerful tool than direct equalization. They also can be a source of tension between the equalization agency, the local assessment district, and local tax districts.

Indirect Equalization

The law may not give the supervisory agency the power to intervene directly in local assessment and taxation. However, unequal levels of assessment among local assessment districts usually are not ignored when a province or state makes payments to local governments like school districts and when the payment formula considers the local property tax base. The equalization agency may be required to factor in local assessment totals so that every district's total valuation is expressed at the same overall percentage of market value. This latter figure is the one used in the aid formula. This procedure is known as *indirect* equalization. The chief difference between direct and indirect equalization is that the former is visible to every taxpayer. Without indirect equalization, local assessment districts would have an incentive to undervalue properties in hopes of receiving larger aid payments, thereby reducing the share of government expenditures borne by local taxpayers.

Equalization agencies also can use the results of direct equalization studies for indirect equalization purposes, so total equalized value would be included in the aid formula. Also as discussed below, equalization studies of the indirect type are used to adjust tax rates locally to reflect differences in levels of assessment. This is done when the tax district is the state or other broad area. Examples are Alberta, Michigan, New Hampshire, and Vermont, which at the time this text was being prepared (early 2008) levied province- or state-wide education property taxes.

As illustrated in Table 7-9, the equalization agency determines the actual level of assessment in each district (column 3) and the factor needed to convert local assessments to the legal standard (which here is assumed to be 100 percent) (column 4). Column 5 is simply column 2 multiplied by column 4. Because the local assessments in districts A and B were below full market value, their equalized values are higher than their assessed values, and the taxable wealth of all the districts also is higher (see the sum of column 6). Ignoring other complexities in aid formulas, local taxable wealth would increase in districts A and B, but only District A's aid payment likely would decrease, as shown in column 7. The important point, however, is that without indirect equalization, taxpayers in district A would receive a free ride.

TABLE 7-9. Illustration of Indirect Equalization

Local Assessment District	Total Local Assessed Value (taxable wealth in $ millions)	Actual Level of Assessment (%)	Indirect Equalization Factor	Total Equalized Assessed Value (restated taxable wealth in $ millions)	Proportion of Total Taxable Wealth (%)	Implied Shift in Aid Shares (%)
A	400	50.0	2.00	800	47	-42
B	400	80.0	1.25	500	29	+12
C	400	100.0	1.00	400	24	+27
All	1,200	70.6	1.42	1,700	100	—

Sometimes, local tax levies are increased or decreased to compensate for inequities in assessment levels. Assume for example, that a state-wide education property tax of 0.005 were levied to fund aid payments for schools. Using Table 7-9 to illustrate how this mechanism might work, without indirect equalization, the taxpayers in each district would contribute $2 million to the aid fund, which would be unfair based on the real value of property in each district. If the fund were fixed at $6 million, fairer contributions from the three districts would be $2.82, $1.74, and $1.44 million, respectively, based on the percentages in column 6. The adjusted tax rates levied against the unequalized local assessed value that would raise those amounts would be 0.00705, 0.00435, and 0.000360, respectively (the adjusted levies divided by the total assessed values).

Initial Assessment Processes

This section briefly surveys the generally accepted administrative policies and procedures that are needed in effective, economical property tax administration. Although real property valuation is discussed first, the work of collecting and organizing data occurs first in practice. Many of the practices described here reflect current standards of practice in Canada and the United States. Different standards would be appropriate in countries with lower levels of property taxation and in countries just introducing value-based property taxes (see Dillinger 1991 and Keith 1993).

Immovable Property Valuation

Because valuation is highly technical, this section provides only an overview of systems for estimating the market value of real property (land and buildings) for property tax purposes. As background, valuation is the activity of *estimating* what values are, and market value is an expected price—the price for a property that would most likely be agreed to in an open market, assuming that the seller and buyer were reasonably well informed and under no unusual pressure.

The science of valuation began to be developed in Europe in the eighteenth century. Theory and practice coalesced during the twentieth century. Three general approaches to valuation (sales comparison, income, and cost), each emphasizing a particular kind of market evidence, became widely accepted (valuation terminology is not standardized internationally; here terms common in North America are used).

The *sales comparison approach* to property valuation uses information on recent open-market sales prices. The aim is to decide how differences in the characteristics of sold property—use, size, location, quality of buildings, and so on—influence their prices. This information is then used to estimate what the properties being appraised (*subject* properties) would sell for. Where there is a large number of recent sales of fairly similar properties, as is often the case with residences and may be the case with smaller office and retail properties, statistical techniques (such as multiple regression analysis) can be used to assign values to each measurable characteristic, and the valuation can be done with a fair degree of confidence. Where sales are infrequent or are spread over a broad territory and where properties tend to be distinctive, the sales comparison approach is both more difficult and less useful.

The *income approach* to property valuation involves estimating the future income stream that can be ascribed to the property over its remaining economically useful life and using a "discount rate" or rate of return on investments of comparable risk to "capitalize" the income stream into a present value as of the valuation date. The basic mathematical relationship is

$$Value = income \div rate.$$

Income is estimated as the rents from the subject property or comparable properties net of taxes, insurance, and operating costs and adjusted for expected occupancy rates. The income approach is theoretically preferred in the valuation of commonly rented properties because it mirrors the thinking of market participants. Practical difficulties sometimes limit the use of the income approach in valuations made for property tax purposes.

The *cost approach* to property valuation involves estimating and combining three components:

$$\begin{aligned} Value = {} & replacement\ cost\ of\ improvements \\ & + accrued\ depreciation \\ & + land\ value \end{aligned}$$

Replacement cost is what it would cost to replace the existing structures and other improvements with new construction of equivalent usefulness but not necessarily the same design and construction technologies and materials. Accrued depreciation (also known as *amortization*) is the loss in value due to physical depreciation, functional obsolescence, and economic obsolescence. Land value is what vacant land with the same location, area, shape, physical characteristics, and allowable uses would sell for in the open market. The cost approach has its problems, but enjoys the position of being the default valuation approach because it was the first mass appraisal approach to be developed and because data on replacement costs are inexpensively available from specialist publishers or database providers, who also serve the insurance and construction industries.

There are many different ways of applying these three approaches to value, and some methodologies combine elements of two or more approaches. Standards of practice require valuers to work systematically, document their work, and communicate their opinions of value clearly. Figure 7-2 identifies the main steps. The *purpose* of a valuation—in this case, providing the basis for apportioning property tax obligations—greatly affects how the valuation should be made. Two factors especially affect valuations for property tax purposes: (1) the need for efficiency in the valuation process and (2) the need to treat taxpayers consistently. Efficiency is warranted because the costs of administering a tax should be kept to a minimum. Relative to most other purposes for commissioning a valuation (such as determining the price of a property or whether the property provides sufficient collateral for a mortgage), the amounts at stake in a property tax valuation (the taxes in question) are low. Consistency is warranted for perceived equity and for quality assurance.

While valuation is only a means to an end in property taxation—the apportionment of property tax obligations—valuations for property tax purposes may have other uses. If there are other value-based taxes, the valuation programs should be coordinated. Certainly the database created to support the valuation program has other uses. These uses might make it possible to allocate the costs of data collection to other programs or to recover a portion of the costs by the sale of data products to the private sector.

FIGURE 7-2. Generalized Valuation Process

1. Define the valuation problem		
1.1 Identify the intended use and users of the valuation		
1.2 Define value(s) to be developed		
1.3 Establish date(s) of value opinion(s)		
1.4 Identify and locate the real estate		
1.5 Identify the property rights to be valued		
1.6 Identify limiting conditions or limitations		
2. Preliminary analysis and plan: select and collect data		

GENERAL (MARKET):
2.1 Market analysis
  2.1.1 Demand components
  2.1.2 Supply components
  2.1.3 Trends
  2.1.4 Forecasts
	SUBJECT PROPERTY:
	2.2 Property analysis
	  2.2.1 Site/improvements
	  2.2.2 Size
	  2.2.3 Age and condition
	  2.2.4 Location
	  2.2.5 Legal (title, use)
		COMPETITIVE PROPERTIES:
		2.3 Comparison analysis
		  2.3.1 Sales
		  2.3.2 Rentals
		  2.3.3 Costs
		  2.3.4 Elements of comparison
		  2.3.5 Units of comparison

3. Develop highest and best use opinion		
3.1 Land as if vacant and available		
3.2 Property as improved (existing or proposed)		
4. Develop indicator(s) of land/site value (as defined)		
4.1 Sales comparison	4.2 Income capitalization	4.3 Subdivision development
5. Develop indicator(s) of improved property value (as defined)		
5.1 Cost	5.2 Sales comparison	5.3 Income capitalization
6. Reconcile value indicators; reach defined value opinion		
7. Report opinion(s) of value(s) (as defined)		

By the beginning of the twentieth century the new science of valuation had been applied en masse to the appraisal of all taxable property in a property tax district in the United States—hence the term *mass appraisal*. When computers became available to assessors in the late 1960s, mass appraisal began to be referred to as CAMA. Now the term *automated valuation model* (AVM) may be used in connection with mass valuation. (Valuation models are discussed below.) In practice, a CAMA system may contain an AVM or it may not; see *Standard on Mass Appraisal of Real Property* (IAAO 2008).

Today, valuers use mass valuation in property tax administration, except for unusual properties, which require the use of individual property valuation techniques. A modern mass valuation program requires a number of linked procedures (which are discussed further below):

- Collection and maintenance of data on the attributes of the inventory of taxable properties
- Collection of evidence of market values, such as sales, rents, construction costs, and so on
- Market analysis
- Development and application of valuation models
- Evaluation of valuation accuracy
- Communication of values to taxpayers, tax administrators, and other stakeholders.

Figure 7-3 is a schematic diagram of all but the last procedure. Property tax administration also requires procedures to link properties to a taxpayer, determine taxability, and collect property taxes. Property tax records are known collectively as the fiscal cadastre (block I, "Data collection and maintenance," in Figure 7-3), and these are discussed after valuation.

Preliminary Analyses

Mass valuation involves a number of preliminary, or exploratory, analyses (block II, "Exploratory data analysis," in Figure 7-3). Areas of inquiry include market patterns and trends, the quality of the data that might be used, and the quality of any existing valuations. The groups of properties (market segments, market areas, or both) to be valued together are identified. Consideration is given to the amount of market evidence available and the types and quality of property attribute data. Recent trends in prices are studied.

FIGURE 7-3. Schematic Diagram of Mass Valuation System

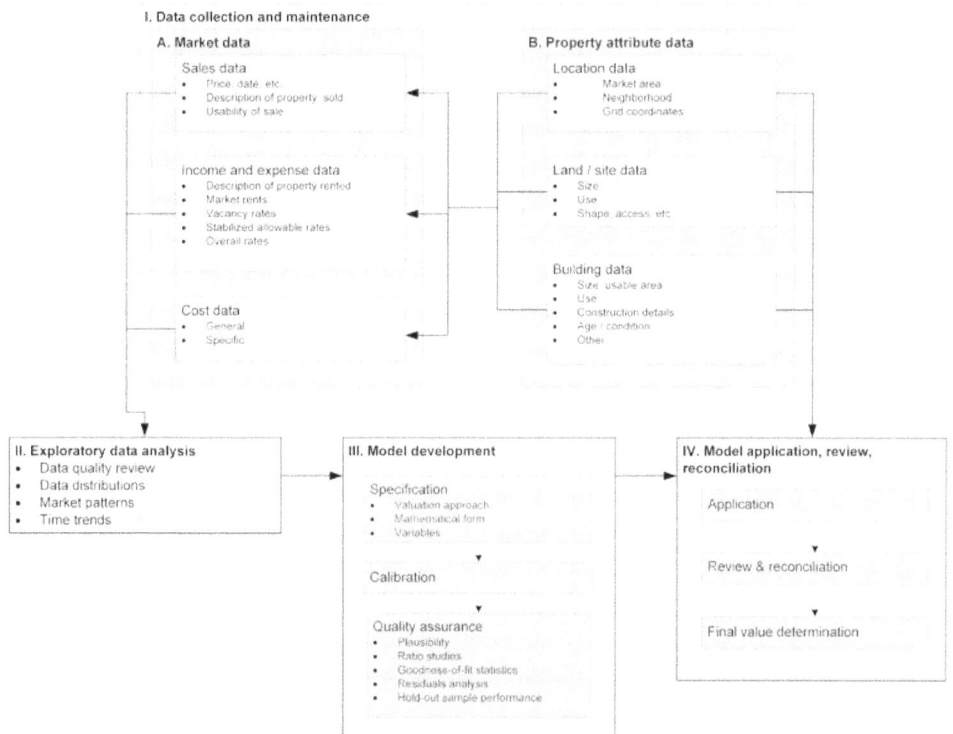

Valuation Modeling

A valuation model is a mathematical representation of the effects of property supply and demand factors on market prices. International experience reveals a range of practices that fit under the umbrella of mass appraisal. In general, however, mass valuation modeling involves model specification and calibration (Figure 7-3, block III, "Model development"). Specification is theoretical and involves deciding which valuation approach to use, which property characteristics likely have a significant effect on property values, and how those characteristics are assumed to affect value. Calibration is the process of estimating the coefficients associated with the variables in a mass appraisal model. Calibration is the empirical, analytical work appraisers and analysts do in developing models. Specification and calibration may be repeated several times as a model is tested and refined. Valuation models vary with the type of market evidence used. Models based on sales prices often are called market models, and they should be used whenever there are sufficient sales. Income models should be developed for properties that typically are rented. Cost models should be developed for use as a fallback approach when there are insufficient sales or rents of the type of property in question. Forms that models can take include the following:

- *Stratified per-unit models.* Stratification can be used to control for differences in location and type of property, and simple average value per unit models can be constructed. These types of models are very common, and they can be satisfactory for highly uniform properties (such as apartments). They reflect only average prices, not the marginal contributions to value of each attribute. Thus they may fail to reflect complex valuation situations.

- *Extrapolation from appraisals of benchmark or beacon properties.* Under this approach, typical properties are valued using single-property appraisal methods and other properties are rated relative to a benchmark (say, a subject property is considered to be 85 percent as valuable as the value of a benchmark). Such an approach is most practical when properties are reasonably uniform.

- *Banding.* Under the Council Tax in the United Kingdom, persons familiar with property markets merely assigned residential properties to value ranges based on their attributes, essentially sidestepping rigorous valuation analyses altogether. Banding is most practical when there is a considerable amount of value evidence or when sales data are scarce.

- *Multivariate models.* These models explain the simultaneous effect of several attributes explicitly. They represent the state of the art of mass appraisal. Because they are highly mathematical, they are not described in detail; see Gloudemans (1999) for an excellent survey of multivariate model building forms and techniques, of which multiple regression analysis is the most prominent.

One caveat with any valuation model is as follows: the value ascribed to any attribute may, in fact, be influenced by attributes omitted from the model. Suppose, for example, that a model for valuing apartments had only two variables: size and location. But suppose that state of repair (condition) was a factor that buyers also considered. Further suppose that the best-repaired apartments tended to be in one neighborhood (zone). In this situation, the coefficient for the location factor would also reflect the value associated with good repair. Thus, when sales over several years are used to calibrate a model, time of sale should be explicitly considered. Otherwise, any changes in price level over time might be mistakenly ascribed to other attributes.

Spatial Analyses Using GIS

Basic uses of GIS were discussed earlier. Here the focus is on the ways in which spatial data can be used in mass valuation.

Cluster Analysis

Cluster analysis is a statistical method used to group properties into homogeneous groups based on multiple property attributes. Essentially, the method seeks to minimize differences in attributes within a stratum and maximize differences between strata. Often geographic proximity is an important attribute, and a GIS makes it easy to compute distances between points, which can be used as a variable in the clustering algorithm. Cluster analysis can provide a statistical alternative to traditional methods for delineating market areas based on purely on appraiser judgment. However, cluster analysis may not produce areas that are demonstrably better than areas delineated using traditional methods.

Response Surface Analysis
Location response surface analysis (LRSA) potentially provides a better method for evaluating the effects of location on property values than simply assigning properties to neighborhoods (zones) or using similar arbitrary classification approaches. Conceptually, a *response surface* is a three-dimensional surface analogous to a contour map. An x-y coordinate plane represents geographic location, and property value is measured on the z-axis. LRSA requires that the coordinates of a point representing each land plot (often the parcel centroid) be contained in the attribute database.

The procedure proceeds in stages. First, a valuation model is specified and calibrated that has *no* location variables. Second, the ratios of estimated values to actual sales prices are plotted on the geographic grid. (Underestimates have ratios below 1.0, and overestimates have values greater than 1.0.) When low ratios are clustered, the analyst looks for value-influence centers (VICs) that increase the value of property (such as proximity to the city center). The same procedure is used for high ratios to detect causes of diminished property value. Third, after the VICs are identified, the distance from each parcel to each VIC is calculated and an appropriate distance variable specified (such as the reciprocal of the distance). Finally, the model is re-run with the distance variables included. The results are evaluated in the same way as before, and the process is repeated until the model builder is satisfied that all significant VICs have been identified.

The chief theoretical advantage of LRSA is that there are none of the discontinuities in values that are associated with neighborhood variables; that is, values change more gradually as distance from a VIC is increased. Practically, LRSA is limited by the distribution of sales geographically. VICs close to underrepresented areas may not be recognized.

Value Review and Reconciliation

It is good practice to review computer-generated value estimates for reasonableness and consistency before they are adopted as the basis for assessments (Figure 7-3, block IV, "Model application, review, and reconciliation"). After the models have been applied, analysts make statistical reviews of preliminary value estimates using ratio studies. If the values do not meet effectiveness targets, the analysts recalibrate the models as necessary. After that, each individual preliminary value estimate is reviewed for reasonableness and consistency with the estimates of nearby and comparable properties; that is, the value estimates should be similar unless the differences can be justified. If more than one estimate of value has been produced for a property (a recommended practice), a choice needs to be made about the most supportable estimate. Reviewers should be provided with guidelines on when and how to override initial value estimates. Field reviews are desirable unless recent images of the properties are available or unless property characteristics data were recently verified

Keeping Values Current

The fairness of value-based property taxes increases when value estimates are in line with current market values. There are basically three options for keeping assessments in line with current market values: (1) indexing or trending existing valuations, (2) recalibrating or updating existing models, and (3) calibrating new valuation models. The assessor can select the strategy most appropriate for the type of property in question. Trending (indexing) can be used as long as uniformity standards for the class of property or area continue to be met. Cost, income, and sales comparison models can be recalibrated using updated market data. However, a full revaluation is required when there have been fundamental changes in the economy. For example, trending may produce satisfactory results in recently developed housing areas, but it may be necessary to do a full revaluation of property in the commercial core. In other words, it is not always necessary to revalue every property every year; assessments need to be changed only when there is a clear indication based on market evidence that valuations no longer meet standards.

Cadastral Data Management

Types of Cadastres

A *cadastre* is a land record system that contains graphical and textual data. A *legal cadastre* contains information about property ownership, and a *fiscal cadastre* comprises the totality of maps and records needed to administer a property tax. There are two basic types of fiscal cadastres: person- (or taxpayer-) based systems and property- or map-based systems. A computerized cadastre based on a relational database management system (RDBMS) allows reports to be organized either way or both ways. Person-based cadastres have ancient origins and basically are lists of persons and information about the taxable properties they are known to possess. Map-based cadastres are a more recent invention. They are needed to administer broad-based property taxes fairly and efficiently. Only by organizing land and building records geographically can a property tax administration be confident that all assessable properties have been discovered and correctly described. Person-based systems are not recommended because they are crucially dependent on owners declaring their property holdings and on tedious efforts to find unknown owners.

A modern map-based fiscal cadastre combines (1) large-scale cadastral maps that accurately depict parcel boundaries and other geographic features; (2) files or registers containing information about land parcels, buildings, and taxpayers; and

(3) a cadastral numbering system that uniquely links the parcels shown on maps with their related records. Successful property tax administration also requires data transfer protocols between related information systems.

Building and maintaining the fiscal cadastre usually are the most labor-intensive and, hence, most expensive aspects of property tax administration. Consequently, these activities need to be well designed and managed. Data management responsibilities encompass the determination of data needs, collection methods, and data storage and retrieval facilities. Work (or business) processes related to building and maintaining the cadastre include the following:

- Compilation of cadastral maps and assignment of property identifiers
- Maintenance of land and building attribute records
- Maintenance of sales records and other evidence of market values
- Maintenance of records of taxpayers (usually owners), taxes assessed, and tax payments.

When movable property is taxable (discussed later), it is necessary to maintain records on persons with assessable movable (personal property) and their holdings. Although these can be linked to real property assessment records, a separate register (roll) of movable property assessments often is made because in rem enforcement usually is not feasible because of the movability of personal property.

Cadastral Mapping

A complete and up-to-date set of cadastral maps (often known as tax maps or assessment maps in the United States) provides the most effective way of discovering (locating spatially) and inventorying real property holdings. The maps help ensure that the property tax administration has accounted for all land and that no land areas are taxed twice. The maps also detail the location, shape, and size of every parcel of land, as they are important determinants of land value. Building records are keyed to land parcel records (and some maps display building footprints). Unit or occupancy records are keyed to building records.

The process of compiling cadastral maps is analogous to completing a jigsaw puzzle. Representations of plots of land in plans and surveys, aerial photographs, descriptions in title certificates and deeds, and the like constitute the pieces of the puzzle. The puzzle has to be complete before the tax administration can be sure that all the pieces are in their proper places and that there are no missing or extra pieces. Solving the cadastral map puzzle requires that every parcel of land be displayed accurately on a map. Newly compiled maps should be digital, as they are a major component of GIS; see *Standard on Manual Cadastral Maps and Parcel Identifiers* (IAAO 2004a) and *Standard on Digital Cadastral Maps and Parcel Identifiers* (IAAO 2003c).

Cadastral Numbers

Written descriptions of land plots, addresses, and parcel cadastral numbers are all used to identify land parcels. The property tax administration or a mapping agency usually designs the cadastral identification (numbering) scheme and assigns (or retires) cadastral numbers as new parcels are created (or as old parcels are eliminated). The purpose of the cadastral number is to provide a convenient way to unambiguously refer to a parcel and to link parcel records. Consequently, uniqueness is an important design criterion.

A unique identifier represents only a single parcel configuration. Whenever a parcel is divided or combined with another parcel, the original cadastral number is *not* used to describe the succeeding parcel or parcels. Each new parcel or parcels has a new number assigned to it, and the previously assigned numbers are retired. Alternatively, suffixes can be assigned to a parent number to indicate a change. Whenever parcel numbers are not unique, market analyses can be confounded and tax liabilities confused. Figure 7-4 illustrates two ways to achieve uniqueness when a parent parcel is split into two child parcels. Similar approaches can be taken when parcels are combined.

FIGURE 7-4. Ways to Achieve Uniqueness in Parcel Identifiers

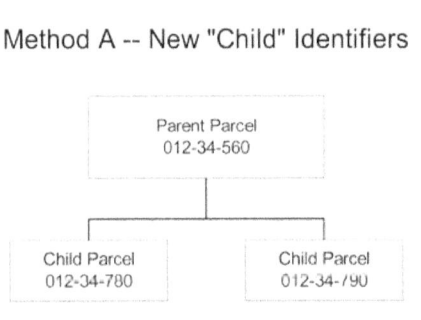
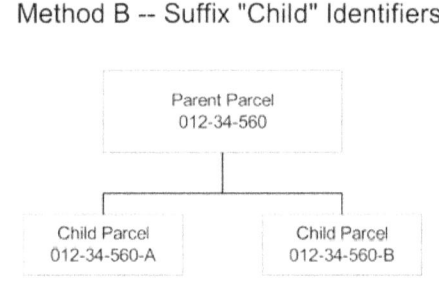

Buildings and other assessable structures and any separately assessable parts of structures also make up a major part of the property inventory. It is desirable to extend the cadastral numbering system to buildings and individual occupancies when they are separately assessed and taxed. At the same time, it is desirable to have a way to link separate parcels that constitute a single economic unit.

Immovable Property Attribute Data Collection
Property Attribute Data Needs

In designing (or redesigning) a property tax system, an initial issue is the data needed for assessment (property identification, valuation, and defense of appealed assessments) and for tax administration (determination of liability for assessment or taxation and the extent of assessability or taxability). Especially in a computerized environment in which systems are to be integrated, the data needs of others in the public and private sectors also need to be taken into consideration if the property tax administration is required to pay for additional data or if the users are willing to pay for the data. In general, data describing to location of properties, the characteristics of land parcels, and the characteristics of buildings and other constructions are needed. The data management program embodies a concern for cost-effectiveness and an effective quality assurance program. It benefits from a well-designed computer system.

Data on the *location* of properties always are needed in a value-based real property tax, because location affects the value of both land and buildings. Location can be described in such ways as the following:

- Belonging to a market area or neighborhood or "zone." These areas usually are delineated by experts in local real estate markets. The areas need to be large enough to ensure sufficient sales or other market evidence for analysis.
- Adjoining a feature that affects value positively or negatively, such as fronting on a body of water or adjoining a railroad track.
- Being within a certain distance of such a feature, such as having a view of a body of water. Altitude differences can have similar effects.

With respect to *land* attributes, a property record usually needs the following:

- The size, dimensions, or both of each land plot (with units of measure, such as square meters, clearly identified)
- If applicable, the dimensions of components of the parcel (such as excess land or various soil classes)
- A land use code (actual use, presumed most economical use, or both)
- Site characteristics that significantly contribute to the desirability of the parcel.

A property record should provide for recording essential *building* and structure elements. The sales comparison and cost approaches to valuation (discussed below) usually need the following data:

- Size
- Quality rating (design, quality of materials, quality of workmanship)
- Year built and condition
- Significant construction features (such as materials used, wall and roof type, and story height for commercial and industrial structures)
- Other components that significantly contribute to desirability or construction costs in the locale.

The cost approach to value has more extensive data requirements. As attribute data needs are identified, it also is necessary to specify how each individual attribute is described and stored in cadastral records. This process requires some analysis and planning if economy, accuracy, and consistency are to be achieved, as background, words, mnemonics, numbers, and images can be used to describe an attribute. Although the data in the cadastral database can be in any form, attribute data must be reduced to a numerical form for analysis by computers. This requires coding. Codes can reduce a lengthy description to a uniform and manageable size.

Data Capture Strategies

Deciding how to collect and maintain data is an important administrative system design task. Options are as follows:

Data Conversion

If after careful evaluation the answers to the four questions below are "yes," conversion of existing cadastral data can be a good option.

- *Relevance of the data.* Are available data well suited to current needs?
- *Coverage, completeness, and accuracy.* For data items considered relevant, are they available for all assessable properties? Are they reasonably accurate? Old computerized data may not be what they seem to be; users of hardwired legacy systems may have stored data in a field intended (and labeled) for another data item.
- *Accessibility.* Are computerized records in a format that can be read? Are paper records well organized, and is the information on them legible?
- *Ease of maintenance.* Will it be possible to keep data elements up-to-date at reasonable cost?

If the answer to some of the questions is "no," reliance on one or more of the other options is advised.

Field Canvasses

A field canvass can be necessary to obtain the data needed for the new property tax system, as field inspections provide an effective, albeit expensive, way to ensure that the information on property attributes is correct. It is generally believed that properties should be reinspected regularly to ensure that attribute data are accurate. About five years is considered to be the maximum interval between reinspections. A rolling reinspection program, in which a fraction of all properties is inspected each year, is a cost-effective strategy. Increasingly, imagery can be substituted for sending inspectors into the field.

In addition to procedures for comprehensive canvasses, procedures for targeted inspections may need to be developed for properties that were recently sold, were issued a building permit, and are under appeal.

Field inspections can be two general levels of detail: a complete collection or

Chapter 7 ■ Components of Model Property Tax Administrative Systems **235**

re-collection of data (with any existing data essentially being ignored) or merely a verification of data. Successful canvasses require well-trained staff, use of appropriate technology, carefully planned logistics, data quality assurance, and public relations.

Taxpayer Returns

Taxpayer returns can be an expedient way of collecting property attribute information quickly and economically, particularly in the early stages of setting up a property tax system (but see the discussion of self-assessment in Chapter 3). They have been successfully used in initial data collection programs in the Czech Republic and in Slovakia, and they are used on an ongoing basis in Turkey. They also can be used to supplement conventional field canvasses. The chief shortcomings of relying on taxpayers for data relate to their ability to provide consistent and accurate descriptions and their willingness to do so. Limiting data requests to simple, objective items can minimize the first problem. The second problem can be addressed with a combination of appropriate incentives and penalties.

Market Data Collection

The three main approaches to valuation (the sales comparison, income, and cost approaches) differ chiefly in the types of market evidence they rely upon. Desirably, data would be collected to support all three approaches.

Sales Data

Data on open-market, arm's-length sales are crucial in all methods for estimating market values but are integral to the sales comparison approach, which is the generally preferred approach when there are sufficient sales. An effective sales data collection and processing system requires the following:

- *Access to sales data.* The law should require buyers and sellers to disclose needed information and ensure that the title agency (legal cadastre) transmits the data it obtains to the property tax administration in a timely manner. However, it is advisable to develop alternative sources, such as private-sector real estate professionals, valuers, and brokers, for confirmation and background information.

- *Confirmation.* Sales data confirmation requirements vary with the general validity of the primary source of sales data. Information from title registration systems usually is more conclusive than information from deed registrations systems. When the source(s) cannot be regarded as authoritative, confirmation is essential, particularly of sales of commercial, industrial, and unbuilt (vacant) parcels.

- *Validation.* An analyst should decide whether a sale matches the criteria of an arm's-length, open-market sale, because only such sales provide reliable evidence of market values. Codes would indicate whether a sale meets usability criteria and, if not, why not. Sales not disqualified for a specific reason would be deemed to be usable. The coding system should differentiate between sales that are not usable in ratio studies but are usable in valuation.

- *Verification of property attributes.* Although it is permissible to transcribe property attribute data from the existing property record when building a sale record, each usable sale should be inspected to ensure key land and building attributes are current, especially when the sale is of a rarely sold type of property.

- *Adjustments.* If changes in price level between the date of sale and the date of valuation warrant, it is desirable to adjust nominal sales prices to the price level on the valuation date. Adjustments should also be considered for such things as the inclusion of movable property in the sale, the use of nonmarket financing, and the presence of nonmarket leases.

- *A sales file.* The sales file constitutes a continuous record of sales and contains a record of *every* sale, including those deemed unusable in ratio studies and in valuation. Each sale record should contain pertinent information about the transaction, especially the sale price and date of sale; the identification of the property transferred; salient property characteristics as of the date of sale; for ratio study purposes, the total appraised value in effect on the sale date; and an analyst's opinion as to whether the sale is usable. It is highly desirable that sales files be computerized, but a computerized file is essential when the number of sales available for analysis exceeds a few dozen.

Rental Property Income and Expense Data

Similar to sales data, rental and operating expense data should be collected by the property tax administration from property owners, managers, and tenants, and those data should be analyzed to determine current market levels, especially when the basis for the property tax is annual rental value. The property tax administration also should monitor building construction costs.

Income and expense records should contain the following:

- A record identifier
- The date the record was created or when the source data were transcribed
- The reporting period, to create a valuation date/assessment year reference
- Property identification, such as parcel identifier and applicable unit (occupancy) identifier(s)
- Key property characteristics, such as use type, location, size (in terms of relevant valuation units), condition/age

- Sale data (when available), such as price, date (should be reasonably contemporaneous with income data), usability code, particulars of financing terms (if applicable)
- Lease data for each lease, such as term of lease, renewal terms, landlord and tenant responsibilities, lease type (e.g., triple-net), unit of measure, rent reviews, and the like.

Movable Property Assessment and Valuation

Movable property (movables, personal property, personalty, or chattels) is not as widely taxed as immovable property (real property). To make compliance by taxpayers easier and to simplify administration, it is necessary to define in law which categories (if any) of movable property are taxable; that is, no attempt is made to gather information about categories of movable property that will not be taxed.

Because movable property is defined by exception, there must be agreement about what constitutes *immovable* property, especially when the conclusion determines what is taxed or the rate of taxation. Examples of where disagreements can occur in practice are as follows:

- *Fixtures.* These are items of formerly movable property that become so firmly attached to a building that they cannot be removed without substantial damage to a building. Thus they usually are classified as immovable property for purposes of taxation (and they ordinarily would be transferred when the immovable property was sold).
- *Trade fixtures.* These are things a building tenant would install in a building and might be expected to remove at the end of the lease. (Reviewing the terms of a lease may help identify trade fixtures.)
- *Industrial plant.* Particularly when chemical processes are involved, there may be no clear distinction between buildings and similar structures and the process equipment.

Definitional problems are as important, if not more so, when *only* immovable property is taxed, because taxpayers seek to have more property classified as movable. (When movable and immovable property is taxed alike, definitional issues are reduced.) Definitional problems also are magnified when different departments of a tax administration assess movable and immovable property. Unless internal communications are good, some items of property may be omitted from taxation and some may be taxed both as movable and immovable property.

Special situations can arise. Buildings on land leased from another would be classified as movable property in some property tax systems (Finland, for example), even when moving the building would be a practical impossibility. In the United States, mobile homes are classified as movable or immovable depending on whether the owner of the home owns the land on which it is situated.

Pipelines, parts of electricity transmission and distribution systems, parts of telecommunication networks, and sometimes parts of railways can be classified in legislation as either movable property (usually to exempt them) or immovable property (to tax them) in a manner similar to that in the Plant and Machinery Order in the United Kingdom. When the entire system is taxed, a value for the entire system is found and allocated to each local tax district based on a legislated formula.

Locating Movable Property for Tax Purposes

The tax district that is entitled to receive the property tax revenue from a piece of immovable property usually is clear; if the property is located within the territorial limits of the district, it receives the revenue (*situs* is the term used to identify this location). The situation is not always clear with movable property. Some movables are more-or-less permanently on the move, transportation equipment, for example. Others may be moved only near the assessment date, either to be located in a district with a low tax rate or to conceal the existence of the property. Raw materials, inventories, and the like also can have several locations during a tax year. Intangibles such as cash, stocks, and intellectual property essentially have no meaningful physical location. Laws attempt to resolve the issue of which district can tax movable property by laying down various rules. The place where the business has its headquarters may be entitled to tax the property, instead of the district where the property is located on the assessment date. The place where a vehicle is licensed may be entitled to the tax. A formula for sharing revenue among competing claimants should be devised. Without clear rules, taxpayers can find themselves facing competing demands, and tax bodies can waste efforts trying to tax property that "belongs" to another.

Discovering and Inventorying Taxable Movable Property

The activity of discovering taxable movable property is as difficult as deciding who can tax it. The basic administrative steps in movable property assessment include (1) compiling lists of potential taxpayers, (2) collecting information from those persons regarding their movable property holdings, (3) reviewing that information with the objective of arriving at an estimate of the current taxable value of that property, and (4) making assessments. Without overt efforts by tax officials to identify probable owners of taxable movables and send them blank reporting forms, a tax on movable property becomes a tax on honesty.

Identifying Owners of Potentially Taxable Movable Property

The basic task in compiling a list of (business) taxpayers is to identify all registered and unregistered businesses with a physical presence (premises) in the assessment district. To the previous year's list, new businesses and newly discovered businesses are added, and businesses that have ceased operations in the district are deleted.

Although registration and licensing requirements vary greatly across the United States, assessors rely heavily on such official sources (in some districts, a business must advertise its creation in a legal newspaper). It also is important to monitor business directories and commercial advertisements, as they provide an indication of the type of movables that a business ordinarily would possess.

Leased equipment can present special discovery problems. The terms of the lease can make true ownership difficult to determine (some leases essentially are financing vehicles). In the U.S., the district entitled to tax ordinary business equipment like computers generally is the one in which the computer is located, not the one in which the leasing company is headquartered.

Declarations
After a business has been identified, it is sent a movable property tax return. Designing these returns requires a balancing of several objectives; they should ask for the information needed to make a fair and accurate assessment. At the same time, they should be easy to complete, and they should facilitate administrative processing (including data entry). Basically, a return asks for (1) the identification of the business and the person filing the return, (2) original costs by category of asset and year of acquisition, (3) information about assets that have been fully depreciated (amortized) but are still in use, and (4) the presence of non-owned movables (such as leased equipment) in the control of the business.

Rather than designing a general-purpose declaration, some assessment districts attempt to design returns better suited to specific industries and to the size of the business. Particularly when assessment calculations are made manually, the return also provides space for the tax official to make changes in reported figures, calculate current costs, and provide for depreciation (amortization). A potential problem is differences between company accounting systems and tax district reporting requirements, which makes both reporting and verification more difficult. Large corporations must maintain records that comply with accounting standards, whereas small, individually owned businesses may maintain no asset records. Businesses that operate in multiple states have the problem of complying with the requirements of each state.

Declarations normally are mailed to the business. Blank forms also can be obtained over the Internet as well as picked up at tax offices. Electronic filing is possible in some places. For existing accounts, some portions of the return may be preprinted to reduce reporting burdens and simplify data entry. Taxpayers can enter changes, additions, and deletions. An assessor's office can use bar coding technology to reduce manual data entry and to ease record matching and document tracking.

Processing Returned Declarations
Particularly when returns are maintained in a physical file, they are organized by the name of the taxpayer, and an arbitrary account number is assigned. Sometimes

returns are first organized by type of business or industry to facilitate comparisons. The taxpayer record also contains information about the property where the movables are physically located.

When a completed return is received by an assessor's office, it is logged either as an existing taxpayer or added to the list of taxpayers. If there are penalties for filing late, the date the return was received also is recorded, so that the amount of any penalties can be properly calculated.

After logging, the return is screened for completeness. Incomplete returns probably are held in abeyance while the situation is clarified. Next the return is screened for reasonableness by comparing it with the previous year's return and with the returns from similar businesses. Any problematic returns are flagged for follow-up action. The assessor's office can modify the assessment or schedule a field inspection or audit.

When the deadline for returns approaches (or is reached), reminders are sent to non-filers. If a business fails to file, the assessor's office usually has the power to assess the business for movables it is presumed to possess.

Valuation and Assessment

In the interest of economical property tax administration, highly simplified valuation procedures are used. Although each of the basic three approaches to value (sales comparison, income capitalization, and replacement cost) can be used in movable property valuation, the distinction between the sales comparison and cost approach is blurred. Prices of new movables generally are regarded as costs under the cost approach, and prices of used movables obtained from secondary markets are regarded as sales under the sales comparison approach. Use of the income capitalization approach basically is restricted to leased equipment.

When they are deemed reasonable, reported original costs for a class of asset acquired in a given year usually are the starting point of most valuation and assessment calculations, as follows:

$$\textit{Tax value} = \textit{original cost} \times \textit{cost trend factor} \times \textit{depreciation factor}.$$

The purpose of the cost trend factor is to approximate what it would cost to acquire the movables on the assessment (valuation) date. The depreciation factor is designed to allow for wear and tear and other factors that reduce the value of the movables. Sometimes composite cost trend-depreciation factors are used to further simplify work. Of course, there can be much debate about what the various factors should be. In rapidly evolving technologies like computing, costs can decline over time rather than rising, as is the usual case.

In the case of depreciation, both the lives of assets and the depreciation methods are an issue. Some equipment is continuously maintained so that it always is in an almost new state, reducing the need for a depreciation allowance. Moreover, most tax systems establish a residual value for movables (i.e., no more depreciation is allowed after an asset reaches a certain age).

As goods move through the streams of commerce, there are three levels of trade that theoretically can influence the value of the goods. That is, the value of, say, a computer in the hands of its manufacturer is lower than the value of the same computer in the hands of a distributor, and the value of the computer in the hands of the distributor is lower still than the value of the computer at the retail/consumer level. This is because the costs associated with placing the good in the hands of a consumer are added to the price. Of course, this concept embodies elements of double and even triple taxation, which partly underlies the movement in the United States to exempt inventories.

Several approaches are used when original costs are not reported (or cannot be discovered through an audit, as discussed below). A completely arbitrary value can be assessed, which would be increased annually until the taxpayer appeals. Although this approach consumes little resources, it is haphazard. Some taxpayers could be undertaxed for years, while others could be overtaxed and fail to appeal out of ignorance. A more defensible approach is to base the assessment on business norms. At least for ordinary businesses, expected values of movables per square foot or meter of building can be developed (these sometimes are called *density studies*).

In the United States at least, assessors can consult commercially published guides on the wholesale and retail prices of high-value used movables such as vehicles. If such items are separately listed in tax returns, typical used prices can be used directly in the assessment process.

Quality Assurance

By the nature of taxable movables, neither tax officials nor taxpayers can be sure that all of them are reported and valued correctly. Consequently, efforts to provide some assurance that movable property assessments are correct are warranted.

Audits

The main tool a tax administration has to ensure that movable property has been correctly reported by taxpayers is the power to audit the returns. Audits should be carried out regularly. Returns that should be audited are those of large businesses, returns with significant changes from prior years, new accounts, and returns that are suspicious for other reasons, such as large departures from norms.

Internal Controls

To minimize the possibility of corruption, procedures should be established to prevent an official from concealing errors. Work assignments should be rotated. In the United States, some state governments study the performance of local officials by essentially reassessing a sample of movable property accounts and comparing the results with the original assessments.

The inclusion of movables in the property tax base can increase perceptions of fairness, particularly for chemical plants and oil refineries, which are very valuable but have few ordinary buildings. With a larger tax base, it is possible to raise a greater amount of revenue with any given tax rate (or reduce the tax rate to raise a given amount of revenue).

A well-designed and administered system for taxing movable property does not discriminate against the honest. It facilitates compliance through vigorous and even-handed efforts to identify potential taxpayers. Well-designed reporting forms with clear instructions help. Publicized field inspections and audits discourage noncompliance, as do appropriate penalties for non-filers and persons who file erroneous returns. Simple valuation models can mirror the market for the type of property in question.

Assessment

Classification of Property for Purposes of Taxation

Property usually must be classified as to whether it is assessable, taxable, and subject to differential taxation. The *task* of classifying property for such purposes requires some care. Principles for defining classes include the following:

- *It is clear to which class every property belongs.* This is achieved by carefully defining the classes and designating one class as including all properties that do not fit into one of the other classes. There are specific, written class descriptions. Classes based on location are defined on maps.

- *Unintended consequences are minimized.* Taxpayers look for simple changes in their activities or their properties that make them eligible for membership in a class that is taxed preferentially. For example, an exemption of the first five acres of rural land encourages people who own such large plots to divide ownership or land holdings. Large differences in the rates between similar classes encourage attempts to avoid higher tax rates. Therefore, proposed class definitions are carefully scrutinized for weak points (loopholes), and attempts are made to eliminate them. This is done by anticipating how taxpayers will react when the class definitions are made official.

- *No class is defined to benefit or discriminate against any specific property or taxpayer.* This is a basic principle of fairness.

- *The classification system is kept simple.* Complex classification systems increase the costs of property tax administration, and they lead to efforts to create additional classes so that more taxpayers qualify for a lower rate of taxation, further increasing complexity.

Identification of Taxpayers

Whether in an in rem or an in personam system for determining liability for taxation, the identification of a taxpayer for each assessable property is one of the main administrative tasks. In the former case, associating a person with a property essentially serves only to facilitate collection by sending the tax bill to the person with a significant interest in the property. In the latter case, the determination of the taxpayer (or taxpayers) is crucial to a legal assessment.

Especially when liability of taxation is in personam and when ownership is uncertain, procedures for determining taxpayers need to be carefully designed. Experience suggests the following principles:

- *State a general rule in law.* Either the owner or the occupant (user) is designated as the taxpayer.
- *Spell out any exceptions to the general rule clearly.* For example,
  - If the general rule specifies that the owner is the taxpayer but the owner is not known with certainty or cannot be located, an occupant could be designated as the taxpayer whether or not the occupant has a usufruct.
  - If the state (government) is the owner but the property is used by another, the user usually is designated as the taxpayer.
  - When the provisions of a lease between private parties makes the occupant responsible for paying the property tax, the assessor as a convenience to the parties can direct tax statements to the occupant.
  - When a property is owned or used by more than one person, the owners or users jointly are designated as the taxpayer, not each individual. This simplifies administration.
  - Special rules may apply to real estate held in customary tenure.

Decisions by an assessor as to the person liable for paying the tax due on a particular property in a given year normally would be grounds for an appeal. If the law allows such appeals, it should also specify the rules for making refunds (including interest) and for assessing the taxes in question to the rightful person.

Administration of Exemptions and Tax Relief Programs

The first task, of course, is to administer legal requirements faithfully. No eligible taxpayer should be denied an exemption (or other relief measure), and no ineligible taxpayer should receive an exemption. It is desirable to review eligibility for exemptions that have been granted periodically.

It is not good practice to accept applications without question or verification; this may require field checks to verify that property is being used for exempt purposes. Sales of exempt properties should be flagged so that exemptions are removed in the next tax year unless the new owner establishes eligibility for the exemption. For reasons of transparency, it is good practice to list exempt properties in assessment rolls.

Roll Preparation

The preparation of assessment or tax rolls involves compiling comprehensive lists of properties, their owners, assessed values, and, in the case of tax rolls, the amount of taxes assessed against the properties. If the data are computerized, record maintenance is easier, and the roll can be produced quickly and accurately.

When an assessment district comprises several, often overlapping tax districts, the property tax administration is responsible for identifying the properties in each district so that those properties can be properly taxed. The usual procedure is to overlay tax district boundaries on cadastral maps or on index maps. Each tax rate area is designated as illustrated. The proper tax rate area code is included in each parcel record. Alternatively, files of the parcels can be maintained in each area. The code identifies a table that lists tax jurisdictions and applicable tax rates.

Notices

The accuracy and equity of assessments depend on well-informed taxpayers, who are given opportunities to audit the work of tax administrators. In addition to making assessment (tax) rolls public, mailing each property owner or taxpayer a notice of every change in her or his assessment in advance of the appeal period is an important component of a communications program. Usually notices of new assessments are mailed shortly before the appeal period. If mortgage companies pay property taxes, procedures should be established to ensure property owners receive assessment notices to protect their appeal rights. Table 7-10 identifies information contained in a good assessment notice according to the IAAO *Standard on Public Relations* (2001b). The standard suggests a tax impact notice be included. Some notices also include other property details.

TABLE 7-10. Content of an Assessment Notice

• Owner's or taxpayer's name and address	• Amount and type of any exemptions
• Cadastral number and property address	• Prior and proposed new assessment
• Legal description (abbreviated)	• Reason for new assessment
• Effective date of assessment	• Date of notice
• Total appraised full market value	• Tax district number
• Class of property and level of assessment if applicable	• Appeal rights, hearing procedures, and dates

Tax Billing and Collection

Collection is the last major phase of property tax administration. If collection procedures are not effective, the work that has gone before will be for naught. Hence property tax collectors have a fiduciary responsibility not only to protect investments that have been made earlier but also to collect the taxes and penalties that have been assessed.

The keys to success in property tax collection are (1) a culture of paying taxes fully and voluntarily and (2) efficient systems. The former can take time and requires consistent, effective propaganda (discussed below). However, the main messages might include the following:

- No one, especially the rich and powerful, can escape paying taxes.
- It is less expensive to pay taxes on time than not to pay them or to pay them late.
- The money is used for good purposes.
- Compassion and relief are available when circumstances warrant (these, of course, must be legally authorized).

Having transparent (open for public inspection) lists of tax assessments, taxes paid, or taxpayers in arrears that can be accessed by taxpayer name or by property can help get these messages across. Those who have paid can find out who has not. Those who have not may succumb to peer pressure.

As with all facets of property tax administration, collection procedures should be economical—for both the tax agency and the taxpayer. An important principle is that tax obligations cannot be sidetracked by appealing an assessment.

Billing

Laws normally govern billing procedures. A property tax bill (which may be combined with an assessment notice) is an individual notice of taxes due. It has the beneficial psychological effect of formally notifying the taxpayer of an obligation to pay property taxes. If properly designed, the bill can facilitate financial control, help persuade the taxpayer that paying the tax is

TABLE 7-11. Billing Information

- **Identification of the office issuing the bill** and the legal authority for issuing the bill.
- **A reference number** such as a cadastral number or an account number—these are important for follow-up and for associating a payment with the correct bill.
- **Date of issue**—important in determining subsequent deadlines and dates, such as when penalties or interest begin to accrue.
- **Name and address** of the taxpayer.
- **A general narrative of assessment and tax matters,** including a summary of assessment and tax calculations—these help explain the basis for the assessment and the details of the taxes due, which may help the taxpayer decide whether the assessment was fair and the taxes are reasonable.
- **Information about any applicable tax reductions** and appeal rights.
- **If applicable, information about any previous tax debts**—this can be an important reminder.
- **Information about ways to pay the bill,** including information about installment payments (if applicable), whether partial payments are acceptable, and information about places where payments may be made and acceptable means for making payments. the possibility of paying in installments—which is helpful information and which may lessen anxiety about affordability.
- **If applicable, coupons** or other ways to record payment or receipt of payments.

worthwhile, and provide information about payment options. What information should a property tax bill contain? Again, the specific content would be determined by the law, but common options are listed in Table 7-11.

Coverage Options

When a taxpayer is liable for the taxes on more than one property in a district, should there be an individual bill for each property or should there be a combined bill covering all properties?

Separate bills are simpler procedurally. There is no need to have a mechanism for assembling multiple assessment records. Under in rem liability, any payment would be linked to a specific property, which would be important in identifying and collecting arrears. Of course, multiple notices must be prepared and delivered, a process that consumes more resources. Along with the billing efficiencies, the combined bill option can be more convenient for some taxpayers. However, it requires an efficient mechanism for assembling the records on all the taxpayer's properties in one place before the notice of liability can be prepared. However, when a payment is past due or when a partial payment is made (and accepted), there are some accounting and enforcement issues to address, notably to which property the payment is credited.

Delivery Options

How should bills be delivered? In some systems, it is necessary to deliver tax bills personally to taxpayers in order to establish the tax obligation. Without personal service (usually requiring the taxpayer to sign a delivery receipt), no obligation to pay is established. Clearly, this system is time-consuming and expensive. Moreover, it facilitates avoidance; it is impossible to serve a notice on a dead person and difficult to serve a foreigner. At the other extreme (common in the United States) is the publication of a notice that tax obligations have been determined. The taxpayer must search a tax roll to find out what he or she owes if a bill is not received. Tax bills mailed to the taxpayer or to the property facilitate compliance. Tax bills also can be sent to the taxpayer's bank, particularly when the property is mortgaged, or combined with another municipal bill, like a utility bill. Ultimately, however, any failure to deliver or receive a bill does not relieve the taxpayer of the obligation to pay the tax.

Collection

A culture of voluntary payment of real estate taxes is easier to achieve if payment procedures consider a taxpayer's convenience. Ways to increase convenience include the following:

- Providing clear information about collection procedures (as discussed above).
- Allowing multiple ways to pay, such as by mail, in person, or via the Internet; accepting cash, check, and credit card payments; combining property tax bills

with mortgage payments or with other bills (such as those for utilities); and permitting payments to be made at various places, including banks, post offices, and the like.
- Allowing installment or partial payments.
- Synchronizing payment due dates with cash flows, such as harvest times in agricultural economies.
- Having collection offices open outside of normal business hours.
- Providing an incentive for prompt payments. A discount could be offered for payments made before a deadline. Other incentives include (1) making property taxes deductible from income taxes, (2) not allowing title to be transferred or a deed to be registered without proof of payment of property taxes (a tax clearance), and (3) allowing mortgage interest to be deducted from income taxes only with proof of payment of property taxes. Early payers could participate in a lottery.

Providing convenient, flexible payment arrangements can complicate tax accounting (although such problems are easily solved in automated systems) and can increase administrative costs marginally. Whether convenience measures make economic sense depends on such factors as the level of taxation and the marginal costs of the measures. For example, small partial payments could be disallowed when the total amount due is very small. Some systems levy no tax at all on any assessment under a minimum amount.

When a payment is made, effective procedures are needed to

- *Accurately account for payments.* Each payment needs to be tied to a particular taxpayer and tax liability. Accumulated receipts and cash should balance. Receipts should be credited to the proper account or fund. An audit trail should be established, so that an independent audit of tax accounting can be made.
- *Providing for cash security.* Safeguards are needed to prevent loss, embezzlement, or theft of cash and other negotiable forms of payments.
- *Tracking arrears.* Arrears are obligations that are past due. On payment deadline dates, a collection office must be able to identify property tax accounts with past-due amounts (as discussed in the next section).

Sanctions and Enforced Collection of Arrears

Tax laws typically provide a variety of sanctions that make failure to pay property taxes expensive and specify the actions the tax administrators can take to collect arrears. Penalties and interest are charged on late payments to encourage timely payment (as are discounts for early payment). For either option to be effective, the rate of interest (or discount) must be higher than market rates of interest. After a stipulated period of delinquency, property tax administrators usually have recourse to direct enforcement actions that involve a legal process. Typically, a demand for immediate payment is issued. If that is ignored, enforcement begins.

Deciding which available enforcement measure to pursue requires careful analysis and execution (and legal advice is desirable). Procedures will be needed to (1) establish tax due dates and identify delinquent accounts when the deadlines are not fixed by law and (2) determine the amount of interest penalties to be charged on late payments.

With effective collection and enforcement efforts, virtually all tax obligations can eventually be satisfied, with collection of over 80 percent of current-year obligations. When very low collection rates are tolerated, any property tax payment that is made essentially is a voluntary contribution, not a tax in the true meaning of the term.

Taxpayer and Stakeholder Relations

Property owners form their opinions about government in general based on their experiences with the offices and officials with whom they come in contact. Property tax administrators come into indirect contact with every property owner through assessment and tax notices and direct contact with many owners when they inquire about their assessments or tax obligations. Effective public information and taxpayer assistance programs are crucial to public acceptance of a property tax and to voluntary compliance. Acceptance is increased when all agencies involved in property tax administration communicate with taxpayers, explaining the rationale for the tax, how it is administered, and taxpayers' rights and responsibilities. Equally important are open and accessible records (except those that are properly held confidential under the law). Property tax administration should be viewed as a public service function—the chief service being an equitable assessment. The tax administration should demonstrate at every opportunity that the tax is being impartially and equitably administered.

Assessors and collectors have several publics—taxpayers, residents, business people, and other government officials. Communication tools and techniques are Web sites, media campaigns, audiovisual materials, press releases and briefings, outreach efforts, and reports.

All people regularly involved in property tax administration should receive training in how to deal with members of the public and how to respond to questions. Taxpayers are entitled to courteous and prompt answers. Of course, all officials cannot be expected to be able to answer any question. They need instruction on which questions they are competent to answer and how to respond to questions that are best answered by others. Certainly misleading or inaccurate answers are to be avoided.

Taxpayers should be made to feel welcome in assessment and collection offices and be reassured that property tax officials are genuinely interested in their needs. Many taxpayers need individual assistance—they seek explanations of assessments, help with a form, or real estate data. Property tax officials can expect to receive many such requests for information and assistance. Systems and procedures need to be established to satisfy these requests effectively and efficiently. They also should anticipate that some taxpayers may be angry, and the staff should be trained to diffuse or deflect anger and provide the service needed.

Review and Appeal

Assessment appeal is an integral part of an assessment system. In property taxation, in contrast to other taxes where administrators audit the assessments of taxpayers, taxpayers audit the work of tax administrators during the appeal process. Despite the care tax administrators take to ensure accurate appraisals, changes in property characteristics can go undetected. Factual errors can go undetected or uncorrected, and judgment errors can be made. Appeal procedures are designed to deal with such problems. They provide taxpayers opportunities to review their assessments and question their accuracy and fairness. In the property tax, it is the taxpayer's responsibility to verify the correctness of his or her assessment. Taxpayers do this by reviewing their assessments and appealing them if they disagree with the assessor's judgment.

The appeal process should be accessible and inexpensive, at least at the initial stages, with later stages reserved for more complex appraisal and legal problems, where expert assistance may be necessary. A convenient, inexpensive assessment appeal system features

- Adequate notice of assessment (discussed above)
- Information about assessments and taxes generally
- Convenient opportunities for an informal discussion of the assessment and the assessment process with the assessor as a prerequisite to lodging a formal appeal
- An opportunity to appeal an assessment to a local, independent, and qualified appeal agency
- An opportunity for a higher level appeal to an administrative or quasi-judicial appeal agency before resorting to the courts.

This structure is for questions on valuation, classification, and taxability; legal questions should be taken to the courts (see the *Standard on Assessment Appeal* [IAAO 2001a] and the Model State Assessment Appeal Act approved by the American Bar Association [1983]).

Informal conferences are an excellent opportunity to increase owners' understanding of property taxation. They provide opportunities to ensure that records are correct and that appraisals take into account all pertinent factors. They also serve to clarify differences of opinion about property value and are useful should the property owner decide to file a formal appeal.

Formal appeals are expensive and time-consuming for both the property owner and the government officials involved in the appeal. For that reason, simple factual errors and misunderstandings are best handled informally.

Even though property tax administrators may lose jurisdiction over assessments during the stages of an appeal process, they retain responsibility for maintaining accurate records of the results of appeals. They also may be responsible for providing administrative assistance to appeal bodies, scheduling hearings, and communicating with appellants about the appeal agency's decision. They also must ensure that the decision is properly reflected on the assessment roll and on appraisal records if the administrator accepts the agency's decision. If the administrator does not agree with the decision, a note needs to be made to change the assessment next year. These activities need to be systematized. It also is useful to compile statistics on appeal activity for planning purposes. The number of appeals is no index of failure.

Practices that can improve the efficiency and effectiveness of appeal hearings are as follows:

- *Use an application form.* Requiring (or encouraging the use of) a form can make it easier for taxpayers to state the essence of their appeal and for the appeal body to consider it. To ensure that the process is open to all, assessors should be willing to help taxpayers with the form if necessary.

- *Register appeals.* Registering appeals helps ensure that appeals are heard, protects future appeal rights, and generally increases the efficiency of the appeals process.

- *Organize hearings so they are convenient to taxpayers while not unduly burdening appeal bodies.* Experience will reveal the best way to organize hearings. The choices are scheduling hearings or holding hearings on a first-come, first-served basis.

- *Hold hearings in public.* Other appellants and onlookers will understand the property tax and appeal system better if hearings are open to the public. If the hearings are conducted well, observers are reassured about the honesty of officials and the fairness of the tax.

- *Stick to the issues in hearings.* Many taxpayers want to complain about taxes or about poor services; these issues should not be discussed during an appeal. (However, if the government has another avenue for dealing with taxpayers' needs, such as a citizen's information center, this avenue should be explained to the taxpayer.) Otherwise, hearings will be overlong, and other appellants will be inconvenienced (not to mention the appeal body members). The chair of a hearing should briefly explain its purpose, outline the rules, and firmly stick to them.

- *Decide appeals publicly and promptly.* Most appeals should be decided during the hearing. In rare cases, an appeal board may agree to postpone a decision to allow the appellant or the assessor time to gather more information or to allow it to consider similar cases.

- *Communicate decisions clearly.* The decision of the appeal board should be communicated orally during the hearing and in writing on a form. Whether an appeal is granted or denied, the right of further appeal should be communicated. Any changes should be reflected in a revised tax bill.

- *Make sure changes are implemented.* Nothing discredits a tax system as much as when appeal actions are not implemented. When an appeal is granted, the change must be reflected in the assessment roll. A special tax bill may need to be issued. If the taxes in question have not been paid, the new amount due (including any interest) should be indicated. Any necessary refund should be issued promptly (to avoid having to pay more interest).

As noted in the discussion of burdens of proof in appeals in Chapter 3, "Fundamental Elements of the Property Tax," there has been a shift from the taxpayer having to prove the assessment wrong to the assessor having to prove that the assessment is correct in some jurisdictions. The rationale for such a shift—not placing onerous burdens on aggrieved taxpayers—has greater force in residential appeals, where many taxpayers lack the sophistication and resources to mount a successful appeal. Although every assessment arguably should be supportable and not arbitrary, the rationale for shifting the burden of proof is less persuasive when the taxpayer has expert representation and third-party appeals are allowed.

In some areas, property tax agents virtually constitute an industry, and the property tax systems there have been characterized as "appeals-driven" or "captured by the tax agents." In the United Kingdom under the Uniform Business Tax, for example, the volume of appeals nearly equals the number of assessments. Some appeals are merely protective, in that the purpose of the appeal is to benefit from any favorable change in policy or practice. Appeals also may be filed speculatively. In some areas of the United States, for example, where many property tax agents work on a contingent basis—that is, they are compensated only if the appeal succeeds—property tax agents sometimes file appeals without the knowledge or authorization of the taxpayer. The sheer volume of appeals sometimes can lead to reductions in assessments even when no compelling reasons for reductions have been presented.

Whatever the merits of an appeal, the assessor must allocate resources to preparing a defense or risk an unwarranted loss in assessed value. Shifting resources to defending assessments under appeal means that those resources are not available for other important tasks (the assessor also may have to hire legal representation valuation experts as well as allocate staff). It has been said that the appeals process is the dress rehearsal for the court case and the need for good preparation for the appeal is crucial. Failing to defend appealed assessments competently risks a general reduction in property tax revenues, shifting property tax burdens to taxpayers who did not appeal (which is a reason for "protective" appeals), or both. In some parts of the United States, taxing bodies have the right to appeal assessments that they consider to be too low, further complicating the defense of assessments (they also may intervene on behalf of the assessor). Sometimes, the assessment on a single property can be subject to appeals from two sides. Off course, the workloads of appeal bodies increase commensurately with the volume of appeals, and some appeal bodies lack the competence to evaluate complex arguments, further complicating the situation. Although reasonable procedural requirements can curtail frivolous appeals, finding the right balance of interests in an appeal system can be challenging, and fixing perceived problems can be difficult.

References

Advisory Commission on Intergovernmental Relations. 1963. *The role of the states in strengthening the property tax.* 2 vols. Washington, DC: ACIR.

Almy, R.R. 1982. Historical patterns and trends in the jurisdictional setting of property tax administration. *Property Tax Journal* 1 (March):75–83.

Almy et al. 1978. *Improving real property assessment: A reference manual.* Chicago: International Association of Assessing Officers.

American Bar Association. Committee on State and Local Taxes. 1983. Model Assessment Appeal Act (Legislative Recommendation No. 1983-4), http://www.abanet.org/tax/groups/salt/legree/1086137.pdf (accessed April 4, 2008)

The Appraisal Foundation. updated annually. *Uniform standards of professional appraisal practice* (USPAP). Washington, DC: The Appraisal Foundation.

Bernhardsen, T. 1992. *Geographic information systems.* Arendal, Norway: Viak IT.

Dillinger, W. 1991. *Urban property tax reform: Guidelines and recommendations.* Washington, DC: The World Bank.

Dornfest, A., and D. Thompson, 2004. State and provincial ratio study practices: 2003 survey results. *Journal of Property Tax Assessment and Administration* 1(1):31–70.

Eckert, J.K., R.J. Gloudemans, and R.R. Almy, eds. 1990. *Property appraisal and assessment administration.* Chicago: International Association of Assessing Officers.

Gloudemans, R.J. 1999. *The mass appraisal of real property.* Chicago: International Association of Assessing Officers.

International Association of Assessing Officers (IAAO). 2008. *Standard on mass appraisal of real property.* Kansas City, MO: IAAO.

———. 2007. *Standard on ratio studies.* Kansas City, MO: IAAO.

———. 2004a. *Standard on manual cadastral maps and parcel identifiers.* Chicago: IAAO.

———, 2004b. *Standard on property tax policy.* Chicago: IAAO.

———. 2003a. *Assessment practices: Self-evaluation guide*, 2nd ed. Chicago: IAAO.

———. 2003b. *Standard on administration of monitoring and compliance responsibilities.* Chicago: IAAO.

———. 2003c. *Standard on digital cadastral maps and parcel identifiers.* Chicago: IAAO.

———. 2002. *Standard on facilities, computers, equipment, and supplies.* Chicago: IAAO.

———. 2001a. *Standard on assessment appeal.* Chicago: IAAO.

———. 2001b. *Standard on public relations*. Chicago: IAAO.

———. 2000. *Property tax policies and administrative practices in Canada and the United States*. Chicago: IAAO.

Jensen, J.P. 1931. *Property taxation in the United States*. Chicago: The University of Chicago Press.

Johnson, M., C. Bennett, and S. Patterson, eds. 2003. *Assessment administration*. Chicago: International Association of Assessing Officers.

Keith, S.H. 1993. *Property tax in Anglophone Africa: A practical manual*. (World Bank Technical Paper No. 209, Africa Technical Department Series). Washington, DC: The World Bank, http://www.gao.gov/new.items/d07731g.pdf (accessed February 5, 2008).

National Association of Assessing Officers (NAAO). 1941. *Assessment organization and personnel*. Chicago: NAAO.

———. Committee on Principles of Assessment Practice. 1938. *Assessment principles: Final report of the Committee on Principles of Assessment Practice*. Chicago: NAAO.

Seligman, E.R.A. 1925. *Essays in Taxation*, 10th ed. rev. New York: The MacMillan Company.

Shannon, J. 1967. Conflict between state assessment law and local assessment practice. In *Property taxation in USA*, R.W. Lindholm, ed. 39–63. Madison, WI: The University of Wisconsin Press.

Silverherz, J.D. 1936. *The Assessment of real property in the United States* (Special Report of the State Tax Commission No. 10). Albany, NY: J. B. Lyon Company.

United States Bureau of the Census. 1975. *State and local ratio studies and property tax assessment* (State and Local Government Special Studies, No. 72). Washington, DC: Government Printing Office.

United States Government Accountability Office. Comptroller General of the United States. 2007. *Government auditing standards: July 2007 revision* (GAO-07-731G). Washington, DC: U.S General Accounting Office, http://www.gao.gov/new.items/d07731g.pdf (accessed February 5, 2008).

Urban and Regional Information Systems Association and International Association of Assessing Officers. 1999. *GIS guidelines for assessors*, 2nd ed. Park Ridge, IL: Urban and Regional Information Systems Association.

Chapter 8
Systems of Government and Taxation: A Global Perspective

This chapter discusses tax systems from a comparative international perspective, giving a context for evaluating a country's tax systems. It examines relationships among such factors as type of government and reliance on taxes. It summarizes selected features of property tax systems.

Types of Government

Governments differ in many important ways. The terms in their names are not always a clear guide, because terms can have different meanings. As an important example, the term *state* usually refers to the sovereign national government, not a constituent of a federal government (as in the United States). As for the distinction between federal and unitary governments, in a federal government powers are constitutionally divided between the central government and subnational regional governments like the states in the United States. In a unitary government, regional or local governments generally derive their powers from the national government (or state). The system is hierarchical: the power of the state surpasses that of any regional or local governments. Unitary governments are more common than federal governments. Of the 161 countries with taxes on property examined in this chapter, 143 have unitary governments, although several, including Colombia, Hungary, the Netherlands, Spain, and the United Kingdom, have devolved substantial power to regional or local governments. Only 18 countries clearly have federal constitutions or are a federation.

Other categories of government can be important in describing or evaluating tax systems, including the following:

- *Central government.* Central government includes all governmental departments, offices, establishments, and other bodies that are agencies or instruments of the central authority of a country. Some agencies may enjoy considerable autonomy in carrying out their assigned functions. Some may be characterized by considerable administrative decentralization.

- *State, provincial, or regional government.* State, provincial, or regional governments are a characteristic of a federal state, but they also are found in unitary states. They exercise a competence independently of central government in a part of a country's territory encompassing a number of smaller localities. Thus in countries where they exist, they occupy an intermediate position between the central government and any local governments that may exist. They may be referred to as states (in Australia, Germany, and the United States), as provinces (in Canada), or as regions (in France and Russia).

- *Local government.* Local governments are entities exercising an independent competence in the various urban and rural jurisdictions of a country's territory. Where they exist, they may include counties, municipalities, cities, towns, townships, boroughs, school districts, and other special-purpose districts.

The combination of all general-purpose governmental units in a country is called *general government.* Governments also may be organized to provide a wide or narrow range of services, although local governments more commonly are special purpose. Governments may surrender some of their sovereignty to supranational alliances, such as the European Union. There also are subnational regional governmental organizations.

Types of Taxes

The single, most complete source of statistics on taxation is the *Government Finance Statistics Yearbook* of the International Monetary Fund (IMF 2007). The CD-ROM edition of the IMF 2007 yearbook contains the *Government Finance Statistics Manual 2001* (GFSM 2001) (IMF 2001), which identifies the following categories of taxes (IMF classification codes are in parentheses):

- *Taxes on income, profits, and capital gains* (111). The two main categories of income taxes are those levied on individuals or families and those levied on businesses or enterprises. Some income cannot be so allocated, so the IMF treats it as a separate category. An area of potential confusion in practice is distinguishing between the income received from rents by a business and the rent that a property can command in the marketplace. Such confusion is lessened if property taxes are deducted from income before an income tax is levied. A capital gains tax is *ad valorem* in nature and may require a valuation. In the IMF, social insurance payments are not classified as taxes.

- *Taxes on payroll and workforce* (112). These taxes are imposed on employers or the self-employed based on either a fixed amount per person or on the size of the payroll.

- *Taxes on property* (113). This category includes taxes on the use, ownership, or transfer of wealth. Thus, they may be recurrent or they may be levied on a transaction or other event. The IMF has identified six categories of taxes on property: recurrent taxes on immovable property (1131, the focus of this chapter); recurrent taxes on net wealth (1132, taxes that, for example, would deduct amounts owed from the assessable value); estate, inheritance, and gift taxes (1133); taxes on financial and capital transactions (1134, including real estate transfer taxes and stamp duties); other nonrecurrent taxes on property (1135); and other recurrent taxes on property (1136, including taxes on movable property). The IMF also classifies some property-related taxes under other categories (such as the example of capital gains mentioned above).

- *Taxes on goods and services* (114). This category includes general sales taxes and value-added taxes. Among the other subcategories are extractive resource taxes, motor vehicle taxes, and excise taxes.

- *Taxes on international trade and transactions* (115). Included here are such things as customs, other import duties, and export duties.

- *Other taxes* (116).

In practice, it can be difficult to classify a tax. However, in any given category, there are two sides to a taxation coin: that which is taxed and that which is not (via exclusions, exemptions, administrative failures, and so on). This survey does not detail such differences; however, they underlie the statistics that are presented later.

Utilization of Taxes

Countries vary considerably in how they utilize taxes. The IMF 2007 yearbook contains data on 145 of the 161 countries known to have taxes on property (out of a potential of as many as 266 "nations, dependent areas, and other entities" according to the Central Intelligence Agency (2008). The data available for any particular country depend on its ability to report data in the format preferred by the IMF (finance statistics reported on an accrual rather than a cash basis in the detail of the IMF classifications). The data are for the most recently reported year, which in most cases is 2004 or 2005 (but could be as early as 1997 or as late as 2006). Data, of course, are reported in national currencies, which complicate international comparisons. Convenient overall comparative measures that do not require currency conversion are (1) taxes as a percentage of gross domestic product (GDP) and (2) taxes as a percentage of governmental revenue.

Data on total taxes as a percent of GDP were available for 71 countries (IMF 2007, table W4). The median percentage was 23.5 in Spain; the maximum was 41.7 percent in Lesotho; and the minimum was 1 percent in Kuwait. Canada ranked sixteenth (29.2 percent), and the United States ranked 51st (20.5 percent). Kuwait illustrates the point that a country may not have to rely on taxes for revenue. See Figure 8-1 (the dotted reference line locates the median).

FIGURE 8-1. Total Taxes as a Percentage of GDP for General Government in Selected Countries

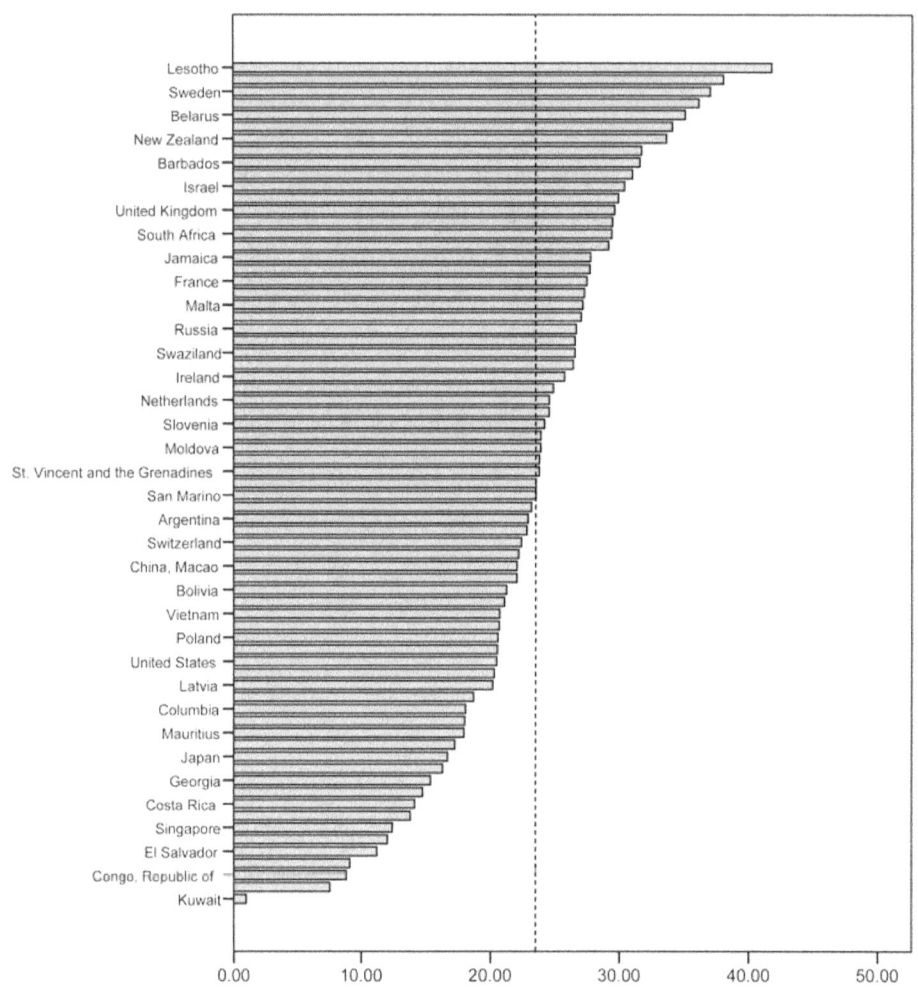

Source: IMF 2007; computations by author.

Comparable data on the main categories of taxes as a percentage of revenue (i.e., data reported on an *accrual* basis for *general* government) are available for 43 countries (see Figure 8-2). Of these, the median percentage was 62 percent (the United States, see the dotted reference line). The maximum was in Denmark (84.4 percent), and the minimum was in Kuwait again (2.7 percent). (Canada was not included in this sample.)

FIGURE 8-2. Taxes as a Percentage of Revenue for General Government in Selected Countries

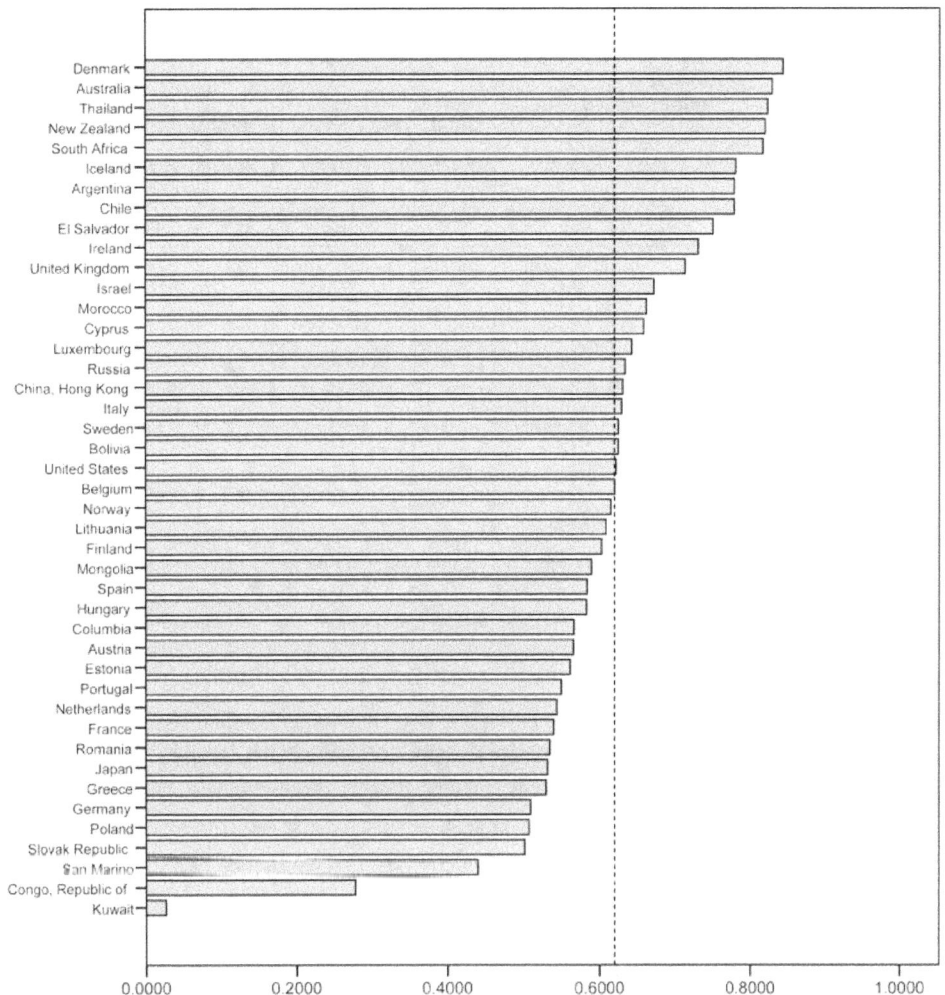

Source: IMF 2007; computations by author.

Details on the IMF's six main tax categories were available for 42 countries in the above set of countries (excluding Japan, except for income taxes). Table 8-1 identifies the country that relied least and most on each type of tax as well as the median country (of the total number of countries for which data were available, which is in parentheses). The percentage associated with each country also is displayed. Based on the medians, taxes on goods and service are most important (45.6 percent), followed by taxes on income, profits, and capital gains (42.2 percent). Taxes on property are a distant third (4.65 percent).

TABLE 8-1. Median, Minimum, and Maximum Utilization of Main Categories of Taxes in Percentages of Total Taxes for General Government in Selected Countries

Tax Category	Number of Countries	Median		Minimum		Maximum	
		Country	% of Total	Country	% of Total	Country	% of Total
Income, profits, and capital gains	43	Israel	42.2	Bolivia	12.7	Denmark	62.0
Payroll and workforce	15	Hungary	0.8	Romania	0.0	Austria	8.5
Property	42	Kuwait Greece	4.7 4.6	Democratic Republic of Congo	0.6	Hong Kong (China)	19.3
Goods and services	41	Germany	45.6	Hong Kong (China)	17.7	Slovak Republic	67.8
International trade and transactions	31	Australia	2.0	Austria	0.0	Kuwait	71.6
Other	31	United Kingdom	0.9	Russia	0.0	Chile	7.4

Note: Percentages equal to 0.0 indicate situations in which the percentage is less than 0.1 (rounded). Source: IMF 2007; computations by author.

By comparison, the United States ranked third, at 61.7 percent, in utilization of income taxes; third, at 15.2 percent, in utilization of taxes on property; 40th, at 22.2 percent, in utilization of taxes on goods and services; and 20th in utilization of taxes on international taxes and trade. Taxes on payroll and workforce and other taxes are not used in the United States (at least insofar as IMF statistics show). Figure 8-3 graphically shows how each of the countries utilizes each type of tax.

As Figure 8-4 suggests, countries with federal governments tend to rely on taxes more than countries with unitary governments. The figure contains two sets of "box plots" of the reliance on taxes by type of government. The left-hand panel contains plots of taxes as a percentage of GDP. The vertical dimension of each box encloses 50 percent of the observations (i.e., from the 25th to the 75th percentiles). The horizontal line inside each box shows the location of the median. The lines, circles, and stars above and below each box show the full extent of the data. The vertical, capped lines enclose observations within 1.5 times the distance between first and third quartiles (the interquartile range [IQR]); the circles identify observations within three times the IQR (known as *outliers*); and the stars locate the most extreme observations (known as *extremes*). The right-hand panel plots recurrent taxes on property as a percentage of total taxes. The right-hand panel clearly illustrates that federal countries tend to make greater use of recurrent taxes on property than most unitary countries.

Chapter 8 Systems of Government and Taxation: A Global Perspective 261

FIGURE 8-3. Utilization of Main Types of Taxes by Percentage of Total Taxes for General Government in Selected Countries

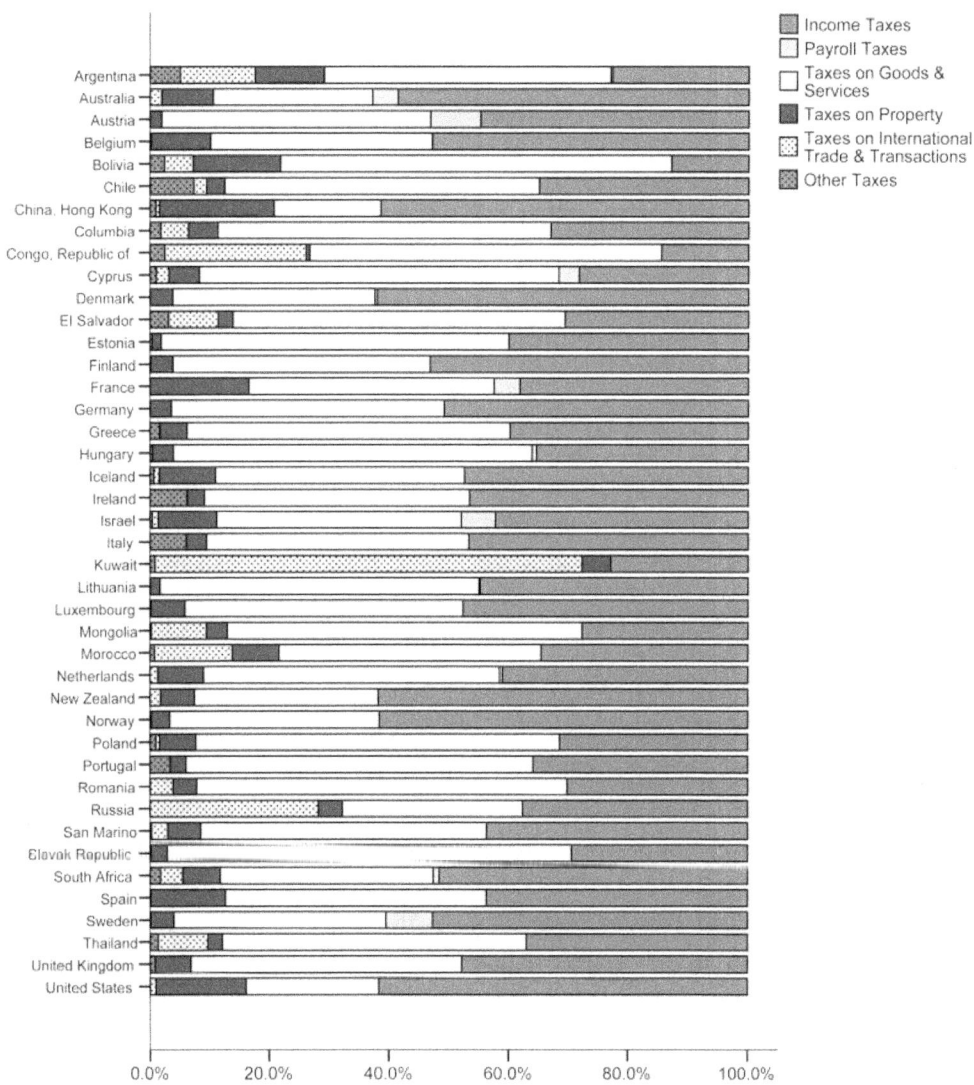

Source: IMF 2007; computations by author.

FIGURE 8-4. Box Plots of the Utilization of Taxes by Type of State

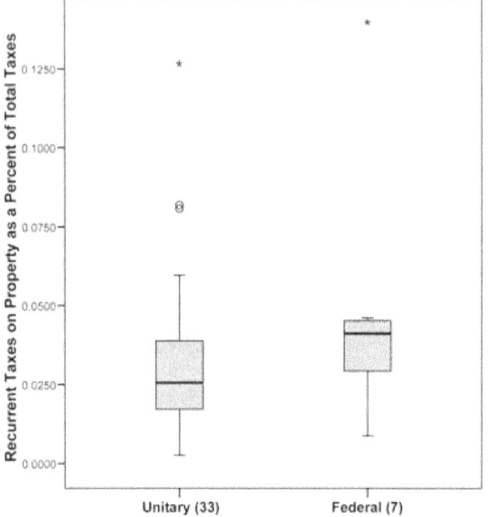

Source: IMF 2007; computations by author

Utilization of Taxes on Property

This section further examines the use of recurrent taxes on property. Two data sets are used. The first is the set of 42 countries analyzed above. The second is a larger set of 161 countries; it includes countries that did not provide general government summaries and countries that reported revenue statistics on a cash basis instead of an accrual basis. The categories examined are (with the IMF classification codes in parentheses): (1) recurrent taxes on immovable (real) property (1131); (2) recurrent taxes on net wealth (1132); (3) other recurrent taxes on property (1136), including movable (personal) property; and (4) recurrent taxes on immovable property combined with other recurrent taxes on property.

Table 8-2 and Figure 8-5 examine recurrent taxes on immovable property and other recurrent taxes on property in the set of 42 countries examined above. (Detail on movable property taxes in the United States was not reported.)

Chapter 8 — Systems of Government and Taxation: A Global Perspective

TABLE 8-2. Median, Minimum, and Maximum Utilization of Categories of Recurrent Taxes on Property in Percentages of Total Taxes for Selected Countries

Property Tax Category	Number of Countries	Median		Minimum		Maximum	
		Country	% of Total	Country	% of Total	Country	% of Total
Immovable property	39	Bolivia	2.8	Democratic Republic of Congo	0.0	United States	14
Other recurrent	13	Italy	0.4	Poland	0.0	El Salvador	1.8
All recurrent taxes on property	42	Netherlands Bolivia	2.8 2.8	Finland	0.3	United States	14.0

Note: Percentages equal to 0.0 indicate situations in which the percentage is less than 0.1 (rounded).

FIGURE 8-5. Recurrent Taxes on Property as a Percentage of Total Taxes in Selected Countries

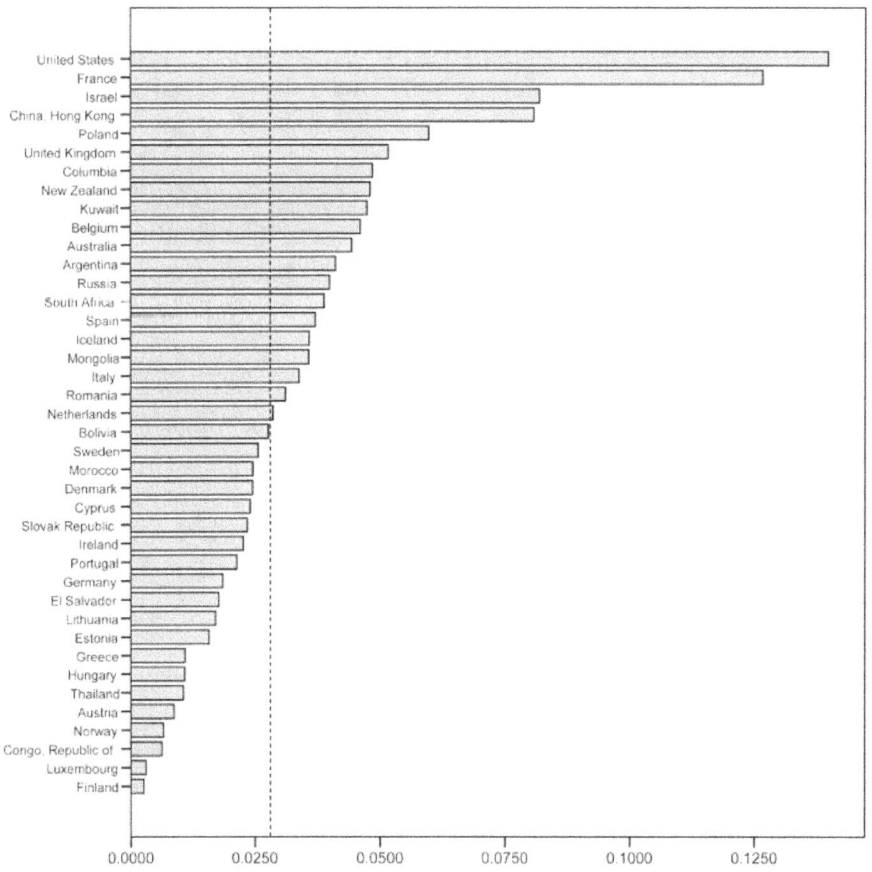

Source: IMF 2007; computations by author.

When data on recurrent taxes on property for all 93 reporting countries are examined, a different picture of what is typical emerges: the median is considerably lower, 1.7 percent (Lithuania and Swaziland) instead of 2.8 percent. For the purposes of characterizing the profiled countries, countries with taxes below the 25th percentile are considered to have "low" property taxes (0.6 percent of total taxes), and properties with taxes above the 75th percentile (3.5 percent) are considered to have "high" property taxes.

Profiles of Property Taxes on Immovable Property

As noted earlier in this chapter and in Chapter 1, "Introduction to Tax Policy," it is a misnomer to speak of "the property tax." This section focuses on recurrent taxes on immovable property but touches on recurrent taxes on movable property as well. Such taxes differ widely in detail, and this section suggests the scope of these differences. Among the 95 countries studied, there are well more than 100 distinct recurrent taxes on immovable and movable property. Virtually every country with a tax on immovable property has a story to tell. The countries represented here were selected because of recent developments or because they have interesting system features.

The profiles in this section draw on data from the IMF 2007 yearbook and from the sources listed in Table 8-3. Some profiles also make use of first-hand observations, country presentations made in courses conducted by the Lincoln Institute of Land Policy (LILP) and the Organization for Economic Co-operation and Development (OECD), and other presentations.

There is a wealth of descriptive and analytical information in the many international surveys of property tax systems. The more recent ones include Almy 2001 (Europe), Bird and Slack 2004 (a sample of 25 countries drawn from around the world), Brown and Hepworth 2001 (Europe), Charles 1996 (Africa plus one paper from Asia), De Cesare 2004 (Latin America), Dos Santos 2004 (Caribbean), Dos Santos and Bain 2004 (Caribbean), Federal Land Cadastre Service of Russia 2001 (Europe), Franzsen and McCluskey 2004 (Africa), Malme and Youngman 2001 (transitional countries in Europe), McCluskey 1999 (a sample of 21 countries drawn from around the world), McCluskey 1991 (a sample of 12 countries drawn from around the world), McCluskey and Plimmer 2007 (central and eastern Europe), and Youngman and Malme 1994 (a sample of 14 countries drawn from around the world). These sources provide information on about 95 countries. Other countries' systems are described in individual works not cited here. The subscription services of the International Bureau of Fiscal Documentation (http://www.ibfd.org/) are important sources of descriptive information.

TABLE 8-3. Information Sources for Countries Profiled

Country	Sources
China	Bird and Slack 2004 and People's Republic of China, State Administration of Taxation 2004
Colombia	Bird and Slack 2004 and De Cesare 2004
Denmark	Müller 2000 and Almy 2001
Estonia	Vallner and Juss 2004; Bahl, Martinez-Vazquez, and Youngman 2008; and Almy 2001
Hungary	Péteri and Lados 2003 and Lados 2003
Latvia	Latvia State Land Service 2008 and Almy 2001
Lithuania	Bahl, Martinez-Vazquez, and Youngman 2008 and Almy 2003
Netherlands	Gieskes et al. 2002; Kathmann and Kuijper 2006; Kruimel 1999; and ten Have 1994
Russia	Malme and Youngman 2001 and Almy 2001
South Africa	Bird and Slack 2004 and Franzsen and McCluskey 2004
Sweden	Färnkvist 2004; Brown and Hepworth 2001; and Almy 2001.
Turkey	Çopur 2005 and Öz 2004
United Kingdom	Brown and Hepworth 2001 and Almy 2001

Perhaps more durable than descriptive information are the insights of practitioners and scholars. Those with keen insights include Bahl, Martinez-Vazquez, and Youngman; Bird and Slack; McCluskey and his various coauthors; Paugham; and Youngman and Malme.

Examples of Diversity

As in Argentina, Australia, Canada, Mexico, Switzerland, and the United States, subnational governments in federal countries often have distinctive systems of property taxation. In contrast, Austria and Germany are examples of federal countries with a single property tax. Diversity also can be found in unitary countries. Some countries have more than one kind of tax. As another example of diversity, land may be taxed differently than buildings. Property owned by natural (physical) persons may be taxed differently than property owned by legal persons.

In 92 of the 95 countries studied, local governments receive some or all of property tax revenues. Central governments receive property tax revenues in 52 countries, and intermediate (state-level) governments receive property taxes in 15.

An important area of difference is the basis of the tax. In the countries studied, 21 had area-based taxes; 31 had annual rental value-based taxes, and 72 had capital value-based taxes. Taxes based on annual rental value tend to account for a larger percentage of total taxes than taxes based on area or capital value. There also are important differences in collection and enforcement. Most countries make a person liable for paying property taxes (*in personam* liability). The United States is among the exceptions that utilize *in rem* liability. This difference manifests itself in the determination of assessable property and in the delivery of property tax bills. Sometimes only legally registered property is assessable; sometimes tax bills must be personally served to be valid.

The countries studied exhibit diversity in institutional arrangements. An important factor of course is whether the government is federal or unitary. In the latter, the central government generally has overall responsibility for property tax administration, although local governments often assist. Responsibility for valuation most commonly rests with the land (cadastre) authority (Federal Land Cadastre Service of Russia 2001, 12).The next most common arrangement for valuation responsibility is with the taxation authority (which generally is under the minister of finance) or the ministry of finance. The United Kingdom (discussed below) assigns responsibility for valuation to a special valuation authority. Netherlands (also discussed below) is among the countries that make local governments responsible for valuation.

Local Autonomy and Administration: Hungary, the Netherlands, and South Africa

Hungary, the Netherlands, and South Africa (together with Colombia and the United Kingdom discussed below) are examples of unitary governments that have devolved policy and administration to local governments. Norway is another.

Hungary

Although Hungary does not rely heavily on recurrent property taxes, it is interesting for the autonomy over policy and practice afforded local governments (of which there are about 3,100 municipalities). Half the municipalities have fewer than 1,000 inhabitants.

In Hungary, modern types of property taxation originated in the mid-nineteenth century. Before socialism, there were obligatory municipal taxes on land and buildings, including agricultural land. Under socialism, there were local government taxes on urban land and buildings and a county tax on agricultural land. During the transition to decentralized local government, municipalities were given the constitutional power to choose from one of four forms of property taxation (see Table 8-4)—or to choose not to impose any property taxes. The four property taxes are as follows:

- A tax on buildings (Residential buildings, nonresidential buildings, or both can be taxed. Municipalities can also choose an area or value basis.)
- A tax on land plots, which also can be taxed on an area or value basis
- A communal tax on private persons, which also taxes land plots on a per-plot basis
- A tax on tourism, which includes a property tax on summer cottages.

Chapter 8 — Systems of Government and Taxation: A Global Perspective

TABLE 8-4. Property Taxation in Hungary, the Netherlands, and South Africa

Country and Name of tax	Base	Basis	Revenue Recipients	Importance	Features of Interest
Hungary	The taxes below are an à la carte menu.				
Tax on buildings (1991)	Residential and nonresidential buildings	Area or value	Local authorities	Overall: moderate (1.1% of total tax revenues)	The upper limits on rates are 900 forints per square meter or 3% of corrected value. Corrected value is 50% of government-determined assessed value, which corresponds to 50% of average observed market value.
Tax on plots (1991)	Land plots	Area or value	Local authorities		The upper rate limit is 200 forints per square meter or 3% of corrected value.
Communal tax on private persons	Owned or rented real estate plots	Plots	Local authorities		The tax on plots is 12,000 forints per plot per year. On enterprises, it is a head tax (poll tax).
Tax on tourism	Includes summer cottages	Area	Local authorities		The tax covers a number of touristic activities (hotels, for example, are taxed on the basis of room-nights). The maximum rate on cottages is 900 forints per square meter.
Netherlands					
Municipal tax (1970)	Land, buildings, and houseboats	Market value (since 1997)	Municipalities	Moderate: 2.8% of total tax revenues	There are separate taxes on owners and users (owner-occupiers are liable for both). Originally, municipalities could choose to base the tax on surface area or market value.
South Africa					
General rate (alternatively, assessment rate)	Land and buildings	Site value or market value of the developed property or a composite rating system	Local authorities	High: 3.9% of total tax revenues (20% of local revenues)	Residential property tax relief is provided in several ways, including rebates. Rural property is not taxed.

All are locally administered, and a single property can be taxed under only one tax. Taxes on nonresidential buildings have been most popular (with municipalities), followed by taxes on land plots, taxes on houses, and taxes on tourism. Altogether, more than half of Hungary's municipalities have adopted property taxes. Only a few have adopted value-based taxes. Factors that affect a municipality's decision to impose a property tax include the uncertainties about property ownership, the size of the potential tax base in light of numerous exemptions, administrative capacity, and the complexity of the systems that supply needed data.

The Ministry of Finance oversees property taxation. Real estate transaction data flow from fee offices (where transfer taxes are paid), to land offices (where titles are registered), and then to municipal tax offices. The fee offices are county-level offices under the notary. Land offices are under the Ministry of Agriculture, and they manage the legal cadastre. Municipalities do not receive transaction price information, because that information is regarded as confidential. This discourages adoption of the market-value basis. In addition, technical departments, which may cover several municipalities, register building permits, local master plans (zoning), and public utility information. The systems used by the various entities are not integrated.

Given the low level of taxation and the high degree of complexity, administrative costs are regarded as high. A 1992 survey revealed that property taxes were more expensive to administer than the business (profits) tax (for which compliance costs probably are higher). As would be expected, administrative costs were relatively higher in smaller municipalities. Overall, the cost of administering the tax on buildings was 13.1 percent of revenues. The ratio ranged from 15.5 percent for municipalities with fewer than 5,000 people to 12.4 percent for municipalities with more than 50,000 people (Péteri and Lados 2003).

According to Péteri and Lados (2003, 3, 6),

> Introduction of local taxes was part of an 'experimental' process, when basic characteristics of local governance, public administration, local finances and municipal financial management went through a transformation. The first 'try' of a modern local tax system was highly controlled, so any failures could have been easily corrected by other elements of intergovernmental finances. After 4–5 years, the assumption was that the system would be redesigned.

Netherlands

The Netherlands is a rare example of a country that moved to a market value-based tax from a system that gave municipalities the option of basing the property tax on either surface area or market value. In several respects, the Dutch property tax resembles those of Canada and the United States.

The Netherlands converted to municipal property taxation in 1970 (replacing a package of central and local government taxes). In 1989, the decision was made to eliminate surface area as a basis for taxation because of the recognized inequities of area as a base and because of the increasing complexity of the coefficients that were applied to different areas in an attempt to improve fairness. A new law on immovable property assessment came into force in 1997 (with values as of January 1995). At the same time, municipalities became responsible for valuation as well as collection. A central government agency, the Dutch Council for Real Estate Assessment, supervises the 458 municipalities. There is an active, hierarchical appeal system, which culminates with a tax court. The court has been active in deciding points of law.

Municipalities have considerable latitude in setting tax rates. Rates depend on funding requirements, and they are subject only to the limitation that tax rates cannot increase by more than 20 percent in a year. Municipalities also may grant certain exemptions. Their acts are contained in bylaws, which require royal assent.

Unusually, the municipal tax had two components: the user tax and the owner tax (and owner-occupiers would be subject to both taxes). Although only owners of residential property are now subject to the real estate tax, both owners and users of nonresidential property remain subject to the tax. Since 1995, houseboats are taxed along with real estate. Agricultural property is exempt.

Initially, revaluations were required every four years. However, revaluations are now performed every year. Valuation systems are technologically advanced. Values are used for other purposes, such as water board levies and in income taxation. Direct debiting of property tax obligations facilitates collection. To increase the efficiency of the system, properties with a value less than 25 thousand Dutch florins are exempt.

According to Gieskes et al. (2002), there are about 1,600 employees involved in property taxation administration. The Dutch Council for Real Estate has 20 employees. In 2006, there were 8 million properties. According to Kathmann and Kuijper (2006), about €160 million was spent in 2006 on administration (40 percent for characteristic data maintenance and administration, 40 percent for analysis and valuation, and about 20 percent for appeal). Tax revenues totaled €5 billion. Thus, the tax cost about 3 percent of revenues, or about €20 per property. The values have significant nonfiscal uses as well.

South Africa

South Africa is of interest because of the importance of property taxation in its history, basis options, and the current place of property taxation in the government structure. Although property taxation is a municipal power under the South African constitution, the central government and provincial governments regulate the tax (the latter through ordinances). A proposed Local Government Property Tax Rates Bill (published in 2003), if enacted, would create a national legal and regulatory framework for property taxation.

Property taxes are administered locally. In 1994, the power to levy property taxes was extended to all local authorities (not only white areas). A lack of capacity has deterred some from attempting to introduce property taxation. Currently, local authorities have a choice in the basis of property taxes: (1) unimproved site value (taxing land only as if unimproved); (2) so-called flat rating, under which both land and improvement values are taxable at a uniform rate, or (3) differential rating, under which land and improvement values are taxed at different rates. The use of these bases is evenly split. Under the proposed law, the second option would become the standard.

Valuers must be registered under the Property Valuers Profession Act (2000), and there are more than 2,000 registered valuers. Most large municipalities have valuation departments; others rely on private sector valuers. The City of Cape Town recently completed a revaluation using advanced CAMA methods.

Interestingly, valuers now estimate and record both unimproved site value, site value, and improvement value (the difference between total value and site value, although the cost approach may be used). Revaluations are required every four or five years, although revaluation requirements are not always met, partly because some former municipalities operated under a regime that required less frequent reassessments. Full property inspections generally are required.

Diversity in Policy, Administration and Practice: United Kingdom

The United Kingdom is of interest for several reasons. It influenced the development of many property tax systems, including those of the United States, Canada, and other members of the British Commonwealth. There are differences in systems among the U.K. countries. England and Wales share the systems summarized here (with some differences in detail). Northern Ireland and Scotland each have distinctive systems. Northern Ireland is notable for its recent conversion from a residential property tax based on annual rental value to a system based on capital market values (see Table 8-5).

Britain's traditional property tax, known as "rates" traces its origins to 1601 and was based on the annual rental values of residential (domestic) and nondomestic properties. This system remained in place until 1990, when residential rates were replaced by the Community Charge, a poll tax, and nondomestic rates were transferred to the central government. The Community Charge tax proved to be disastrously unpopular because of its regressive nature, and it proved to be difficult to enforce because of the mobility of segments of the population. In 1993, the Community Charge was replaced by the Council Tax.

Council Tax

The Council Tax is a residential property tax benefitting the approximately 400 local authorities. It is loosely based on capital value: each of the approximately 22 million properties is assigned to one of eight value strata, or "bands." Table 8-6, which applies to England only, illustrates the banding concept (Scotland and Wales have different bands reflecting the generally lower property prices in those countries). The relative tax that applies to each property in a band is fixed in legislation. However, the local authority annually sets the tax due for properties in Band D.

Chapter 8 — Systems of Government and Taxation: A Global Perspective

TABLE 8-5. Property Taxation in the United Kingdom

Name of Tax	Base	Basis	Revenue Recipients	Importance	Features of Interest
England, Wales, and Scotland					
Council tax	Residential (domestic) land and buildings	Capital value	Local authorities	Overall, high (5.7% of total tax revenues)	The "banding" system, which eliminates the need to determine a specific value for each property—properties must only be assigned to a value category.
Uniform business tax (rates)	Nondomestic premises	Annual rental value	Central government		In essence, the nondomestic tax base is pooled nationally and redistributed to local governments based on their populations.
Northern Ireland					
Rates	Domestic land and buildings	Capital value	Local authorities		The recent conversion from annual rental value to capital value
Rates	Nondomestic land and buildings	Annual rental value	Local authorities		

The value bands in Table 8-6 reflect values in 1991. The Valuation Office Agency (VOA) carried out a council tax revaluation in Wales in 2005. A revaluation of England was scheduled for 2007; however, it has been postponed.

TABLE 8-6. Council Tax Value Bands in England

Band	Value Range (£)	Tax Rate (%)	Value Differential (% of lower limit of band relative to Band D)
A	40,000 or less	67	Indeterminate
B	40,001–52,000	78	56
C	52,001–68,000	89	76
D	68,001–88,000	100	100
E	88,001–120,000	122	129
F	120,001–160,000	144	176
G	160,001–320,000	167	235
H	More than–320,000	200	470

The banding concept has several attractive features. It was implemented quickly. By attempting only to place a property in the appropriate value category, much of the contentiousness of conventional point estimates was avoided. At least as implemented in the United Kingdom, the banding concept also has shortcomings, the chief one being the regressive nature of the band structure. Another shortcoming, at least initially, was the failure to provide for periodic rebanding. As implemented, a property would remain in its band indefinitely, regardless of what happened in the market later. A property can change bands only when physical changes are made that change its value and when it is sold. These defects could of course be remedied.

Nondomestic Rates (the Uniform Business Rate)

The Uniform Business Rate (UBR) is a national tax based on annual rental value. It is collected locally and remitted to the central government, which redistributes the funds to local authorities based on their population. Revaluations are conducted every five years, with the valuation date being two years before.

The taxpayer is the occupier of the property or premises. There are about 1.7 million properties, and the number of appeals following revaluations in 1990 and 1995 approached 1.5 million. VOA (see below) hopes its "right first time" goal with the 2005 revaluation will alter if not overturn this appeals-driven system.

Administration

In England and Wales, a central government valuation authority, the VOA, is responsible for valuation. A counterpart organization, the Valuation and Lands Agency (VLA) was responsible for valuation in Northern Ireland until it was subsumed by Land and Property Services (LPS) in 2007. LPS also is responsible for collection, title registry, mapping, and other services. Both LPS and VOA supply general valuation services and real estate advice to the public sector. In Scotland, valuation is the responsibility of local assessors. Local authorities are responsible for collection in all countries.

VOA has been modernizing its operations. It now has a system for electronic filing of the rental returns required for the Uniform Business Rate. It has explored the use of CAMA for a revaluation of domestic properties for the Council Tax. More than 95 percent of the taxes due annually are collected (99 percent of the UBR). Currently the cost of administering the English property taxes is approximately 3 percent (cost of collection alone about 1.9 percent). Efforts to improve collection efficiency include allowing the direct debiting of taxes from the taxpayer bank accounts. LPS also is highly modernized.

The Northern Ireland Residential Revaluation

Rates, based on annual rental values, were introduced in 1826 in Northern Ireland, and the first valuation took 40 years complete. The last residential revaluation before the conversion to capital values occurred in 1976 (nonresidential revaluation has been more regular, the most recent revaluation occurring in 2003).

Since the last residential revaluation, the complexion of residential real estate tenure changed from renting to owning in Northern Ireland (as in the rest of the United Kingdom). Sales data were comparatively more plentiful than rental data.

Hence, the decision was made to convert the residential property tax from an annual rental value basis to a capital market value basis effective in 2007. The conversion was designed to be revenue-neutral, and changes in burdens were seen as an exercise in restoring fairness. Of the 760,000 properties in valuation list, 704,000 were residential. The revaluation was carried out by a staff of 300, including 100 chartered surveyors (appraisers).

Other Recent Reforms

Arguably, the collapse of the Soviet Union brought about more attempts at property tax reform than any other event in history. At the same time, however, there has been pressure to reform systems of government and taxation in less developed countries. Some of the more interesting and successful reform efforts are described here.

Russia

The Russian Federation is an interesting case study for several reasons. Its original (1991) system of property taxation provided the model for the tax systems in most of the former Soviet Union. The system's elements included a land tax, a tax on the property of physical persons, and a tax on the property of enterprises (see Table 8-7). Deficiencies in the original design of these taxes became apparent with reforms in property ownership, the economy, and government. Russia's size and economic diversity, like that of China (discussed below), make designing a coherent national system especially challenging. Although (also like China) Russia has pursued a gradualist approach to property tax reform, its cadastral revaluation of land is a remarkable achievement.

The Original Tax System

In the Soviet period the concept of "property" did not include land, although it did include buildings as well as movable (personal) property, hence the separate land and "property" taxes. Because enterprises controlled more property, a distinction was between physical (natural) persons and legal persons (enterprises), hence the two property tax laws. Russia also introduced taxes on the transfer of property, gifts, and inheritances in 1991. Rents for the use of state-owned (government-owned) land also have some of the characteristics of taxes. Factors that have influenced property taxation are privatization programs and the decision to allow private ownership of land (previously, only rights to use land existed).

Originally, the land tax chiefly was levied on agricultural land. Consequently, the normative value basis chiefly reflected the relative value of land from an agricultural perspective.

The tax on the property of physical persons chiefly is a housing property tax. In Soviet times, the housing stock was inventoried in order to judge needs and to allocate housing. Housing units also were valued for mandatory insurance purposes. Each

TABLE 8-7. Recurrent Property Taxes in the Russian Federation

Name of Tax	Base	Basis	Revenue Recipients	Importance	Features of Interest
Land tax	Land	Normative value until 2006 when cadastral value became the basis	Regions (although they often share revenues with municipalities)	Overall, high (4% of total tax revenues, with the tax on property of legal persons and the land tax contributing the bulk of the revenue)	As normative values were static following the collapse of the Soviet Union, an attempt was made to maintain revenue yields by indexing the rates to account for inflation. In 2004, the tax code was amended to change the basis to cadastral values, which incorporated market information. Under the cadastral value regime, local authorities decide differential rates, subject to legal maximums (0.3% for residential, agricultural, and utility land; 1.5% for commercial land). The federal government is to become a taxpayer.
Tax on property of physical persons	Buildings	Inventory value (a cost-based value)	Municipalities		The law allows local authorities to fix specific rates within the following ranges: (1) no more than 0.1% for property holding that total less than 300,000 rubles in value; (2) between 0.1% and 0.3% for assessments over 300,000 rubles but no more than 500,000 rubles; and (3) between 0.3% and 2.0% for holdings in excess of 500,000 rubles.
	Motor vehicles, aircraft, watercraft	Engine displacement			Tax rates in rubles per horsepower are keyed to the officially set "minimum salary."
Tax on property of legal persons	Buildings, other structures, and certain movable property	Average book (balance) value	Municipalities		Discretion re rates (maximum 2%); agricultural enterprises are not taxed.
Experimental real estate tax	Land and buildings owned by certain enterprises	Market value	Novgorod		A market value-based real estate tax

municipality had a Bureau of Technical Inventory (BTI), which maintained housing records and made the valuations. The valuations became the basis for the tax on the property of physical persons. Summer cottages and privately owned garages also are taxed. There is an array of exemptions that reflect presumed ability to pay and gratitude for past service to the country. There were 30 million taxpayers in 1994.

The tax on the property of legal persons (domestic and foreign enterprises) is based on "balance value," which is a value carried on the books of businesses. Balance values reflect original costs less "amortization" (depreciation), although they periodically are indexed to reflect inflation. The tax is self-assessed and paid quarterly, with an annual reconciliation. Its base includes buildings, industrial plant and equipment, and some vehicles. Land and certain other classes of assets are not taxable. There were 1.5 million taxpayers in 1994.

Fiscal and Institutional Arrangements
The Russian Federation comprises 89 member regions of various types. Under them are 2,300 districts and 26,000 municipalities (after 2006). The power to tax property rests with the central government. It has assigned the revenues from the land tax and the tax on the property of physical persons to municipalities. However, it retains a percentage of collections to cover administrative costs. The enterprise property tax is assigned to regional governments (*oblasts*), but they may share the revenues with municipalities (e.g., in the Leningrad region). The laws grant regional and local authorities discretion over tax rates. They annually set rates for physical person and enterprise property taxes subject to legal maximums. As shown in Table 8-7, only the enterprise property tax is currently significant. Until 2004, enterprise property taxes accrued to the region (usually Moscow) in which the enterprise was headquartered; now the taxes accrue to the region in which the property physically is situated.

The Ministry of Finance is responsible for property tax policy and for overseeing the property tax system. The Ministry of Taxes and Duties (formerly the State Revenue Service and before that the State Tax Service under the Ministry of Finance) maintains registers of taxpayers and is responsible for property tax collection. The State Tax Service had a staff of 30,000 in 1994. As noted, municipal BTIs originally registered and valued buildings and premises owned by physical persons. Now the Federal Land Cadastre Service is responsible for building valuation along with land valuation. Regional governments provide partial financing for valuation and approve valuation results. Local authorities provide information, a lesser amount of financial support, and "take in" results of valuation activities.

Market Value Reforms
In 1997, the Russian Federation enacted legislation that allows certain local authorities to institute market value-based property taxes on land and buildings as an economic unit. The first to experiment with this form of property taxation were Novgorod Veliky and Tver. Novgorod has introduced the tax on a limited basis—only

40 enterprise taxpayers are subject to the tax. However, interest in expanding the coverage of such a tax remains, and a draft real estate tax law has been introduced in the Duma (parliament). The proposed tax would be based on the cadastral (market) value of land and buildings. It would have differential, locally determined rates in range of 0.05–0.5 percent. Local authorities have been reluctant to embrace the tax because they fear they would lose revenue with the removal of movable property from the property tax base.

Another reform effort has been a project of the Federal Land Cadastre Service to develop cadastral values that reflect market factors for urban land for use in the land tax. All three approaches to value are used. The service developed the valuation methods and software and trained valuers (6,000 have been trained). Valuers are now licensed. Initially (through 2002), the valuations were made by government-owned companies (through 2002). From 2003 onward, licensed companies have done the work.

The project began in 1999 and was 95 percent complete by the fall of 2005. Beginning in 2006, the new values were to be used in taxation. It is estimated that 42 million parcels are subject to the land tax. The creation of computerized registers made it possible for the cadastre service to study the redistribution of land taxes under the old and new regimes.

The Baltic Countries

The Baltic Countries—Estonia, Latvia, and Lithuania—are perhaps the most successful of the former socialist countries to have attempted property tax reforms. Table 8-8 outlines features of current property taxes in the three countries.

All have had land reforms under which nationalized properties were restituted (either by returning properties to their former owners or by compensating them in other ways). Such programs are difficult because of conflicting claims, incomplete records, "illegal" ownership, and the like. All have invested in developing valuation methods based on recognized approaches and in computer technology; in all three countries, assessment data are accessible over the Internet. All three countries also have contributed to an annual review of Baltic real estate markets.

Estonia

Estonia introduced its land tax soon after its independence. Policy considerations drove the decision to tax land only: following restitution, the government wanted to ensure that land that was returned to private owners would be used productively. Taxing land would encourage use; looked at another way, the land tax would discourage leaving land idle, which was feared would happen if absent owners had no expenses associated their land. A practical reason for taxing land and not buildings was that information on all buildings was lacking. Since the inception of the land tax, consideration has been given to introducing a tax on the value of improvements to land (buildings), but no decision to introduce such a tax has been made.

TABLE 8-8. Property Taxation in the Baltic Countries

Country and Name of Tax	Base	Basis	Revenue Recipients	Importance	Features of Interest
Estonia					
Land tax (1993)	Land	Capital (market) value	Municipalities	Moderate: 1.5% of total tax revenues. In Tallinn, the capital, the effective tax rate is about 0.6%.	Taxpayers are landowners or holders of long-term leases or usufructs. Previously the land tax was a shared tax. Now, local councils annually decide rates within between 0.1% and 2.5% (the maximum for agricultural land is 2.0%).
Latvia					
Real estate tax (1997)	Land and commercial and industrial buildings and structures	Cadastral value (since 2000, a market-based capital value)	Municipalities (553)	Moderate: 3.4% of total tax revenues	Currently, residential and agricultural buildings and premises are not taxed. Rates are fixed at 1% of cadastral value. A value increase limit (25%) is in effect from 2008 until 2010.
Lithuania					
Land tax (1992)	Land	Normative value	Municipalities	Overall, moderate (1.7% of total tax revenues)	The land tax rate is fixed in law at 1.5% of value.
Immovable property (building) tax (2006)	Buildings owned by businesses	Market value	Municipalities		The 2006 law superseded a 1994 law under which buildings were valued on a normative basis. The new law introduced an element of local discretion over tax rates; now municipal councils fix the rate within a range of 0.8% to 1% (previously the rate was fixed in law at 1%). The change in valuation basis resulted in a twofold increase in the tax base.

The National Land Board is responsible for assessment. Valuation is governed by a separate law from the law on land tax. About 1,000 urban land market areas (zones) have been delineated, and there are about 5,000 agricultural zones. Data on sales are received directly from notaries, and more than 119,000 sales transactions have occurred. Revaluations were conducted in 1993, 1996, and 2001. Thirty-five public- and private-sector valuers participated on the 2001 revaluation.

The National Tax and Customs Board is responsible for collection. A 98 percent collection rate is achieved, although bills are not issued for obligations less than 20 Estonian crowns (EEK).

Latvia
Along with Lithuania, Latvia did not introduce a market value-based property tax as quickly as Estonia. Both countries have pursued a strategy of gradually introducing market value-based taxes on land and buildings. In 1997, Latvia enacted a real estate tax that superseded earlier land and property taxes based on Russian models. Separate estimates are made of land value and improvement value. The formal basis of assessment is "cadastral value," which is based on models informed by available market information. As in many other countries, obtaining reliable information on sales prices is difficult.

The State Land Service is responsible for the cadastre and for annual mass valuation exercises (it estimates that 94 percent of all properties are registered). Four types of property are valued using mass valuation methods: (1) rural land, (2) urban land under housing, (3) industrial real estate, and (4) commercial and public-purpose real estate. Notably, residential buildings are not yet taxed.

Beginning with 2007, one class will be revalued every year so that all are revalued over a four-year cycle (new industrial real estate values are scheduled for adoption in 2008). Values may be revised between revaluations if necessary. The valuation and tax systems are automated. With the introduction of market-based values, the rate of tax was reduced from 1.5 percent to 1.0 percent. The lack of flexibility in rates has been an obstacle to taxing residential properties. In 2005 and 2006, residential property values appreciated rapidly. In 2007, they began to decline. The decline has prompted concerns from municipalities about declining municipal revenues.

Local authorities (municipalities) collect the tax, maintain ownership information, and determine the use of property for valuation purposes. Notices are sent annually. The State Revenue Service of the Ministry of Finance oversees tax calculation and collection.

Lithuania
Lithuania has both a land tax and a building tax. The land tax, which was first introduced in 1990 (the law was revised in 1992), is based on normative methods. In 2003, a plan to introduce a market value-based land tax was shelved after an analysis of the new values sparked fears of an outcry over increased taxes. Lithuania's building tax system was changed from an "inventory value" basis (essentially a replacement cost basis used in insurance) to a market value basis in 2005 for taxation in 2006. The 2005 values are valid for real estate tax purposes for five years. As with Latvia, residential buildings and units are not yet taxed.

The government of Lithuania has assigned a number of cadastral and valuation functions to a government-owned corporation established in 1997, the State Enterprise Center of Registers (SECR). While SECR receives some funding from the government, it receives fees for title registration services and competes with pure private-sector firms for some surveying and valuation business. The need to operate efficiently and be responsive to a wide range of clients doubtless has contributed to a strategic outlook and progressive approach to problem solving. The State Tax Inspectorate administers the land and building taxes; that is, it keeps track of properties that are exempt, issues tax bills, and collects taxes.

SECR uses modern CAMA methods to produce its market value estimates. Although the cost approach still is used, the SECR developed tools for using multiple regression analysis (MRA) and trained valuers in each of its eleven regional offices in their use in 2002. Thus, SECR has not taken a top–down approach to valuation for property tax purposes; expertise in modern mass appraisal has spread throughout the country, not concentrated in a few persons in headquarters. In total, about 70 specialists are engaged in mass appraisal, of which 40 are valuers working directly in the central office and in branch offices (the other specialists include IT and GIS experts). SECR prepares summary reports of each revaluation for use by Lithuania's 60 municipalities in setting their tax rates (a national summary report also is prepared). SECR estimates that eventually the real estate register will contain 2.3 million land plots and 3.7 million buildings.

The SECR's estimates of market value are used for purposes other than property taxation. For example, its estimates of the market value of land are used in Lithuania's social support program to ensure that persons receiving payments were actually deserving (previously, persons who had extensive property holdings qualified for payments because of low salary figures). The SECR updates its market-value estimates annually.

China

While private ownership of land and land taxation existed in China as early as 594 BC, it is China's recent history with property taxes that is of interest today. Since market reforms began in 1978, China's industrialization and urban development have been extraordinary. Although land currently is state or collective owned, physical and legal persons can obtain the right to use land, and buildings can be privately owned. Existing recurrent taxes (see Table 8-9) reflect this situation. In 1994, revenues from the taxes were assigned to local authorities (cities, county towns, townships, and other designated areas). They were given discretion over tax rates, and they were assigned administrative responsibilities as well.

Taxpayers under the urban real estate tax and the house tax include owners, managers or custodians, mortgagees, and occupants of buildings. However, only foreign entities pay the urban real estate tax, and only domestic entities pay the house tax.

The State Administration of Taxation is generally responsible for tax policy and administration. Under the 1994 reforms, however, local governments are responsible for collecting property taxes. Each city that levies the urban real estate tax appoints a committee on real estate assessment to determine standard values on land and buildings annually. Standard values reflect perceived

TABLE 8-9. Recurrent Property Taxes in China

Name of Tax	Base	Basis	Revenue Recipients	Importance	Features of Interest
Urban real estate tax (1951)	Land and buildings with foreign ownership or investment in designated cities	If owned, capital value; if leased, annual rental value.	Designated cities	Overall, moderate: (2% of total tax revenue in 2002)	If a building is assessed on a capital value basis, the rate is 1.2% of the assessed value (standard value); and land is taxed at 1.5% of the standard value. It the land and building values cannot be determined, the total value of the property is taxed at 1.5% of standard value. If leased, the rate is 15%.
House (building) property tax (1986)	Nonresidential buildings	If owned, residual value (a capital value); if leased or used, gross annual rental value.	Local authorities		The rate applied to residual value assessments is 1.2%; the rate applied to gross annual value assessments is 12%. Residual value is original cost minus 10-30%, with the specific percentage being determined by the province in which the property is located. Unprofitable enterprises may receive temporary exemptions.
Urban and township land use tax (1988)	Land in cities and other specified areas	Area	Local authorities		Taxpayers are users of land. The taxable area is the area actually used. Local tax offices decide the rate per square meter within the allowable range, which varies with the character of the political subdivision in question (the rate range is highest for large cities and lowest for counties, townships, and mining districts).

differences in local market conditions, costs of construction, quality, and use. Provinces and certain municipalities decide the percentage to be subtracted from original cost to determine the taxable residual value under the house tax. Local tax offices have the power to set tax rates within allowable parameters.

Deficiencies and inconsistencies in the current system of recurrent property taxes are recognized. The taxes lack buoyancy, and one aim is to make them the main source of tax revenue for local authorities. Another goal is to treat foreign and domestic taxpayers more equitably. It also is believed that a consolidated market value-based real estate tax would simplify administration especially if operations were computerized. At the same time, a reformed tax must reflect social values and differing degrees of affordability across the country. In 2005, pilot studies were initiated in Beijing, Shenzhen, Chongqing, and Liaoning, as well as in Jiangsu Province and the Ningxia Autonomous Region. The aims of the projects were to obtain practical experience with methodologies and information on the size and composition of the potential tax bases in the areas studied. The latter were crucial to informed property tax policy. The area covered by pilot studies was expanded in 2007, but at the time this text was being prepared (early 2008), the decision to impose taxes based on new assessments had been deferred.

Technological Diversity

The technology of assessment and taxation varies widely from twenty-first century systems that harness computers and GIS technology to systems that rely on less ambitious models. Although the countries examined in this section are not the only representatives of their categories, they demonstrate the various degrees of sophistication in assessment and taxation systems. Other features of each country's system also are presented.

Systems That Use Self-Assessment

As noted in Chapter 3, "Fundamental Elements of the Property Tax," relying on taxpayers to describe and value their properties is regarded as a risky strategy. Yet, elements of self-assessment can be found in many property tax systems. Here two examples are examined.

Colombia

Colombia's property tax system is interesting in a number of respects. Its constitution, which is similar to Hungary's, assigns the right to tax property to municipalities (of which there are more than 1,000). However, the legislation governing property taxation is national. The current tax, the unified property tax, was introduced in 1990 (it replaced four earlier taxes in an effort at simplification and at eliminating double taxation). Of particular interest here is that municipalities can choose one of two methods of assessment, and they have discretion over tax rates within the limits established by law. Although overall reliance on recurrent property taxes is relatively high for Latin America, reliance varies considerably among municipalities.

The law (Law 44 of 1990) allows municipalities to base the tax on cadastral value or on self-assessed value. Bird and Slack (2004) describe differences between Bogotá, which selected the self-assessment method, and Medellín, the second-largest city, which selected cadastral value. Cadastral value is a capital value that incorporates the value of the land and the value of buildings and other improvements considering only their current use. The value of infrastructure and surroundings is included; the value of growing crops is among the things excluded. Revaluations are called for every five years, and in intervening years, values are to be indexed. The index is determined by the national government.

City cadastral departments are responsible for maintaining cadastral registers in the largest cities, and tax departments are responsible for tax administration. A central government cadastral agency, the Agustin Codazzi Geographic Institute (IGAC) under the Ministry of Finance, has responsibility for cadastral systems elsewhere. The IGAC also is responsible for the annual index, which cannot exceed the annual inflation target set by the central bank. Although technically skilled, IGAC has not been able to maintain the revaluation schedule. Also problematic was a collapse of the Colombian real estate market in the late 1990s, as the indexing scheme did not anticipate declining property values.

Under the self-assessment system, taxpayers annually declare their property values and pay their taxes. As implemented in Bogotá, self-assessments also were used in calculating capital gains, which encouraged accurate assessments initially. In addition, each year's succeeding assessment could not be less than the previous year's assessment multiplied by the annual index. Lower values could be declared if the taxpayer could satisfy the cadastral department that a property's value had indeed declined. The volume of appeals was so great that in 2000 general permission for lower values was granted. Because there had been no effort to establish minimum presumptive values (as the law contemplated) or to maintain cadastral values systematically, the foundation for the self-assessment system was undermined.

The unified property tax also permits municipalities to vary tax rates with property use in a progressive fashion, so that the tax rate structure is complex. Residential taxpayers also can qualify for additional preferential treatment. As a result, Bogotá had established 28 general rate categories and 8 preferential residential rate categories. Uncertainties in the assessment base and the complex rate structure have made it difficult for the city to balance revenue needs and receipts. Consequently, Bogotá's cadastral department has been attempting to ensure that all properties are registered in the cadastre and to update cadastral values. Parallel efforts are being made to enforce collection. However, return deadlines vary with type or group of taxpayers, and returns and payments are made to authorized banks, making control difficult. The amount of informal real estate development adds an additional challenge to the self-assessment system. (Cali, the third-largest city, has switched from the self-assessment system to the cadastral value system.)

Turkey

Turkey's land and building tax is an example of the successful use of simple valuation models and self-assessment. Buildings are valued on a replacement-cost-per-square-meter basis with adjustments for age and features (such as elevators and heating). Land also is valued on a per-square-meter basis. Value rates per square meter are updated every four years by an estimation commission. The General Directorate of Revenues of the Ministry of Finance supervises the property tax and promulgates the valuation standards. Municipalities administer and collect the tax.

When a building is newly constructed, or in quadrennial revaluation years, taxpayers are required to obtain a tax return, complete it, and file it with the municipality together with their tax payment. Tax returns contain schedules of building cost rates. They contain minimum, maximum, and average rates (in Turkish liras) per square meter for four types each of residential and nonresidential structures and five categories of construction quality. Depreciation is allowed for ten age categories. The taxpayer calculates the taxable value of each property from these schedules and computes the appropriate tax. Taxable land values are determined in a similar fashion. However, land rates are contained in books that are available in tax offices and other public places. The books contain lists of streets (or street segments when the street is long) with applicable rates organized by municipality.

Although the tax administration is regarded as successful, its strategic direction includes improving the efficiency and effectiveness of tax administration and establishing modern integrated information technology support systems.

Highly Computerized Systems: The Scandinavian Countries

Although they exhibit diversity in property tax system design features (see Table 8.10), the Scandinavian countries are characterized by technologically sophisticated cadastral and property tax systems. Finland and Norway are not described in detail because they make little use of property taxation. In Norway, municipalities can levy property taxes. If they do, they are locally administered. The focus is on Denmark and Sweden because they have long used MRA in the valuation of residential property. However, all the countries are involved in linked systems that use GIS technology and that disseminate data via the Internet.

Denmark

Denmark has three recurrent taxes on property: a land tax, a tax on business property (the service tax), and a tax on owner-occupied dwelling and summer houses (the property value tax). Local governments (counties and municipalities) receive the revenue from the taxes. In 2002, a number of changes to the system were introduced, including controls on increases in the property value tax and the land tax.

TABLE 8-10. Examples of Technological Diversity

Country and Name of Tax	Base	Basis	Revenue Recipients	Importance	Features of Interest
Colombia					
Unified property tax (1990)	Land and buildings	Cadastral value or self-assessed value	Municipalities	26% of local revenue (1999)	Rates for categories of property based on use and other characteristics are determined by municipalities within ranges established in law. The overall range is from less than 0.1% to 3.3%.
Turkey The owner or user is the taxpayer.					
Land and building tax	Land and buildings	Market value	Municipalities	8.6% of local government revenue (2004)	The general rate for residential buildings is 0.1% and for non-residential buildings, 0.2%. In metropolitan areas, the rates are 0.2% and 0.4%, respectively. The general rate for land designated for building 0.3% and for other land, 0.1%. In metropolitan areas, the corresponding rates are 0.6% and 0.2%.
Denmark In each tax, the owner is the taxpayer.					
Land tax (1926)	All land	Capital value	Counties, 275 municipalities	Overall, moderate (2.5% of total tax revenue	The county tax rate is fixed by parliament (at 1%). Municipalities decide the tax rate between 0.6% and 2.4%. There are lower rates for agriculture and forestry, and deferrals for the elderly.
Service tax (1961)	Commercial, industrial, and administrative buildings	Capital value			
Property value tax (2000)	Owner-occupied dwellings and summerhouses	Capital value			This tax replaced a former income tax on imputed rent of owner-occupied dwellings and summerhouses. It is collected by the central government with the personal income tax.
Sweden					
Real estate tax	Land and buildings	Market value	Central government	Overall, moderate (2.6% of total tax revenue)	Assessed values are 75% of estimated market values. Parliament annually decides rates. The rate depends on the category of property (how it is used). New construction receives a temporary exemption.

In 2002, the central government (the Customs and Tax Administration of the Ministry of Taxation) became fully responsible for valuation. Previously, municipally supported valuation committees reviewed valuations produced by the central government. In 1999, about two million properties were valued. Currently, property is revalued every two years on a rotating basis (residential property in one year, commercial and agricultural in the next). The Customs and Tax Administration maintains two valuation systems, and it maintains a sales register. A land valuation system essentially applies the land rates and adjustments decided by valuation experts. A property value system is a CAMA system that uses a statistical package (SAS), to calibrate valuation models. The data are presented in the "base home" structured format. An effort is made to keep the models simple and logical.

The municipalities maintain a valuation and collection register (they collect the land and service taxes). The National Survey and Cadastre is the source of land parcel records in the valuation registers. The municipalities maintain a building and dwelling register, which is the source of building information. The registers are computerized.

Sweden

The legal framework for the Swedish real estate tax (currently a national tax) includes an assessment law and a tax law. The Swedish Tax Board (under Minister of Finance) is mainly responsible for property tax assessment and issues instructions on how assessments are carried out. They are updated before each general reassessment. The National Land Survey (NLS, which is under the Minister of Environment) is responsible for valuation models. The NLS manages a sales price data base that is part of the property information system. Private valuers at the regional level are involved in determination of value levels, zone boundaries, and the like.

The valuation date is two years before taxation. All approaches to value are used, but the sales comparison approach has highest priority, income approach second, and cost third.

Residential land and building values are estimated separately. The mass appraisal model process involves specifying a standard property (norm) for each value zone. A tabular set of adjustment coefficients for deviations from the norm in terms of size, age, and so forth is calibrated for each zone using a combination of statistical analysis and valuer judgment.

The interval between revaluations is influenced by the election cycle; values are not increased just before an election. Since 1988, there has been a system of cyclical reassessments, as follows:

- Commercial and industrial properties were revalued in 1988, 1994, and 2000.
- Family houses were revalued in 1990, 1996, and 2003.
- Agricultural properties were revalued in 1992 and 1998.

Except for industrial properties, assessed values were indexed between revaluations by using regional price indexes. This proved to be controversial, and now simplified general reassessments are made. Each revaluation involves a year of preparatory work and a year of implementation. GIS is used in updating valuation zones. In the preparatory year, a return containing the data in the building register is issued. It also contains the proposed property value. If the owner does not contest the valuation or update the data, he or she is deemed to have accepted the new value.

There are seven main categories of property, and the classes are used in valuation and taxation. The three largest classes and the tax rate in effect in 2004 for each category are as follows:

- One- or two-family houses together with land, 1.0 percent
- Multifamily dwellings and commercial properties, apartments, 0.5 percent, and commercial, 1.0 percent
- Industrial properties and certain fisheries, 0.5 percent.

In recent years an attempt has been made to hold revenues to about 25 billion Swedish crowns (SEK) despite rising property prices.

In 2004, there were approximately 2.3 million one- and two-family dwellings, including 600,000 summerhouses. The number of sales per year ranges between 40,000 and 70,000. Three years of sales are used. There were 115,000 commercial properties and 166,000 industrial properties. In addition, there were 360,000 agricultural and forest properties. The remaining categories of property, which total about 95,000, include mining and extraction resource properties, special buildings, agricultural and forest property (including one- and two-family dwellings on such land), power plants, and waterfall riparian rights.

Issues

The fall of the Soviet Union in 1991 gave impetus to transforming developing and centrally planned socialist economies into market-based economies and representative democracies. Strengthening local government was a common objective. Providing them with dedicated sources of revenue, especially property taxes, was a common strategy. Concurrent efforts to expand the European Union and to deepen the integration among its member states demonstrated that there were many models from which to choose. Reforming real property and financial institutions also was on the reform agenda.

Fiscal Decentralization

A number of factors influence the recent widespread interest in governmental decentralization. The benefits of public services often have spatial limits; that is, individual preferences or needs for public services vary widely, but spatial patterns in those needs emerge as the result of economic and social factors. As a result, decentralization can allocate public services more efficiently. Decentralization in the form of autonomous local authorities tends to promote accountability. Political accountability is difficult for centralized governments to achieve, as can be seen from the collapse of command economies. Administrative decentralization is not sufficient. Large bureaucracies tend to respond slowly to changes in needs. If only to be seen as evenhanded, they tend to seek one-size-fits-all solutions.

Many public finance scholars believe property taxes can be an important component of a balanced revenue system. A tax on immovable property is an especially suitable source of revenue for local governments. A dedicated source of revenue promotes local autonomy. The visibility of property taxes focuses attention on the overall quality of governance and promotes accountability. In many countries, the tax on immovable property is the only tax that affords taxpayers the opportunity to review and challenge not only their assessments but also the assessments on similar or surrounding properties. Moreover, the tax captures for local government some of the increases in the value of land that are partially created by public expenditures. The base is easily identified; the tax is difficult to avoid. Information collected in the course of administering taxes on immovable property becomes part of a valuable fund of information that has numerous governmental and private uses. At the same time, taxes on immovable property receive their share of criticism. They may be regressive (especially when poorly administered), provide insufficient revenue, be difficult to administer, and not be economical when administered by small local governments. Some commonly encountered administrative problems are property omitted from tax rolls, infrequent revaluations, low rates, and low collection efficiency, all of which contribute to low revenue productivity.

Students of property taxation and of fiscal decentralization ponder why property tax reform is so difficult and why there is so little meaningful decentralization in practice. Bahl, Martinez-Vazquez, and Youngman (2008) provides an excellent survey of these issues (see Chapters 1 and 3 in particular).

Tax Harmonization and Competition

The global economy is becoming increasingly integrated. Measures of global integration are growth in trade, increasing capital flows, and the worldwide rise of the Internet.

Analysts who consider the impact of globalization on governmental (particularly local) finance put forward these hypotheses: First, globalization makes it more difficult to tax mobile factors (such as capital, which is taxed under a business income tax) and taxation of immobile factors (such as property) will likely grow. Second, an increasingly mobile tax base (whether individuals or capital) makes it more difficult for one government to tax such factors much more heavily than another government. Thus, one would expect a convergence of tax policies and rates over time. Indeed, this has been a goal of the European Commission. Yet, there is little empirical evidence of these things happening. It is unclear whether the hypotheses are flawed or whether such shifts in tax policies have simply not yet shown up in the data; see Alm, Holman, and Neumann (2002).

An area of concern among members and potential members is the impact of European Union legislation and regulations on a country's property tax policies and practices. It appears that currently the EU has no requirements that deal *directly* with property taxation. Šulija (Bahl, Martinez-Vazquez, and Youngman 2007, 442) observes that the focus has been on indirect taxes (e.g., value-added taxes and excises). European property tax systems certainly have few similarities (Almy 2001 and Brown and Hepworth 2001). However, policies that favor decentralization (such as "subsidiarity") have clear implications for property tax system design. National policies designed to subsidize agriculture and industry may come under scrutiny by the EU. (Conversely, EU subsidies may influence agricultural property prices.) In addition, the EU's 1995 Data Protection Directive may have a bearing on data that can be regarded as public.

Strengthening Private Property and Cost-Effective, Transparent Property Taxation

Strengthening private property institutions is a strategic element of efforts to strengthen market economies. DeSoto (2000) has been a particularly influential exponent of reforming property institutions so that people can gain secure title to the real estate they have. The link between real estate ownership and the legal cadastre on the one hand and the fiscal cadastre and property taxation on the other can be an area of contention. The issue has several aspects. One is the ease, expense, and time required to register ownership. (The difficulty in registering title is monitored on the World Bank Group "Doing Business" Web site, http://www.doingbusiness.org.) In addition to undercutting the development of property markets, barriers to title registration can adversely affect real property taxation. High transfer taxes also are detrimental (Maurer and Paugham 2000). How unauthorized occupation of land and unauthorized construction is dealt with in the title system and in the tax system also can be detrimental. In some property tax systems only completely "legal" properties can be taxed; otherwise, the act of taxation can be seen as recognizing an as yet unrecognized ownership claim or as condoning unauthorized construction. Advocates of reform take the position that title registration and taxation are separate governmental functions. Taxation of an identifiable plot of land or of an actual albeit illegally constructed building does not necessarily signify recognition of a title claim or condone the construction. To do otherwise provides incentives to avoid title registration and to ignore planning and construction regulations by freeing such properties from taxation.

In a similar vein, governments sometimes take the position that only data from official government sources can be used in assessment and taxation even when it is clear that the data are erroneous. Thus, only declared prices will be considered even when under-declaration is widely recognized.

Another barrier to effective property taxation is the policy of requiring personal service of tax bills to establish a tax obligation. This makes it easy for an owner to avoid or evade property taxation by refusing to accept a bill, being away from the property or address of record, or otherwise concealing ownership. Such policies also provide opportunities for corruption. Countries perceived to have higher levels of corruption, as measured by Transparency International's corruption perception index (Transparency International 2004), tend to have tax systems that yield less, as measured by taxes as a percentage of GDP. Why this is so, as with many facets of tax policy and practice, remains to be discovered.

References

Alm, J., J.A. Holman, and R. Neumann. 2002. "Globalization and state/local government finances," http://aysps.gsu.edu/publications/2002/globalization.pdf (accessed August 3, 2008).

Almy, R. 2003. Modernizing property taxes: The case study of Lithuania. *Fair & Equitable* (December 2003). 7–11.

———. 2001 *A survey of property tax systems in Europe*. A report prepared for the Ministry of Finance of Slovenia.

Bahl, R., J. Martinez-Vazquez, and J. Youngman, eds. 2007. *Making the property tax work: Experiences in developing and transitional countries.* Cambridge, MA: Lincoln Institute of Land Policy.

Bird, R.M., and E. Slack, eds. 2004. *International handbook of land and property taxation.* Cheltenham, U.K.: Edward Elgar.

Brown, P.K., and M. Hepworth. 2001. *A study of European land tax systems.* Working Paper Series. Cambridge, MA: Lincoln Institute of Land Policy.

Central Intelligence Agency. 2008. *The world factbook,* https://www.cia.gov/library/publications/the-world-factbook/ (accessed March 23, 2008).

Charles, C.M., ed. 1996. Major property tax issues in Africa. Paper given at a seminar organized by the Municipal Development Programme (MDP) for Eastern and Southern Africa, Harare, Zimbabwe, November 1995, http://www1.worldbank.org/wbiep/decentralization/afrlib/Afproptx.htm (accessed May 15, 2004).

Çopur, T. 2005. Turkish property tax system. Presentation at the OECD course on property taxation, Ankara, Turkey, October 10–14, 2005.

DeCesare, C. 2004. General characteristics of property tax systems in Latin America. Paper presented at the 7th International Conference of the International Property Tax Institute on optimizing property tax systems in Latin America, Guadalajara, Jalisco, Mexico, September 28–October 1, 2004.

DeSoto, H. 2000. *The mystery of capital: Why capitalism triumphs in the West and fails everywhere else.* New York, N.Y.: Basic Books.

Dos Santos, P. 2004. "Survey on the Caribbean tax systems," http://www.caricom.org/jsp/community/cota/general_assembly/18cota-surveyontaxsystems.pdf (accessed August 3, 2008).

Dos Santos, P., and L. Bain. 2004. "Survey of the Caribbean tax systems," http://www.caricom.org/jsp/community/cota/general_assembly/18cota-caricom-tax-system-survey.pdf (accessed August 3, 2008).

Färnkvist, O. 2004. Real estate property valuation and taxation in Sweden. Presentation at the OECD course on property taxation, Ankara, Turkey, May 10–14, 2004.

Federal Land Cadastre Service of Russia. 2001. *Land (real estate) mass valuation systems for taxation purposes in Europe.* (A report prepared and published on behalf of the UN ECE Working Party on Land Administration). Moscow: Federal Land Cadastre Service of Russia.

Franzsen, R.C.D., and W.J. McCluskey. 2004. Ad valorem property taxation in Sub-Saharan Africa. Paper given at the 7th International Conference of the International Property Tax Institute, Guadalajara, Mexico, September 29–October 1, 2004.

Gieskes, J.G.E., R.M. Kathmann, H. Wessels, and J.B. van der Veen. 2002. How the Netherlands approaches property taxation. Panel presentation at the 2002 annual conference of the International Association of Assessing Officers,

International Monetary Fund. 2007. *Government finance statistics yearbook.* CD-ROM ed. Washington, DC: International Monetary Fund.

———. 2001. *Government finance statistics manual 2001* (GFSM 2001). Washington, DC: IMF, http://www.imf.org/external/pubs/ft/gfs/manual/index.htm (accessed June 25, 2008).

Kathmann, R.M., and M.Kuijper. 2006. How to evaluate valuation models? Presentation at the 2006 FIG conference, Munich, Germany, October 9, 2006, http://www.fig.net/pub/fig2006/ppt/ts07/ts07_01_kathmann_kuijper_ppt_0490.pdf (accessed July 26,

2008).

Kruimel. 1999. Property tax systems in the Netherlands. In *Property tax: An international comparative review.* W. McCluskey, ed. Aldershot, England: Ashgate.

Lados, M. 2003. Property taxation in Hungary: Historical introduction. Presentation at the OECD seminar on property tax reform and valuation, Budapest, Hungary, July 7–11 2003.

Latvia, State Land Service. 2008. Cadastral (mass) appraisal in Latvia. Presentation at the Lincoln Institute of Land Policy executive course on a market value-based mass appraisal system for taxation of real property, Riga, Latvia, June 9–13, 2008.

Malme, J.H., and J.M. Youngman, eds. 2001. *The development of property taxation in economies in transition: Case studies from Central and Eastern Europe.* (WBI Learning Resources Series). Washington: The World Bank.

Maurer, R, and A. Paugham. 2000. *Reform toward ad valorem property tax in transition economies: Fiscal and land use benefits.* (Land Use and Real Estate Initiative, Background Series 13). Washington, DC: The World Bank, http://www1.worldbank.org/wbiep/decentralization/ecalib/TGsum1.pdf.

McCluskey, W.J. 1999. *Property tax: An international comparative review.* Aldershot, England: Ashgate.

———, ed. 1991. *Comparative property tax systems.* Aldershot, England: Avebury.

McCluskey, W.J., and F. Plimmer. 2007. *The potential for the property tax in the 2004 accession countries of central and eastern Europe.* (RICS Research Paper Series). vol. 7, no. 17. London, U.K.: The Royal Institution of Chartered Surveyors.

Müller, A. 2003. Importance of the recurrent property tax in public finance, tax policy & fiscal decentralization. Paper presented at the international conference on property and land tax reform sponsored by the Institute of Revenues, Rating & Valuation, Tallinn, Estonia, June 2003.

———. 2000. Property taxes and valuation in Denmark. Paper presented at the OECD seminar on property tax reforms and valuation, Vienna, Austria, September 19–21, 2000 (with updates to 2005).

Organisation for Economic Co-operation and Development (OECD). Center on Tax Policy and Administration. Forum on Tax Administration. 2007. *Tax administration in OECD and selected Non-OECD countries: Comparative information series (2006),* http://www.oecd.org/dataoecd/47/49/37363448.pdf (accessed June 25, 2008).

———. 2007. Taxing power of local and regional governments in OECD countries. abstract, http://www.oecd.org/LongAbstract/0,3425,en_2649_201185_36451569_1_1_1_1,00.html; tables, http://www.oecd.org/dataoecd/28/33/36451568.pdf (accessed June 25, 2008).

Overchuk, A. 2005. Cadastral valuation of land in Russia and the introduction of the new land tax. Paper given at the 2006 annual conference of the International Association of

Assessing Officers, Anchorage, AK.

Öz, S. 2004. The Turkish property tax system. Presentation at the OECD seminar on property taxation, Ankara, Turkey, May 10–14, 2004.

Paugham, A. 1999. Ad valorem property taxation and transition economies. (ECSIN Working Paper No. 9). Washington, DC: The World Bank, http://www1.worldbank.org/wbiep/decentralization/library9/Esw-tax2.PDF (accessed August 3, 2008).

People's Republic of China, State Administration of Taxation. 2004. The introduction of property tax in China. Presentation at the OECD seminar on property taxation, Ankara, Turkey, May 10–14, 2004.

Péteri, G., and M. Lados. 2003. Local property taxation in Hungary. Paper given at an OECD property tax course, Budapest, Hungary.

Sellers, J.M. 2003. National local political economies and varieties of capitalism. Paper given at American Political Science Association Meeting, Philadelphia, PA, August 28–30, 2003, http://www.usc.edu/dept/polsci/sellers/Publications/Assets/National%20Local%20Political%20Economies%20and%20Varieties%20of%20CapitalismAPSA2003.pdf (accessed February 29, 2008).

ten Have, G.G.M. 1994. Taxes: A computer-assisted (mass) appraisal. Paper given at the International Conference on Property Taxation, Mass Appraisal, and Geographic Information Systems, Dublin, Ireland, April 13–15, 1994.

Transparency International. 2004. *Transparency international corruption perception index 2004,* http://www.transparency.org/publications/publications/annual_report_2004 (accessed March 18, 2008).

Vallner, R., and A. Juss. 2004. Estonian report on property taxes. Presentation at the OECD seminar on property taxation, Ankara, Turkey, May 10–14, 2004.

Youngman, J.M., and J.H. Malme, eds. 1994. *An international survey of taxes on land and buildings.* Deventer, Netherlands: Kluwer Law and Taxation Publishers.

Chapter 9
Prospects and Challenges

> *The property tax is a venerable, tough and resilient fiscal institution. It has survived assaults by generations of theorists and reformers, legislators, politicians, and taxpayers.*
>
> —Stocker 1991

This final chapter reviews the role of the assessing officer in property tax policy. It concludes with a discussion of the sustainability and likely future of the U.S. property tax as an institution.

Tax Policy and the Assessing Officer

Possible policy roles for an assessor are as follows:

- Providing the data necessary to craft such policy
- Acting as a the expert interpreter of the derivation and meaning of property tax data
- Serving as a policy advocate for widely accepted property tax principles and practices.

Examples of ways in which assessing officers provide information useful in a policy setting are given in Figure 9-1.

At the outset, the assessing officer usually is considered the administrator or implementer of tax policy. In the U.S. model, formulation of tax policy generally is reserved to the legislative and executive branches, with review by the judicial branch, of state government. While these entities establish the legal framework for the property tax and its administration, assessing officers and tax administrators ultimately administer these laws. Through this administrative process, assessors develop highly specialized knowledge that, if shared, can benefit policy makers, taxing districts, and the public that pays the tax and is served by property tax policies. The IAAO *Standard on Property Tax Policy* (2007) echoes this sentiment, stating in Section 2.1,

> Assessing officers should work continually with the issues involved in property tax administration to increase their knowledge of various property tax systems and should use this knowledge to improve the system.

FIGURE 9-1. Conceptual Approach to Reviewing Property Tax Policies and Practices

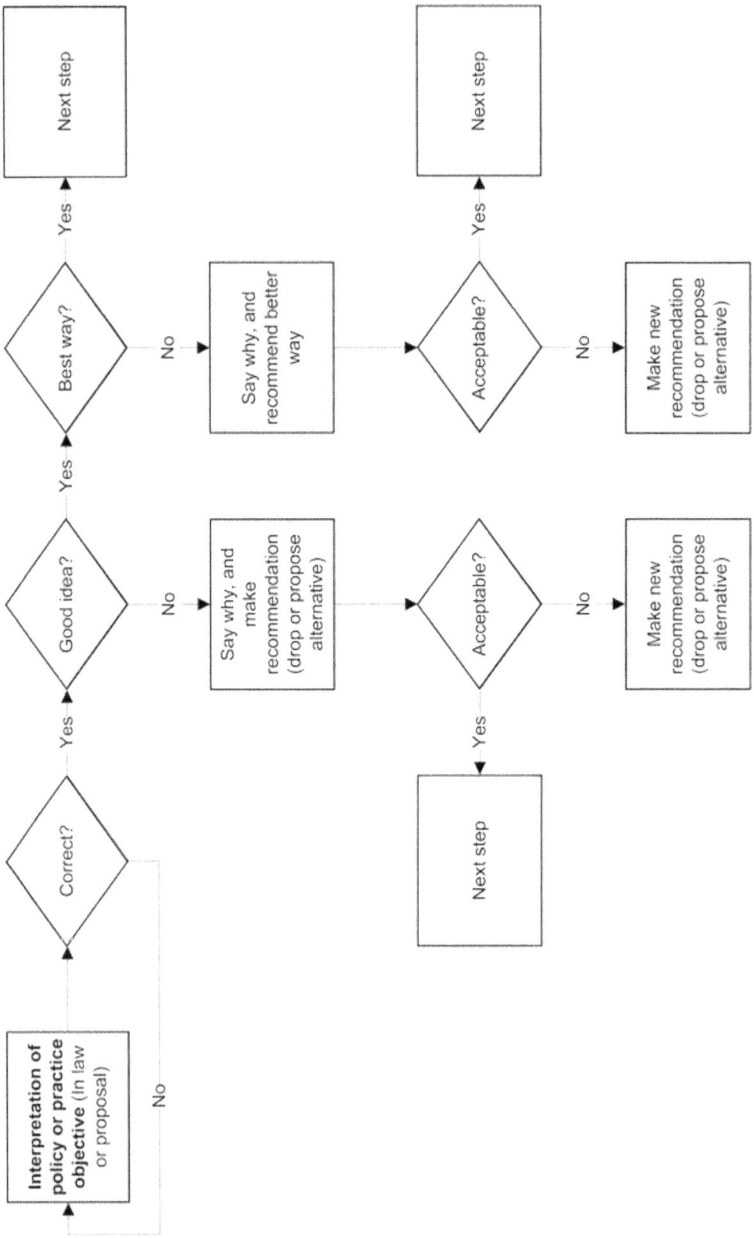

Because systems and roles differ from state to state and comparisons are inevitable, assessing officers should be able to identify widely used patterns to help evaluate their states' systems. A comprehensive recent review of property tax policy information, including roles and responsibilities of the different levels of government involved in property tax administration, is available in the IAAO publication *Property Tax Policies and Administrative Practices in Canada and the United States* (2000).

The legislature can pass laws that are administratively cumbersome and hamstring the assessment process. Alternatively, there can be an effective partnership between the legislative branch and those who administer the property tax. Most states (37) and Canadian provinces (8), for example, have effective sales disclosure laws, which provide assessors with information critical to establishing and testing the quality of assessments based on market value (Dornfest 2004). States have passed open records and truth-in-taxation laws, enhancing the ability of the public to obtain information on the valuation process and making the tax part of the system more visible. Appraiser certification programs have been established, and continuing professional education has been mandated.

Information Clearinghouse Roles
Provider of Property Tax Data

Analysts, citizens, and business people seek information on property tax institutions, assessment methods, and taxable property values from assessors. To the extent possible, the crafting of good property tax policy necessitates that the assessor respond to these inquiries. Publications and Web postings with answers to frequently asked questions on a jurisdiction's property tax institutions and assessment practices facilitate responding to these questions. Furthermore, data on a jurisdiction's property tax values should be kept—in as much detail as legally allowed and possible—in an up-to-date, error-free spreadsheet or database. A description of the information in the spreadsheet and a glossary of terms also should be available to policy analysts or practitioners using these data. If privacy provisions allow it, such information should be posted on a Web site. Table 9-1 provides some conceptual examples.

TABLE 9-1. Examples of Useful Information Sharing by Assessing Officers

Example	Audience	Value
Land records information	Governmental planners and private developers	Assists in understanding distribution of various property types and in analyzing infrastructure needs.
Valuation (taxation) statistics compiled by class of property	Public, legislature	Increases understanding of predominance of various classes of property (greater value if converted to proportional shares of tax burden).
Exemption information, including value, tax effects, and participation rates	Public, legislature	Increases understanding of usefulness and appropriateness of exemptions and tax credits.

For both administrative and general tax issues, legislators need credible, accurate, objective, and timely information to understand all aspects of property taxation. Although assessing officers often understand the administrative aspects of such issues, they should broaden their knowledge of the interrelationships throughout the property tax structure. Then they can help clarify the issues and enable legislators to better understand the problem and focus on the appropriate solution. For example, if assessing officers point out that a newly proposed exemption for farm equipment would shift a significant share of the property tax burden onto homeowners in farming communities, legislators may be able to provide substitute revenue to taxing jurisdictions to prevent the tax shift. Without timely information explaining the interrelation among property classes, exemptions, and the distribution of the tax, legislators can create new exemptions and other changes whose effects are far different than they intended.

Assessing officers must develop ways of responding to lawmakers' concerns. For example, assume these concerns lead lawmakers to provide a new exemption or preferential treatment perceived as increasing fairness and equity. Assessing officers can be responsive by becoming knowledgeable about the issues leading to this conclusion. They can and should address the following points:

- Is the issue real? Does it affect a definable group or type of property, or does it result from a specific and highly unusual set of circumstances unlikely to recur?
- Is the proposal understandable? Can it be administered effectively and accomplish its nominal goal?
- Does the proposal have unanticipated side effects that could create more or new inequities?
- Is there a better way to address the issue at hand?

To answer these questions effectively, assessing officers must develop a thorough understanding of the interrelationships of the various components of the current property tax system. Analysis often requires data so that effects can be quantified. Databases designed for appraising and maintaining land records should be flexible and accessible so that these analyses can be performed without additional resources. Access to data maintained in centralized (state) repositories may also be needed.

In addition to information tailored to respond to specific proposals and situations, assessing officers and legislators need to understand and have available basic property tax facts, such as the proportion of assessed value and property tax paid by different classes of property and the proportion used by different taxing districts. These facts will help the assessor address issues such as those listed in Table 9-1. Tables 9-2 and 9-3 demonstrate the use of these facts to compile information based on actual proportions in Idaho in 2006. (This information can be found on the Idaho State Tax Commission Web site ["2006 Market Values and Property Taxes and the Effects of the Homeowner's Exemption," http://tax.idaho.gov/propertytax/PTpdfs/2006mkt_value_ptax2.pdf].)

The type of information shown in Table 9-2 is especially useful in dispelling common myths about which class of property pays the predominant share of the property tax. Once charts like this have been developed, they should be maintained and updated annually, so that long-term trends can be established and analyzed. Short-term trends are important as well and can be discerned from year-to-year comparisons. The percentage change in property taxes shown in the last column of Table 9-2 demonstrates the effect of a legislative policy change whereby school general maintenance and operations revenue was no longer levied as property tax beginning in 2006. Further, the table shows that, since owner-occupied residential property paid about 41 percent of all property tax in 2006, that percentage of the school tax reduction could be attributed to such residential property. This inference in turn can lead to discussions about replacement funds and whether the same class of taxpayers can expect to pay more or less overall tax.

TABLE 9-2. Proportion of Property Tax Paid by Various Property Classes in Idaho in 2006

Category of Property	Portion of Taxable Value in Category (%)	Estimated 2006 Property Tax Rate (%)	Portion of Property Tax in Category (%)	Change in Property Tax 2005–2006 (%)
Residential*	68.6	0.955	64.0	−10.3
Owner-occupied	38.8	1.085	41.1	−12.8
Other residential	29.8	0.786	22.9	−5.4
Commercial	22.6	1.274	28.1	−10.6
Agricultural	3.8	0.944	3.5	−21.7
Timber	0.8	0.780	0.6	−31.3
Mining	0.7	0.454	0.3	−7.8
Operating (utilities)	3.5	1.012	3.5	−20.8

The type of information shown in Table 9-3 is especially useful in dispelling myths about how much of the property tax is used for various governmental purposes and again shows the dramatic effect of removing most Idaho school general funding from the property tax in 2006. By making data available and accessible and by providing information designed to enhance understanding of the components and structure of the property tax system and its administration, assessing officers can fulfill an important information clearinghouse role. In addition, the information can be used to "...help shape

TABLE 9-3. Who Spends the Property Tax in Idaho

Taxing Jurisdiction	Portion of Total Property Tax (%)	
	2005	2006
Schools	42.7	30.3
Counties	22.7	26.9
Cities	21.8	26.8
Highway districts	5.3	6.6
Other special districts	7.5	9.5

debate, define the administrative requirements of a policy proposal, call attention to problems that might be created by a policy..." (IAAO 2004, 5).

Interpreter of Property Tax Data

Once analysts, citizens, and business people have used tax information provided by the assessor's office, they will ask follow-up questions about these data, hence the recommendation to provide information in an easy, interpretable form. Nevertheless, the assessor should be prepared to offer assistance and appreciate what good teachers learn early on, "There is no such thing as a stupid question."

Policy Advocate

Perhaps the most difficult, controversial, and potentially rewarding role that a property tax assessor can be asked to play is that of policy advocate. This role requires that the assessor be both knowledgeable and policy-connected.

To act as a policy advocate, an assessor needs to be aware of the difference between a positive and a normative statement. A positive statement is based purely on fact and includes no value judgments. An example of a positive statement is, "If homeowners move in and out of a neighborhood with nearly identical homes and if acquisition value is used for assessment, different homeowners will pay different property taxes for the same local services." A normative statement relies on some form of value judgment. An example of a statement requiring an assessor's value judgment is, "Acquisition value assessment is preferred (or not preferred) to market value assessment."

Assessors who analyze property tax policy should try to keep advocacy within the positive realm. When making normative statements in offering policy advice, assessors should acknowledge that this is their opinion and cannot necessarily be supported by the facts alone. Beyond knowing this distinction between positive and normative statements, the assessor should make sure that any normative statements are accurate. This requires that assessors know the specifics of the law and policy-making practices for property taxation in their jurisdiction and state.

Finally, an effective policy advocate needs to think like a policy analyst. Assessing officers should define a policy problem without including a specific solution in the statement of the problem. An example of how to appropriately define a policy problem would be, "The revenues of local governments in the United States are less than what it costs to provide the goods demanded from them." On the other hand, an inappropriate way of defining this policy problem is, "Local governments should raise local property tax rates to cover their shortfalls in revenue." The second statement clearly includes a value judgment and assumes the answer to the policy problem within the statement that defines it.

Once a policy analyst has defined a policy problem in an appropriate manner, he or she should suggest specific alternatives or solutions. For instance, for the above problem of a shortfall in local government revenue, solutions could be to increase local property taxes, sales taxes, fees, and so on or to make citizens more aware of the real cost of local government services in the hope that their demand for them will decrease and so will the shortfall. Once reasonable alternatives have been suggested, they can be evaluated by the policy analyst based on an agreed-upon set of criteria that are equally applied to each alternative. If raising local property taxes is identified as the preferred solution to a revenue shortfall, justification will be more apparent if the solution is developed in a normative manner.

Problems versus Solutions

Sometimes what is perceived as a system problem, requiring legislative remedy, is actually an administrative or communication problem, which can be addressed quite differently. Assessing officers need to understand distinctions between these situations and seek to maintain adequate dialogue with policy makers so there is opportunity to air and address concerns. For example, it is usually better to review office procedures to determine whether eligible farmland is receiving an appropriate exemption or use value, than to have eligible farmland owners seek legislation to broaden the farmland exemption because of administrative misunderstandings and poor communication.

In an attempt to bridge the communication gap, many assessing officers are establishing focus groups, technical advisory committees, stakeholder groups, and the like. Useful information on a Web site is an excellent tool for gaining better public understanding of the property tax system. Professional Web sites with accurate records, digital photographs, building footprints, and supporting maps should not be underestimated; they demonstrate the transparency and consistency of the property tax system. Some assessment agencies have public information officers dedicated to improving communication and standardizing the information that is made available.

The Property Tax as an Institution

The U.S. property tax is a venerable institution, with roots in the colonial era. The tax has evolved substantially, in terms of both tax base and tax utilization. The tax base began with the nearly all-inclusive general property tax of the nineteenth century, was reconstituted as a tax on most real and personal property for much of the twentieth century, and, increasingly, has become a tax on real property (land and buildings) in the early twenty-first century. As noted in Chapter 1, "Introduction to Tax Policy," even more dramatic has been the change in utilization—from a major source of state government revenue to a sustaining source of revenue for local governments, with only limited state use. Even for local governments, property tax use is challenged, and these governments have been pressured by political and populist forces to look for alternative revenue sources. The commentary associated with the information in Tables 9-2 and 9-3 demonstrates one state's experience with and response to these pressures, as the Idaho governor called a rare special session of the Idaho Legislature for one day in August 2006 for the sole purpose of repealing (and replacing with state aid and a 1 percent increase in the state sales tax rate) most Idaho school general property taxes. The enacting legislation can be found at http://www3.state.id.us/oasis/2006spcl/H0001.html (accessed August 7, 2008)

Although Idaho chose a pathway that, at least initially, led to less reliance on property tax for school finance, several states have dealt with local disparities in school property tax revenue by replacing local property taxes with state property taxes, which could be more uniform. The Michigan experience of the mid-1990s provides an example of both a reduction in property taxes and a shift from local to state property taxes (Wassmer and Fisher 1996). This model has since been adopted in at least two additional states (New Hampshire and Vermont) and one Canadian province (Alberta).

All funding choices have multiple layers of effects, some of which are not readily apparent. The Idaho choice appeared to lower reliance on property tax, and did so initially. In the year following the implementation of substitute funding, however, atypically large voter-approved property tax overrides and bonds for schools were approved. Was this an indirect result of perceived additional property tax capacity? Will it lead to further pressures to relieve the property tax?

Although the major Michigan property tax reforms of the 1990s differed from the proposals discussed above, it is valuable to reflect on this example of real-world reform in action.

In FY 1993–1994, local property taxes in Michigan provided two-thirds of the revenue needed in the state for the provision of K-12 public education (Fisher 2007, 363–364). Just one year later, local property taxes provided only one-fourth of the state's public school revenue, while statewide property taxes provided about 7 percent. How did such a radical reduction in property taxation come about in such a short time? A quick examination of the Michigan case offers an excellent example of the economic and political forces that have driven, and continue to drive, property tax reform (reductions) in the United States.

The roots of property tax reform in the United States go back 30 years to the early 1970s, when concerns were raised about inequalities in per-student property tax bases across local school districts that resulted in inter-district inequalities in per-student spending. These perceived inequalities are of special concern because most state constitutions guarantee their residents an "equal" public education. U.S. state courts have responded to this concern by forcing implementation of solutions that have effectively moved states away from their reliance on local property taxes for the provision of local public education. In addition, citing the need to offer a competitive business climate, economic development officials have become increasingly concerned about the degree of local property taxation imposed. Furthermore, as demonstrated by the now-defunct ACIR polls dating back to the 1970s, only about 10 percent of Americans believe that a local property tax increase is the preferred way to raise a small amount of additional local revenue.

A 1999 update of the ACIR survey showed the local property taxes as considered the "least fair" of all state and local taxes and of all U.S. taxes except the federal income tax. In this more recent poll, 29% picked the property tax as least fair, while only 16% chose the state sales tax and 11% chose the state income tax. (Cole and Kincaid 2001)

Thus, state policy makers have sought to reduce schools' reliance on property taxes as a means of equalizing local public school spending, winning voter support, and furthering the cause of state and local economic development. This melding of motives for equalizing local per-pupil spending in public schools, along with increasing pressure from individuals and economic development officials for property tax cuts, goes a long way toward explaining property tax cuts in the United States and Michigan.

At least in the case of Michigan, its significant reduction in property tax reliance to fund public school expenditures would not have occurred without the political environment that existed in that state in 1993.

By 1993, Michigan voters had faced 12 different initiatives that had asked them to approve various forms of school finance and property tax reform. The motivation for these initiatives, at least in part, was the failure of the state's 20-year-old system of power-equalized aid to local school districts to alleviate larger per-pupil spending differences. However, all the initiatives, which substituted some form of statewide tax for a reduction in local property taxes for schools, had been rejected. As an example, in June 1993, Michigan voters rejected Proposal A—by a 54 percent margin—which would have cut local school property taxes by 30 percent and raised the flat rate of the state's personal income tax from 4 percent to 6 percent to replace the lost revenue.

In response to the rejection of Proposal A, in the summer of 1993, Republicans in the state legislature proposed property tax cuts that received strong support from Michigan's Republican Governor Engler, but only lukewarm support from Democrats in the legislature. To the surprise of many, and likely motivated by a growing dislike for the inherent inequity they generate in per-pupil spending, in September 1993, a Democratic state representative proposed the elimination of all local property taxes for public schools beginning in FY 1994–95. Even though no form of replacement revenue was mentioned, the truly radical bill passed, and work immediately began in the Michigan legislature on a way to replace the lost revenue of $6.5 billion (or 20 percent of total state expenditures). A final agreement on possible forms of revenue replacement was not reached until December 24, 1993.

The legislative agreement called for a March 1995 referendum to raise the state's sales tax rate from 4 to 6 percent, to slightly lower the flat rate of state income taxation, to raise the rate of cigarette taxation, to implement an acquisition value system of property tax assessment on primary residential property that would limit yearly nonsale assessment increases to the lesser of inflation or 5 percent, and to institute a system of lower statewide property taxes. If this referendum failed, legislation would automatically go into effect to raise the state's personal income and business tax rates. Perhaps not surprisingly, given the choice, the referendum was adopted by Michigan voters with a 65 percent majority (Wassmer and Fisher 1996).

Sustainability Issues

Although major advantages and disadvantages of the property tax are discussed at length in Chapter 3, "Fundamental Elements of the Property Tax," and Chapter 4, "Role of Intergovernmental Finance," many of these factors are relevant in discussing the sustainability of the property tax. Table 9-4 reiterates some of the key positive attributes of the property tax.

TABLE 9-4. Key Arguments Favoring the Property Tax

Attribute	Discussion
A principal funding source for local governments	No clear or widely acceptable replacement mechanisms are available; the property tax remains key to sustainability of local government autonomy.
Administrative system is in place and operating at higher level of government than local units that utilize the tax	Local units of government do not need redundant collection or enforcement systems, since most property tax administration is centralized at municipal or county level.
Reliable and stable source of revenue	Property tax collections can vary somewhat with the underlying economy, but generally are more resistive to major and rapid upswings or downturns than other tax types. In addition, property tax revenue is the only revenue that can be ascertained for budgeting purposes before it is received.
Important component of a diversified and balanced tax structure	By preventing over-reliance on one type of tax, the property tax becomes a component of a more equitable taxation system that involves all citizens as taxpayers without overburdening any one sector or permitting some sector to escape participation in the costs of government.
Visible, accessible, accountable, and transparent	Property tax records tend to be in the public domain. With the predominance of local administration, appeals are accomplished as the local level and, generally, without requiring significant legal and financial resources. Often, local assessors are elected. In addition, the taxpayer usually is notified of the specific taxing districts that will use the payments and may be invited to budget hearings for these districts.

Property tax is necessary to provide a balanced tax system, with taxpayers reflecting a broad cross section of society and receiving benefits from the tax. Modern property taxes tend to provide revenue for local, rather than state, government, and it is often contended that there "...are no taxes capable of financing our current system of local governments that can be locally levied and administered, except the property tax." (Fisher 1996).

These local governments tend to be small geographically, with considerable autonomy to provide specialized services within a unique service area. Alternative funding mechanisms are sales or income taxes, user fees, and state aid. None of these mechanisms has proven totally adequate, so, despite public dislike of the property tax, no state has eliminated it, and academicians and public policy experts are much less apt to condemn it. In 1934 and 1994 surveys by academic economists, 85 percent of those surveyed indicated that property tax should be retained as a major source of local government revenue. Hence, despite the advent of many alternative funding mechanisms during those 60 years, support for the property tax was unchanged (Slemrod 1995).

From the public policy perspective, the property tax has been labeled, "A good tax under siege" (Brunori 2003). This siege has forced local governments to increase reliance on nontax revenue, notably, intergovernmental aid and user fees and charges. Intergovernmental aid constitutes external revenue, because it is not under the control of the local government that receives the aid. Sustainability of such aid during economic contractions that place pressure on state budgets (from which most of the aid is derived) is dubious at best. Regardless of sustainability, such aid lessens local autonomy and spending restrictions can be attached. While user fees can be efficient means of financing public services, the base of users is limited and therefore the fees are inadequate to meet the demand for widely available services (Brunori 2003).

Aside from administrative issues related to local sales or income taxes, complete state funding would lessen the accountability of local governments and disconnect them from their constituencies. Funding distribution formulas would be difficult to conceive, and tax shifting inevitably would occur. Elimination of the property tax would have the effect of moving—not ending—the arguments about taxation.

Potential Solutions to Aspects of Property Tax Considered Unfair

Regardless of public support for services provided by local governments and the seeming impossibility of funding these services without a major role for the property tax, the public continues to view the property tax as "unfair" or "too high." As an example, the *17th Annual Idaho Public Policy Survey* (Social Science Research Center 2006) reported the following findings:

- Similar percentages of Idahoans believe that they get the most from their tax money at the local (36.1%) and state (33.2%) levels of government.
- 22.6% of Idahoans think that the local property tax is the least fair tax followed by 18.0% who think the federal income tax is the least fair.
- Although 48.2% of Idahoans believe that the local property tax is too high, 42.9% think it is about right.

This reinforces the typical pattern—support for services provided with property tax funding but opposition to the property tax itself. Table 9-5 identifies common reasons for the dislike of the property tax and potential solutions.

TABLE 9-5. Property Tax Issues and Solutions

Issue	Potential Solution
In an inflationary environment, the tax falls on unrealized capital gains and can fall more heavily on fixed-income households.	Target exemptions or tax credits (circuit breakers, deferrals, or others) to fixed- or limited-income households.
Large, lump-sum payments make the amount of the tax more obvious.	Permit and encourage installment payments.
Property appraisals and their relationship to property taxes are poorly understood.	Conduct frequent, highly visible reappraisals; initiate outreach efforts by assessment officials; show estimated taxes on assessment notices.
Appraisals may be perceived as poor quality and therefore inequitable.	Provide visible state or local oversight; perform effective ratio studies; have well-trained and responsive staff.
The tax sometimes has no obvious tie to the type of services being funded; for example, the value of property does not correlate well to the proportionate share of educational services needed.	Hold public meetings to emphasize the balanced system provided by the property tax; explain that without a property tax component for school funding, for example, some property owners would contribute little or nothing to this governmental function.
The tax is too complex and too costly to administer.	Part of the complexity and costs occur because the process is intended to be visible to the public and transparency is encouraged. The public should be encouraged to review records, file appeals, and attend taxing district budget hearings.
Exemptions unfairly favor and distort the tax, often shifting tax burden to real property.	Analyze exemptions thoroughly and ensure broad need and applicability. Consider applications and sunset provisions to ensure re-examination.

Countering a Populist Argument

Populists, including many legislators, often anecdotally point to the fact that some people of limited income end up owning land or property with a high market value and thus end up paying high property taxes. The anecdotes that are relied on are often based on farm land or resort property (such as a home on a lake) that has become more valuable as a result of recent phenomena, such as development or recreational desirability of adjacent parcels.

This situation is not the general case, but rather a special case in which an area becomes gentrified or is in greater demand than previously. This increase in demand raises land and fixed property values in that area. If a market-based system of assessment is used, this raises the property tax payments of people owning property in that area. In most cases, the people who own such property are individuals with higher incomes. However, the case could be made for a rural lake surrounded by properties owned by low- to middle-income residents, which later became popular as a place to build a "trophy" home. In the case of low-income residents living in an established central city neighborhood, high-income individuals sometimes move in, tearing down existing homes and building larger, more valuable homes. This gentrification raises land values for low- and moderate-income individuals in those areas, and they pay higher property taxes if their property is assessed in relation to market value. The important point is that this is more the exception than the rule, and it does not change the overall finding that property taxes as a whole are progressive.

Policy makers are correctly concerned about this exception because it does cause a low-income person to devote a higher percentage of his or her income to these taxes. However, measures such as the circuit-breaker programs (discussed later) are appropriate solutions to dealing with such cases. One counterargument, which is not typically accepted politically, is that formerly low-income people are no longer so after this increase in land values. Their potential income has risen due to the increased value of land in these circumstances. They can tap into this potential income to pay these higher property taxes.

In some situations, low-income people devote a greater percentage of their income to property taxes than high-income people. According to economists, however, this situation does not exist frequently enough to counter the New View conclusion that given a certain level of local services, high property tax rates reduce the value of land (as measured by the selling price or rental rate) in the community. Because high-income people receive a greater portion of their overall income from land holdings than low-income people, high property taxes, or the depressed land values they generate, fall upon high-income people to a greater extent than upon low-income people. This makes the overall system of state and local property taxation in the United States a progressive tax (i.e., high-income people pay a greater percentage of their income in property taxes than low-income people). Furthermore, as pointed out in Chapter 6, tax deferral and circuit-breaker programs can be used to craft a more precise, targeted solution that maintains the underlying market value concepts of the property tax, but grants relief where needed.

Stabilizing the Property Tax

The public tends to support taxes that are predictable and do not change rapidly in short periods of time. A market-value-based property tax meets these criteria as a stable tax, provided the following underlying conditions exist and persist:

- Revenue needs of government supported by property tax do not change dramatically from year to year.
- The proportional share of the tax base represented by a given property (and its market value) does not change substantially from year to year.

In stable markets, without infrastructure crises, these conditions tend to remain true. However, U.S. infrastructure needs are growing, and in the years immediately preceding 2007, in any case, market value increases were extreme in many areas. This was particularly true for the housing market, and property tax systems based primarily on current market value have demonstrated increases in the proportional share of tax borne by this sector. Regardless of whether such situations stabilize in the long run, there is always pressure for immediate relief, especially for homeowners.

Common legislative responses to these situations have included the following:

- Limits on assessed value increases
- Limits on total property tax increases
- Truth-in-taxation systems
- Circuit breakers, tax deferrals, and homestead exemptions.

These measures are discussed in detail in Chapter 6. However, some additional comments are warranted as part of this discussion of potential remedies that assessing officers and policy makers may wish to review or propose (Youngman and Malme 2005).

- *Expanding the circuit-breaker concept.* While the premise of a circuit-breaker program is that it is needs based, such programs can be broad or narrow, depending on the income and benefit limits that are chosen. Notably, many states have not changed income or benefit limits rapidly enough to keep up with inflation and tax shifts. Some states have adopted automatic inflation adjustment procedures, which have the advantage of not requiring additional legislation each time an adjustment is necessary.
- *Combining tax deferral with tax forgiveness.* Recently, at least one state has combined tax deferral with forgiveness, meaning that part of deferred taxes never needs to be paid back.
- *Creating a default tax deferral program.* At the time this text was being prepared (early 2008), several states were considering default-based tax deferrals

for homeowners. Under such a concept, delinquent property taxes and interest automatically accrue with respect to primary residential property.

- *Expanding homestead-type partial exemptions.* Many such exemptions are based on specific dollar amounts (i.e, $20,000 in value) that are changed infrequently through legislative action. Recently, at least one state (Idaho) changed its law to require annual adjustment tied to the federally established housing price index applicable to that state. This type of adjustment tends to enable such partial exemptions to keep pace with property appreciation (at least regionally, if not locally) and tends to mitigate tax shifting during periods with significant market value increases.

- *Rate classification.* Although rate classification is constitutionally prohibited by some states' uniformity clauses, some states, such as Massachusetts, have limited the permitted shift from commercial to residential property that otherwise would occur (in some areas) by specifying different (lower) maximum property tax rates for residential and commercial classes of property.

- *Alternative tax collection methods.* The difficulties of lump-sum payments for taxpayers are well-known. These problems can be eased by allowing credit card use or more frequent payment schedules.

- *Frequent reassessment.* Frequent reassessment of property means smaller, less dramatic shifts and changes. Values upon which taxes are based are also more understandable to taxpayers.

In reality, some taxpayers have unreasonable expectations that property taxes *always* need to be lower while public services are still high. These taxpayers assert that taxes are too high without considering that utilities, home maintenance, cable television, and many other economic issues are contributory factors. If assessing officers and legislators rush to accept these quick fixes to reduce criticism, they will only make the system weaker. In some states, for example, the 3 percent cap on value increases was touted as an end to controversy. Yet within a year or so after the 3 percent cap was in place, there were complaints that it was too high and proposals were presented to lower it to 2 percent or 1 percent or to freeze it.

The Future of the Property Tax

Property taxes are likely to continue as a major source of local government tax revenue for the foreseeable future, not only in the United States but also in other countries with a strong interest in effective, accountable local government. This is not to say that current property tax institutions will not continue to be challenged. Politically empowered groups will continue to seek relief from what they perceive as a high level of property taxation or from higher taxes occasioned by either increases in government spending or increases in market values. The array of fiscal controls and relief measures likely will increase as different governments respond to such challenges in various ways. The link between assessed values and property taxes actually paid and the current market value of properties may become ever more tenuous.

The market value standard likely will remain economically and professionally prized. Advances in valuation methods, the use of information technology (particularly the use of GIS), and methods for analyzing tax burdens likely will draw on current market prices. Both value estimates and perceptions of patterns in tax burdens will become more objective. Pressures to strengthen both standards of practice and the qualifications of property tax officials likely will continue, perhaps resulting in a virtuous circle of continued improvement in technical performance. Technical and professional advancements will make it easier for scholars and policy makers to employ a coherent framework for policy analysis that may enable them to avoid "…long-term consequences that will make government more remote and even less responsive" (Fisher 1996).

Of course, it is impossible to forecast future economic and political upheavals or their effects on the property tax as an institution. Future asset-price bubbles like that seen in the United States housing market in the first decade of the twenty-first century certainly could prove destabilizing. That phenomenon, however, aroused interest in whether nonresidential property was being assessed as accurately as residential property. That may lead to a similar line of inquiry about the gradual narrowing of the property tax base in the United States since the nineteenth century.

The property tax base has been moving away from intangible and toward tangible assets, particularly focusing only on real property, and not on movable property. Hence, intangibles, such as intellectual properties, represent a large and growing amount of wealth that is less and less subject to property tax. Studies have shown that, since 1977, there has been a marked decrease in the ratio of potentially taxable property to GDP, as the value added by intangible assets is ignored in the property tax base (for good practical reasons, particularly for a local tax). Although this finding does not suggest elimination of the property tax, it does portend continuing narrowing of the property tax base (Tannenwald 2002).

However, increasing mobility associated with globalization can be expected to diminish the importance of taxes "…that are more affected by the mobility issues of capital and trade (e.g., the corporate income tax)" (Alm, Chen, and Wallace 2003). This in turn could increase the importance of property taxes, which are based on less mobile sources. Thus, the quest for wise property tax policy and practice likely will continue, not only in the United States but around the world. Policy makers and practitioners can benefit from the lessons learned from these experiments. Beleaguered assessors also can take heart from defenders of the property tax, such as Brunori (Brunori 2005).

References

Alm, J., S. Chen, and S. Wallace. 2003. State and local governments' susceptibility to globalization. *State Tax Notes*.

Brunori, D. 2003. *Local tax policy*. Washington, DC: The Urban Institute Press.

———. 2005. Assess this: Why you should stop whining and learn to love the property tax. *Fair & Equitable* 3 (11): 3–5.

Cole, R.L. and J. Kincaid. 2001. Public Opinion and American Federalism: Perspectives on Taxes, Spending, and Trust. *Spectrum: The Journal of State Government*, Summer, 2001, as cited in: Fisher, R.C. *State and local public finance*, 3d ed. 13 (318). OH: Thomson, South-Western.

Dornfest, A., and D.C. Thompson. 2004. State and provincial ratio study practices: 2003 survey results. *Journal of Property Tax Assessment and Administration* 1 (1):31–70.

Fisher, G.W. 1996. *The worst tax?: A story of the property tax in America*. Lawrence, KS: The University Press of Kansas.

Fisher, R.J. 2007. *State and local public finance*, 3rd ed. Mason, OH: South-Western College Publishing.

International Association of Assessing Officers (IAAO). 2004. *Standard on property tax policy*. Chicago, IL: IAAO.

———. 2000. *Property tax policies and administrative practices in Canada and the United States*. Chicago, IL: IAAO.

Slemrod, J. 1995. Professional opinions about tax policy: 1994 and 1934. *National Tax Journal* 48 (1):121–147

Social Science Research Center. 2006. *17th Annual Idaho public policy survey*. Boise, ID: Boise State University, April.

Stocker, F.B., ed. 1991. *Proposition 13: A ten-year retrospective*. Cambridge, MA: Lincoln Institute of Land Policy.

Tannenwald, R. 2002. Are state and local revenue systems becoming obsolete? In *National League of Cities Metropolitan Policy Program*. Washington, DC: The Brookings Institution, pp. 15–17.

Wassmer, R.W., and R.C. Fisher. 1996. An evaluation of the recent move to centralize the finance of public schools in Michigan. *Public Budgeting and Finance* 16 (3): 90–112.

Youngman, J., and J. Malme. 2005. Stabilizing property taxes in volatile real estate markets. *Land Lines* (Cambridge, MA: Lincoln Institute of Land Policy) (July).

Appendix A
Regressivity versus Progressivity of the Property Tax

The issue of who ultimately pays property taxes is usually broken down into a comparison of whether people with high incomes devote a larger, smaller, or equal percentage of their income to this expenditure than people with low incomes. This determination of income incidence is an important factor in society's evaluation of the fairness and ultimate desirability of using property taxation as a revenue instrument for the provision of government services.

The academic debate on this issue has been divided into three camps: the traditional view, the new view, and the benefit view. The traditional and new views separate the forms of property that are taxed into land (immobile factors) and structures (mobile factors), and rely on separate market (supply and demand) models of land and structures to predict the final income incidence of property taxation. For these analyses, land and structures are assumed to have both an owner (supplier) and a renter (demander). If someone owns a piece of property and uses it for his or her own purpose, that individual takes on the role of both owner and renter. The traditional and new views reach different conclusions on income incidence based upon the models' different underlying assumptions. One important assumption in both the traditional and new views, nevertheless, is that the local provisions of goods and services are not affected by local changes in the property tax rate. Local governments rely on alternative revenue sources to provide the same level of services when the rate of property taxation is cut.

The Traditional View

The traditional view of who pays property taxes assumes that the supply of land in a jurisdiction levying a property tax is fixed. Thus, if a tax on land is put in place, the after-tax return of the land falls by the full amount of the tax, and the owner of land bears the full burden of the tax. The traditional view also assumes that the supply of structures in a jurisdiction is infinitely elastic at a market rate of return, which is determined throughout the economy. This means that a city can continue to get builders to put up additional structures in its jurisdiction, as long as the return on these structures equals the market rate of return generated everywhere. In this case, if a property tax is levied on structures in a jurisdiction, the rate of return from a structure (determined by the rental income stream) in that jurisdiction must rise by the full amount of the tax. If it does not rise, then existing structures will no longer attract investors in the jurisdiction and no new structures will be built there. This reduction in the supply of structures drives up rental rates in the jurisdiction. As a result, those who demand these structures, or renters, pay the full property tax.

Under the traditional view, the land portion of property taxes is borne by landowners in proportion to the fraction of income they receive from land rents. Because high-income people receive a larger portion of their income from land rent than low-income people, this portion of the property tax is considered progressive (high-income people devote a greater percentage of their income to it than low-income people). Following the model used in the traditional view, the structure portion of the property tax is borne by people in proportion to the fraction of their income devoted to housing. Because in any given year low-income people devote a greater portion of their income to housing expenses than high-income people, the structure portion of the tax is viewed as regressive. There is some evidence, however, that the structure portion of this finding changes if examined over a lifetime of housing consumption (in which low- and high-income people are more likely to devote equal percentages of lifetime income to housing). Most ignore this lifecycle finding and conclude that the structure portion of the property tax under the traditional view is regressive. Because the percentage of property tax revenue collected from structures is larger than the percentage collected from land, the conclusion reached using the traditional view is that the property tax is regressive in its income incidence.

The New View

Alternatively, the new view considers property taxation to be a general tax on capital (which includes both land and structures) throughout the United States, with some jurisdictions taxing above the average rate observed in the country and some taxing below it. Under the new view, property tax effects are divided into two separate categories: the general tax effect and the excise tax effect. The general tax effect indicates—to the extent that the supply of land and structures in the United States is fixed—that the average rate of property taxation in the country depresses the return on these assets by the full amount of the tax. The excise tax effect recognizes that jurisdictions tax property at a rate above and below the average rate in the country. If possible, owners of structures will thus move them out of high-property-tax-rate jurisdictions into low-property-tax-rate jurisdictions. This mobility is expected to continue to occur until the after-tax return on structures is equal across jurisdictions. The result is a complicated adjustment process that can lower (raise) structural values and wages in the short term in high- (or low) property-tax jurisdictions, and lower (or raise) land values and employment in high- (or low) property-tax jurisdictions in the long term.

Under the new view, the general tax effect of property taxation in the United States is borne by people in proportion to the fraction of income they receive from property rents. As in the land portion of the traditional view analysis, this makes it a progressive tax. Because most conclude that the general tax effects are greater than the excise tax effects, the conclusion from the new view is that high-income people devote a larger percentage of their income to paying property taxes than low-income people. This overall progressive determination of the income incidence of property taxation is the opposite of the overall regressive finding derived under the traditional view.

Both the traditional and new views of property taxation ignore the fact that if a taxpayer pays higher property taxes to a jurisdiction, he or she may get a greater level of local services from that jurisdiction. If people and businesses are mobile across taxing jurisdictions, they will seek jurisdictions that offer the mix of local government services that they desire at the lowest local expense (including local property taxes). This raises demand for land in local jurisdictions that provide desired local services at a low local charge and raises land prices in these jurisdictions. In turn, this mobility lowers demand for land in local jurisdictions where desired local services are only obtained at a high expense and lowers land prices in these jurisdictions. Under certain conditions, mobility and the capitalization of the local fiscal package into local land values can make the property tax more like a local fee for local government services.

The Benefit View

If this is the case (i.e., paying for a given set of local services with low property tax rates and high land prices, or paying for the same given local services in another jurisdiction with high property tax rates and low land prices), the result is that property tax can become a benefit tax. Because "you get what you pay for," this benefit view of property taxation concludes that there is no need to consider the income incidence of the property tax.

As Youngman (2002) points out in her clear interpretation of the benefit view, the concept of regressivity itself must be reexamined when the tax is analyzed as a payment for services. For example, it could readily be established that food, shelter, and other basic necessities require a diminishing proportion of income as household income rises. Increased discretionary income means that a lower proportion of income is devoted to nondiscretionary necessities. However, that assumption does not imply that food or shelter prices are best analyzed as regressive taxes, or that society would be better served by substituting a different price system for these commodities. If the tax is viewed as part of consumer activity, the focus of the inquiry has shifted from a one-way payment—the government's collection of a specific amount from each taxpayer—to a market exchange of money for goods and services.

A major assumption of the benefit view is that residents choose a residence in a particular city in a metropolitan area in part based upon the local services they receive for the property taxes they pay. If low-income people are mobile (an important assumption that is often not the case), they cannot live in a community that has high property taxes and high services unless they really sacrifice and give up a lot of their other consumption. This is the same reasoning that says low-income people cannot have expensive clothes, restaurant meals, cars, and so on. For these privately provided goods, they purchase what they can afford, and there is no discussion of purchases in these markets being regressive.

Similarly, under the benefit view there is no discussion of regressivity of local property taxes as a fee for service. The concern is with low-income people having enough resources to purchase the necessities of life, not the property tax itself. The benefit view is relevant only if people have many communities to choose to live in, as in a large metropolitan area, and if they are mobile among these communities. Because this is often not the case, the benefit view is not the best overall way to think about property tax incidence.

Lifetime Effect

There is an ongoing debate about whether the property tax is regressive for defined segments of the taxpaying population who have limited ability to pay at certain times of their lives. For example, the tax may represent a disproportionately high share of income for older persons or others now on fixed incomes but formerly with greater income with which to pay the tax. This "lifetime" nonregressive nature of the tax of course misses the snapshot view of regressivity in the present for such a group. Circuit breakers and other possible solutions to this problem are discussed in Chapter 6, "Analysis of Selected Property Tax Features."

Discussion

Given these three alternative views of how to treat the incidence of property taxation, it is not surprising that a populist debate still exists about whether people with high or low incomes devote a greater percentage of their income to paying property taxes. Because most existing policy makers were taught the traditional view, property taxation is often described as regressive in political discussions. On the other hand, the consensus among public economists, who favor the more complex new view, is that the property tax is best considered progressive. Then again, there are public economists who believe in the capacity of mobility and capitalization to turn the property tax into a benefit tax. For a more complete description of this debate, see Youngman (2002).

Beyond the important concerns of whether property taxation in general is best considered a regressive or progressive tax or whether the income incidence of property taxation should be ignored, the new and benefit views of property taxation described above offer valuable theoretical approaches to considering the impact of various real-world changes in property tax; these are summarized in Table A-1.

Table A-1. Models for Analyzing a Hypothetical Change in Property Taxation

Property Tax Policy Change	Model to Use	Expected Results
The average rate of property taxation in the United States declines with no change in the level of state and local government services (revenues necessary to continue to provide these services are made up in other ways).	New view—general tax effect	This rate decrease results in an increase in the return from owning property in the United States and benefits owners of property if the supply of property in United States is fixed (definitely the case for land). High-income people benefit from this change more than low-income people because a greater percentage of their income comes from property ownership. But if this reduction in property taxation brings more mobile property into the United States (machines, buildings, and so on), benefits in the form of higher wages or greater employment extend to workers who use the additional property.
A state cuts its rate of property taxation to half the national average rate of property taxation, but does not cut back its provision of government services (revenues necessary to continue to provide these services are made up in other ways).	New view—excise tax effect	Buildings, machinery, and inventories are usually moved to a state that lowers its rate of property taxation because the rate of return on this property rises if the rate of property taxation on it is cut. Workers and homeowners are less likely to move between states because of property tax changes. The buildings, machinery, and inventory that move into the lower-property-tax state require land to locate on and land values are driven up in the state. This benefits high-income people more than low-income people because they derive a greater fraction of their overall income from land rents. At the same time, there is now a greater housing stock in the state that has cut its rate of property taxation, and prices and rental rates on housing should fall and wages paid to the fixed labor force in the state should increase.
A city, which was previously taxing property within its boundaries at a rate similar to that of other cities in its metropolitan area, cuts its property tax rate in half and finances the cut with an increase in local sales taxes and fees. It provides the same level of local government services after this change.	New view—excise tax effect	It is likely that buildings, machinery, and inventory can be moved between cities in a metropolitan area. If the rate of return on this mobile property rises in one city because of a property tax cut, mobile property will migrate to that city. It also is likely that workers and homeowners will seek employment and residence in the city with lower property taxes. All these occurrences will increase the price of land in the city with lower taxes as mobile property owners, employees, and home buyers seek it out. This will benefit high-income people more than low-income people because they are more likely to have owned this land before the tax cut. There will now be more residents and workers in the city with low property tax. However, wages paid in the city will eventually be the same as elsewhere in the metropolitan area because employee mobility between cities in the metropolitan area causes them to equalize.
Voters in a built-up bedroom community of a metropolitan area vote to raise their rate of property taxation to fund an increase in local library services that a vast majority of residents in the community support.	Benefit view	Homeowners in the community view this local property tax increase as a fee for a service they desire (no different than if they went to the local bookstore to buy desired books). This policy change does not cause property owners to leave or enter the community. Land values in the city remain the same. There is no reason to think about how this change affects high-income or low-income people differently because most in the community desired it. For the few who did not wish to pay more property taxes for more local library services, they have the option of leaving the community for another in the metropolitan area with lower property taxes and less local library services.

Reference

Youngman, J.M. 2002. Enlarging the property tax debate—regressivity and fairness. *State Tax Notes* (October 7):45–52.

Appendix B
Economic Effects of Property Taxation

Related to the debate about whether property taxes are best viewed as benefit taxes (see Appendix A) is the policy issue of how much the taxation of property distorts investment and consumption decisions. If property taxes always act as benefit taxes, then no distortion can occur. However, most public economists agree that the benefit view fully applies only where mobility among alternative jurisdictions is possible and where state and local fiscal packages are perfectly capitalized into local land values.

The taxation of property is expected to generate greater economic distortions when there is a greater differential in property tax rates among jurisdictions and a shorter time period under consideration. In a short time period, economic distortions can arise because land values are less likely to have fully adjusted to differences in fiscal packages. In these situations, given that Jurisdiction A has a higher rate of property taxation than Jurisdiction B and that Jurisdictions A and B both offer the same package of local government services and charge residents the same fees and other taxes, Jurisdiction A is likely to have fewer business buildings and machines, as well as exhibit a lower upkeep of existing residential structures. This also causes businesses in Jurisdiction A to pay lower wages and employ fewer people.

These economic distortions send shivers down the spines of economic development officials within a jurisdiction and bring unhappiness to politicians who run on the voter-desired platform of jobs, jobs, and more jobs for a jurisdiction. Thus, not surprisingly, state and local policy makers in the United States have reacted by reducing overall reliance on property taxes, granting targeted property tax abatements, and allowing tax increment financing (TIF, the increment in property tax revenue growth that a zone within a jurisdiction gets to keep in the zone for the funding of capital projects within the zone). A TIF makes the property tax more like a benefit tax for businesses residing in the zone.

In addition to property tax abatements and TIFs, other alternatives are available for reducing economic distortions generated from property taxes. One possibility is property tax revenue sharing among jurisdictions in a metropolitan area. As practiced in the Minneapolis–St. Paul Metropolitan Area, 40 percent of the growth in a city's locally generated property tax revenue is placed in a regional fund that is then redistributed to all cities in the area based on their percentage of the property tax base relative to the entire region. This reduces the economic distortions generated by local property tax differentials in a metropolitan area by discouraging business and residential mobility due to high property tax rates, low local government service levels, or both. Because more fiscally attractive communities are likely to be at the periphery of an urban area, such a plan could also reduce urban sprawl.

Another alternative to reducing the economic distortions generated through property taxation is the adoption of a property tax roll that splits the taxation of land values from other forms of property. Such an idea—first proposed in 1879 by Henry George and currently used in some jurisdictions in Pennsylvania—taxes the land component of property at a higher rate than the structure/machine/inventory components. Because land is immobile while structures, machines, and inventories can be very mobile, this split in taxation can discourage mobility away from high-property-tax/low-government-service jurisdictions. Oates and Schwab (1998) found evidence supporting this assertion for Pittsburgh. Both split-rate taxation, which taxes land at a higher rate, and the alternative, which taxes land at a lower rate, as practiced in programs intended to preserve land used for agriculture, are discussed in greater detail in Chapter 6, "Analysis of Selected Property Tax Features."

Reference

Oates, W.E., and R.M. Schwab. 1998. The Pittsburgh experience with land-value taxation. In *Local government tax and land use policies in the United States: Understanding the links.* Northhampton, MA: Edward Elgar.

Appendix C
Legal (Statutory) Incidence versus Economic Incidence

The legal incidence of a tax reflects which person is statutorily responsible for paying the tax. For example, a sales tax might be legally placed on the merchant, an income tax on a worker, and a property tax on the property owner. However, prices may change because of the tax, so legal incidence analysis often does not reveal who is really paying the tax. Who pays the tax is a function of the economic incidence. Economic incidence is determined by analyzing the change in private real income that is caused by the tax. The difference between legal and economic incidence is a measure of the amount of the shifting of the tax burden. These concepts can be illustrated with the following short-term examples.

Example 1. The Incidence of a Unit Sales Tax

Figure C-1 illustrates the incidence of a unit sales tax. With the assumed supply and demand elasticities, a unit sales tax would raise the supply schedule from S to S' because at each price the producer will now supply less as a result of the tax and at each quantity the producer requires a higher price to get the good to market (t is

FIGURE C-1. Incidence of a Unit Sales Tax

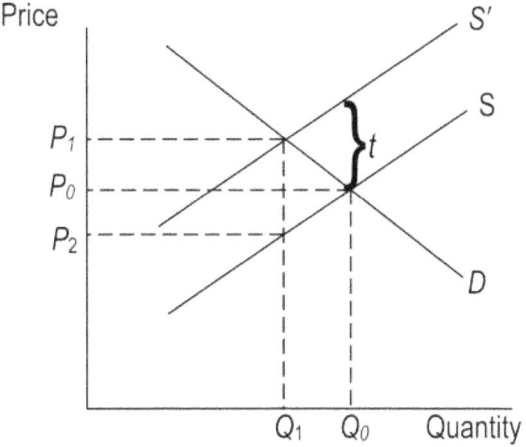

the amount of the unit tax). With no change in demand, this would cause a price increase from P_0 to P_1. P_1 is the price that the consumer pays. However, P_2 is the net amount that the seller receives (i.e., the net of tax amount). In this case, the tax is shared between the buyer and seller, even though the legal incidence is entirely on the seller. Further, the quantity purchased also falls, from Q_0 to Q_1. The extent of this sharing depends on the relevant elasticities of supply and demand.

Example 2. The Incidence of Social Security Tax with Respect to Wages

If, in the short term, the supply of labor is fixed (at S), the aggregate labor market equilibrium would be as shown in Figure C-2. The Social Security tax would lower the demand for labor curve from D to D'. The equilibrium wage would fall from W_0 to W_1, and the entire tax would be borne by labor. This is despite the legal belief that in the United States this tax is shared by business and labor. Because the payroll tax disappears at a particular income level, the overall incidence of this tax is regressive.

FIGURE C-2. Incidence of Social Security Tax with Respect to Wages

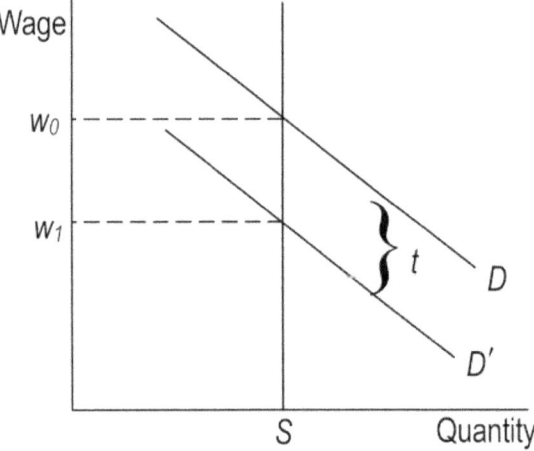

Example 3. The Incidence of a Land Tax

With a fixed supply of land and if land is considered an asset, a land tax is capitalized into the price of that land; that is, the price of the land drops because of the tax. When the tax is first imposed, the owner of the land bears the full burden of the tax. When that owner attempts to sell the land, he or she will be able to sell it only at the after-tax price. The new buyer pays this lower price, and so, even when the buyer pays the land tax in the future, because he or she was able to purchase the land at the lower price, the new owner is not bearing the tax—it is forever fixed on the original owner. (Note that this is a simple example. The discussion of property taxes in Chapter 4, "Role of Property Tax in Intergovernmental Finance," more thoroughly analyzes the necessary conditions for capitalization to occur and presents the debate about whether the property tax is really a benefit charge [Fischel 2002; Hamilton 1975]).

References

Fischel, W.A. 2002. Capitalization and home values: An introductory explanation. *State Tax Notes* (May 6):507–521.

Hamilton, B.W. 1975. Zoning and property taxation in a system of local governments. *Urban Studies* 12:205–211.

Appendix D
Partial versus General Equilibrium Analysis (Sector Analysis)

Up to this point, the discussion of incidence has been short term and focused only on the particular item being taxed; this is partial equilibrium analysis. Although the general conclusion of partial equilibrium analysis—the legal incidence of the tax is irrelevant in terms of who actually bears the tax's burden—remains correct, the analysis can be made more sophisticated by adopting a general equilibrium viewpoint. General equilibrium analysis takes a larger view of taxation: it allows behavioral responses to occur over a longer period of time, and it examines how different markets can be interrelated (Harberger 1962).

For example, suppose a tax is placed on tickets to a football game. Again, assuming ordinary supply and demand elasticities, partial equilibrium analysis indicates that the burden of that tax will be shared between the fans and the team's owner. There may be fewer fans attending at the higher priced ticket rate. However, some of these fans who would have attended the game may now go to an automobile race. There will be an increase in demand for race tickets, and the price of these tickets might well increase. Then, some of the marginal race fans might well switch back to the football game, and so on. Ultimately, there is likely to be a different set of equilibrium prices at both football games and car races, and race attendees will be affected by the football tax. Tracing this even further, if salaries of players and drivers depend on attendance, these too will be affected. Also, the salaries of workers in firms that make football and race products, ranging from team jackets to specialized engines, might be affected. Some of these effects might happen relatively quickly; others may take a long time to be fully recognized.

Moving to a general equilibrium analysis greatly complicates the examination of any specific tax. A tax on one sector can cause consequences in other sectors—a tax on residences might affect business construction, for example. Careful analysis must attempt to consider potential general equilibrium effects. Care must be taken that the assumptions underlying the examination of these effects are reasonably accurate (assumptions of relevant supply and demand elasticities, assumptions of the timing of the effects, and assumptions of production functions) and that the partial equilibrium analysis is not paralyzed because the general equilibrium framework is too difficult to implement.

Behavioral Effects

Although many potential behavioral effects can be attributed to taxes, there are four potential changes in behavior that make useful examples. The four following examples assume a general equilibrium framework (although not necessarily a complete general equilibrium analysis).

Example 1. Shift in Consumption Patterns due to a Sales Tax

When an item is taxed, in many cases, the price of that item increases, and the equilibrium quantity purchased falls. Assuming that households continue spending the same amount of money on consumption items and depending upon the relevant elasticities, households may have more or less money to spend on other consumption goods. In either case, consumption of these other goods is likely to change; a tax on apples is likely to reduce the amount of apples purchased and also affect the amount of oranges purchased. At times, taxes are deliberately used to induce these types of changes. Alcohol and cigarettes are often heavily taxed because society thinks that these products are unhealthy and that the taxes will raise their prices and lower their consumption. A cynic might argue that these products are also taxed because consumers are not very responsive to price increases in them and because these taxes will reduce consumption only slightly and still generate a good deal of tax revenue. In addition, the revenues raised from these taxes might be used to offset the negative externalities of alcohol and cigarette consumption. A further complication is the introduction of border effects. In these cases, if adjoining jurisdictions do not impose the same sales tax, the jurisdiction with the higher tax might experience a loss of sales as consumers travel to the jurisdiction with the lower tax to make purchases. Although the use tax is supposed to take care of this problem, in reality it rarely does for most small purchases.

Example 2. Shift in Savings versus Consumption Patterns due to a Sales Tax

The best way to avoid a sales tax is to not consume, that is, replacing an income tax with a sales tax stimulates savings. In current discussions at the national level, arguments are sometimes advanced that replacing the income tax with a value-added consumption tax increases savings.

Example 3. Shift in Work versus Leisure Choices due to an Income Tax

The supply of labor is assumed to be fixed in the short term. However, in the long term, it may be that the income tax might encourage workers to work less and spend more time in leisure. For example, if the income tax rate were 100 percent, then workers would not work at all. On the other hand, higher tax rates might stimulate workers to work longer hours to maintain their current consumption patterns.

Empirical results seem to indicate that males between 20 and 60 years of age are not very responsive to tax changes, while married females tend to be more responsive (Rosen 2002). Further, many workers do not have control of their time and so cannot respond to the tax change. An example of this choice analysis is the Laffer Curve, developed by the economist Arthur Laffer, which argues that as taxes increase, tax revenues increase only to a particular point and then begin to decrease (see Figure D-1). Although this is obviously true, Laffer further argued that the U.S. economy was to the right of the peak (point A) and a cut in tax rates would be self-financing. This is sometimes called supply-side economics. However, most empirical work indicates that the U.S. economy is operating to the left of the maximum revenues (Fullerton 1982). This does not mean that income taxes should not be cut; rather, it indicates that cutting taxes will not stimulate an increase in work that would generate enough revenues to finance the tax cut.

FIGURE D-1. Example of Laffer Curve

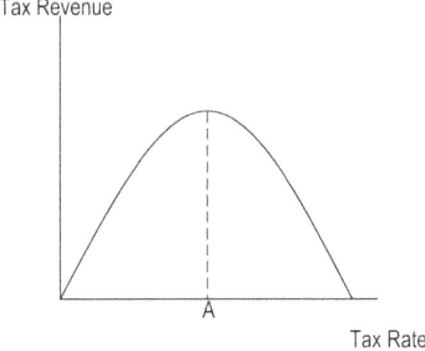

Example 4. Shift in Investment Patterns due to a Property Tax

A property tax on a particular type of asset might influence how that asset is used. For example, it may be argued that a tax on land (but not on improvements) might encourage the landowner to more quickly or more intensively develop that property. Conversely, in some areas of the United States, rural land is deliberately under-assessed as long as it remains rural, even if it is on the urban fringe. This under-assessment is designed to encourage the owners not to develop the land.

These behavior effects, in a general equilibrium setting, have tax revenue consequences. Typically these consequences are ignored in forecasting revenues; that is, forecasters typically assume a static partial equilibrium framework. When these consequences are included in the analysis, that is, using a general equilibrium framework, these revenue estimates often change. Using a general equilibrium framework is often called dynamic analysis. However, dynamic analysis is heavily dependent on myriad assumptions, and so results must be treated with a good deal of care.

References

Fullerton, D. 1982. On the possibility of an inverse relationship between tax rates and government revenues. *Journal of Public Economics* 19(1):3–33.

Harberger, A. 1962. The incidence of the corporation income tax. *Journal of Political Economy* 70(3):215–240.

Rosen, H.S. 2002. *Public finance*, 6th ed. Boston, MA: McGraw-Hill/Irwin.

Appendix E
Criteria for Evaluating Effects of Taxes

In addition to understanding the underlying principles and characteristics of a tax system, such as stability and acceptability to fully evaluate the effects of taxes, particularly with respect to incidence, additional factors such as efficiency and equity must be understood and analyzed. These factors are outlined below.

Efficiency

When a perfectly competitive market is at equilibrium for all goods, services, and factors, then at least in theory it is impossible to make any individual better off (in his or her own judgment) without making someone else worse off. Then any change caused by a tax leads to a movement away from this position. There would be an efficiency loss caused by the tax that increases by the square of the tax rate. For example, if the tax rate doubles, the efficiency loss quadruples.

Consumer surplus represents the difference between what the consumer is willing to pay for a particular amount of the good and what the consumer actually does pay. The measure of a tax efficiency loss can be approximated by the loss of consumer surplus that occurs because of the behavior responses. A simple example for a sales tax follows. (Note, however, that the concept of loss of efficiency is also true for income and property taxes.) Any time that there is a change in behavior, which leads to a new equilibrium that is different from the optimum, there is a loss of efficiency. Consumer surplus is approximated by a measure of the area under the demand curve, but above the initial equilibrium price. This is true for a product constrained by the perfectly elastic supply curve at the price of the product (see Figure E-1) in which $P_0 Q_0$ is the initial equilibrium. As Figure E-1 shows, when the tax is added to the price, there is a loss of consumer surplus of the trapezoid $P_0 P_1 Z Y$. Rectangle $P_0 P_1 Z U$ represents the tax revenue collected at the new equilibrium, $P_1 Q_1$. Triangle UZY represents a loss of consumer surplus that just disappears. This is the loss of efficiency and is sometimes called the deadweight loss or excess burden of the tax. Algebraically, this can be measured as

$$\tfrac{1}{2} \eta\, P_1 Q_0 t_2$$

where η is the absolute value of the price elasticity of demand for the product and t is the tax rate. (If the supply curve is upward sloping, there is also some producer's surplus created, and the formula is slightly different; see Rosen [2002, 292].) This is a powerful argument for a broader base that would allow a smaller tax rate to exist.

FIGURE E-1. Loss of Consumer Surplus

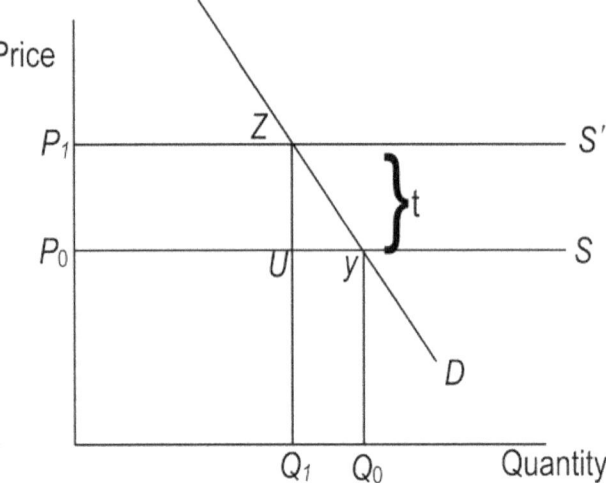

Equity

One approach to equity is the benefit principle. According to this theory, an equitable tax system is one in which consumers of a government service pay for the service. For example, if a person uses a community swimming pool, he or she pays a user fee to enter the pool. If direct user fees are difficult to calculate, sometimes a tax on a complementary product can be used—a tax on gasoline is often partially earmarked for highway repairs or construction. Thus the tax is being imposed using the benefit principle. Note that the charge is independent of income.

A second approach to equity is the ability-to-pay approach to taxation. This is the rule that taxpayers should finance government activities in accordance with their ability to pay. Taxation based on the ability-to-pay principle rests on two assertions. The first, referred to as horizontal equity, calls for equal treatment of taxpayers who are the same in all relevant economic aspects. This means that two economically identical taxpayers would pay the same tax. There are two problems with this criterion. First, there may be differences in policy makers' judgments as to what constitutes all *relevant* economic aspects. For example, in the United States, if two households are identical in wage income but one has a blind member while the other has a deaf member, the household with the blind member pays less in taxes—a value judgment passed by Congress. Second, there may be some looseness in the meaning of *being treated equally*. For example, suppose there are two identical families in terms of income received. Yet one chooses to buy a house using a mortgage while the other chooses to rent an apartment of identical size. In the United States, the family that buys the house may pay less in taxes because of the mortgage interest deduction. Again, this is a policy decision.

A second ability-to-pay assertion is that taxpayers with a greater ability should pay more. This is referred to as vertical equity, and it essentially means that taxpayers who are in unequal economic positions should be treated differently. In practice, this means that low-income people should pay less in taxes than high-income people. Again, there are difficulties in implementation. For example, how much more in taxes should high-income people pay? If taxes are measured in total dollars, it is certainly possible to have high-income people pay more but still have a regressive system. An additional consequence of using ability to pay as a criterion is that it leads to most of the tax revenue coming from high-income people who then have an incentive to lobby to distort the tax laws for their own benefit.

At a minimum, the incidence of taxes should be accurately calculated so that the effects of tax changes can be appropriately discussed. Often tax policy is made by appealing to either the horizontal or the vertical criteria, yet little is known about the incidence of the tax.

In general, most tax policy writers believe in a balanced system, approximately equal amounts among sales, income, property, and other fees and taxes. In this case, the system is more likely to be stable in terms of the revenue generated. However, Kleine and Shannon (1986) argued that different state value systems result in different state-local revenue systems. For example, if the highest goal of the state is to attract high-income individuals and investors, then a state should have a low personal or corporate tax. If the state's desire is to have a progressive tax system, then progressive income taxes should be used. Or if political accountability is the central consideration, then most public services should be financed at the local level, through local taxes. Differences in state economies may also affect this balance; for example, some states have much greater opportunity to export taxes (to tax tourists) or are border states that might worry about taxpayers shopping across the state's borders.

References

Kleine, R.J., and J. Shannon. 1986. Characteristics of a balanced and moderate state-local revenue system. *Reforming state revenue systems*. Denver, CO: National Conference of State Legislatures.

Rosen, H.S. 2002. *Public finance*, 6th ed. Boston, MA: McGraw-Hill/Irwin.

Glossary

Much of the material in Fundamentals of Tax Policy *was drawn from Course 402 "Property Tax Policy" including this Glossary, which has been updated with minor changes. The contributions of earlier authors are gratefully acknowledged.*

A

Abatement—(1) An official reduction or elimination of one's assessed valuation after completion of the original assessment. (2) An official reduction or elimination of one's tax liability after completion of the assessment roll.

Acquisition Value System of Property Tax Assessment—A system of valuing property at its market value as of the last transfer of ownership or of the last major physical change. A property is placed on the tax roll at its acquisition value. Values usually are permitted only limited annual increases, but may be updated when major physical changes occur or when the property is sold. The system established by California's Proposition 13 is an example.

Ad Valorem Tax—A tax levied in proportion to the value of the thing being taxed. The property tax is an ad valorem tax.

Appeal—A process in which a property owner contests an assessment either informally or formally.

Appraisal—The act of estimating the money value of property.

Assessment—The official act of discovering, listing, and appraising property.

Assessment Level—The common or overall ratio of assessed values to market values.

Assessment Progressivity (Regressivity)—An appraisal bias such that high-value properties are appraised higher (or lower) than other properties in relation to market values.

Assessment Ratio—(1) The fractional relationship an assessed value bears to the market value of the property in question. (2) By extension, the fractional relationship the total of the assessment roll bears to the total market value of all taxable property in a jurisdiction.

Audit—A systematic investigation or appraisal of procedures or operations for the purpose of determining conformity with specifically prescribed criteria.

Audit, Performance—An analysis of an organization to determine whether or not the quantity and quality of work performed meets standards. Ratio studies are an important part of performance audits of an assessing organization.

Audit, Procedural—An examination of an organization to determine whether established or recommended procedures are being followed.

Average Tax Rate—Total taxes paid divided by the total base.

Average Total Cost—The total cost to produce something divided by the number of units produced.

B

Benefit-Based Taxes—Taxes linked, often by earmarking, to the consumption of particular government services.

Block Grants—Grants that are designated for a broad set of uses, such as economic development. They are not as restrictive as categorical grants, with broader goals, more discretion, and fewer administrative requirements. However, block grants are not as flexible as revenue sharing.

Border Effect—Tax administration problems that arise because shoppers or commuters can evade or avoid certain taxes by crossing the border from one taxing jurisdiction to another.

Buoyancy—The ability of tax yields to rise (and fall) with the economy and with revenue needs. Buoyancy is a characteristic of value-based property tax systems, but assessed valuations must be updated as the underlying market values change.

C

Capitalization—Used in terms of the value of land being lower in a jurisdiction with a high tax/low public service fiscal structure; alternatively, in terms of the value of land being higher in a jurisdiction with a low-tax/high-public-service fiscal structure.

Categorical Grants—Grants that are designated for a particular use, such as development of municipal parks.

Charges—Non-tax revenue from fees and reimbursements for current services.

Circuit Breaker—For qualifying property owners, a credit or rebate of specified amounts of property taxes incurred whenever such taxes exceed specified percentages or amounts of household income. In instances in which renters are included, rent or rent equivalents substitute for property taxes.

Classification—The act of segregating property into two or more classes for the application of different effective tax rates.

Classified Property Tax System—A system intended by law to tax various kinds of property at different effective tax rates. Common approaches are establishing by law either that property is to be uniformly assessed but taxed differently by class, or that property is to be taxed at a uniform rate but assessed at different assessment ratios by class.

Coefficient of Dispersion (COD)—In ratio studies, a measure of uniformity calculated as the average percentage deviation from the median ratio.

Coefficient of Variation (COV)—A standard statistical measure of relative dispersion of sample data about the mean of the data. In ratio studies, a measure of uniformity calculated by expressing the standard deviation of the ratios as a percentage of the mean ratio.

Consensus Forecasting—Collective agreement by a group of knowledgeable individuals in the finance department about a future revenue/expenditure stream.

Consumer Surplus—The amount by which consumers' willingness to pay for a commodity exceeds the sum they actually have to pay.

Credit, Property Tax—An offset against the property tax payment for taxpayers who meet certain criteria or whose properties have certain characteristics or are used for specified purposes; a direct reduction in a tax payment rather than in a tax base.

D

Delphi Forecasting—A multiple-step method that involves predictions of expert individuals that are then reconsidered after other expert individuals comment on the forecasts.

Differential Taxation—A legislated difference in effective tax rates between groups of properties classified according to use, value, or some other criterion. Differentials may be affected by applying different legal assessment ratios, tax rates, or both. Systems that provide differentials are generally known as classified property tax systems in the United States.

Dillon's Rule—Legal interpretation that maintains that local governments are not power centers in their own right, but derive all their powers from state governments.

Direct Taxation—Taxes that are imposed on the household that is meant to bear the burden.

E

Economic Incidence—A change in the distribution of real income induced by the tax.

Economies of Scale—Unit costs fall as the scale of production rises. For example, if it costs $8,000 per student to educate a high school student in a school with 500 to 800 students, but only $6,000 in a school with 1,000 to 2,500 students, then economies of scale exist.

Economies of Scale in Production—The average total cost to produce something continually falls as more of it is produced, and it can be beneficial to have only one producer (a natural monopoly). This is usually due to a large fixed cost of production.

Effective Tax Rate—For property tax, the tax rate expressed as a percentage of market value; will be different from the nominal tax rate when the assessment ratio is not equal to 1.

Efficiency—An allocation of resources such that no one person can be made better off without making another person worse off; includes both productive efficiency (no wasted resources) and allocative efficiency (resources are allocated to meet consumer demand).

Elasticity (Tax)—A measure of the responsiveness of tax yields to changes in economic conditions. The yield of an elastic tax increases rapidly in a growing economy. The yield of an inelastic tax increases slowly. Often measured by the formula:
Percentage change in tax ÷ Percentage change in personal income

Equalization—The process by which an appropriate governmental body attempts to ensure that all property under its jurisdiction is assessed at the same assessment ratio or at the statutorily required ratio(s). This process may be direct, involving adjustments to taxable values of individual properties, or indirect, usually involving adjustments to overall values for property classes or jurisdictions. Such adjusted

Glossary

overall values are then used to determine the proper distribution for state aid to local governments or to create uniform effective tax rates.

Equity—(1) In assessment, the degree to which assessments bear a consistent relationship to market value. Measures include the coefficient of dispersion, coefficient of variation, and price-related differential. (2) In popular usage, a synonym for tax fairness. (3) In ownership, the net value of property after liens and other charges have been subtracted.

Exemption—A specified category of income or spending that is not included in the tax base. In property taxation, an exclusion of part or all of the value of a category of property from taxation.

Expert Forecasting—Collective agreement by a group of knowledgeable individuals that extends outside of the finance department about a future revenue/expenditure stream.

Externality—Produced when the costs (benefits) faced by a producer (consumer) of a good/service do not represents all of the costs (benefits) generated from production (consumption).

F

Fairness—See Equity.

Federal Conformity—The extent to which a feature of state or local tax law is the same as federal tax law.

Federalism—Form of government in which power is constitutionally divided between a center or national government, and states or regional centers.

Federalism, Coercive—A degenerative form of cooperative federalism in which the Federal Government dominates state and local governments.

Federalism, Competitive—A system of government in which competition among governments is a major means of coordinating actions by the governments. The national government competes with states, states compete with each other, and local governments compete with each other.

Federalism, Cooperative—A system of government in which there is interdependence among the different types of government (for example, between national and state governments).

Federalism, Dual—A system of government under which the national government and the states have separate sets of responsibilities.

Federalist System of Government—A system of government in which the distribution of power is shared between a central authority (Federal Government) and the constituent units; each of the constituent units (state and local governments) is more or less self-governing.

Fiscal Capacity—A measure of the own-source revenues a state could raise if it had a "representative tax system" and applied the national average tax rate to its own amounts of the major sources of taxes and charges.

Fiscal Comfort—An index that combines fiscal capacity and fiscal need measures into a single measure. Determined from the ratio of fiscal capacity to fiscal need.

Fiscal Effort—"The ratio of each state's actual tax collections to the taxes it would have collected under the representative tax system" (Tannenwald 1999).

Fiscal Federalism—An approach to federalism that emphasizes the nature of the goods and services that government provides and derives the structure of government from that analysis. (Sometimes the term is used in a more general sense to refer to the financial analysis of federal systems of government.)

Fiscal Need—A measure of would-be revenue requirements if a state had a "representative expenditure system" and supplied the national average level of services to its own amounts of "workload" variables.

Flat Tax—A tax with a single rate applying to all income for a specified tax-exempt level. Note that the existence of a tax-exempt level of income means that the burden of the tax can still be progressive.

Fractional Assessments—Assessments that by law or by practice have assessment ratios different from 1. Usually the assessment ratio is less than 1, and if assessment biases are present, different classes of property may have different fractional ratios. Fractional assessments are often condemned as offering a way to obscure assessment biases.

G

General Equilibrium—The study of the interrelationships among various sectors.

Glossary

General Revenue—All government revenue except from government-operated public utilities, government-operated liquor store revenue, and for unemployment compensation, employee retirement, workers' compensation, or other government trust funds.

General Sales Tax—A tax levied as a fixed percentage on the dollar value of a broad category of retail purchases.

H

Homestead Exemption—Exclusion of part or all of the value of a residence, usually an owner-occupied primary residence; a reduction in the property tax base.

Horizontal Equity—Individuals/households in equal economic situations should be treated the same. In property assessment, properties of the same value should be valued the same.

I

Incidence—Usually refers to the persons who ultimately bear a tax burden as opposed to the persons on whom the tax is initially imposed.

Income Incidence—The determination of the percentage of a person's income that is devoted to paying a tax. For a given tax, if this percentage rises (falls) as income rises, the tax is considered progressive (regressive).

Indirect Taxation—Taxes that are imposed on a commodity that are then shifted to the household.

Individual Income Tax—A tax levied on the net income of individual. In most cases these are broad-based and include income from labor and other sources, but the Census definition includes distinctive taxes on income from interest or dividends.

Intergovernmental Revenue—"Revenue received from other governments as grants-in-aid, shared revenues, payments in lieu of taxes, or a reimbursement for the performance of services for the paying government" (Hoffman 2002).

L

Level of Assessment—The common or overall ratio of assessed values to market value. This may be a statutory ideal or may be determined by application of inferential statistics developed using ratio studies.

Leviathan—Often used as a metaphor for a government striving to grow as large as possible. Dictionary definitions include a sea monster mentioned in the Old Testament; a huge marine mammal, such as a whale, or anything of huge size.

Levy, Property Tax—(1) The total amount of money to be raised from the property tax as set forth in the budget of a taxing jurisdiction. (2) Loosely, by extension, the millage rate or the property tax bill sent to an individual property owner.

Lump-Sum Grant—A grant that does not depend upon how much the recipient government spends on a particular service.

M

Mandates—Federal regulations that impose costs on state and local governments. There are also state mandates on local governments.

Marginal Tax Rate—The proportion of the last dollar of income taxed by the government.

Market Value—Market value is the major focus of most real property appraisal assignments. Both economic and legal definitions of market value have been developed and refined. A current economic definition agreed upon by agencies that regulate federal financial institutions in the United States of America is:
The most probable price (in terms of money) that a property should bring in a competitive and open market under all conditions requisite to a fair sale, the buyer and seller each acting prudently and knowledgeably, and assuming the price is not affected by undue stimulus. Implicit in this definition is the consummation of a sale as of a specified date and the passing of title from seller to buyer under conditions whereby:

- The buyer and seller are typically motivated;
- Both parties are well informed or well advised, and acting in what they consider their best interests;
- A reasonable time is allowed for exposure in the open market;
- Payment is made in terms of cash in United States dollars or in terms of financial arrangements comparable thereto;
- The price represents the normal consideration for the property sold unaffected by special or creative financing or sales concessions granted by anyone

Glossary

associated with the sale.

Matching Grants—A matching grant provides a certain amount for each dollar spent by the recipient government. For example a 50 percent matching grant would provide $1 to the recipient government for each $1 it spent on a particular function.

Millage, Mill Rate—A tax rate expressed as mills per dollar. For example, a 2 percent tax rate is $2 per $100, $20 per $1,000, or 20 mills per $1. One mill is one-thousandth of $1, or one-tenth of one cent.

Miscellaneous Revenue—Nontax, noncharge revenue derived from interest earnings, special assessments, sale of property, or other sources.

N

Naïve Forecasting—Assuming that historical relationships hold constant, this year's revenues are a constant function of last year's revenues.

Natural Monopoly—A monopoly, or a single producer of a good, that arises due to economies of scale throughout the relevant range of production of the good. This results in a continually declining average total cost to produce and the least expensive way to produce the good being a single producer.

Neutral/Neutrality—Refers to a tax that does not distort economic decisions. Closely related to the concept of efficiency, the situation in which patterns of consumption maximize the general welfare of society.

Nexus—The legal question of what constitutes sufficient presence in a state or jurisdiction to be held responsible for paying or collecting a tax.

Normative Statement—A statement that involves the use of value judgments and whose merits cannot be evaluated on facts alone.

O

Own-Source Revenue—Government funding that only comes from within the jurisdiction under consideration. For local governments, this means that it excludes revenue received from federal and state intergovernmental grants; it may include taxes, current charges, and miscellaneous revenue collected by the jurisdiction. Alternatively, general revenue minus intergovernmental revenue.

P

Partial Equilibrium—Models that study only one market (or sector) and ignore possible spillovers into other sectors.

Per Capita—Divided by the number of people in the population.

Positive Statement—A statement that involves the use of no value judgments and whose merits can be evaluated on facts alone.

Price-Related Differential (PRD)—A statistical measure of vertical property tax equity. The PRD is calculated by dividing the mean ratio by the weighted mean ratio in a ratio study. If the result exceeds 1.03, assessments are considered regressive. If the result is less than 0.98, assessments are considered progressive.

Privilege Tax—A special tax on the right to start, expand, or continue a business (syn. franchise tax).

Progressive Taxation—A tax system under which a taxpayer's average tax rate increases with income.

Progressivity—*Income Progressivity* refers to a situation in which people with higher incomes pay a higher percentage of income in taxes than persons with lower incomes. *Assessment Progressivity* refers to a situation in which effective property tax rates on higher value properties are greater than effective property tax rates on lower value properties. The opposite of Regressivity.

Proportional Taxation—A tax system under which a taxpayer's average tax rate is the same at each level of income.

Proposition 13—The 1978 California property tax limit proposition that replaced current market value with acquisition value as the basis for property taxation.

Public Good—A good/service that once produced can be jointly consumed, and it is difficult to keep a nonpayer from consuming. This is the opposite of a private good (such as an apple) that as a whole cannot be jointly consumed, and another can easily be stopped from consuming.

R

Rate-Driven Levy—The property tax rate to be applied is specified in the budget or tax levy ordinance of a taxing jurisdiction, in contrast to the usual situation in which the total revenue to be raised is specified, and the rate is calculated.

Ratio Study—A statistical study of the relationship between appraised or assessed values and market values; based on an analysis of the ratio derived by dividing the appraised or assessed values of property by the market values of such property. Sale prices or independent appraisals are used as proxies for market values.

Real Dollars—Adjusted for inflation relative to a reference or "base" year. Divided by the price index for the current year relative to the price index of the base year.

Regressive Taxation—A tax system under which a taxpayer's average tax rate decreases with income.

Regressivity—*Income Regressivity* refers to a situation in which people with lower incomes pay a higher percentage of income in taxes than persons with higher incomes. *Assessment Regressivity* refers to situations in which effective property tax rates on lower value properties are greater than effective property tax rates on higher value properties. The opposite of Progressivity.

Representative Expenditure System—A method of constructing national average rates of expenditure for many categories of outlays as the ratio of each type of spending to a corresponding "workload" measure such as population, number of pupils, vehicle-miles traveled, or poverty counts.

Representative Tax System—A method of constructing national average rates of tax for many types of taxes and charges as the ratio of each type of revenue to a corresponding measure of the tax base.

Revenue Elasticity—How sensitive the revenue from a particular tax is to (a) cyclical changes or (b) trends in overall economic activity.

Revenue-Sharing Grants—Grants that can be used for almost any governmental purpose. For example, a municipality receiving a revenue-sharing grant might use the grant for fire prevention, welfare, or garbage pickup.

S

School Aid Equalization—A system of state revenue sharing to local schools based upon guaranteeing that each school district has the same property tax base per student upon which to levy local property taxes to fund per-student expenditure on public education.

Selective Sales Tax—A tax levied on the purchase of a specific type of good or service.

Specific Taxation—A tax imposed per unit of the product.

Spillover Effects—Benefits or costs of a good or service that accrue to individuals who do not pay for that good or service (same as externality). Spillovers can be positive (beneficial) or negative.

Statutory Incidence—The legal burden of the tax.

Sumptuary Taxes—Excise taxes designed to discourage the consumption of specific items, such as cigarettes or liquor. Colloquially referred to as sin taxes.

Sunset Provision—A provision within a statute creating a law or agency and providing for the automatic termination of that law or agency at a fixed date in the future.

T

TANF—Temporary Aid to Needy Families (TANF) is commonly referred to as welfare and replaced Aid to Families with Dependent Children (ADFC) in 1996. TANF is administered through a federal block grant to states that requires state welfare programs where most recipients must work within two years of receiving assistance, limits most assistance to five years total, and lets states establish "family caps" to deny additional benefits to mothers for children born while the mothers are already on public assistance.

Tax Assignment—A theory that determines which tax or revenue instruments should best be employed by the national government, which should best be employed by state governments, and which should best be employed by local governments.

Tax Avoidance—Altering behavior in such a way as to reduce legal tax liability.

Tax Burden—Economic costs or losses resulting from the imposition of a tax. Burden can be determined only by detailed economic analysis of all economic changes resulting from the tax. In popular usage, the term often refers to the initial incidence rather than ultimate economic costs.

Tax Elasticity—Measure of the responsiveness of tax yield to changes in economic conditions; often measured by the formula:
percentage change in tax ÷ percentage change in economic base
with the economic base often being personal income.

Tax Evasion—Not paying taxes legally due.

Tax Incidence—Refers to the eventual distribution of the burden of a tax.

Tax Incidence Analysis—Economic analysis that compares the way different taxes affect the distribution of income; requires analysis of the impact of taxes on the market for the taxed item and the market for all factors (land, labor, and capital) used in producing the taxed item.

Tax Increment Financing (TIF)—The idea that property taxes, or other revenue, resulting from the increase in a tax base (for example, property values or retail sales) in a specific area can be used to repay the costs of investment in that area. Funds may be invested in various programs, such as public infrastructure improvements or land write-down subsidies to private investors.

Tax Policy Analysis—The process of gathering and interpreting economic data to provide information that can be used by policy makers to formulate tax policy.

Truth-in-Taxation (Full Disclosure) Requirements—Legal obligations for local government officials to make taxpayers aware of assessment increases, levy increase proposals, and the like and to give taxpayers an opportunity to participate in public hearings on the changes.

U

Uniformity—In property taxation, the principle that the same tax rat is applied to every property.

Unit Tax—A tax levied on the quantity purchased as opposed to the dollar amount purchased. Examples are cigarette taxes per pack and gasoline taxes per gallon.

Unitary Government—A hierarchical system of government in which state and local governments are de facto departments of the national government.

Use Tax—A companion to the general sales tax designed to cover out-of-state purchases.

Use-Value Assessment Laws—Laws that require or permit appraisal and assessment of property based on a particular restriction or use. Typically, use value laws are applied to agricultural land, timber land, or historical sites, permitting assessments to be lower than market value and thereby lessening the proportional share of property tax paid by these classes of property.

V

Vertical Equity—Distributing tax burdens fairly across people with different abilities to pay.

W

Wealth—Valuable material objects that are owned, either individually or collectively; that is, all tangible property. Note: In popular usage the term "wealth" is synonymous with "property" and, as such, embraces intangibles as well as tangible property. This usage is considered incorrect by economists and is not recommended. Intangible property, with the possible exception of goodwill, patents, and the like, is not a real source of income, but only a means of distributing income derived from the two primary sources, tangible property and persons. The adding together of tangible property and intangibles to secure total wealth results in multiple counting of the same values. Some authorities consider nonrepresentative intangible property as wealth, but this usage has received only limited acceptance.

Welcome Stranger Assessment—The practice of systematically assessing recently sold properties on the basis of their sales prices, while failing to reassess similar properties that have not recently sold.

References

Hoffman, D. 2002. *Facts and figures on government finance*, 36th ed. Washington, DC: Tax Foundation.

Tannenwald, R. 1999. Fiscal disparity among the states revisited. *New England Economic Review* . (Boston: Federal Reserve Bank of Boston) (July/August):3–25, http://www.bos.frb.org/economic/neer/neer1999/neer499a.htm (accessed January 24, 2008).

Index

A

abatements   64, 186, 188 (table), 317
ability-to-pay principle   28, 30, 328
accountability   47
accuracy standards for appraisals   214
acquisition value system   175, 182
ad valorem taxes
   definition   30
   early development   11
   vs. specific taxes   7
administrative practicality   31
adjusted gross income (AGI)   99
Advisory Commission on Intergovernmental Relations (ACIR)   151, 156, 196, 301
advocacy   298
affordability   32, 49
Alaska   88, 93, 99
Alberta
   performance monitoring   219
   shift from local to state property taxes   300
   tax administration   51
alcoholic beverage taxes   107, 157, 334
allocation of resources   24, 29
analytical studies   133
annual rental value   61, 272
appeals   52, 68
   system features   249–252
   tracking and managing with CAMA   212
Appraisal Foundation
   standards of practice   15
   USPAP   46, 194
appraisers, qualifications   57, 215
arrears   247
Articles of Confederation   11
assessment administration   15
   appeals   52
   billing and collection   52, 244
   budgeting   201
   CAMA   210
   centralized vs. decentralized   195 (table)
   computer support   210
   data collection   205, 207
   efficiency   203, 204
   employees   202, 202 (table), 203, 215
   equalization actions   219, 222
   exemptions and tax relief programs   243
   identification of taxpayers   242
   Iowa   198
   NAAO   196–198
   organization   203
   planning   200
   policy setting   199
   procedural matters   45
   professional ethics   204
   quality assurance   241
   ratio studies   206, 214
   roll preparation   244
   rules and procedures   205
   security procedures   205
   standards   204, 214, 215
   supervision   213, 214 (table)
   Texas   198
assessment districts   197, 195 (table)
Assessment Shared Services Environment (ASSET)   219
attribute data collection, for immovable property
   data capture   234
   field canvasses   234
   land   233
   location   233
   taxpayer returns   235
Australia   67
automated valuation model (AVM)   226

B

balanced revenue system 31
Baltic countries 276–279, 277 (table)
base-year assessment 62, 170
behavioral effects 130, 324
benefit principle 28, 31, 328
benefit taxes 110, 112
billing 52, 69, 244–246
    coverage options 246
    delivery options 246
    information on tax bill 244 (table), 245 (table)
block grants 114
border effects 96, 108, 112
British Commonwealth, see United Kingdom
budget-based rates 48
budget-driven property tax systems 166–169, 167 (table), 168 (table)
building permits, tracking with CAMA 211
buoyancy, as benefit of uniformity 31, 62

C

cadastre
    mapping 231
    identifiers 209 (table)
    types of 230
California
    Alameda County 178
    Educational Revenue Augmentation Fund 178
    Los Angeles County 176, 177 (figure)
    Proposition 13 10, 13, 45, 63, 119, 175, 176–178
    Orange County 178
    San Mateo County 176
Canada 26, 55, 116, 198
capital value 61
capitalist system 20
categorical grants 114
chattel, see personal property
cherry-picking, see sales chasing
China 279–281, 280 (table)
cigarette taxes 108, 109 (table), 108, 157, 324
circuit breakers 64, 160, 186 (table), 306
Civil Rights Act of 1871 39 (table), 46

classification of property
    categories 6
    differentials 63
    direct vs. indirect 6
    effect on property taxes 181 (table)
    fractional assessment ratios 181, 182
    legislative 40
    principles of 242
    systems of 181
    U.S. Census Bureau system 6
close-ended grants 115
cluster analysis, in GIS 228
coefficient of dispersion (COD) 208, 232 (table)
coercive federalism 76
collection 52, 69, 244–247
Colombia 281–282, 284 (table)
Colorado 94
comity 37 (table), 40, 46
Comity Clause (of the U.S. Constitution) 37 (table)
Commerce Clause (of the U.S. Constitution) 37 (table), 41, 45
Committee on Assessment Organization and Personnel, NAAO 197
Committee on Principles of Assessment Practice, NAAO 196
Communist countries
    land taxes 6
    restitution programs 4
Community Charge (U.K.) 270
comparable property selection, with CAMA 212
competition 21, 22, 119
competitive federalism 77
computer-assisted mass appraisal (CAMA) 210–212, 226
Connecticut 101, 117
consensus forecasting 131
Constitution of the United States
    Comity Clause 38 (table)
    Commerce Clause 38 (table), 41, 45
    Due Process Clause 38 (table), 41
    Eleventh Amendment 39 (table), 45
    Equal Protection Clause 38 (table), 44, 45, 175
    Fourteenth Amendment 38 (table), 39 (table), 44, 175
    Import-Export Clause 38 (table), 41

Index **347**

influence on property tax law   37
local governments   3
power to tax   11
Privileges and Immunities Clause   38 (table)
Sixteenth Amendment   37, 99
Supremacy Clause   38 (table), 45
Tenth Amendment   37, 39 (table), 75, 195
Consumer Price Index (CPI)   136 (table)
consumer surplus, loss in efficiency   327
consumption, as a tax base   157
cooperative federalism   76–77
corporate franchise taxes   113
corporate income taxes   104
  state rates   105 (table)
  Texas   105
  Washington   106
cost approach   224, 233, 240
cost-effectiveness   31
Council of Europe, European Charter of Local Self-Government   195
Council Tax (U.K.)   55, 228, 270, 271 (table)
county funding sources   84 (figure)
credits   186 (table)
current market value, *see* market value basis
current-use value   61
Czech Republic   55, 235

D

data collection   128, 205, 207, 235, 236
data management, with CAMA   210
decentralization   287
deductibility   100, 117, 158
deferrals   64, 186 (table), 306
Delphi forecasting   131
demand economy, *see* economy
demand elasticity   130
democracy   19
Denmark
  equalization grants   49
  exemptions   60, 67
  land tax   180
  PILOT programs   49
  property taxes   283–285, 284 (table)
  revaluation   62

density studies   241
depreciation, in movable property valuation   240
descriptive studies, in policy analysis   129
differential property tax systems   63
Dillon's Rule   78
direct equalization   46, 219
discrimination in assessment   44
disincentives   65
disparity ratio   176, 177 (figure)
District of Columbia   139, 139, 155
double taxation   12
dual federalism   76
Due Process Clause (of the U.S. Constitution)   39 (table), 41, 46

E

econometric forecasting   132
economies of scale   74
economy   20
education   24, 73, 74, 76
efficiency
  effects of taxes   327
  neutrality fosters   29
  productive vs. allocative   21
elasticity
  definition   161
  demand   130
  income, examples   162 (table)
  rate, examples   162 (table)
  revenue   98
Eleventh Amendment (of the U.S. Constitution)   39 (table), 45
emergency relief   65
emerging democracies   4
eminent domain   80
enforcement   52, 69
Equal Protection Clause (of the U.S. Constitution), see Fourteenth Amendment
equality   43
equalization   46
  compensating for fiscal differences   49
  effect on distribution of property taxes   220 (table)
  effect on effective tax rates   221 (table)

grant calculation mechanisms   50
grants to local governments   49
in assessment administration   219
indirect equalization   222 (table)
revenue sharing   124
school funding   16, 121
supervision and   50
uniformity vs. wealth   121
equilibrium   29, 323–326
equity   28
effects of taxes   328
effect of value constraints   173
horizontal vs. vertical   28
estate and inheritance taxes   78
Estonia   54, 67, 276, 277 (table)
European Union   286, 288
excess burden   29
excise taxes   107, 110, 111 (table), 158
exemptions   64, 182, 183 (table)
abatements   64, 187, 188 (table), 317
administration of   66, 243
circuit breakers   64, 160, 306
controls on   185
de facto exemptions   185
deferrals   64, 186 (table), 306
differentials   63
disincentives   65
emergency relief   65
from sales tax   89, 94
full   184 (table)
general   7
homeowner   42 (table)
homestead   64, 307
in property taxation   42, 183 (table)
incentives   65
indirect   66
institutional   65
nongovernmental organizations   66
partial   183, 307
personal   64
transitional relief   65
expert forecasting   131
externalities   22, 73

F

4-R Act, *see* Railroad Revitalization and Regulatory Reform Act of 1976
faculty taxes   99
fairness   28, 61, 241
federal grants-in-aid, *see* grants
federalism   3, 73, 75–78, 114, 255
Federation of Tax Administrators   91, 99, 139
fiscal capacity, cross-state differences   151, 153 (table)
fiscal comfort, *see* index of fiscal comfort
fiscal federalism, theory of   73, 74
"fixed annual general charge"   67
fixed rates   47
flat grants   116
forecasting
behavioral effects   324
in policy analysis   130
issues   130
qualitative techniques   131
quantitative techniques   132
revenue forecasting   130
Foreign Commerce Clause (of U.S. Constitution), *see* Commerce Clause
foreign countries
recurrent property taxes   263 (figure)
taxes as percentage of GDP   258 (figure)
taxes as percentage of revenues   259 (figure)
utilization of taxes   260 (table), 261 (figure), 262 (figure), 263 (table)
foundation grants   115
Fourteenth Amendment   38 (table), 39 (table), 44, 175
fractional assessment ratios   181, 182
France   26, 49, 57, 62

G

gambling taxes 108
gasoline taxes 107, 110, 111 (table), 110
general equilibrium analysis 323, 324, 325
general property tax 12
general revenue, definition 133, 134 (table)
General Revenue Sharing program 114
George Washington University 156
geographic information systems (GIS) 212
   cluster analysis 228
   maps 213
   location response surface analysis (LRSA) 229
Germany 62
globalization 287
good, public vs. private 21
government intervention, in response to market failure 25 (table)
grants
   block 114
   calculation mechanism 50
   categorical 114
   flat 116
   foundation 115
   general revenue sharing 114
   guaranteed tax base 115
   intergovernmental 114
   matching vs. lump-sum 114
   open-ended vs. closed-ended 115
   school aid 115
Great Depression 12, 88
gross domestic product (GDP)
   in selected countries 258 (figure)
   relation to government spending 26 (table), 27 (table)
   ratio to taxable property 308
   utilization of tax 262
guaranteed tax base grants 115

H

Hawaii 99, 139
Holmes, U.S. Justice 80
home rule laws 78
homestead exemption 64, 306
horizontal equity 173, 328
hotel room occupancy tax 41, 112
Hungary 266, 267 (table)

I

IAAO
   Assessment Administration 204
   Assessment Practices: Self-Evaluation Guide 198
   Glossary for Property Appraisal and Assessment 170
   Property Tax Policies and Administrative Practices in Canada and the United States 294
   Standard on Administration of Monitoring and Compliance Responsibilities 213
   Standard on Facilities, Computers, Equipment, and Supplies 202
   Standard on Mass Appraisal of Real Property 206
   Standard on Property Tax Policy 8, 168, 170, 175, 213, 215, 293
   Standard on Ratio Studies 206, 213, 215, 221
   standards of practice 15
Idaho
   local government tax authority 139
   partial exemptions 307
   proportion of property tax by property class 297 (table)
   public policy survey 303
   sales tax 88
   school general property taxes 83, 300
   spending by jurisdiction 297 (table)
   State Tax Commission 139
   State Tax Commission Web site 296
   study of value constraints 174
   truth-in-taxation program 170
Illinois 88, 221
immovable property 31, 59

attribute data collection 232
  in movable property valuation 237
  valuation 223
  vs. movable property 4
impact fees 113
Import-Export Clause (of the U.S. Constitution) 38 (table), 41
incentives 65
incidence *see* tax incidence
income approach 224
income capitalization approach 240
income tax 80
  administration of state income tax 103
  corporate 104
  deductibility 100
  individual 99
  state corporate rates 105 (table)
  state rates 102 (table)
  shift in work vs. leisure choices 324
index of fiscal comfort 153 (table)
indirect equalization 222, 222 (table)
indirect relief 66
information clearinghouse role of assessors 295–305, 295 (table)
in personam taxation 58, 242
insurance value 61
in rem taxation 58
intangible assets 308
intangible property 4, 12
intergovernmental grants, *see* grants
intergovernmental revenue 114, 134, 134 (table)
International Monetary Fund 5, 257
International Valuation Standards Committee 194
Interstate Commerce Clause (of the U.S. Constitution), *see* Commerce Clause
Ireland 62
Internal Revenue Service (IRS) 103
Israel 170

J
Japan 170

L
Laffer Curve 325
land tax
  Communist countries 6
  Denmark 283
  Estonia 276
  incidence 321
  site value 180
land value models, with CAMA 211
Latvia 277 (table), 278
legal structure, for taxes 9
legal systems 36
levy 48
lien 59, 64
limits on property taxation 118
Lithuania 55, 277 (table), 278
Lincoln Institute of Land Policy 175, 264
local government
  number in U.S. 76 (table)
  revenue history 88
  revenue sources 86 (table)
location response surface analysis (LRSA), in GIS 229
lump-sum grants 114
lump-sum payments 307

M
mandates, federal 117
maps 213, 231
market data collection 235
market failure 25 (table)
market value basis 61
  advantages and disadvantages 171 (table)
  assessment 62, 230, 304
  attribute data collection 233
  in property taxes 305, 307
  valuation system 170
Maryland 196, 197
mass appraisal 210, 226
  schematic diagram 227 (figure)
Massachusetts 117, 307
matching grants 114
means testing 64
Memphis, Tennessee 94
Michigan, tax reform in 1990s 83, 300–302

Index **351**

Minneapolis–St. Paul Metropolitan
  Area 317
Minnesota
  Department of Revenue 139
  study of value constraints 174
  tax incidence studies 155
mixed-market economy, *see* economy
Montana 186, 187 (figure), 196, 197
mortgage interest deduction 158
motor fuel taxes, *see* gasoline taxes
movable property 59
  assessment and valuation 237
  declarations 239–240
  discovering and inventorying 238
  identifying owners 238
  locating 238
  vs. immovable property 4
multiple owners 58
multiyear processing, with CAMA 211
municipality funding sources 81 (figure)

N

National Association of Assessing
  Officers (NAAO)
  Committee on Assessment
    Organization and Personnel 197
  Committee on Principles of
    Assessment Practice 196
national basis test 40
National Environmental Policy Act 118
National Governors' Association 74
naïve forecasting 131
Nebraska 108
Netherlands 268
  exemptions 67
  revaluation 62
  property taxes 267 (table)
  tax administration 51
neutrality in taxation 29
New Hampshire 116, 300
New Zealand 67
nexus 97, 120
No Child Left Behind Act 74
non-exempt classes 42
nonprofit organizations 79
nonrecurrent taxes, vs. recurrent 6
normative approach 128, 298
North Carolina 64

Northern Ireland 45, 270, 272
notices of assessment 244, 244 (table)

O

open-ended grants 115
openness 33
Oregon 93
Organization for Economic Cooperation
  and Development (OECD) 5, 264
out-of-state sellers 96, 97, 120
own-source revenue
  definition 134
  comparison by state 145 (table)
  for selected years 143 (table)
  state and local government
    share of 140 (table)

P

parcel identifiers 232 (figure)
partial equilibrium analysis 323–326
partial exemptions, *see* exemptions
Pennsylvania
  local income taxes 119
  Pittsburgh, site value taxation 180
  property tax 318
performance budgeting 201
performance monitoring, by supervisory
  agencies 217
perimeter sketching, with CAMA 211
personal income 140 (table), 147 (table),
  149 (table)
personal property 4, 59, 89
photographic images, with CAMA 212
PILOT (payment in lieu of taxes)
  programs 49, 116
Pittsburgh, Pennsylvania 180
policy analysis 133, 298
political leadership 35
Portugal 55
positive approach 128, 298
price-related differential (PRD), in ratio
  studies 210
private sector 21, 55
Privileges and Immunities Clause (of the
  U.S. Constitution) 38 (table)
privilege taxes 113
procedural audits 217
program budgeting 201

progressivity
  definition 29
  of property tax 160, 311–316
  price-related differential (PRD) 210
  redistribution 78
  unit sales tax 319
property taxes
  administration of 50, 53, 194, 200
  affordability 49
  area-based systems 59–60
  as an institution 299
  based on personal income
    by state 149 (table)
  billing 52, 69, 244 (table), 245 (table)
  budget-based rates 48
  budget- vs. rate-driven
    systems 166–169, 167 (table),
    168 (table)
  categorization 59
  collection 52, 69, 244–246
  controls 172, 173 (table), 174 (table),
    179 (tables), 182
  economic distortions of 317
  effect of classification 181 (table)
  effect of value constraints 172–185,
    173 (table), 174 (table), 182
  enforcement 52, 69
  equal protection 44
  establishing liability 58
  exemptions 182–185
  external linkages 54 (table)
  fixed rates 47
  in foreign countries 264
  incentives 65
  issues and solutions 304 (table)
  key arguments favoring 302 (table)
  levy 48
  local government revenue 82
  multiple owners 58
  non-value bases 60
  per-capita compared to other
    taxes 14 (figure)
  populist argument 304
  private sector 55
  qualifications of officials 57
  revenue compared with other
    taxes 14 (figure)
  self assessment 56
  shift in investment patterns due
    to 325
  significance in local government
    revenues 13 (figure)
  single vs. compound rates 48
  site value 180
  sustainability 302
  system controls 179 (tables)
  viability 49
proportional taxation, definition 29
Proposition 13 in California 10, 13, 45,
  63, 119, 175, 176–178
public acceptance 32, 67, 204
public relations 216, 248, 299

Q
quality assurance 241

R
Railroad Revitalization and Regulatory
  Reform Act of 1978 (4-R Act) 39
  (table), 181
rate classification, 307
rate-driven property tax
  systems 166–169, 167 (table),
  168 (table)
rate-setting mechanisms 47–49
ratio studies 206
  appraisal accuracy standards 214
  arithmetic mean 208
  coefficient of dispersion (COD) 209,
    209 (table)
  data analysis 209 (table)
  data assembly 207
  evaluation of results 210
  median 208
  price-related differential (PRD) 210
  stratification 207
  weighted mean 209
rational basis test 40
reappraisals 199
reassessments 199, 221, 307
recurrent taxes, vs. nonrecurrent 6
redistribution function of
  government 23
regression analysis 132

Index 353

regressivity
  definition   29
  lifetime effect   314
  of alcohol taxes   107
  of property tax   160, 311–316
  of sales tax   94
  of tobacco taxes   108
  price-related differential (PRD)   210
relational database management system (RDBMS)   230
remote vendors, *see* out-of-state sellers
rental property income and expense data   236
resource allocation   24, 29
revaluations   62
revenue, state and local government   140 (table), 143 (table), 145 (table)
revenue elasticity   98
revenue forecasting   130
revenue sources, *see* sources of revenue
revenue trends, analyzing   136
Rhode Island   100
roll preparation   244
Russia   273–277, 275 (table)

S

sales chasing   199, 210, 217
sales comparison approach   223, 235, 240, 285
sales tax
  benefit-based   107
  consumption-based   88
  consumer services   93
  example of unit sales tax   319
  excise taxes   107
  general   88
  in largest city in each state   95 (table)
  local revenues   104
  retail rates   94
  services   91 (table), 120
  shift in consumption patterns   324
  shift in savings   324
  state rates   89 (table)
  types of   80
sales tax policy
  border effects   96
  political acceptability   99
  regressivity   94

revenue elasticity   98
Streamlined Sales Tax Agreement   98
Streamlined Sales Tax Project   97
Scandinavian countries   283–286, 284 (table)
school finance   16, 24, 83 (table), 83, 114, 116 (table), 122 (figure), 123 (table), 69, 178, 300–302
sector analysis   323
selective sales taxes, *see* excise taxes
self assessment   56
services, taxes on   91 (table), 120
SILOT (services in lieu of taxes)   116
site value system of property taxation   180
Sixteenth Amendment (of the U.S. Constitution)   37, 99
Slovakia   55, 235
Smith, Adam   27
Social Security tax, incidence   320
socialist system   4, 20, 80
South Africa   267 (table), 269
Soviet Union   4, 20, 286
sources of revenue   79 (table), 81 (table), 84 (figure), 86 (table), 133, 134 (table)
special assessments   113
special district funding   84 (figure)
split-rate taxation   318
stability   31
stabilization function of government   23
standards of practice   15, 46, 194
state aid   114–117, 116 (table)
statistical analysis, with CAMA   211
Streamlined Sales Tax Agreement   98
Streamlined Sales Tax Project   97
subsidiarity   195
sumptuary taxes   107
supervisory agencies
  equalization actions   219
  functions   51
  performance monitoring   217
  procedural audits   217
  reassessment orders   221
  technical assistance   216
supply and demand   20 (figure)
supply-side economics   325
Supremacy Clause (of the U.S. Constitution)   38 (table), 45
sustainability issues   302

Sweden   26, 62, 284 (table), 285
Switzerland   4

T

tangible property   4, 15
tax credits   186
tax base   15, 162
tax base sharing   49
tax burden
   analysis by initial incidence   157
   based on personal income
      by state   149 (table)
   comparison by state   147 (table)
   definition   138
   lifetime effect   314
   per-capita overall by state   151 (table)
   property tax by state   147 (table)
   studies   155
tax-exempt bonds   117
tax expenditures   158, 159 (table)
tax incidence
   and tax burden   138, 156
   benefit view   313
   definition   138
   District of Columbia studies   155
   initial vs. ultimate   159
   legal vs. economic   319
   lifetime effect   314
   Minnesota studies   155
   new view   312
   sector analysis   313
   technical issues   161
   traditional view   311
tax increment financing (TIF)   68, 187, 188 (table), 189 (table), 317
Tax Injunction Act of 1937   38 (table), 46
tax limits   15
tax policy
   analyzing the effects of   127
   and the assessor   293
   conceptual approach   294 (figure)
   implementation   9
   public policy   2
tax relief mechanisms   186 (table)
   abatements   64, 187, 188 (table), 317
   circuit breakers   64, 160, 186 (table), 306
   collection methods   306
   credits   186 (table)
   de facto exemptions   185
   deferrals   64, 186 (table), 306
   differentials   63
   disincentives   65
   emergency   65
   forgiveness   306
   full exemptions   184 (table)
   general   7
   homeowner   42 (table)
   homestead exemption   64, 306
   incentives   65
   indirect   66
   institutional   65
   partial exemptions   183, 307
   rate classification   307
   reassessment   307
   TIF   68, 193, 188 (table), 189 (table), 317
   transitional   65
Temporary Assistance to Needy Families (TANF)   114
Tenth Amendment (of the U.S. Constitution)   37, 39 (table), 75, 195
Texas   105, 198
thematic maps, with GIS   212
time series forecasting   132
tobacco product taxes, *see* cigarette taxes
transitional relief   65
transparency   30, 33, 67
Treaty of Maastricht   195
trend analysis   132
Tribal Commerce Clause (of the U.S. Constitution), *see* Commerce Clause
truth-in-taxation   63, 66, 118, 169
Turkey   56, 235, 283, 284 (table)
town meeting   19

U

Uniform Business Tax (U.K.)   50
uniformity   30, 43, 121
unit sales tax   319
unitary system   3, 47, 75, 255
United Kingdom
   Council Tax   55, 228, 270, 271 (table)
   land tax   180
   Plant and Machinery Order   238
   tax administration   52, 271
   tax base sharing   49

Uniform Business Rate 272
Uniform Business Tax 50
Valuation Office Agency (VOA) 272
value bases 61
user fees 78, 113
U.S. Census Bureau
  classification of taxes 6
  classification of revenue 136
  informational tables 139
utility franchise taxes 113

V

valuation modeling 227–229
Valuation Office Agency (VOA) (U.K.) 272
valuation systems
  acquisition value 171, 176
  annual rental value 61
  area-based systems 60
  base-year appraisal 62, 170
  Canada 169
  capital value 61
  constraints on assessed value 172, 173 (table), 174 (table), 182
  controls on distribution of burden 172
  cost approach 224, 233, 240
  current market value 171 (table)
  cyclic reappraisal 170
  fractional assessment ratios 181, 182, 221
  frozen valuation 171
  generalized process 225 (table)
  income approach 224
  indexing 62
  Israel 170
  Japan 170
  market value 61, 170, 171 (table), 304
  mass valuation 226
  multiple value estimates, with CAMA 211
  responsibility for 51
  revaluation 62
  sales comparison approach 223
  self assessment 56
value bases 61
value constraints 172–175, 173 (table), 174 (table), 182
value indexing 62

value influence centers (VIC) 229
valuers, *see* appraisers
Vermont 100, 300
vertical equity 173
viability 49
vouchers, for education 24

W

Washington 106
wealth
  as underpinning for tax 8
  net worth 158
  vs. uniformitiy 121
Web sites
  Montana 186 (figure)
  provider of data 295
"welcome stranger" assessing 44, 199
West Virginia 181
Wisconsin 12, 99
work flow management, with CAMA 211
work maps, with GIS 213